Photoshop® 7.0 for Screen Printers

Joli Ballew

Wordware Publishing, Inc.

Library of Congress Cataloging-in-Publication Data

Ballew, Joli
    Photoshop 7.0 for screen printers / by Joli Ballew.
      p. cm.
    Includes index.
    ISBN 1-55622-031-6
    1. Computer graphics. 2. Adobe Photoshop. I. Title.
    T385.B3545 2003
    006.6'96--dc21
                                    2003009305
                                         CIP

ISBN 1-55622-031-6

10 9 8 7 6 5 4 3 2 1
0305

All inquiries for volume purchases of this book should be addressed to Wordware
Publishing, Inc., at the above address. Telephone inquiries may be made by
calling:

(972) 423-0090

Dedication

For my daughter, Jennifer, whose intelligence, perseverance, kindness, and fortitude inspire everyone around her.

Contents

Contents

Contents

Contents

Contents

Acknowledgments

Several people made this book possible. First, thanks to Jim Hill, publisher at Wordware Publishing, who gave me the opportunity to write the book, and Wes Beckwith, my developmental editor, who kept everything organized and on the right track. In addition, technical editor David Helmsley worked diligently on the manuscript seeking out technical errors, while editors Heather Hill and Beth Kohler edited for grammatical ones. It takes quite a few people to make a book work, and I had a great team.

I'd also like to thank a few people who, over the six months and ten hours a day I spent writing this book, sent me everything from faster computers to software to personal tips about screen angles, halftone dot patterns, and moiré. Thanks to James Jones at Intel for the new computer, Fred Schoeller from Arts & Letters for the clip art, J.D. Burke from Metroplex Screen for the printing tips and for generally letting me "hang out," Scott Fresner of the U.S. Screen Printing Institute (www.screenprinters.net) for FastFilms, and Cosmo at North Texas Graphics (www.NorthTexasGraphics.com) for letting me try out my test screens on your presses. I also have a wonderful agent, Neil Salkind, who at every turn is encouraging and positive and always available when I need him.

A group thanks to all the people who answered my questions on the screen printer's e-list (screenprinters@screenprinters.net) and spent their personal time answering queries and giving advice. You were great!

Of course, without the support of my family, I'd never have had the time to write a book like this. I have the most supportive and encouraging family in the world, and I love them very much.

Introduction

There are between 20,000 and 30,000 registered screen printing companies in the U.S. and many thousands more worldwide. Additionally, there are thousands of companies that are run from backyards, garages, and storage facilities. All of these screen printing companies have one thing in common—they all use some type of graphics program to create artwork, work with client files, and print out specialty prints and color separations for their film and screens. Many of these artists use some version of Photoshop; unfortunately, there isn't a single book available on the subject...until now!

This book details how to use Photoshop 7.0 in a screen printing company. Screen printers have different needs than offset print facilities, advertising companies, artists, photographers, or web designers, and most books on Photoshop don't address these needs. As you know, most Photoshop users don't need a thorough explanation of four-color separations and how to print them on PostScript printers, but screen printers certainly do; in fact, it is the heart of the process.

In this book, I detail how to use Photoshop 7.0 in a screen printing facility. I've made certain assumptions, such as you either have a working screen print facility or are just starting one, you have a working knowledge of computers, and you have Photoshop 7.0 installed or will install it soon.

The Book's Unique Features

This book consists of six sections. Part I is written for those new to Photoshop and details the toolbox, the menu bar, the palettes, the options bar, and how to personalize the workspace. Even if you use another version of Photoshop, you'll find that this section is informative and a must-read. Part II covers creating artwork and logos. It starts with basic tasks like coming up with ideas and ends with building a complex image from scratch using layers. Part III is all about working with client files and includes information on opening, importing, scanning, and working with client-created artwork. Part IV details some of my favorite tools, how to work with third-party clip art, and how to add special effects.

Part V, the heart of the book, explains how to perform all kinds of color separations, including spot color, process color, indexed color, and simulated process color. This is invaluable information for any screen printer. You also learn how to create artwork for sublimation, heat transfers, and similar substrates. Finally, in Part VI, I cover how to print all of these separations and include everything you need to know about screen angles, line count, dot gain, halftone dot patterns, and more.

In addition to these topics, there are chapters on the following screen printing-specific tasks:

- Using the File Browser to open and merge files
- Personalizing the workspace for optimum screen printing applications
- Adding shapes, text, and colors for logo creation best suited to screen printing (one to four colors)
- Editing photos for more successful heat transfers
- Using paths and vector masks to create logos and designs
- Working with text and numbers
- Using the Eraser tools
- Understanding color models and color modes
- Working with e-mailed files
- Understanding file types
- Working with digital cameras, scanners, and various disks
- Using the Magic Wand, Lasso tools, Clone Stamp tool, Pattern Stamp tool, and more

The CD

This book includes a companion CD. The CD contains logo designs that can be used as templates for your own work, some sample artwork and photos that contain layers, and samples of logos and designs that incorporate applying filters and other special effects. In addition, almost every chapter has exercises and chapter projects. The files that you need to work through these projects are on the companion CD.

And Finally....

I hope you find this book informative and useful. I've tried to incorporate all you need to know to get started with Photoshop, create artwork, perform color separations, and print them successfully. I've consulted many print shops (including my own, of course!) and fused all of the suggestions, tips, and tricks together in this book.

I can be reached at Joli_Ballew@hotmail.com, and I look forward to hearing from you!

Part I
The Photoshop Interface

Chapter 1

The Toolbox

The toolbox is the heart of Photoshop 7.0, where you'll find the tools you need to create your artwork and perform editing tasks. From the toolbox you can access the Selection tools, Shape tools, Type tools, Crop tools, and Eraser tools. These are basic tools that any screen printer or graphic artist needs. There are other tools available, of course, and the purpose behind this chapter is to familiarize you with all of them.

As a graphic artist, some tools are more important to you and your specific industry than others. For instance, if you have a manual, four-color, four-station screen printing press and no PostScript printer, chances are good that you won't use the Gradient tool as often as you'll use the Paint Bucket or Type tools. If you have automatic presses and create and output process color creations, you'll probably use the Gradient tool a lot more. If you run an offset print shop and print multicolored business cards, brochures, and booklets and you have a $15,000 PostScript printer at your disposal, you'll probably spend quite a bit of time with brushes, the Crop tool, and tools such as Sharpen, Dodge, and Burn.

In this chapter, I briefly introduce all of the tools in the toolbox and how to access them. No matter what field(s) of graphic arts you are in, make sure you've familiarized yourself with the tools located here before moving forward with this book and the program. Throughout the book, most of these tools are detailed in depth.

 Note:

If you've been using Photoshop for a while (earlier versions of Photoshop, anyway) and you purchased this book more for the topics related to screen printing and graphic arts than how to locate tools in the toolbox, you might think you can skip this chapter. However, because the toolbox offers new tools not found in earlier versions of the software, it is a good idea to skim the chapter anyway.

The Toolbox

Figure 1-1 shows Photoshop 7.0's toolbox. The top-left tool (the rectangular Marquee tool) is selected and indented. The toolbox that is shown in the figure is the default toolbox with the default icons.

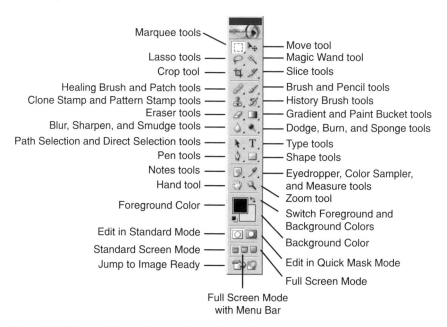

Figure 1-1: The available tools and their default callouts

 Tip:

To see the name of a tool in the toolbox, simply use the mouse to hover over it.

 Caution!

If your toolbox doesn't look exactly like this one, it's because you've been using the program and thus changed the defaults! Many of the tools in the toolbox have hidden tools, and the last choice made from a particular set of tools determines what icon shows in the toolbox.

Notice that many of the icons in the toolbox have arrows in the bottom-right corner. This signifies that there are additional tools located "under" the icon. Figure 1-2 shows the hidden tools available from the Type tool.

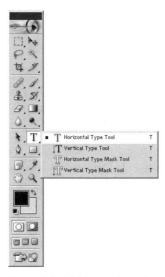

Figure 1-2: Hidden tools in the toolbox

Experiment for a moment before moving on; hover the mouse over each of the default tools to see the names of each of them. In the next section we discuss how to choose them.

Selecting Tools

As mentioned earlier, there are tools and there are hidden tools; they are all located in the toolbox. As shown in Figure 1-2, for instance, the Type tool actually offers four tools: the Horizontal Type tool, the Vertical Type tool, the Horizontal Type Mask tool, and the Vertical Type Mask tool. As mentioned previously, the icon in the toolbox changes, depending on the tool chosen last. Because of this, the icon showing in the toolbox on your computer screen might not match what's showing in Figures 1-1 or 1-2.

 Tip:

To select a tool from the toolbox, simply click on it. You'll get whatever tool the icon shows. To see the hidden (or additional) tools, either right-click on the tool's icon or click and hold the icon for a second until the options show themselves.

To select any tool and familiarize yourself with the toolbox, perform the following steps:

1. Choose **File>New** and then choose **8 x 10** from the Preset Sizes options drop-down list. (You'll have to click the down arrow to see the options.) Verify that the Contents option is set to White and that the Mode is RGB Color. Click **OK** to create a new file.

2. Choose **Window>Workspace>Reset Palette Locations** to revert the work area to its default settings.

3. Click the mouse on the Marquee tool icon in the toolbox and hold. It's the top tool on the left side, as selected in Figures 1-1 and 1-3. Four choices will appear.

4. From the four choices, choose the **Elliptical Marquee** tool. Notice the icon changes to the one shown in Figure 1-3.

Figure 1-3: The Elliptical Marquee tool and its icon

5. Right-click on the Marquee icon and choose the **Rectangular Marquee** tool from the list. Notice the icon changes again.

6. Click on the **Move** tool. It is located to the right of the Marquee tools. Click and hold on this icon, an arrowhead. Notice that no additional tools appear. There are no hidden tools for this choice, thus there is no arrow in the bottom-right corner of the icon.

7. Continue in this manner until you've chosen each of the tools and viewed the additional tools underneath each. When finished, leave this file open for the next exercise in this chapter.

Selecting tools from the toolbox can be achieved by right-clicking or clicking, holding, and choosing from the list of choices, as shown in this example, but the tool that is "on top" or showing can also be selected by quickly clicking on the icon and thus bypassing the list options.

Additionally, tools can be chosen using the keyboard. Look back at Figures 1-2 and 1-3. In the list of choices, there are letters as well as the name of the tool. In the Marquee tools, the letter M is listed; in the Type tools, the letter T is listed. Pressing these letters on the keyboard selects these tools. Try it!

1. With an open file, press the **M** on the keyboard. Look at the toolbox and notice the Marquee tools are chosen.

2. Press the **T** on the keyboard. Notice that the Type tools are now chosen.

3. Press the **U** on the keyboard. Notice the Shape tools are chosen.

Try these others (which are in order from the toolbox):

- L for the Lasso tools
- C for the Crop tool
- J for the Healing Brush and Patch tools
- S for the Clone Stamp and Pattern Stamp tools
- E for the Eraser tools
- R for the Blur, Sharpen, and Smudge tools
- A for the Path Selection and Direct Selection tools
- P for the Pen tools
- N for the Notes tools
- H for the Hand tool
- V for the Move tool
- W for the Magic Wand tool
- K for the Slice tools
- B for the Brush and Pencil tools
- Y for the History Brush tools
- G for the Gradient and Paint Bucket tools

- O for the Dodge, Burn, and Sponge tools
- I for the Eyedropper, Color Sampler, and Measure tools
- Z for the Zoom tool

Knowing how to select tools from the toolbox is only half the battle—knowing which tool to select, why, and how to use it is another story.

 Note:

Because the icons for the toolbox change constantly, there is no set name I use for a specific tool throughout this book. Therefore, I use instructions like, "Click on the Paint Bucket tool; it's the sixth tool down on the right in the toolbox."

The Available Tools

In this section I introduce each of the tools in the toolbox, but only briefly. As you work your way through the book, you'll become more familiar with these and begin to understand how each tool can be used effectively in your field. Refer back to Figure 1-1 and the callouts listed there if necessary.

 Tip:

Working with both hands (keyboard and mouse) is a great way to increase your efficiency with Photoshop 7.0. To remind you to try, the titles of the remaining sections are named appropriately.

If you want to experiment with these tools:

If you want to experiment with the tools introduced in this section, open the file Figure of Wall.jpg from the Chapter 1 folder of the CD-ROM included with this book:

1. Place the CD in the disk drive and choose **File>Open** from the menu bar.
2. Browse to the Chapter 1 folder on the disk from the Look In window of the Open dialog box.
3. Double-click (or single-click, depending on your system) on the file to open it. If prompted, choose to convert the file to your computer's color working space.

4. When clicking on the various tools, notice that the options bar changes each time a new tool is chosen. (The options bar is located directly above the toolbox and is detailed fully in Chapter 4.)

5. When finished, do not try to save your changes to the disk; it won't work! If you want to save your changes, choose **File>Save As** and save anywhere on your hard drive.

 Note:

Many of the tools introduced here have their own sections and chapters, but a few do not. In the following sections, I note briefly either how to use the tool or what chapter details it fully.

M for the Marquee Tools

There are four Marquee tools: Rectangular, Elliptical, Single Row, and Single Column. These tools allow you to select portions of an object, file, photo, or subject for editing. These selections must be either elliptical, rectangular, circular, or 1 pixel wide or thick. There are other selection tools that offer greater flexibility, such as the Lasso tools, which are detailed in the next section. Once an area has been selected, any of the editing tools can be used to manipulate the selection. You can deselect the area using Select>Deselect.

 Tip:

To use the Marquee tools, drag the mouse around the area you want to select. Let go of the mouse to complete the selection process.

L for the Lasso Tools

There are three Lasso tools: the Lasso tool, the Polygonal Lasso tool, and the Magnetic Lasso tool. The Lasso tool lets you draw around an object freehand, using curves and lines. The Polygonal Lasso tool lets you draw around an object using straight line segments and can be used freehand to draw curves when the Alt key is held down while dragging. The Magnetic Lasso tool lets you draw around an object and have the drawn lines snap to the object (based on calculations determined by color differences in the object and the background). While using this tool, you can click with the mouse to create points manually. As with the Marquee tools, you can deselect an area using Select>Deselect.

✎ **Note:**

The Lasso tools are detailed in Chapter 16, and are selection tools like the Marquee tools.

C for the Crop Tool

The Crop tool lets you remove extraneous portions of an image or file by cropping out a specific portion of the image. This is quite useful when you've imported a client file and need to pare it down a bit to only work with what's relevant or to organize and/or center an object for creating a screen or plate.

 Tip:

To use the Crop tool, drag the mouse around the area that you want to select. To remove what's not selected, click the check mark on the options bar to accept the change. The Crop tool is detailed in Chapter 16.

J for the Healing Brush and Patch Tools

The Healing Brush lets you correct imperfections in images such as dirt, smudges, and even dark circles under a subject's eyes. You can match the background texture, lighting, and shadows or shading to "cover up" these flaws. The Healing Brush tool is similar to and used similarly to the Clone Stamp tool detailed in Chapter 18.

 Tip:

To use the Healing Brush, first select a brush from the options bar, create a sampling point using the Alt+click command, and then drag the mouse over the part of the image to correct. By clicking with the mouse and dragging, you'll paint over the imperfections with the color, texture, and shading of the sampling point.

The Patch tool lets you choose a part of the image and use it as a sample for repairing another part of the image; it is similar to the Healing Brush tool. The Patch tool combines the selection power of the Lasso tools with the correction properties of the Healing Brush and other cloning tools. Figure 1-4 shows the power of these cloning tools, as well as others.

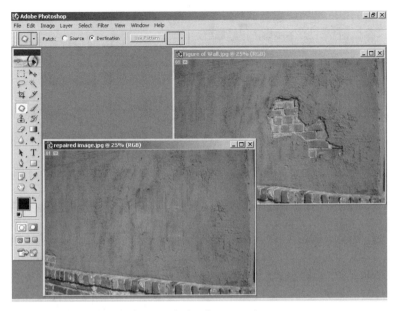

Figure 1-4: Correcting a photo with the cloning tools.

 Tip:

These tools are detailed fully in Chapter 18.

S for the Clone Stamp and Pattern Stamp Tools

The Clone Stamp tool lets you duplicate any area in an image and "paint" that area over any other part of the image. The Pattern Stamp tool allows you to paint with a specific pattern from the pattern library or your own pattern creations. Using the Clone Stamp tool is similar to using the Healing Brush; using the Pattern Stamp tool simply involves choosing a pattern and applying it to the image by dragging the mouse.

 Tip:

These tools are detailed fully in Chapter 18.

E for the Eraser Tools

There are three Eraser tools: the (generic) Eraser tool, the Background Eraser tool, and the Magic Eraser tool. The Eraser tool simply erases to the background layer, while the Background Eraser tool lets you erase to transparency in a single-layered image or in such a way to maintain the integrity of the foreground and other layers if multiple layers are involved. Both of these tools work by dragging the mouse.

When you click once with the mouse, the Magic Eraser tool erases all pixels similar in color to the area on which you clicked. Figure 1-5 shows a photo that originally had a blue background and now has a new picture where this background was removed using the Magic Eraser. By removing the blue background, the image can be used for printing only the sunflowers (with no background) on coffee mugs, mouse pads, T-shirts, or other goods that are a solid color where the blue isn't warranted or needed. This type of color removal allows the background color of the shirt or other material to show through once the sunflowers are printed on it.

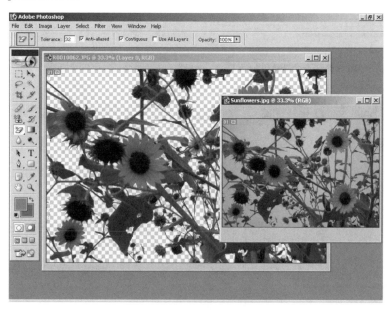

Figure 1-5: Using the Magic Eraser tool

Tip:

The Eraser tools are detailed in Chapter 10.

R for the Blur, Sharpen, and Smudge Tools

These tools do exactly what you'd think; they blur, sharpen, and smudge images on the screen. These tools are used to sharpen and soften edges or smudge an image or area.

 Tip:

To use these tools, set the options in the options bar and simply drag the tool over the part of an image to edit.

A for the Path Selection and Direct Selection Tools

You'll use the Path Selection and Direct Selection tools when you want to edit the paths that you've created. Paths allow you to create custom outlines of shapes for various uses, including creating a custom shape, using the shape or path as a mask to hide areas of a layer, or using it as a clipping path.

 Tip:

Paths and masks are detailed in Chapter 21, along with an introduction to these tools.

P for the Pen Tools

The Pen tool has several tools that are hidden under it, including the (generic) Pen tool, the Freeform Pen tool, options to add or delete anchor points, and access to the Convert Point tool. The Pen tool is used for drawing, as is the Freeform Pen tool. As lines and curves are drawn, anchor points are created that define the line, its endpoints, and its curves. Using the additional Anchor Point tools, the points that make up the line or curve (and thus their shapes and attributes) can be edited.

Tip:

Using the Pen tools is similar to using the Line tool detailed in Chapter 8, but the characteristics of the lines drawn are much different. In Chapter 21, the Pen tools are introduced. Reading both chapters is necessary to understand all aspects of both the Line and Pen tools.

N for the Notes Tools

Both written and audio notes can be added to Photoshop files. These notes can work in tandem with other Adobe products, such as Adobe Acrobat Reader.

 Tip:

To use the Notes tools, set the options in the options bar for author name, font, size, etc., then click anywhere in the document. A box will appear that allows you to insert your notes. You can see the note by double-clicking on it. To add audio notes, click Start to record and click Stop when finished.

H for the Hand Tool

The Hand tool allows you to scroll through an image that doesn't fit completely in the viewing window. It's like using the scroll bars at the bottom and right side of the window, except you do the moving with the mouse by dragging. When the Hand tool is chosen, the cursor becomes a hand.

V for the Move Tool

The Move tool allows you to move an entire image or the selected part of an image to align layers and distribute layers in an image. To move only a selected part of an image, use the Marquee tools to make the selection, and then use the Move tool to move the selection. There will be a box around the image during and after moving. This box can also be used to transform the selection and edit its shape and size.

 Tip:

To use the Move tool, make a selection in the image or select a layer from the Layers palette. Then, with the Move tool chosen, use the mouse to click and drag the box that surrounds the object to move it, and use the Edit>Transform options to manipulate its attributes such as size and shape.

W for the Magic Wand Tool

The Magic Wand tool allows you to make a selection automatically, based on a color, without having to physically trace the outline. Options for the Magic Wand are set in the options bar. Figure 1-6 shows this type of selection in progress. Note the outline around the sunflower; this dotted outline is often referred to as "marching ants."

Figure 1-6: Selecting using the Magic Wand

Once an object is selected, the object can then be copied and pasted into the same document or another one or used on its own layer for editing (and sometimes color separating) the file. Figure 1-7 shows the selection after pasting it into a new document. The sunflower can now be used independently from the original picture for various applications.

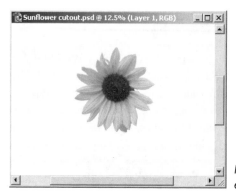

Figure 1-7: Applying a selection after editing

 Tip:

The Magic Wand tool is detailed in Chapter 16.

K for the Slice Tools

Slices are generally used to define areas of an image that will be used later for animating a web page, as links to URL addresses, or for rollover buttons. For the most part, slices aren't used much in screen printing and similar fields.

 Tip:

For more information on slices and the Slice tools, consult Adobe Photoshop Help.

B for the Brush and Pencil Tools

The Brush tool and Pencil tool are both available from the toolbox. These tools allow you to select a brush, choose its characteristics including size, shape, spacing, roundness, hardness, angle, diameter, mode, opacity, and more, and then use the brush for various types of artwork. Some common ways of using brushes in our fields include touching up artwork, filling in around edges of artwork (to create cleaner film), covering up blemishes and other unwanted items on the image (to avoid unnecessary marks on vellum and screens), and hand drawing custom artwork. The brushes can also be used to add a texture to a logo or create logos for paint companies and the like. (Consider a large single brush stroke with the words "A Stroke of Genius" or something similar written over it; this is a quick way to create a logo for a paint company.)

Tip:

Brushes will be introduced in Chapter 7.

Y for the History Brush Tools

There are two history brushes: the History Brush and the Art History Brush. The History Brush allows you to paint over an area in an image that you've previously changed and revert that particular part of the image to its original state. For instance, you can use the Eraser tool to erase an area of an image, and if you don't like it, you can use the History Brush to brush over that area to bring back what was originally there.

The Art History Brush allows you to change an image to make it look like some other type of artwork—artwork that is older, such as impressionist artwork, an oil painting, or a watercolor. These changes are unlike filters and similar tools because they allow you to brush over only part of the image to make the changes and do not apply the change to the entire image or layer.

 Tip:

The History Brush tools are introduced in Chapter 7.

G for the Gradient and Paint Bucket Tools

The Gradient and Paint Bucket tools allow you to fill a selected area or layer with a color or gradient. There are almost an infinite number of colors and gradients from which to choose. The Paint Bucket tool fills an object with a solid color, and the Gradient tool fills the object with a range of colors that fade into each other. The Paint Bucket tools are common tools used with true spot color printing; gradients are common tools used with spot color prints created using halftone screens and process color printing. Either can be used to create a background for any artwork, such as creating a colored or gradient background to be used on a mouse pad or can cooler.

 Tip:

The Paint Bucket tool is discussed in Chapter 7, and the Gradient tool is discussed in Chapter 20.

O for the Dodge, Burn, and Sponge Tools

The Dodge and Burn tools are used to lighten and darken areas of an image or print. By adding or removing light from an image, offset printers can create better images (and thus better negatives) for creating their plates. The Sponge tool is used similarly and can decrease or increase the contrast of the image. Better images mean better prints, films, and negatives!

 Tip:

Each of these tools is applied to an image by setting the options in the options bar and then dragging the mouse over the area to be edited. There is more on correcting photos in Chapter 16.

T for the Type Tools

As mentioned earlier, there are four Type tools: the Vertical Type tool, Horizontal Type tool, Vertical Mask Type tool, and Horizontal Mask Type tool. These tools are used to add words to the file. With a Type tool selected, you can set options for font, size, color, alignment, and more. Of course, text is generally the most common thing we as screen printers and graphic artists use when working up a logo or print for a company, client, or team. Thus, an entire chapter is dedicated to it.

 Tip:

The Type tools are discussed in depth in Chapter 9.

U for the Shape Tools

There are several Shape tools: the Rectangle, Rounded Rectangle, Ellipse, Polygon, Line, and Custom Shape. Shape tools are used by graphic artists for creating logos, setting type boundaries, creating custom artwork, creating trademarks, and more. Shapes are vector images too, meaning they can be resized without distortion. Photoshop comes with many custom shapes, including animals, check marks, hands, feet, puzzle pieces, pens and pencils, phones, international symbols, and more.

Tip:

Chapter 8 is dedicated to using the Shape tools.

I for the Eyedropper, Color Sampler, and Measure Tools

The Eyedropper, Color Sampler, and Measure tools all offer ways to be more precise with your image and editing. The Eyedropper and the Color Sampler tools allow you to match a color exactly by clicking on an area of the image, and then it offers information about that color. The Measure tool calculates the distance between two points in an image and offers information about them too, such as distance from a point to the x- or y-axis and total distance traveled to get from point A to point B.

 Tip:

The Eyedropper and Color Sampler are discussed further in Chapter 11.

Z for the Zoom Tool

The Zoom tool works much like any zoom tool in any other graphics program. Simply choose the Zoom tool and click on an area of the image to zoom in or out.

When the Zoom tool is chosen, the options in the option bar change and offer Zoom In, Zoom Out, choices to resize the window to fit on the screen, and other options. You'll use the Zoom tool often to zoom in on small areas for editing or zoom out to see the "bigger" picture.

 Tip:

Right-click on the image after choosing the Zoom tool to zoom in or out, fit to screen, see the actual pixel size, and see the print size.

Additional Tools in the Toolbox

There are a few other items in the toolbox (at the bottom), including the foreground and background color pickers (detailed in Chapters 3 and 11), and buttons for Edit in Standard Mode or Edit in Quick Mask Mode. There are also icons for toggling between working in standard screen mode (what you see by default), working in full-screen mode with a menu bar, and working in full-screen mode without a window bar. Full mode displays the file on the entire computer screen and minimizes the menu bar. To switch between these modes, simply click the appropriate icon.

Finally, you can jump to Image Ready, an application that ships with Photoshop 7.0 and is used mainly for web design. Additionally, at the top of the toolbox, you can click on the Photoshop logo to jump to Adobe Online.

 Tip:

To change the foreground and background colors, simply click on the appropriate icon in the toolbox and select a new color from the Color Picker. There is much more about this in Chapter 11.

Summary

In this chapter you learned about the toolbox and the available tools. The toolbox holds all of the tools that a screen printer or graphic artist needs including erasers, text tools, pens and brushes, cropping tools, shapes, and more.

Selecting tools was also covered. There are three ways to select tools: by clicking and holding down the toolbox icon and choosing from the list, by clicking on the icon in the toolbox quickly and accessing the default (last chosen) tool, or by using the keyboard.

Finally, each tool available in the toolbox was detailed briefly. If the tool is detailed in another chapter, this was also noted.

Chapter 2

The Menu Bar

In addition to the toolbox, another important interface feature is the menu bar. The menu bar contains several headings: File, Edit, Image, Layer, Select, Filter, View, Window, and Help. It is shown in Figure 2-1. Each of these menu options offers its own set of tools, including options for enhancing photographs, editing artwork, rotating and duplicating images, adding, deleting, and working with layers, working with filters, and personalizing the workspace (just to name a few).

Figure 2-1: The menu bar

In this chapter, I introduce these menus and discuss what can be found under each. Most of the options are intuitive or similar to other graphics programs that you have used. For instance, you'll want to look under the File menu if you want to do something *to* a file, like Open, Close, Save, Print, Revert, or Exit. You'll want to choose the Edit menu for basic editing tasks, such as Cut, Copy, Paste, and Transform. Use the Image menu to perform tasks on images, such as Duplicate, Crop, Trim, Rotate, etc.

Note:

This chapter is meant to serve as an overview of what's available from the menu bar and to note where and when tools will be explored in detail.

Tip:

Don't let the number of options in the menus intimidate you; after a little experimenting, you'll find many options that you're familiar with, including Cut, Copy, Paste, Browse, Open, and Save.

File

As previously mentioned, the File menu is very similar to the File menu in other software programs. Photoshop's File menu is shown in Figure 2-2. You can choose to open a file, save a file, and browse for a file, and you can print, print a single copy, or print with a preview. You can import or export files or save a file for the web. There are additional options that are native to Photoshop though, such as Automate and Place, but all of the options are for working with an entire file and are generally input/output in nature.

Figure 2-2: The File menu

The options from the File menu are detailed throughout this book. For instance, Chapter 6 details using the File>Browse command, which is used to browse through the images and client files on your computer using thumbnail images. Chapter 13 deals with the File>Import command, which is used when opening files from other applications, and using the File>Save As command for saving a file for e-mailing a recipient or saving as another file type. All of the Print commands are detailed in Chapters 27, 29, and 30, and the options available here play a huge role in graphics industries. Throughout this book, choosing an option from the File menu is denoted as File><Command>.

 Tip:

One of the many helpful options in the File menu is File>Open Recent. The resulting choices show the last ten files you've worked with in Photoshop.

Edit

The Edit menu has several
options for editing your work.
When working with an image or
a file, Photoshop keeps a history
of the steps that you've taken
while editing the file, such as
using a Brush tool, using the
Paint Bucket tool, and even cropping or deleting parts of the
image. The Edit menu com-
mands can then be used to undo
the last step taken or "undo an
undo" by choosing Step Forward.
You can cut, copy, and paste a
selection from the clipboard, fill a
layer with a color or pattern,
check the spelling of text, and
transform images in any number
of ways. Figure 2-3 shows the
Edit menu.

Figure 2-3: The Edit menu

The Edit menu is also the place to configure custom color settings or
set preferences for file handling, cursors, the display, transparency and
gamut, units and rulers, memory and image cache, and more. The preferences options are also shown in Figure 2-3.

Throughout this book you'll use options from the Edit menu when
creating logos (Chapter 7), using the Shape tools (Chapter 8), adding text
and numbers (Chapter 9), and working with colors (Chapter 11). The
Edit menu works like other programs do regarding Cut, Copy, Paste, and
Undo. Choosing an option for the Edit menu is denoted as
Edit><Command>.

 Tip:

One of the many helpful options in the Edit menu is Edit>Purge. This command
allows you to clear the memory and cache by deleting the stored information in
the clipboard and histories. Purging the memory and cache will make the program
perform better and faster.

Image

You'll use commands from the Image menu to perform actions on an image. There are several choices, as shown in Figure 2-4.

From here, you can make adjustments to the image concerning color, hue, saturation, and other attributes, as well as changes to the color mode, as shown in Figure 2-4. Color modes are detailed in Chapter 11, while color adjustments are detailed in Chapter 16. Other options allow you to duplicate, trim, rotate, crop, and trap the image and change the image size too. Throughout the book, these tools are incorporated into projects and examples. Choosing an option from the Image menu is denoted as Image><Command>.

Figure 2-4: The Image menu

 Tip:

One of the many helpful options in the Image menu is Image>Image Size. From the Image Size dialog box, you can quickly change the overall size of the image as well as its resolution.

Project 2-1: Getting Familiar with the Menu Bar

In this project, you use the menus discussed so far to open and save a file, edit the file, print a copy of the file, edit the file's colors and other attributes, and more. If you've never used Photoshop before, this exercise is mandatory!

1. Open Photoshop and choose **File>Open**.

2. In the Open dialog box shown in Figure 2-5, click the down arrow in the Look In window and click on the **C** drive (or the root drive that contains the program files for your computer).

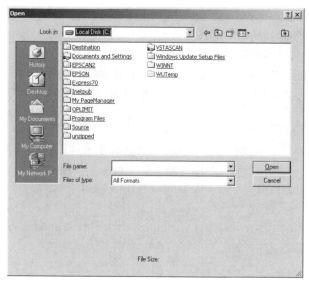

Figure 2-5: Using the Open dialog box

3. Double-click on the **Program Files** folder (or the folder that contains them if it's different from this one). Then click on the **Adobe** folder and the **Photoshop 7.0** folder.

4. Click on the **Samples** folder. You'll see the sample files listed, as shown in Figure 2-6. Click on the **Eagle.psd** file to open it.

Figure 2-6: Locating the sample files

5. Choose **File>Save As**. Save this file to your hard drive so that any changes you make to the file won't be accidentally saved to Photoshop's sample files.

6. In the Save As dialog box, click the down arrow in the Save In window and locate a folder in which you'd like to save your Photoshop files. You might choose the My Pictures folder or the My Documents folder or create a new folder just for Photoshop files.

7. In the File Name window, type **Eagle_Copy**. Click **Save**.

8. To print a single copy of the image without configuring any settings (Photoshop will ask for the default settings automatically), choose **File>Print One Copy**.

9. To edit the file's colors and attributes, make the following choices:

    ■ Image>Adjustments>Auto Color

    ■ Image>Adjustments>Auto Contrast

    ■ Image>Adjustments>Color Balance. Then in the Color Balance dialog box, move the sliders for cyan, magenta, and yellow to manually change the appearance of the image. Click **OK**.

    ■ Image>Rotate Canvas>180 degrees

    ■ Edit>Step Backward

10. Choose **File>Revert** to revert back to the last time you saved the file, which was its condition in step 7.

Now that you've been properly introduced to the basic menu options, let's move forward with some of the more complex ones.

What if I accidentally save over the original sample files?

If you accidentally save over the sample files and want to return them to their original state, close the Photoshop program if it is running, put in the Photoshop 7.0 CD, and choose to install. Work through the installation as you normally would. When prompted as to what type of installation you want to perform (Typical or Custom), choose Custom. Uncheck everything but the Samples folder.

Layer

In order to understand the options for the Layer menu, you have to understand layers. A picture from a digital camera is a single-layered image, as was the eagle in the Eagle.psd file that you opened in Project 2-1. Each time you edited the image, the entire image changed. If you now add text to that image, you're adding that text as a second layer. The text isn't part of the original image, and thus the text can be edited independently of the image. The opposite is true too; the image (layer) can be edited independently of the text.

Layers are covered in Chapter 12, "Layer Basics," and the Layer menu is what you use when working with layers. From this menu option you can add new layers, delete layers, add duplicate layers, group and ungroup layers, and more. There is much more on layers later in the book. Choosing an option from the Layer menu is denoted as Layer><Command>.

 Tip:

One of the many helpful options in the Layer menu is Layer>New>Layer. Choosing this allows you to create a new layer with additional content, add layers that act as masks or gradients, and more.

Select

You are probably already familiar with the Select>All command in your favorite e-mail or word processing program. In Photoshop, the Select All command can be found under the Select menu. The select options let you do more than select all of an image though; you can deselect an image or a selection, reselect an image or selection, and even select the inverse of what's selected! You can also use the Select>Color Range command to select only a specified color or color subset, soften edges around a selection using the Select>Feather command, and more. Choosing an option from the Select menu is denoted as Select><Command>.

✓ **Tip:**

One of the many helpful options in the Select menu is Select>Color Range. You can use the Color Range dialog box to select only the colors that match the sample you take with the Eyedropper tool. The selected colors can then be removed, copied, or edited. The Color Range command is what you'll use when color separating artwork.

Project 2-2: Using the Select>Color Range Command to Remove Colors from a Single-Layered Image

Working with single-layered images, such as pictures obtained from digital cameras or scanners, can be trying, especially if one or more colors need to be removed or separated. The Select>Color Range command can help you with this task and works best when there are distinct differences in colors in an image. Using the Eagle.psd file from the previous project, perform these steps to see how powerful this tool is:

1. With the Eagle_Copy.psd file open and in its original state, choose **Select>Color Range**.

2. Click, hold, and drag using the top of the Color Range dialog box to position the boxes so both boxes can be viewed simultaneously, as shown in Figure 2-7. (At this point, Invert should not be checked.)

Figure 2-7: Configuring the work area

3. Use the mouse to click on a green area of the eagle image. Notice that the cursor changes to an eyedropper.

4. Slide the Fuzziness slider in the Color>Range dialog box to between 45 and 50, or type in the number.

5. Click **OK** in the Color>Range dialog box.

6. Choose **Edit>Cut**. The image is now background-free and can be used in a number of ways by graphic artists.

Filter

Applying filters is covered in Chapter 20, "Special Effects." As shown in Figure 2-8, there are *many* filters to choose from. This example shows the Artistic filters, and the Watercolor filter is chosen.

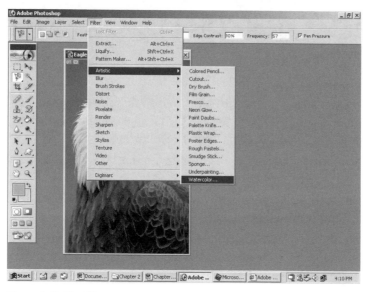

Figure 2-8: The Filter menu

Filters allow you to change the look of an image or layer simply by choosing the desired look from the menu options and configuring any dialog boxes that appear. Figure 2-9 shows a watercolor effect applied to a photo. Sometimes, applying the right effect can offer exactly what a client wants, with very little effort.

Figure 2-9: Applying effects

If you'd like to experiment with filters, close the Eagle_Copy file using File>Close (there's no need to save the changes, so click No when prompted to save) and then perform the following steps:

1. Place the companion CD that came with this book in the CD-ROM drive.

2. From the **File>Open** menu, browse to the CD-ROM drive and open the **Chapter 2** folder.

3. From the Chapter 2 folder, open the file **Downtown.jpg**. If prompted, choose to convert the file to your computer's working color space.

4. Choose **Filter>Artistic>Watercolor** and in the Watercolor dialog box move the sliders for Brush Detail, Shadow Intensity, and Texture. You can see a preview of the effect in this dialog box as well. Click **OK** when finished.

5. Choose **Edit>Step Backward** if you'd like to experiment with any other filters.

You'll find that after experimenting a little bit, there are several filters that can be useful to you as a screen printer, CAD cutter, sublimation technician, or offset printer. For instance, the Sharpen filters can help define an image's corners and edges and are useful with images that are blurry. You can also use the selection tools to select only a part of an image to sharpen. Filter>Render>Lighting Effects can be used to simulate a light source that isn't really there, noise filters can be used to make an image appear dirty or old, and textures can be used to make the image appear as though it's been printed on another type of material such as burlap or canvas.

View

The View menu offers many options for viewing your work. Figure 2-10 shows the View menu and the Proof Setup options. As a screen printer, these options will come in handy if you want to view a plate while the artwork is in progress. You can also show a grid on the image, show rulers, and zoom in and out on the artwork. Throughout this book we use options from this menu as needed. Choosing an option from the View menu is denoted as View><Command>.

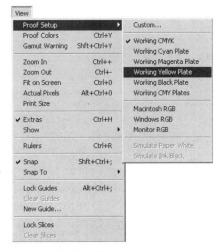

Figure 2-10: The View menu

 Tip:

One of the many helpful options in the View menu is View>Zoom In. Zooming in on a part of the image will make tracing around a selection easier.

Window

The Window menu is mostly for organizing what you see in the Photoshop interface. You can cascade or tile the open files, save a particular workspace configuration or recall a saved one, revert to the default configuration, remove or show the toolbox, status bar, or options bar, show or hide the file browser, and show or hide any of the available palettes. In the next chapter you'll learn all about palettes, including how to arrange them and save a custom palette configuration. Choosing an option from the Window menu is denoted as Window><Command>.

 Tip:
One of the many helpful options in the Window menu is Window>Workspace>Reset Palette Locations. Choosing this option reverts the workspace and the Photoshop interface to its defaults.

Help

The Help menu is one that you should explore in depth before going too much further. This menu has several options, including Photoshop Help, which brings up the extensive help files that are included with the Photoshop software. These files are quite comprehensive and have information on all aspects of Photoshop. (Unfortunately, there isn't much there for screen printers, thus the need for this book!)

You can also choose Help>Export Transparent Image for a wizard to assist you in performing this exporting task or Help>Resize for the Resize Image Wizard. Help>System Info brings up a dialog box that contains your particular system information, including how Photoshop is configured. Finally, there are options for support, updates, registration, and Adobe Online. In the last project in this chapter, we explore these options. Choosing an option from the Help menu is denoted as Help><Command>.

Project 2-3: Getting Help

It's easy to get help in Photoshop by using the built-in help files. In this project, you'll spend some time exploring these files as well as downloading updates, getting support online, and visiting Adobe's web site.

 Note:

You'll need an Internet connection in order to access the online help files.

1. Choose **Help>Photoshop Help** or press **F1**.
2. From the Help window, choose **Using Help**.

 Note:

I think it's funny that the help files have a help file; I included it here for your pleasure.

3. Click **Viewing Topics** to see how the help interface looks and how to view a topic. Work your way through the other options here.
4. When finished exploring, close the help window.
5. Back inside the Photoshop interface, choose **Help>Registration** to register your software. Registering allows you to access more of the online support options.
6. When prompted, choose to create an Adobe online account (optional). Doing so allows you to purchase upgrades online and track orders and registrations. Creating an account also enables you to create an Adobe login name and password, which allows you access to tips and tricks, notification of new products, free trials, access to the Photoshop Expert Center, and more. You'll get an e-mail on how to access these expert centers.
7. To manually set up Photoshop to automatically notify you of updates, choose **Help>Adobe Online** and click **Preferences**. Choose to look for updates once a month, once a week, or once a day.
8. To download the latest updates manually, choose **Help>Updates**.
9. To get help online, choose **Help>Support**. Here you can get support from online training, access user forums, and sign up for e-mail updates.

Photoshop is full of things that can benefit screen printers, CAD cutters, sublimation production shops, sign makers, and other graphic artists. Some of these include the ability to increase productivity by generating a workspace for specific jobs, managing colors, working between programs, previewing RGB colors for CMYK output on various devices, molding text to fit an underlying shape, adding copyright data to images, blending layers of images, silhouetting images, and more.

Unfortunately, one book can't cover all of this, but Adobe does a great job getting most of it on their web site. Register, create an online login name and password, and visit the Photoshop Expert Center. There, you can find step-by-step tutorials on various tasks that aren't covered in the help files or in this book. Figure 2-11 shows the Photoshop Expert Center.

Figure 2-11: The Photoshop Expert Center

Summary

In this chapter you learned all about the menu bar options and their respective drop-down lists. Many of the menu bar titles, such as File, Edit, View, and Help, do some of the same things that these options do in other programs. For instance, the File menu is used to perform actions on an entire file, such as opening, closing, saving, or printing. You can quicken the learning process by exploring all of the menu bar lists before moving forward.

Chapter 3

The Palettes

The palettes in Photoshop 7.0 are located on the right side of the interface. They are contained in rectangular boxes and offer tools to help you modify, monitor, and edit images. Palettes are stacked together, and each rectangular box holds two or three separate palettes. Figure 3-1 shows the default configuration for Photoshop 7.0 and how it looks when the program is opened in the recommended resolution of 1024 x 768 pixels.

Figure 3-1: The default placement for the palettes

The four rectangular boxes on the right contain the palettes. Unfortunately, you can't really see much in this image because at this resolution, everything is pretty small. However, it does give you a feel for how your screen should look. If your screen doesn't have all four of these boxes, you do not have your monitor configured for the optimum resolution (1024 x 768) and are running it at 800 x 600 or lower instead. If possible, change the resolution to 1024 x 768 so that all of the proper elements can be seen.

 Note:

In this chapter, I use a screen resolution of 1024 x 768 since we're working with palettes and it's the optimum setting. But for many shots in the book, the resolution is set at 800 x 600. Using this lower resolution for the screen shots makes for better viewing by the reader. This might cause some minor differences between the screen shot and what you see on your screen, but for the most part, you won't notice any difference at all.

Default Palettes

There are four default boxes that contain palettes, as shown in Figure 3-1. Each box contains two or three separate palettes that are docked together. The first one contains the Navigator and Info palettes.

Navigator and Info

These two palettes are docked together because they are both used for obtaining information about an open file. The Info palette displays color information about the color directly underneath the mouse pointer and displays additional information depending on the tool chosen. As a graphic artist, this information can be quite useful when matching a color or working between different color models. The Navigator palette allows you to quickly change the viewing area of the file on which you are working.

The Info palette offers information including the following:

■ When working with a file, an exclamation point is shown if the color is outside of the color gamut configured for the Info palette.

■ X and Y values are shown when using the Crop tool, the Marquee tools, the Zoom tool, and the Line, Pen, and Gradient tools.

■ Readouts can be configured to show values for actual color, proof color, grayscale, RGB color, web colors, HSB, CMYK, and lab colors, and total ink, or opacity. There are two sets of readouts, both of which can be set.

Let's explore these palettes and view colors for an RGB file:

1. Open the **Harvest.psd** file from the Samples folder stored in the Adobe program folder. (This procedure was detailed in Chapter 2.)

2. Make sure the Navigator and Info palettes are chosen, as shown in Figure 3-2. If you cannot see these palettes, choose **Window> Workspace>Reset Palette Locations**.

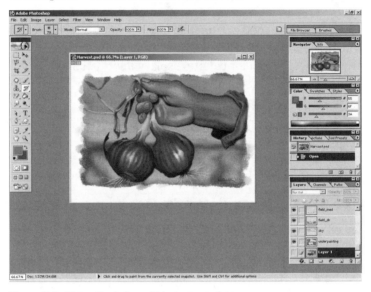

Figure 3-2: Using the Info and Navigator palettes

3. Click the **Info** tab to access the Info palette.

4. Click the right arrow in this palette to see the additional options, and choose **Palette Options**.

5. From the Info Options dialog box, make sure (or change if needed) the first option is RGB color and the second is CMYK color. Click **OK**.

6. Select the **Eyedropper** tool from the toolbox.

7. Hover the mouse over a color in the image. In the Info palette you can see the values for the color. Move the mouse around to see the values of the other colors.

8. Shift+click on the image to add a sample color in the Info palette. You can then compare the colors from this selection to other areas of the image. You can add up to four sampled colors here.

9. Click on the **Navigator** tab. Use the slider bar to zoom in or out, or click on the zoom icons in this palette.

There is much more on colors later in this book; this chapter is only meant to familiarize you with the available palettes.

Color, Swatches, and Styles

These palettes are docked together because they all have to do with the colors in the foreground and background of an image or the style of the selected layer. The Color palette displays information on the current foreground and background colors and allows you to change the colors as desired and/or base the colors on different color models. The Swatches palette also allows you to choose a foreground or background color but also lets you add or delete colors from the Swatches library of colors. The Styles palette lets you apply a preset style to a selected layer, which can be the foreground or background, or load different libraries of styles.

Project 3-1: Creating a Custom Foreground and Background Color

Photoshop 7.0 uses foreground and background colors to determine what color will be applied when a specific tool is chosen and used. The foreground color is used when paint tools are chosen and when fill and stroke tools are selected. When using a brush or the Paint Bucket tool, the foreground color will be applied. The foreground color is also used by some of the special effect filters. The background color is used when creating gradient fills, when creating a new file using the background color, or when filling in an erased area of the image.

You can use the Color and Swatches palettes to create a new foreground and background color, to edit the colors based on different color models, and to see alerts concerning colors that are out of the printable color spectrum for the color model that you've selected.

In this project, you'll create a custom foreground and background color through various methods, including using sliders, using the Swatches palette, typing in specific values, and using the Eyedropper tool. You will probably be called upon at some point to create a specific color for a client who needs his colors matched exactly, needs the colors guaranteed the same every time, or needs to have colors match some industry specification. (Of course, getting the printer to print this exactly or match it from your shop's ink selection is another story, but we save that discussion for later!)

1. Close any open files. If the Harvest.psd file is open, close it without saving the changes. Choose **File>New** to open a new file. Choose **1024 x 768** and **RGB Color**, and select **Background Color** from the Contents section of the New dialog box. Click **OK**.

2. A new file will open, and the color of the new file will be filled with the background color that is currently configured. Locate the Color, Swatches, and Styles palettes, and if they aren't there, choose **Window>Workspace>Reset Palette Locations**.

3. Choose the Color palette by clicking on its tab; you'll want the RGB colors and sliders to be showing. Verify that these color sliders are showing by clicking the right arrow and viewing the additional options, as shown in Figure 3-3. If you need to, choose this option.

4. In the Color palette, select the background color box by clicking on it. A black outline will show around it.

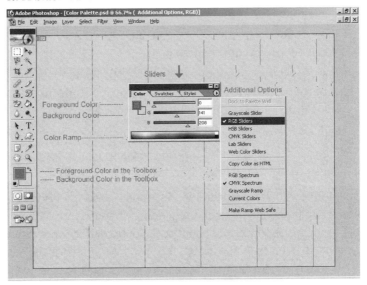

Figure 3-3: The Color palette and its components

5. Hover the mouse over the color ramp and click on a new color. Notice that the sliders move and the color denoted in the background color box changes. (This activity does not change the

background color of the file; it only changes the background color in the toolbox for the next use.)

6. Next, move the sliders manually. Notice that the color denoted in the background box changes again. You can change the amount of red, green, and blue.

7. Double-click on the background color in the Color palette. Select a new color from the Color Picker that appears by clicking on the desired color.

8. Type in numbers in the RGB boxes to create your own color based on color values. The numbers can only be between 0 and 255.

 Tip:

Each of these steps can also be applied after selecting the foreground or background color in the Color palette, as well as from the toolbox.

9. Click on the additional options and notice how many color models there are. Select **CMYK** and then **Web Color Sliders** to see additional options.

10. Click the **Swatches** tab. Select a color from the swatch choices and watch the foreground color change.

11. Click the additional options under this tab. There are several libraries of colors to choose from. Select **Pantone Solid to Process** and click **OK** when prompted to load the new library.

12. Double-click on any color to see its name and Pantone number.

13. When finished exploring, choose the additional options again and choose **Reset Swatches**. Click **OK** when prompted.

If you are new to screen printing and graphic work, all of these color options might seem a little overwhelming; if you are an old hand at the art, you might be so excited about these options that you can hardly stay in your seat. Whatever the case, there is more on colors and swatches later in this book; for now, knowing how to access the palettes and select a color or two is all you really need to understand.

History, Actions, and Tool Presets

The palettes stored in the third default palette box are the History, Actions, and Tool Presets palettes, as shown in Figure 3-4.

✖ **Caution!**

Your default palettes won't look like this if you're using 800 x 600 resolution; change to 1024 x 768 if you haven't done so already. This can be achieved by accessing the display properties from inside your operating system files, usually located under the Display icon in the Control Panel.

In the following figure, the History palette is selected, which shows the list of steps taken to create the image shown in Figure 3-3. You can see that type was added, a custom shape was added (the arrow), and an item was transformed (specifically, rotated). The History palette helps you correct errors (by storing what you've done to a file previously) and allows you to "go back" to a point before a particular edit was made by simply clicking on the appropriate step.

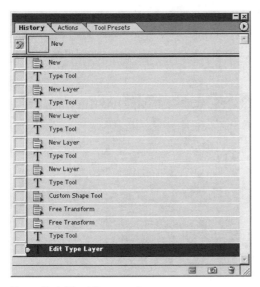

Figure 3-4: The History palette

The Actions palette lets you record, play, edit, and delete specific actions or load action files. Action files can include adding text effects, image effects, and production actions, such as changing a custom RGB file to grayscale or saving a file as a JPEG, and will increase the efficiency in which you perform oft-repeated tasks. You can also purchase actions from third-party vendors and software manufacturers, and these actions will usually perform extremely complex sets of instructions.

Finally, the Tool Presets palette lets you load, save, and replace tool preset libraries for quick reference. Saving custom preset tools allows you to reuse custom tools without recreating them each time. Creating a new tool preset is easy; just choose a tool, configure the options you want to set for the tool, and choose New Tool Preset from the additional options available from the Tool Presets palette.

 Tip:

When you begin to create logos and artwork, keep the History palette and the Tool Presets in the interface. Refer to the History palette often for a quick and painless way to revert back any number of steps to "undo" actions performed. Use the Tool Presets to quickly access preconfigured tools.

Layers, Channels, and Paths

The last default palette box contains three palettes (Layers, Channels, and Paths) and is shown in Figure 3-5. In this figure, multiple layers are shown.

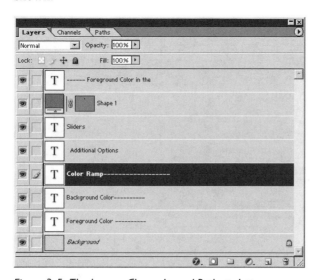

Figure 3-5: The Layers, Channels, and Paths palettes

Caution!

Your default palettes won't look like this if you're using 800 x 600 resolution; change to 1024 x 768 if you haven't done so already.

 Note:

Layers, channels, and paths are all rather complex concepts in Photoshop and are detailed in various chapters throughout the book. For now it is only important to understand a little about layers and that layers can be edited here.

Layers are like transparencies, which are clear plastic sheets of material that can be printed on. The transparencies can be printed and stacked on top of one another to form a complex picture, and single transparencies can be removed from the stack for editing or removal. When you create artwork in Photoshop 7.0, you can create it on layers similar to these transparencies—text on one layer, background image on another, and perhaps a selection pasted from another file on another. These layers can then be edited independently of each other, making the editing process more efficient and precise.

Viewing a Multilayered Image

To see an example of a multilayered image, open the MorningGlass.psd file from the Samples folder of the Adobe program files on your hard drive. Choose the Move tool from the toolbox, and click on any of the layers in the Layers palette. You will see that this picture is made up of multiple layers, each playing a distinct part in the image itself.

Additional Palettes

There are additional palettes available that aren't shown on the interface by default, including the Brushes palette, the Character palette, and the Paragraph palette. The File Browser can also be added, which allows you to access, open, and see the properties of any file quickly and easily.

The Brushes Palette

The Brushes palette can be opened using Window>Brushes. From here, an artist can create or access thousands of types of brushes and configure them to meet any drawing need. You'll use brushes when you create logos and artwork, and you can even use the airbrushes to create air-brushed artwork.

Caution!

Make sure that a brush is chosen when accessing the Brushes palette, or all of the brushes will be grayed out!

The Character and Paragraph Palettes

The Character palette can be opened using Windows>Character. The Paragraph palette opens with it, or you can use Window>Paragraph if you like. With these palettes, the offset printer, logo designer, CAD cutter, or sign maker can format the text used in a file. This includes choosing or changing the font, font style, and font size, as well as making precise changes to text, such as leading, kerning, scale, and baseline shift. Paragraphs can also be formatted, including indentation, orientation, and hyphenation rules. Many of these attributes can also be changed from the options bar while adding the text itself; all of these points are covered in Chapter 9, "Working with Text and Numbers." Since I haven't discussed adding type yet, I'll save this discussion for later.

The File Browser

The File Browser, while technically a palette, is a little different from the other palettes discussed in this chapter. The File Browser allows you to search your physical drives (hard drive, CD drive, DVD drives, digital camera drives, floppy drives, and zip drives) for files that you've either previously created or you need to import. The File Browser is discussed in depth in Chapter 6, "Using the File Browser and Opening Files."

Pop-up Palettes

Some palettes are not available from the Window menu choices and appear instead when a specific tool is chosen and being configured. These palettes are called pop-up palettes for this reason. Let's look at a few of these types of palettes:

1. Close any open files. Then choose **File>New** to create a new canvas to work with.

2. Choose **RGB Color, 1024 x 768**, and a **white** background.

3. Choose **Window>Workspace>Reset Palette Locations** to revert the workspace to its defaults.

4. Select the **Brush** tool from the toolbox.

5. Click on the down arrow to the right of the word Brush in the options bar; it is the second down arrow on the bar.

6. The resulting drop-down list is called a pop-up palette. Click the right arrow to see the additional options. I've chosen to view my pop-up palette using the Large Thumbnail option, but you can choose whatever option is best for you, as shown in Figure 3-6.

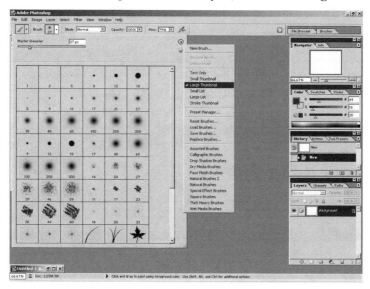

Figure 3-6: Pop-up palettes

7. The brushes showing in Figure 3-6 are the default brushes. From the additional options list, choose **Assorted Brushes** and click **OK** when prompted.

8. Click the **Gradient** tool in the toolbox.

9. From the options bar, click on the down arrow next to the gradient to see another pop-up palette. Again, click the arrow for additional options.

10. From the toolbox, choose the **Custom Shape** tool.

11. Click the down arrow next to the word Shape on the options bar to see the pop-up palette for the custom shapes. When finished, close the file.

As you can probably surmise from the multitude of palettes and options, there are literally thousands of configurations possible for brushes, tools, palettes, and other items. In the next section, you learn how to customize the palettes in the work area and save a workspace.

Moving, Adding, and Removing Palettes

Customizing the workspace is an important part of Photoshop's offerings, and the palettes are quite flexible. The palettes can be added or removed from the workspace, and most of the palettes can be resized as well. They can be docked together in different configurations or docked to the Palette Well located on the options bar.

Moving the Palettes

Palettes are moved like any dialog box in most software programs; just click and drag from the title bar. Resizing is done similarly; just drag from the bottom-right corner. Figure 3-7 shows the title bar and resizing area.

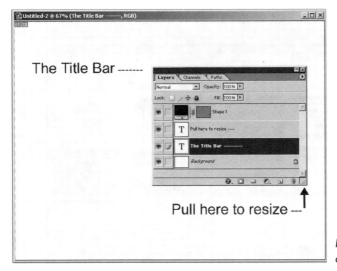

The Title Bar ·······

Pull here to resize ---

Figure 3-7: Moving and resizing

The Window > <command> Options

The Window commands offer quick ways to show or hide specific palettes or revert to the default workspace or a saved one. From the Window menus, place a check next to the palettes you wish to see in the workspace, and remove the check to remove them from the workspace. Adding and removing the check mark is achieved by clicking it.

Docking the Palettes Together

If you don't care for the way the palettes are docked together, you can change them. To separate a palette from its docked companions, simply drag the palette's tab to another area on the screen. Figure 3-8 shows a workspace where all of the palettes have been undocked from their grouped positions. Of course, this isn't an effective way to work, but it proves the point.

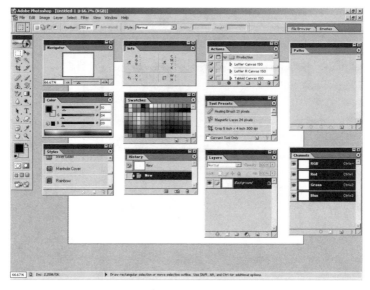

Figure 3-8: Undocking

The tabs can also be dragged off of the screen to the Palette Well, detailed next, or dragged to another palette and grouped elsewhere. Figure 3-9 shows all of the default palettes grouped together as one.

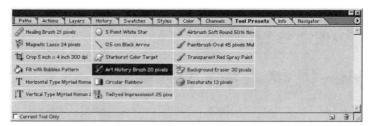

Figure 3-9: Grouping

The Palette Well

The palettes that are in the workspace can be removed from the work area by dragging them to the Palette Well. The Palette Well is located on the options bar in the top-right corner of the interface, as seen in previous figures (Figure 3-8, where it holds the File Browser and Brushes palettes). Using the same dragging technique as detailed in the previous section, palettes can be dragged from the work area to the Palette Well. This effectively removes the palette from the work area, while keeping the palette handy and easily accessible. The palettes can be dragged back onto the workspace from the Palette Well whenever necessary.

 Caution!

You won't be able to see the Palette Well if you have the resolution of your monitor set for 800 x 600—yet another reason to increase the resolution to 1024 x 768 (or higher).

Saving the Workspace

Once you have the workspace just the way you want it, you can save that configuration using the Window>Workspace>Save Workspace command. Type in a name for the workspace in the Save Workspace dialog box, and it becomes available from the Window>Workspace choices.

✎ **Note:**

In Chapter 5, "Personalizing the Workspace," we create a workspace specific to your needs as a screen printer and artist.

Palette Tips and Tricks

There are several tips and tricks out there for palette configuration, and although they're documented in Photoshop's help files, they're worth repeating in the last bit of space here.

Open a new or existing file and try these tips and tricks:

- To show or hide the toolbox, the options bar, and all of the palettes, press the Tab key.

- To show or hide only the palettes, press the Shift+Tab key combination.

- Display various palette menus by clicking on the right arrow in most palettes.

- Use the minimize and maximize options on each palette to make it smaller or larger.

- To always start with the default palette positions, choose Edit>Preferences>General and deselect Save Palette Locations.

- When using pop-up sliders, type in a number for the value to achieve a precise move.

- When using pop-up palettes, set the thumbnails to Large Thumbnail if you want to see the name, size, and sample of each.

- Use the additional options in a palette to rename or delete an item such as a brush.

- Leave the History palette in the workspace so it's easily accessible.

After working with the palettes for a while, you'll discover what you use and what you don't. Armed with that knowledge, you can more effectively personalize the workspace.

Summary

In this chapter you learned all about palettes, including how to use them, how to access additional options, group and ungroup them, dock to the Palette Well, and access pop-up palettes. The palettes play an important role in personalizing the work area and working with files and artwork. Even though you can personalize the workspace, for now consider leaving it as-is until you are comfortable with what is available by default.

Chapter 4

The Options Bar

The options bar is another part of Photoshop 7.0's interface and changes each time a tool is chosen from the toolbox. Figures 4-1, 4-2, and 4-3 show the options bar for various tools. From here, the tool can be configured.

Figure 4-1: The options bar when the Type tool is chosen

Figure 4-2: The options bar when the Brush tool is chosen

Figure 4-3: The options bar when the Pen tool is chosen

In this chapter, we take a look at some of the common option bar choices, such as Style, Show Bounding Box, Auto Select Layer, Mode, Opacity, Brush, and more. Many of these options are shown for multiple tools, such as Opacity and Brush, while others are only available for a specific tool, like Resize Windows To Fit when using the Zoom tool.

 Note:

As with the remaining chapters of this book, not every option is covered. Photoshop can be overkill for screen printers and graphic artists, as they most likely don't create images for the web or use filters and gradients much in their artwork. In this chapter, I only cover what is relevant to the graphic artist.

Common Options from the Options Bar

In order to use the tools successfully, you need to understand what's available and what the words and options mean. A word like "opacity" might not mean much to the layperson, but it is certainly one every Photoshop user should know!

 Tip:

You can drag the options bar anywhere on the screen that you'd like by pulling from the far left corner.

Style

The Style option from the options bar is a common one indeed. This option is available when you choose the Marquee, Pen, Art History Brush, or Shape tools. Clicking on the down arrow next to the Style button brings up either a pop-up palette or a drop-down list where choices can be made about the style of the layer or tool with which you are working. The styles choice is also one of the default palettes, as described in the previous chapter.

Figure 4-4 shows the pop-up palette that appears when clicking the style arrow on the options bar and also shows a simple example of applying a style to a shape. In this figure, the rectangle has been added and has had a style applied to it, specifically a blue neon rollover style with its fill opacity changed. Text was added later. This image would be difficult to screen, and was originally created to be placed on tote bags using heat transfer methods.

Figure 4-4: Style choices from the options bar

 Tip:

You might have noticed that the Palette Well is not available from the options bar. This is because the screen resolution has been changed from 1024 x 768 to 800 x 600, making the buttons appear larger than they would normally.

Show Bounding Box and Auto Select Layer

My two favorite options from the options bar are Show Bounding Box and Auto Select Layer. You see both of these options when you choose the Move tool, and you see the Show Bounding Box option with the Path Selection tool. As a screen printer, I suggest that you keep both of these boxes checked. Checking them allows you to see the bounding box that surrounds a selected object, which in turn makes it easier to move, resize, and rotate a selection. The Auto Select Layer option automatically selects the layer you intend to work with.

Figure 4-5 shows the rectangle and its bounding box and layer selected. The small squares that surround the rectangle can be used to move and resize the rectangle, and the Layers palette (also shown) denotes which layer is currently selected.

Figure 4-5: The bounding box and selected layer

 Note:

You can see from the Layers palette that there are effects applied to the rectangle and its layer. This is because a style was applied to the layer. Clicking on the small cursive "f" in the Layers palette can be used to easily change these attributes.

Mode

Mode appears more often on the options bar than almost anything else, including when the Healing Brush, Pencil, Brush, Clone Stamp, Pattern Stamp, History Brush, Art History Brush, Eraser, Paint Bucket, Gradient, Blur, Sharpen, Smudge, and Sponge tools are chosen. This tool has many uses, and its choices and effects on an image differ depending on the tool chosen.

Basically, the mode options allow you to control how you want pixels to be affected by the application of the painting or editing tool you choose. Modes, also called blending modes, are generally used for creating special effects. Figure 4-6 shows the mode options when the Brush tool is chosen.

Figure 4-6: Mode options

As shown in the figure, there are multiple modes to choose from. While it is not necessary to go through a detailed explanation of all these modes (you'll probably never use many of them), a brief explanation of a few is certainly in order here.

Some modes you might use include:

- **Normal**: This mode is the default mode for painting and editing for most of the tools. Normal mode simply replaces the underlying pixels with the pixels you add to the image by painting or brushing. It is merely uncomplicated replacement of color.

- **Multiply** and **Screen**: When using multiply mode, the foreground color is combined with the original colors in the image to decrease the brightness in the areas in which you are painting. This produces darker images by emphasizing the darker colors. Screen is just the opposite and works in tandem with lighter colors.

- **Light modes**: There are several light modes, including vivid light, linear light, pin light, soft light, and hard light, and each applies light to the image in different ways. Most produce special effect type lighting.

- **Hue**: Hue paints with the foreground shade only and is good for applying tint to areas of an image.

- **Clear**: This mode changes solid-colored pixels to transparent pixels when using the Paint Bucket, Brush, or Pencil tools when using the fill command or the stroke command. Changing pixels to transparent removes them from the image. (You can't choose the clear option if the layer is locked.)

Don't worry too much about the huge number of modes shown in Figure 4-6. Most screen printers don't spend much time applying modes for creating special effects or lightening or darkening images. Most of the time, you'll use the Image>Adjustments>Curve command to change the colors in an image; it's fast, easy, and a common tool for screen printers. Using this option offers a preview of the color changes made as well as the ability to set target colors including midtones, shadows, or highlights. There are several other options that can be set manually as well, and these are discussed throughout the book.

Brush

The Brush option from the options bar comes up quite a bit too. In fact, you'll probably use the brush options more than just about anything else on the options bar. The brush options appear when the following tools are shown: the Healing Brush, Brush, Pencil, Pattern Stamp, Clone Stamp, History Brush, Art History Brush, Eraser, Background Eraser, Blur, Sharpen, Smudge, Dodge, Burn, and Smudge tools. (The brush presets are available when tools are chosen as well and are discussed later in this chapter.) The Brush option lets you configure the painting tool that you are working with by selecting the attributes it will have for its size, texture, shape, and more.

Project 4-1: Using the Brush Options from the Options Bar to Clone an Area of an Image

Let's take a look at some of the Brush tools and how you might use them in a screen printing environment to clone a specific area of an image:

1. Open the file **Flowers1.psd** from the Chapter 4 folder on the companion CD.

2. If you've moved the palettes around, reset them using **Window>Workspace>Reset Palette Locations**.

3. Choose the **Clone Stamp** tool from the toolbox or press **S** on the keyboard. If using the keyboard, verify you've chosen the Clone Stamp tool and not the Pattern Stamp tool from the toolbox.

4. From the options bar, click the down arrow in the Brush window. Next, click the right arrow to show the additional options. These are both shown in Figure 4-7. Choose **Reset Brushes**. Click **OK** when prompted.

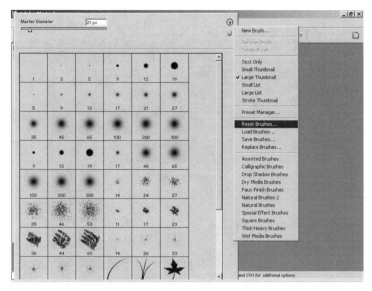

Figure 4-7: Using the brush options

5. Choose brush number **19**, a hard, round brush, by double-clicking on the brush.

6. Change the master diameter to 50 by moving the slider bar or typing in the number **50** in the master diameter window. Hit the **Enter** key to close it.

7. Press the **Alt** key on the keyboard and click in the center of the bottom sunflower to create a sampling point. When pressing the Alt key, the cursor will change to a target shape.

8. Position the cursor in the top-right corner of the picture. You'll be cloning the original sunflower there. Click and notice that there is now a cross over the area from which you took the sampling point, the middle of the sunflower, as well as the outline of the brush you are working with. Use this cross to carefully trace around the sunflower and to create a clone of the original flower. Figure 4-8 shows two pictures; the first is the original, and the second is the clone stamp in progress. If you look closely, you can see the circle that represents the brush and the cross that represents the cloned point.

Figure 4-8: Using a brush in combination with the Clone Stamp tool

9. You can repeat these steps to create many sunflowers. Figure 4-9 shows just how much a single photo can be changed.

 Note:

A file called Flowers2.psd is also in the Chapter 4 folder on the companion CD and contains an image with several cloned sunflowers, as you might have created in this exercise.

Figure 4-9: Using a brush in combination with the Clone Stamp tool

This is just one of the uses for a brush. As mentioned in the introduction of this section, many tools offer brushes as a way to use the tool effectively. You'll want to become proficient in using, selecting, and configuring brushes.

Opacity

Opacity is available on the Layers palette for working with a fill or a layer and from the options bar when working with the Brush, Pencil, Clone Stamp, Pattern Stamp, History Brush, Art History Brush, Eraser, Magic Eraser, Gradient, or Paint Bucket tools. Opacity can also be set when blending options are chosen.

Opacity is used to specify how transparent a layer should be either on its own or in regard to other layers. To see how opacity functions, work through the following project for creating a gradient layer.

Project 4-2: Creating a Background for a Business Card, Decal, or Mouse Pad (Understanding Opacity)

In this project, we create a gradient layer that can be used as a background for a business card, truck or car decal, sign, coffee mug, mouse pad, or process (or simulated process color) T-shirt. In doing so, we learn about opacity and brushes (and maybe even a little bit about layers). We first configure opacity using the Layers palette and later with the options bar.

 Note:

Configuring opacity with the Layers palette first gives you a better understanding of what exactly opacity is.

1. Choose **File>New** and configure the settings as shown in Figure 4-10.

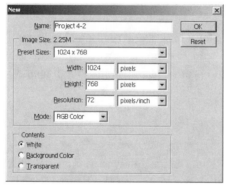

Figure 4-10: Creating a new file

2. Choose **Layer>New Fill Layer>Gradient**. Click **OK** in the New Layer dialog box.

3. In the Gradient Fill dialog box, choose **Linear** from the Style choices by clicking on the down arrow.

4. From the Gradient choices, select a gradient that you like. Leave the other options the same. Click **OK**.

5. Locate the Layers palette; it should be visible in the work area. If it is not, place a check next to the Layers choice in Window>Layers. This palette is shown in Figure 4-11.

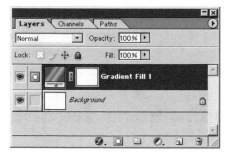

Figure 4-11: Using the Layers palette to configure opacity

6. Highlight the layer that contains the gradient, as shown in the figure. In the Layers palette, click the right arrow beside the word Opacity, and move the slider to the left. Let go of the mouse and notice the depth or thickness of the colors on the layer change. If you move the slider all the way to the left, the gradient layer becomes transparent and doesn't show at all; all the way to the right and there is no transparency at all.

7. Set the opacity at **40** percent by typing in the value in the Layers palette.

8. Select the **Brush** tool from the toolbox.

9. Choose **Layer>New>Layer** and click **OK** in the New Layer dialog box. Notice in the Layers palette that the additional layer has been added. We apply a brush to this layer.

10. Choose the **Brush** tool, and from the options bar click on the down arrow next to the brush to bring up the brush pop-up palette.

11. Click the right arrow in this pop-up palette and choose **Reset Brushes**. Click **OK** when prompted.

12. Choose the **Scattered Leaves** brush (number 95) from the brushes pop-up palette by double-clicking on it.

13. On the options bar, make sure the opacity is set to **100** percent.

14. Click on the image to add the falling leaves.

15. Change the opacity to **75** percent and add more leaves, to **50** percent and add more leaves, and finally to **25** percent, adding more leaves.

16. This background can now be saved and used as a background for a landscape company, a tree service, or similar industry simply by adding a bit of clip art and some text.

The purpose of this project was to familiarize you with the options bar and how to use it and to give you some experience selecting and working with brushes. If you watched the Layers palette while you were working, you probably even learned a little about layers along the way.

Adding or Subtracting from a Selection or Shape

When adding shapes or making selections, you can do much more than just add a distinct shape or make a single, simple selection. You can choose to add to, subtract from, or select what intersects with the previous selection or shape by choosing the correct option from the options bar or use the default of simply adding a new selection or new shape. Figure 4-12 shows a design that was created using the tools in Photoshop 7.0, as well as the location of the add and subtract to shape options on the options bar.

 Note:

If you haven't seen this checkerboard background yet, it's a transparent background. There's nothing behind the logo and artwork, which enables film or vellum to be created without any further editing.

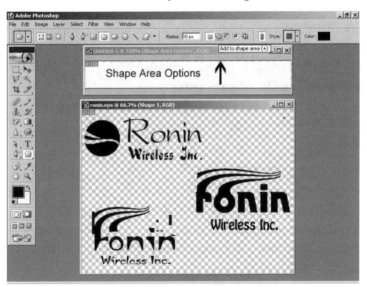

Figure 4-12: Creating custom logos using the add to, subtract from, and intersect options

Adding to, subtracting from, and choosing only what intersects in the original shapes and paths added to the image is necessary to create logos such as these. By using these tools, original artwork can be drawn using simple shapes and paths. To understand how these tools function, work through the following example:

1. Open a new file that is large enough to experiment on, at least 800 x 600. Choose a white or transparent background.

2. Choose the **Ellipse** tool from the toolbox. Verify that the shape layers icon in the options bar is selected, not the paths option. This icon is second from the left in the options bar and looks like a square with four handles, one on each corner.

3. Hold down the **Shift** key and drag the mouse on the screen to draw a circle. Click when finished and then let go of the Shift key.

4. Choose the **Rounded Rectangle** tool next. Make sure the default of **Create New Shape Layer** is chosen from the options bar and draw a rectangle that overlaps the original circle.

5. Choose the **Ellipse** tool again, and draw another circle. Choose **Add to Shape Area** from the options bar.

6. Choose the **Rounded Rectangle** tool next. Draw a rectangle that overlaps this circle.

7. Choose the **Ellipse** tool again. Choose **Create New Shape Layer** from the options bar and draw another circle.

8. Choose the **Rounded Rectangle** tool and choose **Subtract from Shape Area**. Draw a rectangle that overlaps this circle.

9. Choose the **Ellipse** tool again. Choose **Create New Shape Layer** from the options bar and draw another circle.

10. Choose the **Rounded Rectangle** tool and choose **Intersect Shape Areas** from the options bar. Draw a rectangle that overlaps this circle.

11. Choose the **Ellipse** tool again, and choose **Create New Shape Layer** from the options bar and draw another circle.

12. Choose the **Rounded Rectangle** tool, and choose **Exclude Overlapping Shape Areas** from the options bar. Draw a rectangle that overlaps this circle.

Figure 4-13 shows logos created using the same technique detailed in this example. Most were created by drawing a circle first and then a rectangle or by using simple shapes and text.

Figure 4-13: Sample artwork

You can use the add to, subtract from, and intersect options when making selections too. They're located further to the left on the options bar and used similarly. After an initial selection has been made using any selection tool, just click the Add to Selection button to add the next selection to the previous one(s). You can also choose the Subtract from Selection or Intersect with Selection options.

 Tip:

When making selections, you don't have to use these buttons if you don't want to. After an initial selection has been made, hold down the Shift key to add to the previous selection or the Alt key to subtract from it. The cursor changes with a + or – to reflect this choice.

Tool Presets

Each tool in the toolbox has its own icon in the left corner of the options bar, and there is a down arrow beside it. Clicking on this arrow brings up the tool presets. Here, you can save and reuse tools and tool settings, as well as load, edit, and create libraries of tools you use most often. Figure 4-14 shows the tool preset options and the additional options.

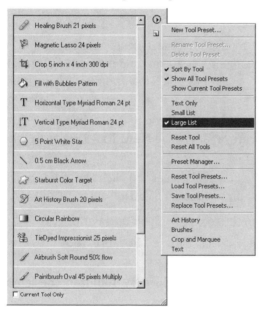

Figure 4-14: Tool presets

To choose a tool preset, create a tool preset, or change how presets appear in the pop-up palette, work through the following steps.

To choose a tool preset:

1. Click the tool presets in the options bar (it's the down arrow next to the tool's icon located furthest to the left).

2. Double-click on a tool in the toolbox to select it.

To see additional options, change how you view the presets, and load new tool presets:

3. Click on the tool presets again, and this time, click the right arrow to see the additional options. (You will see something similar to Figure 4-14.)

4. If you like, change the view to **Text Only, Small List**, or **Large List**.

5. Choose **Load Tool Presets** from the additional options. From the choices, choose **Text**. Notice that the tool presets change automatically to all text tools and presets. (You can load the other sets too.)

6. Choose **Reset Tool Presets** and click **OK** when prompted to return to the default tool set.

To create a new tool preset:

7. Select a tool from the toolbox that most closely matches (or is exactly) the tool you'd like to create and add it to the tool preset list. Configure any additional options you'd like the tool to have from the options bar.

8. Click on the create new tool preset icon in the toolset pop-up palette underneath the right arrow, or choose **New Tool Preset** from the additional options menu.

9. Type in a name for the new tool preset and click **OK**. The new tool will appear in the tool preset pop-up palette.

To change what appears in the tool preset pop-up palette:

10. To load all preset tool libraries, choose **Show All Tool Presets** from the additional options menu.

11. To sort the presets by tool, choose **Sort By Tool** from the additional options menu.

12. To show only the active presets for the tool currently selected, choose **Show Current Tool Presets** from the additional options menu or check the **Current Tool Only** box.

13. To add or delete tools from a preset tool library, choose **Preset Manager** from the additional options menu. Click on any tool to delete or rename it. (I'd suggest not doing this for now, at least not until you are familiar with all of the tools.) Once the library is configured the way you like, choose **Save** and name the new library.

 Tip:

Creating your own preset tool library can be quite helpful if you use the same tools often to perform specific tasks. Revisit this part of the chapter after you've finished this book and create a library of *your* favorites using the Preset Manager available from the additional options.

Other Common Terms and Options

There are several options that you'll see off and on when accessing tools and using the options bar. Words like tolerance, anti-aliased, contiguous, flow, and others will pop up depending on the tool selected. These words are defined briefly here:

 Tip:

Bookmark this page and refer to it when using tools and the options bar. This section is meant to serve as a reference and should be referred to when questions about the options in the options bar arise.

- **Feather:** Feathering is the process of blurring edges around a selection. Blurring the edges helps the selection blend into another object, file, or selection when it is moved, cut, copied, and/or pasted. Feathering causes loss of detail and should not be used with spot color artwork. However, feathering can be useful when working with photos, especially if you plan to cut from one photo and paste into another.

- **Anti-aliased/Anti-aliasing:** Anti-aliasing is the process of smoothing edges around a selection. It differs from feathering in that it does not blur the edges but instead softens them by blending the colors of the outer pixels with the background pixels. This results in no loss of detail. You must choose anti-aliasing before selecting; it cannot be added after a selection has been made.

- **Width and Height:** This allows you to set the width and height for a marquee or shape by manually typing in the dimensions. Width and height can also be set this way for the Crop tool and Slice tool.

- **Align and Distribute options:** These options allow you to align and distribute layers or selections within an image. There are several ways to align or distribute objects: top, vertical center, left, horizontal center, and right.

- **Edge Contrast:** Use this option with the Lasso tools to define the lasso's sensitivity to the edges of the selection you're trying to lasso. Values can range from 1 percent to 100 percent. A lower value detects low-contrast edges (those that don't have much contrast with their backgrounds), and a higher value detects edges that contrast sharply with their backgrounds. Configuring this prior to and during a selection can make selecting an object manually much more efficient. (Combine with the Zoom tool for best results.)

■ **Pen Pressure**: If you use a stylus tablet, you can set Pen Pressure. This allows you to draw on the tablet and have the resulting amount of pressure you use while drawing applied to the tool you're using on the screen. Pen Pressure is available with several tools, including the Pen and some Brush tools.

■ **Frequency**: Use this option with the Lasso tools to determine at what frequency or how often anchor points are added as you trace around the object. Values between 0 and 100 can be used, and higher values add more anchor (fastening) points. Frequency is available when using the Pen tool too; the values there can range from 5 to 40.

■ **Impressionist**: This adds an impressionist effect (like Monet's art) when the box is checked while using the Pattern Stamp tool.

■ **Tolerance**: This option is available with several tools and is used to set how "tolerant" a tool is with regard to the colors with which it is working. For instance, when using the Paint Bucket tool to fill an area with color, the tolerance level determines how close the color must be to the original color (where you click) before it gets filled. Values can be between 0 and 255. A lower number only fills colors very similar to where you click; a higher number fills a broader range of colors. Tolerance can also be set for the Magic Eraser tool, the Art History Brush tool, and the Magic Wand tool.

■ **Use All Layers**: To apply the tool to all of the layers in the image, place a check in this box. For instance, when using the Magic Wand to select a specific color, you can choose to apply the selection to all of the layers in the image instead of the default of only the active layer.

■ **Contiguous**: This is used with tools such as the Magic Eraser, the Paint Bucket, and the Magic Wand to specify how colors will be selected, applied, or erased. When Contiguous is checked, the resulting selection only includes pixels that are adjacent to each other. Otherwise, all pixels of the preferred color are selected.

■ **Resolution**: Resolution determines how many pixels are shown per unit (such as inch or centimeter) in an image. Higher resolutions contain more pixels (thus more detail) than lower resolution images. You can set the resolution when you crop images.

- **Front Image and Clear:** Used with the Crop tool, Clear removes all text from the text boxes, while Front Image uses the settings from the front image for width, height, and resolution settings.

- **Source (Sampled or Pattern):** This is used when repairing flaws in images (perhaps with the Healing Brush) to determine how exactly an image will be repaired. Sampled uses pixels from the current image, and Pattern fills the area with a pattern you select from the pattern pop-up palette.

- **Aligned:** Aligned is used when repairing flaws in images (such as with the Healing Brush or Clone Stamp tool). Place a check in the Align box if you need to release the mouse button while working and still keep the sampling point; sampled pixels are thus applied contin-uously. Uncheck the box to apply the pixels from the original sam-pling point each time.

- **Source and Destination:** These are used with the Patch tool to specify what pixels should be repaired (Destination) and with what pixels (Source).

- **Use Pattern (Pattern):** This offers a pop-up palette from which a pattern can be chosen to fill the selected area and patch it.

- **Auto Erase:** Available with the Pencil tool, a checked Auto Erase box allows you to paint the background color over areas of fore-ground color. This, in essence, erases what has been previously drawn with the foreground color.

- **Toggle the Brushes Palette:** This allows you to toggle the Brushes palette on and off. This is a small button located on the far right of some options bars, such as Burn, Dodge, Sponge, Blur, Sharpen, and Smudge.

- **Flow:** Flow is used to specify how quickly paint is applied when using a Brush tool like the Airbrush. A heavier flow lays on more paint more quickly; a lower flow lays on less.

- **Airbrush:** The Airbrush option simulates traditional airbrush tech-niques by gradually adding paint similar to a spray paint gun or a spray paint can.

- **Area:** Area is used with Art History Brush to specify the painting area diameter.

- **Limits:** Limits allows you to choose from Contiguous, Discon-tiguous, and Find Edges when using the Background Eraser tool.

Contiguous erases colors that are next to the original sample, Discontiguous erases underneath the brush, and Find Edges looks for and finds the edges of an image and erases to those edges.

■ **Protect Foreground Color**: When erasing, check this box to protect the foreground color from being erased.

■ **Sampling**: Sampling is used with the Magic Eraser tool to specify how pixels will be erased (Continuous, Once, or Background Swatch). Continuous erases as you drag, Once erases only the colors where you first click, and Background Swatch erases only colors that match the current background color.

■ **Reverse**: This reverses the chosen gradient's colors and is used with the Gradient tool.

■ **Dither**: Dither reduces visible banding related to gradients when using the Gradient tool.

■ **Transparency**: To use a transparency mask for the gradient fill, place a check in the Transparency box. Doing so allows you to specify gradient transparency (which is kind of like opacity for solid fills).

■ **Strength**: Strength is used with the Blur, Sharpen, and Smudge tools and specifies how strong the stroke should be. Lower numbers reduce the strength; higher numbers increase the strength.

■ **Range**: This is used with the Dodge and Burn tools and allows you to select a tonal range to lighten or darken (midtones, highlights, or shadows).

■ **Exposure**: This sets the amount of exposure (coverage) used by the Dodge and Burn tools.

■ **Sample Size**: The eyedropper can be used to take a sample of a color for multiple uses, including choosing a foreground color, using the Healing Brush, and using the Background Eraser. The sample size of the eyedropper can be changed in the sample size window. It is usually best to keep the sample size small. You can choose from Point Sample, 3 by 3 Average, or 5 by 5 Average.

■ **Actual Pixels/Fit on Screen/Print Size**: Used with the Zoom and Hand tools, these options allow you to configure how the image should look on the screen after modifying it previously.

■ **Resize Windows to Fit**: This option resizes the active window to fit in the workspace area.

- **Ignore Palettes**: When using the Zoom tool, check this box if the Zoom options available on the options bar should ignore the palettes that are currently located in the workspace.

 Note:

Pen, Shape, and Type options have their own chapters and are discussed there.

The Palette Well

The Palette Well is available on the options bar only if the screen resolution is set at 1024 x 768 or higher. The Palette Well is located on the far right of the options bar. (In this chapter, the Palette Well isn't shown in any of the screen shots because the resolution of my screen is 800 x 600 for better images for this book.) Figure 4-15 shows the Palette Well in its default state.

Figure 4.15: The palette well

The Palette Well offers a place to dock palettes that you don't want on the screen but still want to have access to without having to use the Window menu. To dock a palette, simply drag it from its place in the workspace to the Palette Well. Once in the Palette Well, click once on the appropriate tab to open the palette. Once opened, the palette can be dragged back onto the screen from its highlighted tab.

You can also change the order of the palette list in the Palette Well by right-clicking on any tab and choosing to move it left or right, or beginning or end. Additionally, each palette's additional options have a choice to dock to the Palette Well automatically (without dragging).

 Tip:

In the next chapter we create some workspaces that are personalized for specific industries, jobs, or clients. Use the Palette Well to dock palettes that you'd like to keep available but out of sight.

Summary

In this chapter, you learned about the options from the options bar. Some common options include Style, Show Bounding Box, Auto Select Layer, Mode, Opacity, Brush, and adding to or subtracting from a selection or shape. There are other less-common options also; these options were detailed for use as a reference toward the end of the chapter. Refer to this chapter often when questions arise concerning an option on the options bar.

Chapter 5

Personalizing the Workspace

Now that you understand all of the interface elements, let's personalize, configure, and save a workspace for a specific job or industry. Perhaps you are a screen printer working mainly with spot color images and logos and you rarely use styles. You can remove the Styles palette from the interface and save the resulting configuration. If you have specific clients that require mainly text-related jobs, you can create a workspace that contains the Character and Paragraph palettes and open this workspace each time that client's file needs work.

In essence, Photoshop can be configured to suit the needs of just about any industry or artist. The suggestions in this chapter can help you decide what your particular space should look like. As you streamline your business, you can also streamline the interface.

In addition to configuring the interface to meet the needs of the task at hand, you'll also need to configure preferences from the Edit menu, configure the Preset Manager, configure the color settings, and calibrate your system. These are generally one-time tasks, and are necessary to get Photoshop and the machine up and running and ready for handling your screen printing needs. Calibration and configuring color settings are very important parts of personalizing the system, and in-depth projects are included to assist you with these tasks.

Removing the Toolbox, Options Bar, and/or Status Bar

When working with certain artwork, you might find that the toolbox, options bar, and/or the status bar impede your work by taking up much-needed space on the screen. These items can be removed in several ways.

The Window menu has a list of all of the items that can be shown in the Photoshop workspace, and there are checks by those that are showing. To remove the item from the workspace, simply uncheck the item from the Window menu. Figure 5-1 shows the Window menu with all of the items unchecked. As you can see from the image, the workspace is clear of all palettes, the toolbox, the options bar, and the status bar.

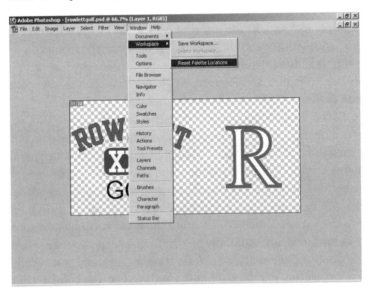

Figure 5-1: Removing everything from the workspace

You don't have to remove everything, certainly, and you can pick and choose what you want to leave in the workspace. For most of your work though, you'll want to leave the options bar, the toolbox, and the status bar checked and available.

Tip:

To reset the palettes, choose Window>Workspace>Reset Palette Locations, which is also shown in the previous figure. Everything will return to its original place except for the status bar, which will need to be checked from the Window menu.

You can also clear the workspace of all palettes and tools by pressing the Tab key on the keyboard. This toggles the workspace from what you see in Figure 5-1 to what you have configured by default. The Shift+Tab key removes all of the palettes.

 Note:

When you close Photoshop, the positions of the palettes are saved. The configuration will be the same the next time Photoshop is opened.

Docking in the Palette Well

Use the Palette Well to dock palettes that you want to keep handy but don't want on the screen. This was discussed in Chapter 4 but deserves a reminder here. Once you have the toolbox, the options bar, the status bar, and the palettes the way you want them, you can save them using the Window>Workspace>Save Workspace command.

Creating a Text-Based Workspace

There are plenty of industries that are generally text based, such as off-set print shops, graphic design shops that create yard signs, banners, and magnetic signs for cars, CAD cutters, and printers that create business cards, print ads, menus, and similar items. While many of these artists have word processing programs that they use for much of their work, and perhaps even vector-based programs such as CorelDRAW or Adobe Illustrator, Photoshop can play an important role too, especially since Photoshop has included vector-based text in the latest versions of the software. For those artists who use Photoshop for their print work, a text-based workspace certainly increases efficiency.

There are several palettes designed particularly for working with text, including the Character and Paragraph palettes. From the Character palette, a language can be chosen for checking the spelling in a file, and font, font size, and other text attributes can be set. The Paragraph palette can be used for configuring how paragraphs of text should be laid out.

In addition to these, the Styles palette can be useful, as text effects can be applied from there, and the Layers palette is useful since adding text also adds layers to the image and those layers can be chosen and manipulated using this palette.

Finally, consider adding the History palette and the Actions palette. In the additional options for the Actions palette, add the text effects actions. A sample palette is shown in Figure 5-2.

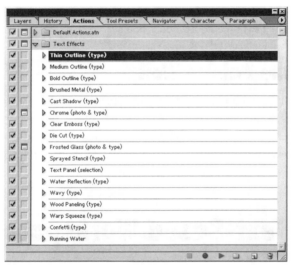

Figure 5-2: A sample text-based palette

Even though I've put all of the palettes together in a single box, you can separate them into two, three, or even four boxes and configure them to fit on the screen however you want. Once you've arranged the text-based workspace the way you want it, choose Window>Workspace>Save Workspace and name the new workspace Text-Based. The new workspace will appear in the Window>Workspace options and will be available anytime you need to work with text.

 Tip:

You can even dock the palettes in the Palette Well if desired, thus keeping the work area clean.

Creating a Screen Printing Workspace

Screen printers use some palettes for almost every job and other palettes very rarely. Since there's no point in having the workspace cluttered with unnecessary palettes, in this section we set up a workspace that suits most screen printers' needs.

There are a few palettes that you should certainly include: the Layers palette, the Channels palette, the Info palette, and the Tool Presets palette. The History palette is also important but only if you are comfortable with it. Some prefer to use the Undo command from the Edit menu. I'd also suggest keeping the File Browser in the Palette Well so that client files are easily accessible.

You probably won't do as much with the Navigator palette, the Styles palette, the Swatches palette, or the Actions palette, so you can remove those. You can open those when necessary from the Window menu. Figure 5-3 shows a sample screen printing workspace (it's the way mine is configured).

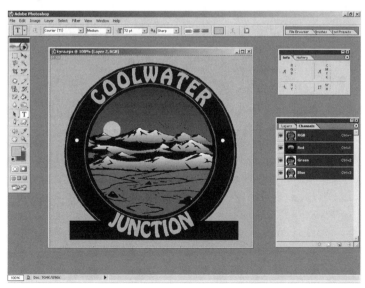

Figure 5-3: A screen printer's workspace

Tip:

Some palettes are docked together, such as the Info and Navigator palettes. If you remove the Navigator palette from the workspace by unchecking it from the Window menu, the Info palette is removed as well. To remove a single palette that is docked with others, drag it from its docked state and then click the close (X) button on the palette to remove it.

In this figure, the File Browser, Brushes, and Tool Presets palettes are docked in the Palette Well, the Info and History palettes are docked together, and the Layers and Channels palettes are docked together. This workspace has been saved as Screen Printer-based.

Creating a Client-based Workspace

When clients come to the shop to bring in their own artwork for printing, I open up the client-based workspace that I've configured. It contains the File Browser for navigating to the floppy, zip drive, or CD the client might have brought with them, the Navigator and Info palettes so we can talk about colors and the size of the image, Swatches so they can see the colors available, and Brushes so touch-ups can be made to photographs and other artwork on the fly.

Figure 5-4 shows a sample client-based workspace, which currently has the toolbox closed so the Navigator palette, File Browser, and client file can be seen clearly. The Brushes palette is docked to the Palette Well. If any editing needs to be done to the image, the Window>Tools option isn't far away, nor is the screen printer workspace configured earlier.

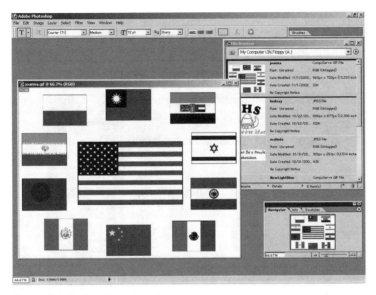

Figure 5-4: A client-based workspace

 Tip:

In addition to this workspace, consider connecting a large TV to your monitor so that the client can see what's on your screen on a larger scale.

Creating an Artist's Workspace

Artists require different workspaces than screen printers. Artists will certainly need layers but perhaps not channels. Performing tasks on channels is the job of the screen printer or the person in charge of color separating the artwork. Unlike a screen printer, the artist requires easy access to brushes, swatches, styles, color, paths, and actions, as well as tool presets and possibly even the Character and Paragraph palettes. Artists of this type will probably not need the File Browser on the screen or even in the Palette Well unless they're incorporating artwork from several open files at the same time. If you've got a serious artist or graphic designer on your staff, consider letting him or her create a custom workspace and save it.

Figure 5-5 shows a workspace configured for a graphic artist in my company. A similar workspace might work for yours. As with the other sections in this chapter, it's still a matter of personal preference, but each offers a good place to start, especially when an employee is in training.

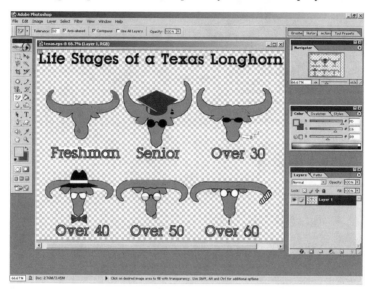

Figure 5-5: An artist's workspace

In Figure 5-5, the Palette Well contains the Brushes, History, Actions, and Tool Presets palettes. The other palettes include Navigator, Color, Swatches, Styles, Layers, and Paths.

Figure 5-6 shows the workspaces configured in this chapter.

Figure 5-6: Workspace choices

Editing Preferences

Photoshop comes preconfigured with preferences that its creators feel
suit most users. As you already know though, a screen printer isn't the
average user! Changing these preferences is a big part of personalizing
the workspace and can prove to be quite useful. However, the configuration changes that you make to the Edit>Preference choices will apply to
all of the saved workspaces configured on your computer, so if multiple
people use the computer, make sure you keep those users in mind when
making changes.

There are plenty of things to change, and in the following project, I
walk you through making these changes. There are a few that can be
quite helpful to a screen printer or graphic artist, and you'll be prompted
to make the change. However, if you feel the change isn't necessary or
doesn't fit your organization's needs, certainly leave the default or
choose another option.

Project 5-1: Setting Optimal Preferences

To configure the preferences in Photoshop for optimum results in a
screen printing facility:

1. Choose **Edit>Preferences>General**.

2. From the General menu, notice the Color Picker is Adobe, History
    States is set to 20, and the Redo Key is set for Ctrl+Z. Leave the
    color picker the same, but reduce the History States if you have less
    than 128 MB of RAM on your computer. Change the key combination
    for the Redo (Undo) command if desired. If you'd like to hear a beep
    after Photoshop completes a task, place a check in the **Beep When
    Done** box. Leave the other options the same in the General options.

3. Click the **Next** button to bring up the next set of preferences: File
    Handling. If you do not plan to use earlier versions of Photoshop for
    opening the files you save, you can uncheck **Always Maximize
    Compatibility for Photoshop Files**. It is checked by default.

4. If you do not want to share files in a workgroup, uncheck **Enable
    Workgroup Functionality**. Otherwise, leave this option checked.

5. Type in a number in the **Recent File List Contains** box if you want the recent files list to show anything other than ten recent files. Click **Next**.

6. In the Display and Cursors preferences, verify that Brush Size is chosen. This allows the cursor to show the actual brush size of the brush that you've chosen.

7. When working with large files, check **Use Pixel Doubling**. This will not change how the image prints but will make image refreshing faster after changes are made. For normal size files, leave this unchecked. Click **Next**.

8. At the Transparency and Gamut preferences, configure grid size and grid colors if you desire, and click **Next**.

9. In the Units and Rulers preferences, change inches to centimeters if you use the metric system.

10. In the same dialog box, leave the print resolution at 300 pixels/inch for now; you'll configure the print resolutions each time you print depending on your needs for a particular image. Do recognize that the preferences can be set here though, and consider changing the print resolution later if desired. Leave the screen resolution at 72 pixels per inch, as this is the standard for most monitors.

11. In the Guides, Grid, and Slices preferences, you can change the color of the guides, ruler grid, and slices. The style can be changed as well, from lines to dotted lines to dots, depending on what you're changing. Change as desired. Click **Next**.

 Note:

Guides are the lines that appear over an image when making a selection. Points snap to this guide, and these guide lines aren't printed when the image is sent to the printer. Grid lines are the lines that appear when using the rulers.

12. In the Plug Ins and Scratch Disks preferences, place a check in the **Additional Plug Ins** directory if you plan to have or do have additional third-party plug-ins. These can consist of actions, special effects, and even color separation tools. Leave scratch disks alone for now.

13. In the Memory and Cache settings preferences, leave all settings the same. Click **Next**.

14. Click **OK** to apply the settings.

This file is saved as a preference file. Preference files are stored by Adobe and your operating system and called upon each time you open Photoshop. The preferences include the palette locations too, as well as if you have rulers or grids showing when you close the program.

 Note:

Occasionally, the preference file can become corrupted and all preferences will be lost. If this happens, repeat these steps to recreate the preference file. (This doesn't happen often but does happen enough to warrant mentioning it here.)

Using the Preset Manager

The Preset Manager is a dialog box that allows you to manage all preset items in one place. Changes made here affect all of the presets that you'll see when accessing them from any area of Photoshop. Presets can be both configured and saved for the following:

- Brushes
- Swatches
- Gradients
- Styles
- Patterns
- Contours
- Custom shapes
- Preset tools

You can access the Preset Manager using Edit>Preset Manager. The brushes library will open by default. There is a right arrow (as in other palettes) that offers additional options, including how the brushes are viewed and additional palette libraries that can be loaded.

You should configure the presets to meet the needs of your organization. For instance, when configuring my presets, I appended square brushes, thick, heavy brushes, and calligraphic brushes because I use those brushes regularly. You'll know what to add and remove after you've used Photoshop for a while too.

In the following project, we learn how to configure the Preset Manager to meet your needs. Work though the project to further personalize your copy of Photoshop.

Project 5-2: Configuring Presets

To configure and save presets that meet your particular needs as a screen printer or graphic artist, work through this project.

1. Choose **Edit > Preset Manager** to open the Preset Manager dialog box.

2. Make sure **Brushes** is chosen in the Preset Type window.

3. Click the right arrow to configure the view settings. I prefer Small Thumbnail for the brushes collection.

4. Click **Load** to see the brush libraries. From the choices, select any you wish to append (add to) the existing library. For this project, add all four: **Dry Media**, **Special Effect**, **Thick Heavy**, and **Wet Media**.

5. Click once on a brush and then click the **Save Set** button. Name the set **All Loaded Brushes** and click **Save**. This new set will now be available from the Load choices.

6. Click the right arrow, choose **Reset Brushes**, and click **OK** when prompted. The defaults will appear again.

7. Click the right arrow and append any brush collection that you think you'll use often. (You can also choose OK to open and/or save only that library or a combination of libraries.) Configure the library the way you want it to look most of the time.

8. Click the down arrow in the Preset Type window and select **Swatches** from the drop-down list. Ctrl+2 also works.

9. Click the right arrow to choose the swatch option that matches the color scheme you use most often. As with the brushes options, you can append, open, or save as desired.

10. Click the **Load** button to browse to any presaved swatch information that you've obtained from a supplier or to load any preconfigured swatches included with Photoshop. If you are unfamiliar with these options, don't append or change anything here; you'll learn more about color in later chapters.

11. Click the down arrow in the Preset Type window and select **Gradients**. Configure the gradients as desired. I prefer the Simple gradients, but the configuration is up to you.

12. Click the down arrow in the Preset Type window and select **Styles**. Styles can be applied to text, layers, and selections, and you'll have to decide what style library you prefer. If you aren't sure, don't make any changes.

13. Click the down arrow in the Preset Type window and select **Patterns**. Configure as desired.

14. Click the down arrow in the Preset Type window and select **Contours**. Contours are used to configure how effects such as drop shadow, inner glow, outer glow, bevel, emboss, and others are applied to an image. It is unlikely that you'll be applying these effects often, so for now, leave the defaults.

15. Click the down arrow in the Preset Type window and select **Custom Shapes**. I prefer to load all of the custom shapes so that they're available each time I access them. To do this, click **Load** and choose **All**. (Of course, you can append or load any library that you want here, as with brushes and other presets.)

16. Finally, click the down arrow in the Preset Type window and select **Tools**. Click the **Load** button or the right arrow to see the libraries and to add them or load them. I prefer to add the Type tools, since I use text often, but Art History, Brushes, Crop, and Marquee are also available.

17. Click **Done** to apply the changes to the presets.

To test your new presets, click a tool in the toolbox that you've made changes to—Brushes, Text, Gradient, Shapes, etc. From the options bar, notice what changes have been made to the available presets in both the options bar and the pop-up palettes.

System Calibration

System calibration is one of the most important elements of this chapter. While you can always reset brushes, move palettes around, or open a saved workspace, system calibration is a one-time task that enables you to personalize your system in a way no other personalization option can. Calibration brings a device like a monitor, scanner, or printer to an absolute standard that ensures consistency across devices. Calibrating is especially necessary when files are being passed from one person to another; what a client sees on his computer compared to what you see on your computer or the service bureau sees on its computer can differ. In order to be sure that what you are seeing in a file is what you should be seeing, your monitor will need to be calibrated.

System calibration (in particular, monitor calibration) is important in other aspects as well. You don't want to spend hours getting a photograph's hue just right (or so you think from the colors on your monitor) and then have it print out all wrong on the printer. This happens a lot in our business and is a major problem. In addition to printing-gone-bad, how can you guarantee to a customer that the file you are creating and the file he is viewing is actually the color it's supposed to be (or will be)? The answer, of course, lies in calibration of your system.

Project 5-3: Calibrating Your System

In this project, we calibrate your monitor. Dim the lights, close the window blinds, and get rid of any shadows or tints that might be disrupting or distorting the natural shade and view of the monitor. Locate and have ready some transparent tape; you'll find out why very soon!

1. Open the Control Panel and locate the Adobe Gamma icon. The Control Panel is part of your operating system and is not part of Photoshop. From Windows, choose **Start > Control Panel**. Double-click the **Adobe Gamma** icon.

2. Check **Step by Step (Wizard)** as shown in Figure 5-7 and click **Next**.

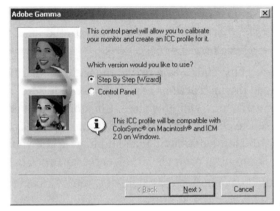

Figure 5-7: Opening the Adobe Gamma Wizard

3. You can click the Load button to choose a specific monitor profile, but a good starting point will already be created and available. Figure 5-8 shows the description of a monitor calibration for my monitor. It can be renamed if desired. Click **Next**.

Figure 5-8: Monitor calibration starting point

4. In the next wizard box, you'll have to adjust the physical brightness and contrast controls on you monitor. These can be dials or buttons, and they will be located on the monitor itself. First, locate the contrast control and set it to its highest setting.

5. Next, locate the brightness control and adjust it so that the black box showing in the dialog box is as dark as possible (without being black), while still keeping the outside box white. Click **Next**.

6. In the next wizard box, click **Next** unless you are positive that the information given is incorrect. You can double-check this information in your monitor's information booklet. Click **Next**.

7. Uncheck **View Single Gamma Only** in the next wizard box. Position the pointers so that the center box fades into the lined frame. This might take a little practice! Click **Next**.

8. In the next wizard box, click **Measure** to measure the hardware white point. Read the instructions and click **OK**. The screen becomes black with three white squares. Click on the left and right squares to make the center square neutral gray. The right square will make it grayer; the left square will make it bluer. When you think the center square is a neutral gray, click the center square. Click **Next**.

9. Click **Next** again and choose to save the new monitor calibration's color space profile.

10. Once completed, each time your monitor and computer boots up, the monitor will be calibrated. Place the tape over the controls on the monitor to prevent the knobs or dials from being changed.

Not all monitors will react well to this sort of calibration. Some options might be disabled or grayed out if your video card doesn't support them. Older monitors might have contrast or brightness controls that aren't functioning properly. Additionally, flat screen monitors can react poorly. Because of this, you might have to work a little with the Adobe Gamma Wizard to get the calibration correct and work in accordance with your monitor and/or video card. For most folks though, the calibration works as planned and should be performed at least occasionally to verify that the system is calibrated properly.

Configuring Color Settings

There are some other settings that should be configured besides calibration settings. Photoshop's creators didn't create and configure the default settings so that screen printers would be ready to print. In fact, Photoshop's default settings are configured mostly for those who want to print photographs onto paper. That's not what we're after as a group, as we need to print on films, acetates, vellums, and other materials. Not only do we print on different materials than "regular" Photoshop users, but we have to consider dot gain, screen attributes, ink attributes, profile mismatches, the working color space, and even how much softness we'll get after printing on a shirt or other material. To customize Photoshop so that it is more screen-printer friendly, work through this last project for configuring color settings.

Project 5-4: Configuring Color Settings

This project offers ways to configure and customize color settings on any computer or operating system using the color settings available in Photoshop. These settings are the best choices for screen printers but can also be applied to other industries.

 Caution!

There are many, many different theories on how to set dot gain, working spaces, and color management policies in this Color Settings dialog box. The theories differ also for automatic versus manual printing presses. The settings stated here are general in nature. You'll learn how to tweak these settings for spot, index, and process color prints in the printing chapters later in this book. For now, work through these steps exactly as detailed.

1. Select **Edit>Color Settings**. The default Color Settings dialog box is shown in Figure 5-9.

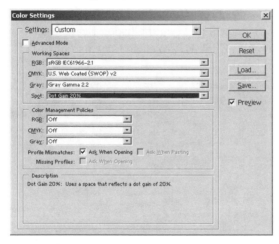

Figure 5-9: The Color Settings dialog box

2. In the Working Spaces choices, notice that an sRBG working space is chosen under RGB (in most cases). That's because this is the native color space for many scanners, inkjet printers, and monitors. This color space has a smaller gamut than other color spaces and should be changed. Choose **Apple RGB**. Yes, you should choose this no matter what, even if you aren't working on a Mac.

3. Next, in the Working Spaces section, click the down arrow next to CMYK and choose **Custom CMYK**. This will allow you to specify custom ink settings, dot gain settings, and more.

4. In the Custom CMYK dialog box, rename the custom settings if desired. I prefer to leave the name the way it is, as it is very descriptive and changes as the values change in the Custom Settings dialog box.

5. From the Ink Colors drop-down list, choose **Custom** if you have specific ink values to input. If not, select an option from the list if it is available and meets your company's specifications. If you don't have either or you aren't sure what to pick, choose **SWOP (Newsprint)**. This choice most closely matches standard process colors provided by many ink companies.

6. Continuing in the Custom CMYK dialog box, change Dot Gain to **35** percent for automatic presses and **40** percent for manual ones. Choose **GCR** if most of the image is neutral in color and light in most areas; choose **UCR** when the design has lots of black. Standard settings for the remaining options are: Black Generation—Light, Black Ink Limit—85 percent, and Total Ink Limit—250 percent. This limits how much ink will print on the paper. Leave UCA Amount at 0. (See Figure 5-10.) Click **OK** to close the Custom CMYK dialog box.

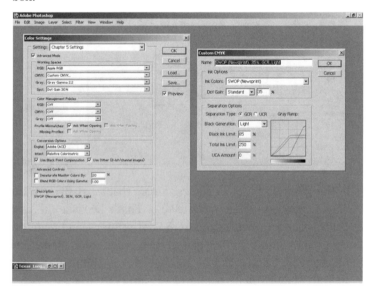

Figure 5-10: The Custom CMYK dialog box

Note:

There are different theories on how these settings should be configured. Some users will set Total Ink Limit to as high as 300 percent and configure Black Generation to Medium. You'll have to work with your equipment to see what's right for you.

7. (Optional) Back at the Color Settings dialog box, load any ink profiles you've received from your supplier or ink dealer that you have previously saved to your hard drive. If you have these profiles, click on the down arrow next to CMYK in the Working Spaces area, and choose **Load CMYK**. Change Files of Type to **CMYK** setup, and locate the ink values. Click on the file and click **Load** to load these specific ink value numbers.

8. Back at the Color Settings dialog box, click the down arrow next to Spot and configure the dot gain to 30 percent. This will allow you to preview the image with dot gain in a spot color image.

9. In the Conversion Options area, verify that the Engine type is Adobe (ACE).

10. In the Advanced Controls, verify that Desaturate Monitor Colors By is unchecked.

11. Click **Save**. Name the color settings you are saving and click **Save** again.

12. In the Color Settings Comment dialog box, type in **T-Shirt settings** or some other descriptive name if desired. Click **OK** twice.

Photoshop will remember these settings for you. These settings will allow you to get the most out of the program and, as you've seen, even allow you to download ink color values from a supplier and automatically input those into the program's customization settings. Before ending this chapter, let's take one last look at the Edit menu.

More about the Edit Menu

There are a few more options from the Edit menu that allow you to further customize Photoshop: Define Brush and Define Pattern. Both allow
you to create a new item for the Brushes palette or the Pattern palette.

Defining a Brush

Defining a new brush for the brush library is simple; just make a selection with the Rectangular Marquee tool and choose Edit>Define Brush.
Work through the following example:

1. Open the **Texas_Longhorn.psd** file from the Chapter 5 folder on the
    companion CD.

2. Select the **Rectangular Marquee** tool from the toolbox.

3. Select one of the longhorns by drawing a rectangle around it. (If you
    mess up, choose **Select>Deselect** and try again.)

4. With a single longhorn selected, choose **Edit>Define Brush**.

5. Type in a name for the new brush and click **OK**.

6. Select the **Brush** tool from the toolbox.

7. From the options bar, open the Brushes palette. Scroll down to the
    last brush to see the new brush that you just defined.

8. Open a new file using **File>New**. Choose a white background, RGB
    color, and make it at least 8 x 10 in size.

9. Select the **Brush** tool again, and select the new longhorn brush from
    the Brushes palette.

10. Set the color, opacity, and other settings and click once on the new
    file. You can even set the brush size.

11. Click once on the new file canvas to draw with the new brush. Figure
    5-11 shows the new longhorn brush in action.

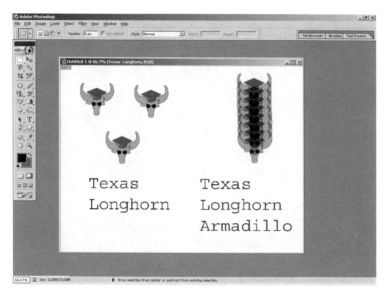

Figure 5-11: Creating and using a newly defined brush

Defining brushes can be used like a permanent copy and paste if you'd like. I use the longhorn quite a bit, so saving it as a defined brush makes it available and predrawn. You can create brushes from personal artwork, clip art, and even text. These brushes can then be saved to libraries to establish shortcuts for creating common logos and artwork for clients.

Defining a Pattern

Patterns can be defined the same way as brushes. Just select a portion of a file, the entire file, or any part of a flattened image using the Rectangular Marquee tool. Or choose Select>All, Edit>Define Pattern, and follow the same directions as in the previous example. Patterns can then be used to quickly produce a background layer when creating images or files for clients. Some common backgrounds include cloudy skies, mountain ranges, light-colored images of logos that are scattered across a page, ocean scenes, and similar images. Figure 5-12 shows a pattern that I've defined for my company, and I use it as stationery, for backgrounds on flyers, for images to send out as advertisements, and even for printing on promotional materials. (I change the opacity depending on the need.)

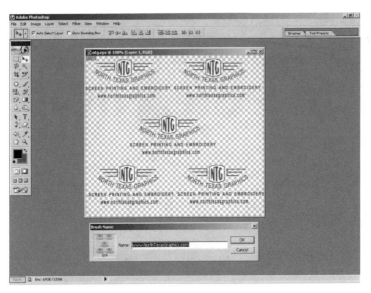

Figure 5-12: Creating and using a pattern

Summary

In this chapter you began personalizing your version of Photoshop 7.0. You learned to create different workspaces for different jobs and industries, including workspaces designed around printing text, screen printing, clients, artists, and more. You also learned how to configure the Preset Manager to create and save libraries of preset items like brushes, styles, and tools. Most importantly, you learned how to calibrate your system and configure color settings that more closely reflect what you, as a screen printer, need. Finally, you learned to create custom brushes and patterns using the Edit menu.

Chapter 6

Using the File Browser and Opening Files

The File Browser can be accessed from the default Palette Well or by using the File>Browse or Window>File Browser commands. This browser lets you access the images on your hard drive, CD drive, floppy drive, additional or removable hard drives, zip disks, and digital cameras. It provides easy access to all of the images on your computer and any images stored locally for your business on CDs or external drives.

Besides opening and accessing files, the File Browser can be used to view and sort files as well. Files can be organized into existing folders or folders you create. Files can also be renamed, moved, deleted, rotated, ranked, and more. You can even see information about an image such as the date the file (or image) was created, its file format, width and height, resolution, color profile, and copyright.

File Browser Basics

The File>Browse command offers a quick and easy way to open the File Browser. Once opened, the browser will look similar to what's shown in Figure 6-1. The figure also contains callouts for the names of the sections in the File Browser (for future reference).

In the following figure, I've chosen to display the pictures using the Details view from the additional options choices, but this is not the default. Your File Browser might not look exactly like this. Additionally, the File Browser has been dragged away from the Palette Well.

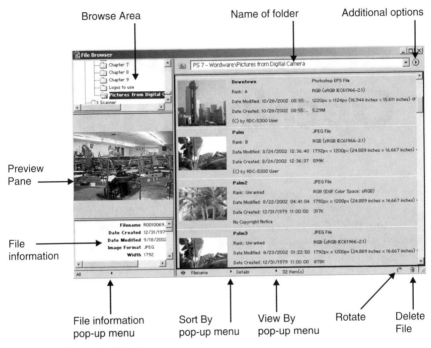

Figure 6-1: Using the File Browser

Of course, your files might not be pictures. As a screen printer, your files will consist of logos that you've designed, files that your clients have given to you to redesign, and files waiting to be printed. Later in this chapter, we learn how to organize your files in folders so that you can locate them easily and work more efficiently. In Figure 6-1, the name of the folder is PS 7 — Wordware\Pictures from Digital Camera. Figure 6-2 shows an example of the File Browser with logos displayed instead; the name of this folder is PS 7 — Wordware\Logos to Use. The logos shown in Figure 6-2 were created in Photoshop for actual clients.

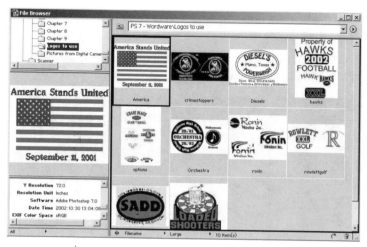

Figure 6-2: Locating logos

 Note:

The view in Figure 6-2 is Large Thumbnail view. Figure 6-2 used Details view. You can change the view from the additional options by clicking on the right arrow in the File Browser.

Browsing for an Image

Now that you know what the File Browser does and looks like and what its parts are named, it's time to actually use the browser to locate a file on your hard drive. In order to locate a file though, you have to know where you've saved it or where it's located.

A hard drive is separated into folders determined by the operating system. Additional folders can be added. The C drive is generally the root drive and contains these folders. A represents the floppy disk drive, and (almost always) D represents the CD-ROM drive. You can have other drives too; I have a zip disk (E), a CD-RW (I), and a digital camera and removable card (G and H). If you aren't sure how your hard drive and additional drives are laid out, go to My Computer or look on the C drive for information.

To use the File Browser to locate files and images on your computer:

1.   Open the File Browser using **File>Browse**.

2. Locate the browse area and drag the bottom of the window down to enlarge the window.

3. Select **My Computer** (PC) or the root drive (Mac). See Figure 6-3. You'll be able to see the drives on your computer.

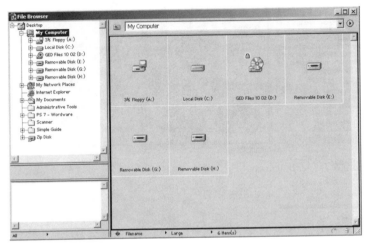

Figure 6-3: Browsing for a file

Note:

In this figure, there is a floppy drive A, a root drive C, a CD drive D, a zip disk E, a digital camera G, and removable disk H.

4. Double-click on the drive that contains the image or file that you want to open. Watch the browse area of the File Browser to see the structure of your drives.

5. Double-click again if necessary, or expand the folders in the browser to locate the files. You will see thumbnails of the files available.

Tip:

If you don't see the folders in the right pane, as shown in Figure 6-3, place a check next to Show Folder in the additional options of the File Browser. Remove the check if you don't want to see these folders.

Opening an Image

Once you've located the file, you can open it in several ways. For most folks, double-clicking on the file is the most comfortable. However, there are other ways. With the file selected:

- Press **Enter** or **Return**.
- Drag the file from the browser to the workspace.
- Right-click and choose **Open** from the Palette menu.

If you are working with the File Browser from the Palette Well and double-click or press Return or Enter to open an image, the File Browser will disappear back into the Palette Well. To keep this from happening, hold down the Alt key (the Option key on a Mac) while double-clicking.

 Tip:

Multiple files can be selected by holding down the Ctrl key while selecting files (Cmd key on a Mac).

Personalizing the File Browser

As shown in the first two figures of this chapter, the look of the File Browser can be personalized and the views of the thumbnails can be changed dramatically. Clicking on the additional options in the File Browser brings up these choices. They're shown in Figure 6-4.

From the additional options:

- Uncheck **Expanded View** to remove the browse area, preview pane, and file information pane.
- Use **Select All** to select all of the images in the folder.
- Select a thumbnail option that suits your needs—Small Thumbnail, Medium Thumbnail, Large Thumbnail, Large Thumbnail with Rank, and Details.

Figure 6-4: Selecting additional options

■ Choose **Refresh** to view recent changes made to the File Browser that have yet to be shown.

You'll change the view often depending on what information you need. I usually prefer the Details view because I can see a small thumbnail as well as information about the last date modified (important if a client calls), its rank and color information, and the date it was created.

 Note:
There are two other ways to open the File Browser: the Palette Well and the Window>File Browser command.

Organizing Images

If you own a small screen printing shop or are just getting started, keeping track of client files and images probably isn't that difficult. After all, you might only have a hundred or so files. However, as your shop grows, you could have thousands of files, and if you're not careful, those files could be scattered everywhere!

For this book, I created two folders: Pictures from Digital Camera and Logos to Use. In reality in my own screen printing business though, I have many other folders, and you should too. In the following sections, you'll learn how to organize your existing files by renaming, deleting, ranking, and moving them, as well as how to create a folder structure for new and existing files.

Deleting

The first step in organizing files is to delete any that you don't need. This not only frees up space on your hard drive, but it also makes browsing for files more efficient. First, there aren't as many files to create a thumbnail of, which helps the computer work faster, and second, you don't have to look through unnecessary files that you'll never use. You can delete files from the File Browser simply by right-clicking on them and choosing Delete from the menu choices.

Only delete files that you know you'll never use again. Just because you created a logo that a particular client rejected doesn't mean that another client won't accept the same logo at another time. Consider moving files that you might need again to an external drive or folder created specifically for such artwork.

Renaming

Go through existing files and rename them with names that are intuitive. You probably won't remember what CS stands for a year from now, and renaming the file to Crime_Stoppers now makes recognizing the file a year later much more promising. You might also con-
sider a name plan, such as an intuitive name followed by the company name (like baseball_alcatel or anniversary_foodbank). Most operating systems these days can handle long file names, so try to create names that will mean something to you later.

Renaming files is as simple as clicking on the name in the File Browser and typing in a new one. You can also right-click on the file in the browser, choose Rename, and then type in a new name. Notice the Delete, Rename, and Rank options, among others, in Figure 6-5.

Figure 6-5:
Right-click options

Using the Batch Rename Command

There is another way to rename files, and it is located in the additional options of the File Browser. The Batch Rename command allows you to rename multiple files simultaneously.

In order to rename multiple files at once, you'll need to select multiple files. You can do this by highlighting a folder in the browse area or selecting multiple files using the Ctrl (Cmd on a Mac) key in the File Browser's main window. When highlighting a folder, all files inside the folder will be renamed; when highlighting specific files in a folder, only those files will be renamed.

To use the Batch Rename command:

1. Select the files to be renamed as detailed above.
2. Click the right arrow in the File Browser to see the additional options and choose **Batch Rename**.
3. In the Batch Rename dialog box, choose to rename the files in the same folder or to move them to a new folder by checking the appropriate choice. Click the **Browse** button to locate the new folder if desired.
4. From the drop-down lists, choose a specific rule that should be used when renaming the files. Choices include the document name, date, serial number, and extension. Choose up to six, but make sure you put the extension as your last choice in the string. You can see what the names of the files will look like while you are choosing them.
5. If desired, choose to make the files compatible with other operating systems—Mac, UNIX, Windows. Click **OK**.

 Caution!

Make sure that the extension is *last*, or your files will be renamed in a way that Photoshop won't recognize. For instance, if you rename the file filename.psd02, with the serial number last, Photoshop will think the file type is psd02, which it won't recognize!

If for some reason you didn't heed the warning and accidentally configure the batch rename with the extension in the middle of the new file names instead of at the end, all of the renamed files will disappear from the File Browser. You can get them back to their original states by exploring to the folder on the hard drive from the operating system's browse feature (such as Windows Explorer or the Mac Finder). Once at the folder, you'll have to rename the files manually (or use another batch operation) to place the extension at the end of the file's name.

Ranking

Files can be ranked A, B, C, D, or E, and you can assign those letters to stand for anything. The files can be ranked by importance or quality—A being the most important or of the highest quality—but they'll have to be re-ranked often as these attributes change. Files can be ranked by type, such as A for all of your school files, B for small business files, C for large company files, D for delinquent files, and E for excellent idea files. Of course, you probably have some sort of idea how things work best in your shop and could create a ranking structure that suits your needs better than this, but you get the idea.

Ranking files is easy too. Just right-click on the file in the File Browser and assign it a rank from the choices.

Creating Folders

This is the most important part of the organization process—creating new folders. You can create a new folder inside the File Browser by right-clicking in the File Browser window and choosing New Folder from the drop-down list. You can then rename the folder as desired and drag or save files in it as needed.

Although file structure and organization preferences differ wildly from one company to the next, consider the following folders for organizing the files at your shop (files can be moved from one folder to the next quite easily, as detailed in the next section):

- **Logo Ideas**: With subfolders named 1-color, 2-color, 3-color, 4-color, process color, indexed color, teams, companies, churches, schools, reunions, graduations, parties, birthdays, fundraisers, etc.

- **Completed Project Files**: With subfolders created for each client, subfolders separating files by month or year, subfolders by city or state, or subfolders by type of client (school, church, business)

- **Work in Progress**: With or without subfolders, this folder could contain files that you are currently working on or those that are in the print queue.

- **Images to Redesign**: With or without subfolders, place images a client gives you that need redesigning here. This could be a subfolder of the Work in Progress folder.

- **Templates for Team Logos**: Most team and sports logos can be reused simply by changing the name of the team or sport. Place all team and sports logos here and create subfolders for types of teams (baseball, hockey, basketball, tennis, etc.) These can be accessed often, especially when a new logo needs to be created.

- **Clip Art**: If you have a large enough hard drive, copy clip art disks to the drive into subfolders created here. In doing so, you have quick and easy access to the clip art without having to put the physical clip art disk in the drive. The hard drive works much more quickly than a CD, and you can keep the original disks in pristine condition if you don't have to access them often.

■ **Archives**: Create subfolders named for the month and/or year and place client artwork files in the folders once the month or year is up. Doing so makes for easy backup and offers a place to store the files until they're needed again.

There are certainly thousands of other folders that can be created, and each shop will have its own needs. These are just ideas to get you started. The point is, don't just lump all of your files in a single folder (or worse, save them in various folders haphazardly). Creating folders makes backing up files easier and moving archived files to external drives more efficient.

 Note:

You don't have to create new folders from inside Photoshop if you don't want to; you can create new folders from the operating system itself. Creating a new folder on a PC is as simple as right-clicking just about anywhere in the file structure and choosing New>Folder. Additionally, many windows have a new folder icon in them, and simply clicking on this icon will create folders. For Macintosh users who use a two-button mouse, the technique is the same. One-button Mac users will need to use the key combination Apple+N or choose File>New Folder.

Moving

Once the files are created, you can move files from one folder to the next by dragging the file from its original position to a new one. Figure 6-6 shows a picture of a neon sign at the local sports club T-Daddy's. This picture (originally in the digital pictures file) will now be used to create a logo for the restaurant and needs to be moved to another area.

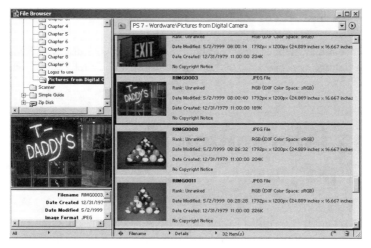

Figure 6-6: Locating the file to move

To move a file from one folder to the next:

1. Locate the file in the File Browser.

2. In the browse area, locate the folder where you'd like the file moved (don't click on it, just use the scroll bars to locate it).

3. Click on the image and drag (the cursor will change to a hand) until its outline is hovering over the file you'd like to place it in. The folder you are moving the file to will change to black, as shown in Figure 6-7.

4. Let go and the file is moved.

Figure 6-7: Moving a file

Organizing your files now might seem like a daunting task, especially if you have several thousand. However, it is well worth it to create a file structure and move everything to its correct place. It will increase productivity and efficiency and help your computer work more quickly.

Caution!

If you move around a lot of files, consider defragmenting your drives afterward. Start the defragging process at night though, because it could take a few hours to finish.

Getting Information about a File or an Image

The last pane on the right of the File Browser contains information about the selected file. There's probably more information there than you'll ever need, but it's there just in case. From here, you can see information such as the date that the file was created, the date last modified, and the filename among other things. Image size, color mode, resolution, color profile, and even the model of the camera (if it is a camera file) can be seen. You can even find out if the camera's flash went off when the picture was taken!

There are two types of information you can display: All or EXIF. EXIF displays information obtained from a digital camera, such as date and time, resolution, ISO speed rating, f-stop, compression, and exposure time. All details similar information. You can toggle between the two from the bottom of the File Browser window.

 Tip:

You can add information to a file using the File>File Info command if a file is open and active.

Additional File Browser Options

There are a few other options available from the File Browser interface. There's a Sort By menu at the bottom of the File Browser window, a View By menu, Rotate options, and a trash can for dragging and deleting files quickly. From the additional options, you can refresh the view, purge the cache, and export the cache, among other things. In this final section, you'll learn about these remaining options.

The Interface

On the bottom line of the interface, you can toggle between viewing all of the file information or only the EXIF information from the digital camera, as detailed earlier. There are other choices including options for sorting your pictures. Click the Details tab to see the options for sorting, including: filename, rank, width, height, file size, resolution, file type, color profile, date created, date modified, copyright, and ascending or descending order. I personally prefer to sort my files by date modified in ascending order so that I can easily view my most recently edited and access files.

The View By options also located on this bar include small, medium, large, large with rank, and details, the same options offered in the additional options menu choices.

Rotating the images shown in the File Browser can be achieved by clicking on the rotation icon on the bottom bar. Here, you can rotate the thumbnail of the image in increments of 90 degrees clockwise. To rotate counterclockwise, hold down the Alt key while clicking on this icon.

Note:

Rotations done in the File Browser are only applied to the thumbnail until the image is next opened in Photoshop.

The Additional Options

A few of the options in the additional options choices need a little explanation. Unless you know quite a bit about computers, you probably don't know what purging, refreshing, caching, and exporting cache mean. It all has to do with memory and hard drive space and how Photoshop works with your computer to remember what it's supposed to be working on and doing for you!

Purge Cache

Cache is an area of the hard drive where information is stored about the thumbnails, metadata, and ranking information in your images. By storing this information in memory, Photoshop is able to load previously viewed pages, such as folders and files, in the File Browser quickly. You can purge the cache and delete this information using the Purge Cache option in the additional options area. This will free disk space, making room for other more important information. After the purge, thumbnails will be regenerated, but ranking and metadata will be lost.

You should use this command at least occasionally, perhaps once a week. The problem is that after a few days of working with Photoshop, the cache part of the hard drive can become filled with thousands of bits of information. While this makes for faster browsing, it can slow down other aspects of your computing tasks.

 Tip:
Consider purging the cache in the Web Browser too.

Export Cache

If you burn a lot of CDs, you can use Export Cache to enhance how you'll use the CD in the future. Exporting the cache allows you to save the thumbnail icons so that when you put the CD in the drive later and open it with the File Browser, the thumbnails are already created and appear instantly. You can now burn and use a CD without having to generate thumbnails each time you use it.

Refresh Desktop View

Refresh Desktop View is also an option from the additional options and can be accessed by pressing the F5 key. Refreshing reloads the File Browser with the most recent information, including file names and rankings. When files are renamed, they aren't automatically moved to their correct position in the list. Refreshing the browser puts the new files in their correct place.

Reveal Location in Explorer or Finder

Finally, if you need to see the actual location of the file you're working on and where it is stored on the hard drive, choose the Reveal Location in Explorer or Reveal Location in Finder command from additional options. Making this choice opens up Explorer or the Finder to the place where the file is being stored on the hard drive.

Summary

In this chapter you learned about the File Browser. The File Browser enables you to access files quickly and see all of the files in all of the drives on your computer. This includes any zip drives, removable drives, floppy drives, or digital cameras seen as external drives. The File Browser can also be used to rename, sort, rotate, delete, and preview thumbnails of files, as well as view file information including the name, date created and modified, color mode, and more.

Part II
Creating Artwork and Logos

Chapter 7

Getting Creative

In Part II of this book, "Creating Artwork and Logos," we discuss how to create files and images using the tools available in Photoshop. Specifically, I cover the Shape tools, Type tools, Eraser tools, and coloring tools. We also discuss layers and color profiles. This chapter will serve as an introduction to these tools and concepts.

Here, we discuss how to focus in on your client's ideas to create artwork that meets their needs. We also learn to use the Paint Bucket tool, Image menu commands such as Duplicate, Rotate, Crop, and Trim, and Edit menu commands such as Cut, Copy, and Paste, among others. Common brushes are covered as is the Pencil tool and tips and ideas for creating designs wisely (which comes in handy if you're new to the screen printing business).

Coming Up with Ideas

It's hard to say where ideas come from, but generally my ideas for artwork come first from listening to the client describe what they think they want and then combining that information with what they've said they want to spend. Most clients have something in mind as far as clip art, text, price, and number of colors and if they want something that's just text and spot color or something photorealistic. If it's your job to find out what they want and create it, this section is a must-read. If your job doesn't entail creating the actual artwork, meaning you are on the production end and/or are provided with camera-ready artwork, you can skip this part of the chapter.

Understand What the Client Wants

Clients generally want one of four things: They want to give you camera-ready artwork, they want to give you artwork that they've created, they want to draw something for you and have you create it for them, or they want you to create something "neat" by reading their minds. The easiest is the first of the four, of course, but generally the other three are more common, and the information usually comes to you by phone, e-mail, on a napkin or a piece of notebook paper, or—worse—by fax. However you get it, you will have to tweak it, create it, or recreate it.

The first step in minimizing how much time it takes to create the artwork (which is quite a big deal in this industry) is making sure you know exactly what the client wants, not only regarding the design but also regarding the price. It does no good to create a four-color design when the client only wants to pay for one screen fee or one setup charge or only wants to spend x-amount of dollars for the shirt or hat. This information is just as important as whether they want a photorealistic image or a spot color one, or even their team mascot.

Table 7-1 lists several questions you should ask your clients when they arrive at your office with artwork in mind that they want you to create from scratch. You can jot down notes here and attach any information they might have with them.

 Note:

Table 7-1 is available in the Chapter 7 folder of the companion CD as a text file and can be printed out for reference. It is also included as an Excel file where you can add in your own fees and calculations and save to your computer for reference and printing.

Table 7-1: Questions to ask before creating artwork for a client

Question	Answer/Related Fees/Notes
Do you have any idea as to what you think you might want the design to look like?	Yes/No
Do you have any clip art or a picture of what you want?	Yes/No
Do you want it printed on the front, back, or both?	Front/Back/Both
Do you envision a photorealistic print or a one- to four-color design?	Photo/1/2/3/4

Question	Answer/Related Fees/Notes
Is there a specific font that your school or company requires you to use?	Yes/No
Is there a team mascot you'd like to use?	Yes/No
If there is lettering, do you want it to be curved around the artwork?	Yes/No
If there is lettering but no specific font, do you have a font type in mind?	Playful/Strong/Block/Plain/Italic/Other
What colors of ink do you want on the front?	-
What colors of ink do you want on the back?	-
Will/should/do the colors fade into one another or are they separate?	Fade/separate/touch at the edges
Do you understand about screen charges?	Yes/No
How much do you want to spend per item?	-
How much time should I put in on this artwork?	I hr/2 hr/other
Do you understand our fee for artwork?	Yes/No
What color material should the design be printed on?	-
Do you have a specific brand name you prefer?	-
Does someone other than you have to okay the artwork?	Yes/No
What is your e-mail address?	-
Fax number?	-
Home number?	-
Are you ordering enough to receive a price break on quantity?	Yes/No
Other information	-

This list helps define exactly what the client wants, and it gets away from the "just design something that you think I'll like" scenario. You will probably have a good idea what the client has in mind after asking these questions. Armed with the correct information, you're now ready to get to the task of designing it. Now, what happens when a client brings artwork?

Working with a Client Disk

Working with a client who brings in his or her own artwork on a disk or printed out on paper is just as common as those who come in with nothing. These clients come to the office with artwork they've created and saved or printed, or they might send it via e-mail. Sometimes the artwork is usable just the way it is, but more often than not, it requires attention. Unfortunately, clients rarely understand the reasons why the artwork isn't usable as-is and often balk at paying artwork fees for recreation or tweaking.

When a client arrives with artwork, she should immediately be made aware that artwork she provides will most likely need work. At the very least, it will need to be color separated, and photos will need to be worked with for optimal color, hue, saturation, tint, color levels, and other attributes. You'll need to outline your charges for the work before starting.

 Caution!

Although you can require that all artwork come to your business as camera-ready artwork (ready for press), you'll lose a lot of business from folks who don't have any idea what that means.

For future reference, inform the client what type of artwork you *do* like. If they have Photoshop, Illustrator, or CorelDRAW, ask them to create their artwork in those programs and save it for you as an EPS file, PSD file, or whatever you prefer to work with. Although it will take time, you can "train" your clients to bring you the artwork in a specific format, thus making your job easier. Chapter 13, "Acquiring Files from Disks," goes into depth about working with client files, as does Chapter 14, "Acquiring Files from Scanners."

Sometimes It's Faster Just to Recreate It....

If the design that the client brings on paper or disk is a simple one, it might be easier just to recreate it in-house. We do that quite a bit at our company, as it allows us to create the file in the format we want, at the resolution we want, and using vector clip art and text that we keep in our art libraries. We have templates for teams of all kinds, clip art that can be edited directly to personalize it, artwork that can be changed quickly to incorporate a new client, and different types of numbers that are ready to go. This makes for a better print, better film, better screens, and a happier client. (If you have the money, a library of vector-based clip art is always a good investment.)

Sometimes too, the price for recreation (an hour of artwork) is actually cheaper than working with a client file. Many companies charge for scanning and working from a client disk, and all charge for color separation. When you create it yourself, these tasks either aren't required or can be performed much more quickly. As you gain confidence with Photoshop, you might find that you'd much rather work on a file you created than try to fix a JPEG someone created by scanning an image of their web page's logo!

E-mail the Artwork for Verification

Once you've created the artwork, it'll need to be okayed by the client. This can be done by fax or snail mail, but it is becoming more common to e-mail it. E-mailing artwork differs depending on the mail program you use, but generally, e-mailing works like this:

1. Save the file to the hard drive as a JPEG if it's a photorealistic image or a GIF if it's vector based and has only a few colors. These files are small and can be sent and received quickly, and most users will be able to open them without incident. If you save and e-mail as a Photoshop file, not only will it be large, but the client won't be able to open it unless he has the program installed on his computer.

2. Right-click on the file and choose Send To>Mail Recipient, or explore to the file and highlight it. Then choose File and zip and e-mail, or File then Send To. (I keep a file on my desktop that's called Email. I save all files there; they stay organized and I know I've e-mailed them.) Note that this is done using an operating system, specifically Microsoft Windows, not Photoshop.

3. The e-mail program that you use should get the file ready for sending, and once it comes up, all you need to do is type in a message and click Send.

Basic Tools and Commands

Once you think you have an idea of what the client wants, you can begin designing the logo or the artwork. Designing the artwork is, of course, a pretty big reason why you purchased this book! In the following sections, we finally get started putting Photoshop's tools to work, and we begin with the easiest of all tools—the Paint Bucket tool.

The Paint Bucket Tool

The Paint Bucket tool is located in the toolbox and is the sixth tool down on the right. It might be hidden if the Gradient tool was selected last. The Paint Bucket tool is used to fill a selection or a layer with color. When using the Paint Bucket tool, you click in an area of the selection or layer on the color you want to fill. The Paint Bucket tool will fill all adjacent pixels that are similar to the color on which you clicked. The color used will be the foreground color configured in the toolbox. Patterns can also be applied by selecting Pattern instead of Fill from the options bar.

Project 7-1: Changing the Color of a Building in a Photograph

You can use the Paint Bucket tool to fill any selected area of color, including areas of clip art images, backgrounds, entire layers, or any part of an image that contains an area of color that is similar. You can even use the Paint Bucket tool to fill inside hollowed lettering. In this project, we change the color of a building in a photograph and maybe even learn a little about modes!

To use the Paint Bucket tool, perform the following steps:

1. Open the file **Lime Green Building.psd** from the Chapter 7 folder on the companion CD.

2. Click on the foreground color window from the toolbox. Choose any shade of purple from the Color Picker dialog box that appears and click **OK**.

3. Select the **Paint Bucket** tool. The cursor will change to a paint bucket. Figure 7-1 shows the image, the Paint Bucket tool selected, and the opacity bar.

Figure 7-1: Painting a building using the Paint Bucket tool

4. Specify the opacity for the Paint Bucket tool from the options bar. For this step, change it to **50** percent.

5. Click between the sign that says Lime and the flag. The Paint Bucket tool will change the color of this part of the building.

6. Change the opacity to **100** percent and click in the lime area to the right of the flag. Notice the difference between the coverage.

7. Change the mode in the options bar from Normal to **Hard Light** and click in the remaining area of lime in the building (the bottom right of the photograph). Notice again how the color changes.

8. From the Edit menu, choose **Undo Paint Bucket**, pick a different mode, and repeat. Continue in this manner to apply the different modes.

 Note:

Modes change how the pixels you add react to the existing pixels in the image. Modes are discussed further in Chapter 20.

9. Choose **File>Revert** to return to the file's original state.

10. Use the Paint Bucket tool at 100 percent opacity and using Normal mode to change all of the lime colors to purple in the picture.

Use Edit>Undo to undo a paint bucket fill, and change the tolerance level in the options bar to increase or decrease the pixels that are affected. Higher levels paint more area and offer more tolerance to the colors filled, while lower levels paint fewer areas and offer lower tolerance for pixels filled.

11. When complete, choose **File>Save As** to save the file to your hard drive, or simply close the file without saving.

Use the Paint Bucket Tool to Fill with a Pattern

The Paint Bucket tool can be used to fill with a pattern too. In this exercise you can experiment with the different patterns available. You can use the Paint Bucket tool and both patterns and fills to easily create a background for new artwork. To use the Paint Bucket tool on a new file and apply a fill or a pattern:

1. Select **File>New**, and choose a white background, RGB color, and 1024 x 768.

2. Select a foreground color from the toolbox.

3. Select the **Paint Bucket** tool.

4. Click once inside the new file to apply a solid-colored fill. Choose **Edit>Undo Paint Bucket** to remove it.

5. From the options bar, change the fill option from Foreground to **Pattern**.

6. Click on the arrow in the options bar next to the word Pattern and select a pattern from the list by double-clicking on it. As with other pop-up palettes, there are additional options and pattern libraries that can be loaded.

7. To apply the pattern, click inside the new file.

8. Experiment with the available patterns by loading and applying the patterns. Remember to choose **Edit>Undo** each time so that the pattern applied isn't stacked on top of the last one.

Patterns make nice backgrounds when a stock background won't do. There are several realistic pattern libraries, including nature patterns and rock patterns. Patterns can be applied to pictures, text, selections, layers, and other items too. Figure 7-2 shows the Textured Tile pattern from the rock patterns library applied to the lime building at 75 percent opacity at normal mode.

Figure 7-2: Applying a pattern

I use the Paint Bucket tool as a fill tool much more often than as a pattern tool. That's because I create a lot of spot color artwork. However, these patterns can be used quite cleverly for process color work by adding backgrounds and patterns to lettering and logos. An extremely simple logo is shown in Figure 7-3, which includes only text and a pattern background. This could easily be printed on tote bags, mouse pads, stationery, and more.

Figure 7-3: Uses for a pattern

Common Image Commands

When creating artwork, there are several image commands that you'll use often. These include Crop, Duplicate, Rotate, and Trim. These are basic image commands that you'll use when working with files, especially those that include selections that have been added or pasted to the image or those files that contain multiple layers.

Image > Crop

The Image>Crop command is used to crop out a part of any image that you've previously selected with the Crop tool from the toolbox. Generally, I click on the check mark in the options bar to complete a cropping, but you can also choose Image>Crop to apply it. There are many reasons to crop an image:

- It reduces the file's overall size, which uses less hard drive space and memory resources and can be e-mailed more quickly.

- To zoom in on a particular area, thus creating a defined focal point for the viewer

- To remove flaws in the photo or image

- To remove distractions from the image

- To create two or more pictures from a single picture

- To change the viewpoint by cropping out a selection and then inserting it into another picture or background

Image > Duplicate

Duplicate is used to duplicate an entire image and is useful when you want to make changes to a file such as a photograph without applying any changes to the actual file that's saved on the hard drive. In fact, it's safe to say you should *always* work on a copy (duplicate). Making a copy is easy; just choose Image>Duplicate and then name the copy in the Duplicate Image dialog box. Consider naming the image the same as the original with the word "copy" listed after it.

Image > Rotate Canvas

Rotating an image is quite common too, especially if you are using a digital camera to obtain your images. Some digital cameras take every picture in landscape orientation, and if you rotate the camera, you end up having to rotate the image when you open it in Photoshop. You can rotate an image in 90 degree increments or any other increment for that matter, but you really only get optimal results if you rotate in 90 degree bits.

From the Image>Rotate Canvas menu, you can also choose Flip Canvas Horizontal and Flip Canvas Vertical. If you use a heat transfer machine, you most likely need to perform this flip to print out the image correctly on the paper. Figure 7-4 shows the longhorn file flipped and ready for printing.

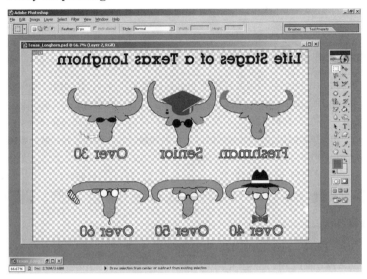

Figure 7-4: Rotating and flipping

 Caution!

You won't have to flip an image for all heat transfer work. Make sure you are aware of what exactly needs to be done, what side of the paper the design prints on, and other items before hitting the Print button.

Image > Trim

The Image > Trim command automatically trims an image (which is like cropping) based on attributes that you specify in the Trim dialog box. This trimming can be based on transparent pixels in the image, the top-left pixel color, or the bottom-right pixel color. With that choice made, the trimming can be done from the top, bottom, left, or right sides of the image or a combination of these. Figure 7-5 shows the Trim dialog box.

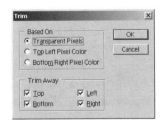

Figure 7-5: The Trim dialog box

Trimming an image improves the image's layout and optimizes the file size by centering it and removing unnecessary pixels. This is a great way to finish off artwork after editing it and give it a more professional look.

Common Edit Commands

Edit commands that you'll need to become familiar with might be familiar to you already. Undo, Step Backward, Cut, Copy, Paste, Check Spelling, and Clear are all important and oft-used commands. Their names are intuitive; many of these commands are available in other software programs that you may have.

Edit > Undo and Edit > Step Backward or Edit > Step Forward

Undo, Step Backward, and Step Forward are all used for correcting mistakes. Many users prefer this to the History palette since it's always available and easy to get to. The Undo command is usually accompanied by the name of the last tool used, such as Undo Paint Bucket or Undo Trim. Undo simply moves back one step and reverses the last action taken. The Undo command is not available after a file has been saved.

Step Backward is a little different from Undo and is used to revert to a previous state even after a file has been saved. Consider this: You work on a file for hours, and then you make a state change such as flattening the layers, trimming the image, or some other drastic measure. You save the file and then realize you shouldn't have made the change. The Undo Trim and Undo Flatten Image commands are no longer available. How can you possibly revert to before the mistake? That's where the Step Backward command comes in. With Step Backward, you can revert to a previous state, even after you've saved the image with the new state change.

Finally, Step Forward allows you to move forward one state. Moving forward is the opposite of moving backward and will only be available after using the Step Backward command from the Edit menu.

Edit > Cut

Cut is a command that is used in many software programs, including word processing software, to remove a selection from the file. You can cut text, layers, and manual selections and thus remove them completely from the image. Cutting places the deleted selection onto the clipboard, where it can then be pasted into the same image or another one.

Note:

Since Cut, Copy, and Paste are available from other software programs, you can generally cut or copy from another application like Adobe Illustrator, CorelDRAW, Arts & Letters, or other graphics program and paste directly into Photoshop.

Edit > Copy and Edit > Copy Merged

Copy does the same thing that Cut does, except it leaves the image on the original file or image, while at the same time placing it on the clipboard for later use with the paste commands. Copying a selection, layer, or text allows you to quickly place the information in another file or the same one without having to recreate it.

The Copy Merged command makes a merged copy of the visible layers in an image or selected area and places it on the clipboard. This command allows you to copy multiple layers at once.

Tip:

Depending on what you're copying, the system could seem to hang for a minute, especially if you are running low on RAM or copying a large amount of data. Be patient!

Edit > Paste and Edit > Paste Into

Pasting is done after a selection has been cut or copied to the clipboard. Pasting is putting what's in memory and stored on the clipboard into the active file. The Paste command pastes the selection into another part of the image or into a new image as a new layer. The Paste Into command pastes a selection into another part of the image or into a new image as a new layer, and the destination's selection border is converted into a layer mask. You can then decide if you want to apply the mask or discard it.

Understand that when a selection is cut or copied from a file of a specific resolution and then pasted into a file or image that is of another resolution, the pasted selection will look a little out of scale. If you are cutting, copying, and pasting under these circumstances, make sure you resize the image first so that the pasted image will fit appropriately into the new one.

After completing the paste action, choose Edit>Purge>Clipboard to remove the selection from the clipboard, especially if the data or image pasted is quite large. Keeping an unnecessary amount of data stored on the clipboard when it isn't needed can slow down the computer and cause your next cut or copy to be placed on the virtual RAM portion of the hard drive. Retrieving information from the hard drive instead of RAM takes quite a bit longer and can cause unnecessary slowdowns.

 Tip:

Dragging a selection to a new file or image or another area of the same image can be done instead of using the Cut, Copy, and Paste commands. Dragging saves system resources since the clipboard isn't used in the move.

Edit>Clear

The Clear command enables you to delete a selection without placing that selection on the clipboard. It's similar to the Cut command. Make sure that if there are multiple layers in an image, you've selected the layer you want to work with from the Layers palette.

Edit>Check Spelling

The Check Spelling command checks the spelling in a document. You'll only be able to check spelling for words that you input using the Type tools; you won't be able to check the spelling on a file that has been flattened or saved as a JPEG or GIF or anything similar. Use this command after you've added text and are still working on the type layer itself.

Experimenting with Brushes

You'll use brushes a lot with Photoshop. Brushes can be configured when using many of the tools, including the Healing Brush, Art History Brush, Brush tool, Pencil, History Brush, Eraser tools, Dodge, Smudge, Sharpen, Blur, Clone Stamp, Patch, and more. You've already been introduced to the Brushes palette, appending or replacing brush libraries, and viewing the brushes, but you have yet to really apply those techniques using a brush. In the following sections, we get our hands dirty and do some painting!

The Brush Tool

The Brush tool is available from the toolbox and is the fourth one down on the right side. The Brush tool is used for painting with the foreground color onto a layer or selection. You can use the Brush tool to brush over parts of an image that need tweaking, add an airbrush quality to an image, or paint any area with color.

Some uses for the brush include:

- To paint with sampled pixels from an image or pattern to cover up flaws in photographs or artwork
- To change a regular photograph into another style of art by brushing with stylized strokes such as watercolor, sponge, oil, pastel, chalk, and others
- To airbrush or spatter paint onto an image for use as graffiti, to soften the edges of an image, to create artwork for motorcycle gas tanks, trucks, or similar work, or to create caricatures
- To write using a calligraphic brush for artwork that will be printed for invitations or other special events
- To add noise to an image for the purpose of covering up flaws in the image itself or to make the image easier to print
- To accent edges, add texture, or distort an area of an image
- To erase any part of an image using any Eraser tool
- To smudge or focus in on an area of an image
- To clone an area of an image

Thus, using the Brush tool is necessary when performing many, many tasks. In the following example, you can experiment with applying some of the brushes while using various tools. While working, think about how you could incorporate this into your own fields.

Project 7-2: Using the Brush Tools

Perform this exercise to become familiar with using brushes:

1. Open a new document with a white background, RGB color, and 1024 x 768 preset size.

2. Click on the foreground color, and choose a bright color that will show well against the white background.

3. Select the **Brush** tool from the toolbox.

4. From the options bar, click on the arrow in the tool preset picker to show the tool presets. From the additional options, choose **Reset Tool Presets**, as shown in Figure 7-6. Click **OK** when prompted.

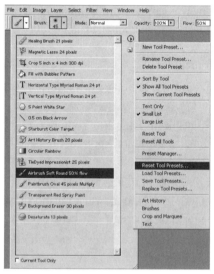

Figure 7-6: Working with brushes

5. From the tool preset picker, select **Airbrush Soft Round 50% Flow** (also shown in Figure 7-6).

6. Click and drag the brush across the new canvas to apply the paint. Try to write something in cursive to get the graffiti look from this tool.

7. From the options bar, change the size of the brush to **20 px** and apply the brush again. The smaller the number, the smaller the brush.

 Tip:

Use this tool to soften hard edges of a photograph or airbrush out flaws in an image.

8. From the options bar, open the Brush pop-up palette by clicking on the down arrow.

9. From the additional options in this palette, choose **Reset Brushes.** Click **OK** when prompted.

10. Double-click on brush number **55**, Wet Sponge. Draw with the new brush on the canvas.

11. Experiment with other brushes. Change the opacity in the options bar, the flow, and the mode.

Project 7-3: Using the Brush and Zoom Tools to Enhance a Logo

Continue from the last exercise or begin here to enhance a logo that has already been created or submitted.

12. Open the file **Pawsable_Paradise.psd** from the Chapter 7 folder on the companion CD that accompanies this book.

13. Use the Zoom tool to zoom in on the dog and cat at the bottom of the picture. Both are shown in Figure 7-7.

Figure 7-7: Zoom in to work with brushes more easily.

14. Click on the **Eyedropper** tool in the toolbox and click on the blue background just above the animals to pick up that color and change the foreground color to this blue.

15. Click the **Brush** tool and select the **Soft Round 9** pixel brush.

16. Use this brush to color in the dog's collar, and then zoom back out to see the result.

17. From the Brush pop-up palette in the options bar, choose the **Grass** brush and add some grass underneath the animals.

18. Leave this file open; we use the History Brush tool shortly.

You'll use the brushes from the options bar quite often. As you work through the book, you also learn to incorporate opacity and fill for effect. For now, think of all of the artwork you can touch up using the Brush tool just in its default state!

The Pencil Tool

The Pencil tool is used just like the Brush tool. However, instead of drawing soft brush strokes or brush designs, it is used to draw hard-edged straight or freehand lines. Drawing with the Pencil tool is a freehand action; if you want straight lines, hold down the Shift key before drawing.

To draw lines using the Pencil tool (use the Pawsable_Paradise.psd file again):

1. Select the **Pencil** tool from the toolbox.

2. Select a foreground color using the Eyedropper tool to match a color in the file specifically or by choosing a color from the color picker. I'll choose to match the blue in the lines that make up the outline.

3. Choose a brush from the options bar and configure settings. For Figure 7-8, I chose the Hard Round 9 pixel brush.

4. Click once and hold down the mouse where you'd like the first line to begin.

5. Hold down the **Shift** key and drag the mouse to draw a straight line. Let up on both the Shift key and the mouse when finished.

6. Repeat steps 3 and 4 to draw the remaining straight lines.

7. To draw a line freehand, do not hold down the Shift key while dragging.

Figure 7-8 shows how lines can be added to the Pawsable_Paradise.psd file. Leave this file as-is and don't save it yet; you'll use it in the next project.

Figure 7-8: Using lines

Experiment a little more with the Pencil tool, and see what happens when you hold down the mouse button and continue drawing without letting up on it. Also, spend some time with different opacities and blends. You can also use View>Rulers to place rulers on the screen for assistance in drawing measured widths and distances. As with any tool that offers the brush pop-up palette on the options bar, the brush can be configured as desired.

✎ Note:

When drawing with the Pencil and Brush tools, the lines are drawn on the active layer. Consider working on a copy so that the original file stays unchanged.

The History Brush

The History Brush can be used to remove what you've painted on a layer using the Pencil and Brush tools in the previous section. We use this brush now to remove what you've added to the Pawsable_Paradise.psd file so far in this chapter.

Project 7-4: Using the History Brush

To experiment with the History Brush and learn to remove previously applied modifications, use the Pawsable_Paradise file you edited in Project 7-3 (it should still be open):

1. Select the **History Brush** tool from the toolbox; it's the fifth one down on the right. You can also choose this tool by pressing the Y on the keyboard (or Shift +Y if it's currently hidden).

2. From the options bar, select the brush size that you used when drawing lines in the last exercise—this was probably the Hard Round 9 pixel brush.

3. Verify that opacity is at 100 percent and blending mode is Normal.

4. Drag the mouse over the lines that you drew with the Pencil tool. They'll disappear. This is because the History Brush removes what you've previously painted on the file's layer. (Technically, it uses the original layer or image as the "source" and reverts to that state.)

5. Change the opacity to **50** percent, and change the brush to one of the airbrushes.

6. Drag the mouse over the collar previously filled in with color or over the grass that you added earlier.

The History Brush will work as long as the file is open. The History Brush won't work if you close and save the file as a JPEG, GIF, or other compressed file or if you flatten the layers of the image before saving. Make sure you've applied this brush as needed before closing the file.

The Art History Brush

The Art History Brush allows you to paint over a picture or design with a brush to give it an artistic look and feel, like that of older artistic masterpieces. By using different tolerance options, paint styles, and brush sizes, you can simulate texture as well. In order to use the Art History Brush, you have to choose a point in time from the History palette to use as the specified history state or source data. (This is similar to the History Brush, except the source data state must be manually selected.)

Project 7-5: Using the Art History Brush

To use the Art History Brush:

1. Open a file to apply the Art History Brush to. The Sunflower.psd file is a good choice if you don't have one and is located in the Chapter 7 folder on the companion CD. This is the file I use in this example.

2. Choose **Window>History** to open the History palette if it isn't already on the workspace.

3. Select the **Art History Brush** from the toolbox.

4. From the Brush palette available from the options bar, load the **Dry Media Brushes** from the additional options. Click **OK** or **Append** when prompted.

5. Choose the **Permanent Marker Medium Tip** from the available brushes.

6. Make sure the mode is set to Normal and that opacity is at 100 percent. Set the style to **Tight Short**.

7. Change the area to **50 px**. This will increase the painting area. Set the tolerance to **5** percent. (A lower tolerance lets you paint more strokes; a higher tolerance limits the strokes. A lower tolerance will let you see the effect more quickly.)

8. From the History palette, click to the left of the first and only layer listed to use this layer as a starting point for the brush to sample from. An Art History Brush will appear in the small window in the History palette.

9. Drag the mouse slowly over the sunflower picture, starting with the sunflowers themselves and working outward in a circular motion.

 Tip:

Depending on how much RAM and other system resources you have, it might seem like the Art History Brush stops working occasionally. This is not the case; it's just that you're making changes faster than the computer can apply them. Let go of the mouse, let the computer catch up, and then click and drag again if this happens.

10. Experiment with other opacities, modes, styles, areas, and tolerances to see how these changes affect the image. Keep in mind that these changes are pixel-based and differ dramatically from one image to another.

You might not use the Art History Brush very often as a screen printer, but you might as a graphic artist in another field. Understanding what's available is half the battle though, and you might come across a client someday who wants you to create a watercolor, oil painting, pastel, chalk, or charcoal rendition of their artwork or photograph. Figure 7-9 shows how the above example turned out with my Art History Brush application.

Figure 7-9: Using the Art History Brush

Caution!

As you'll soon find out, screen printing artwork that has had special effects applied or effects such as the Art History Brush will be more difficult than screen printing images that do not have these effects applied. These tools are best used in our industry to repair or correct flaws, or to make flaws in the image less noticeable.

Using Color and Design Wisely

Since we're on the subject of being creative, creating artwork from scratch, using the basic tools, and generally getting started with the whole idea of doing things artistically using Photoshop, it is certainly a good time to talk about creating artwork that's easy to print using a screen printing press. If you are new to screen printing, you'll want to simplify the print process as much as possible by designing artwork that is uncomplicated and easy to work with; if you've been printing for some time, you probably already know what's easy to print and what isn't, as well as what your equipment's limitations are.

 Tip:

Of course, you'll always have to give the client what they want, but you'll also discover quite quickly what you can't do. You're not going to be able to print an award-winning photorealistic design on a two-station manual press or if you only have an inkjet printer with no PostScript capabilities. If that's the case, you'll have to create spot color prints exclusively and ship out all of your process color jobs. Keep this in mind when creating artwork and accepting jobs.

About the Images in This Chapter

In Figure 7-9, there are many colors. Printing something like this using a manual four-station press would be difficult at best. Printing it on an automatic press as process color would work better. In contrast, printing something like the Rocks and Things logo in Figure 7-3 would be pretty easy since there are really only two or three colors, the background is noisy with lots of dots haphazardly placed in the image, and the font has clearly defined edges. You could even use the color of the shirt as a background and reduce the logo to one color with a border and some background noise.

The design in Figure 7-4 would work well as a heat transfer or a screen print and could also be easily transferred using sublimation techniques. Figure 7-4 is a spot color design; all of the colors and lines are clearly defined and a screen can be created for each of the colors in it. For true spot color designs, stencils (screens) are created for each color in the image, and those screens define exactly what will be printed on the shirt. With a true spot color design, halftone screens don't need to be created. Unlike spot color designs with highlights or gradients or process color designs, you don't need a PostScript printer to create the film or vellum.

Figure 7-7 and the Pawsable Paradise file have a gradient as a background. This needs to be printed out using a PostScript printer and needs to be color separated. It will also be printed on the film or vellum using halftone dots so that the colors will fade into one another when the actual printing occurs on the press. This would be a more difficult item to print for someone new to the industry but certainly manageable in Photoshop and with a four-color press and appropriate printer. (You might also want to consider an index print for this design since it has only a few colors.)

So where should you begin if you're new to the industry? Spot color designs that are one or two colors and where the colors don't touch at all is a good place to start. This type of design helps you learn Photoshop and understand your press and equipment's capabilities, as well as gain clients who only want simple designs.

When Colors Don't Touch

The easiest artwork to print on a manual press is artwork that is spot color and whose colors don't touch. The simplest of spot color designs are those that are one color or contain between one to four colors that don't touch and can be easily separated. Each color has its own screen, and no PostScript printer is necessary.

Figure 7-10 shows a single spot color design whose colors and edges do not touch. Printing this requires a single printout on vellum or film and a single screen. There is no need to color separate or create process or indexed color printouts and no need for halftones, so any inkjet printer that can lay down the ink will do. This is the easiest of prints and is a great place to start for newbies in the field.

Figure 7-10: Single spot color design

 Note:

This design and logo is included on the companion CD.

When Spot Colors Touch

Spot colors that touch or overlap are the next easiest to design and print. (In this section, I'm still referring to true spot color images, those that do not blend or fade.) You still can get away with not having a PostScript printer; you can use a two- or four-station manual press, and you can print out film or vellum to create simple stenciled screens. Of course, this makes the actual printing process a little more complex; for colors that touch, you have to have your press and screens aligned well so everything lines up like it's supposed to. You'll want to put the colors on in a specific order if they overlap; for instance, dark ink will usually print over light ink, but the reverse isn't always true. You might have to flash in between also, and you might have to use an underbase. You'll have to take the design into account too and take extra steps if the colors fit together incorrectly in production. Additionally, you can't have more colors than you have stations on your press, since you can't take the shirt off and put it back on again and maintain registration and alignment.

Figure 7-11 shows a design where the colors touch. Printing this requires that the colors be separated and each color printed separately. There are plenty of chapters in this book dedicated to color separations;

for now, it's only important that you understand the differences between types of prints.

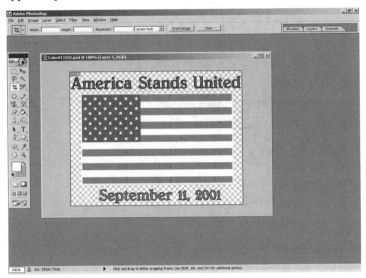

Figure 7-11: Colors that touch

In this example, there are four colors: red, white, blue, and black. America Stands United is in blue with a black outline, the date is in red with a black outline, and the flag is made up of red, white, and blue. (This design was printed on white shirts, so the color white was never actually printed.)

When Colors Blend, Process Color, Fake Process Color, and Indexed Color

For printing any other design, including photos, photorealistic images, spot color artwork with gradients or highlights, artwork where colors blend into each other, and any kind of process color or indexed color print, you need a PostScript printer and a fair knowledge of separations, dot gain and loss, ink types, undercoatings, and color channels. You need to be somewhat experienced with your equipment. Part V of this book, "Color Separations," and Part VI, "Printing," detail how to color separate and print out this type of artwork. It'll take some practice! Figure 7-12 shows an image that requires a process color print.

Figure 7-12: Process color print

✔ Tip:

Until you've worked through the projects in this book and created process artwork successfully, consider sending out your process color jobs to an experienced printer.

In this figure, the background is black, the outer circle is a light blue, the sky fades from orange to red using a gradient, and the mountains fade from green into white using a gradient. There are many colors in this image that will need to be created by blending colors and inks together, making this print quite complex.

Summary

In this chapter you learned about creating artwork. Specifically, we discussed understanding what a client wants and how to use basic tools and commands such as the Paint Bucket tool, the Brush and Pencil tools, the History Brush and Art History Brush tools, and the Image and Edit commands. These tools are used just about every time you create something in Photoshop, and some of the commands are common to other programs. For instance, Cut, Copy, and Paste are used in other software programs, and you can paste into Photoshop after cutting or copying from another program.

You also learned how to use color and design wisely if you're new to screen printing. Single spot color prints and two- to four-color spot color prints are the easiest, and the film or vellum can be created even if you don't have a PostScript printer. Process color, indexed color, and artwork whose colors blend into one another require extra attention, including color separating them. Color separation is covered in depth in the last few sections of this book.

Chapter 8

Using the Shape Tools

The Shape tools, available from the toolbox, are used to create vector shapes for logo or design creation. Using these tools, you can easily draw rectangles, ellipses, circles, polygons, and lines and choose from custom shapes. As each Shape tool is chosen, the options bar changes to reflect the choice. From the options bar, tool-specific options can then be set. Using the tools is a pretty straightforward process, so in this chapter we focus on using them to create actual client-based designs.

 Note:

Vector-based means that the shapes are drawn using mathematical formulas and thus won't be pixelated like raster-based images. There's no need to switch to a vector-based program anymore when creating shapes and text, since Photoshop has incorporated this feature into its latest versions.

Rectangle Tools

If you're new to Photoshop, designing artwork for clients, and especially screen printing, creating artwork using the Shape tools is a great place to start. Creating artwork that contains shapes and text is not only easy to produce but easy to print also. Vector-based shapes can be resized without distortion, so you can use the same artwork for a truck decal and a business card without having to rework the design.

In Project 8-1 we use the Rectangle tool to create a common logo for an athletic group, coach, or team. You'll add a couple of letters here to complete the design, but the text chapter is next, so I won't go into too much depth about that just yet.

Project 8-1: Creating the Famous XXL Logo

The design in this project can be changed to fit the needs of any client simply by typing in their name instead of the XXL we'll add here. Later, we look at some examples of how this design was changed to meet other clients' needs.

1. Choose **File>New**. Choose RGB color mode, 1024 x 768 preset size, and transparent background. (For most of your work, you'll want to create a transparent background, but often in this book I use a white background so it shows up better in print.)

2. Locate the Shape tools from the toolbox and choose the **Rounded Rectangle** tool. You can also hold down the Shift+U keys to toggle through the available tools.

3. From the options bar, change the radius to **10 in.** by typing the number into the radius window. This specifies the corner radius.

4. Change the foreground color to black in the toolbox by clicking on it and using the color picker.

5. Place the mouse in the top-left corner of the new file and drag to draw the rounded rectangle. Let go of the mouse when the rectangle is the size you want.

✖ Caution!

Don't panic because the edges look pixelated; as soon as you move on to the next tool, it'll straighten out!

6. Choose the **Horizontal Type** tool from the toolbox. It's directly above the Shape tools.

7. Click once inside the rounded rectangle.

8. From the options bar, select a large font size (for this project, I've used **350 pt**) by typing it in the font size window. The options bar is shown in Figure 8-1.

9. From the options bar, choose white for the text color (see Figure 8-1).

10. Choose **Arial** as the font type (see Figure 8-1). If you have a more "collegiate" font, such as Yearbook, use that for better effect.

11. Type in **XXL**.

12. Select the **Move** tool from the toolbox (top-right tool), check **Auto Select Layer** in the options bar, and click on the text.

 Tip:

If you need to go back and correct anything, like the size of the font, the shape of the rectangle, etc., use the History palette (Window>History) to go backward and correct errors.

13. Position the text in the center of the rounded rectangle and save the file.

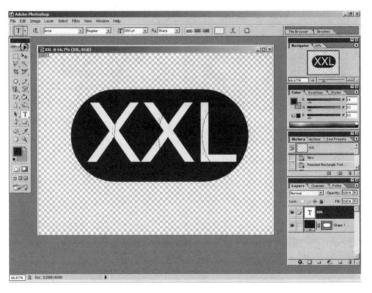

Figure 8-1: Creating the XXL logo

This design has two colors. The rounded rectangle is black, and the print is white. When printed though (without color separating the artwork first), the printout will only have black on it. The lettering will be transparent. A printout like this on film or vellum can be used to create a single screen. With this type of design, all you need to do is print the one color on the shirt and the letters XXL will be whatever color the shirt is, since there will be no ink there!

Of course, you can color separate the design before printing it out, thus creating two screens. One screen will be the circle with the XXL cutout, and the other will be the XXL lettering for printing another color on the shirt. Either way, it's an easy way to create a logo for a client. Figure 8-2 shows some other uses for this type of design.

Figure 8-2: Modifying the XXL logo

 Note:

Again, I've made the background white instead of transparent so the design will print better in the book. You'll want to use a transparent background that these were originally created on.

More about Rectangles

Drawing a rectangle is just like drawing the rounded rectangle detailed earlier. The options bar is the same as well, except the radius option isn't available. Radius has to do with circles, and while a rounded rectangle has a circular shape around its edges, regular rectangles do not.

You can draw a square instead of a rectangle either manually or by holding down the Shift key while drawing. Additionally, the color of the shape just drawn and still selected can be changed from the options bar.

Options Common to All Tools

With a little experience with rectangles under your belt, let's take a look at some options that are available for rectangles and other Shape tools. These additional options are located on the options bar and allow you to create shapes that follow precise specifications.

Figure 8-3 shows the additional options for the Rectangle tool. This is a drop-down list that can be accessed from the down arrow in the middle of the options bar. Here, you can tell Photoshop how you'd like the rectangle to be drawn by default: unconstrained (which is the default), as a square, as a user-specified fixed size, as any proportion of width and height, to draw the shape from the center instead of the default top-left corner, or to snap the shape to pixels (pixel boundaries).

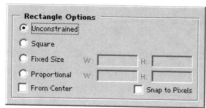

Figure 8-3: Rectangle options

The options for ellipse and polygon are a bit different, but certainly intuitive. For an ellipse, drawing as a circle is an option, while snap to pixels isn't (pixels are square, not round.). For polygons you can set the radius, choose to smooth the corners, create a star, and indent sides of the polygon.

Additionally, the options discussed in earlier chapters including Create New Shape Layer, Add to Shape Area, Subtract from Shape Area, Intersect Shape Areas, and Exclude Overlapping Shape Areas are also available. For more information on these options, see Chapter 4, "The Options Bar."

Ellipse Tool

The Ellipse tool is used in a similar way to the Rectangle and Rounded Rectangle tools and are drawn on the page the same way. Holding down the Shift key while dragging causes a circle instead of an ellipse to be drawn. Circles and ellipses can be used to create simple logos and designs. Figure 8-4 shows a logo created using an ellipse, a single piece of clip art, and some lettering.

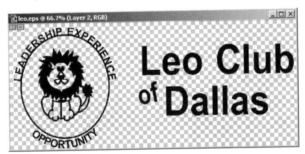

Figure 8-4: Using ellipses

Polygon Tool

The Polygon tool has a few more options than the Rectangle and Ellipse tools do, including the ability to choose how many sides you want your polygon to have. Polygons are closed shapes, like triangles, squares, rectangles, and octagons, and have three or more sides. You can create a polygon with 100 sides if you want, although it'll look more like a circle.

The polygon tools come in handy when you want to create your own shapes or a shape that precisely matches a client's existing logo or artwork. As mentioned in the last chapter, sometimes it's easier to recreate a logo for a client than to work with a low-resolution web graphic or JPEG file.

Another common use for the Polygon tool is to create a graphic that is the same size and shape as a sublimation blank. (*Sublimation* is the process of printing out artwork using an inkjet sublimation printer and adhering it to a sublimation substrate using a heat transfer press.) Sublimation blanks come in all shapes and sizes: key chains, luggage tags, coffee mugs, Christmas ornaments, clocks, nameplates, etc. A design can be created to match the material's shape exactly.

Project 8-2: Using the Polygon Tool

In this project, we learn to create a polygon that is a star, which can be used later as a background print for a sublimation Christmas ornament blank. After drawing the polygon, you can insert a photograph of your favorite family member, use the Type tools to add text, add a little clip art, and make a very personal Christmas ornament.

To use the Polygon tool:

1. Open a new file and choose the **Polygon** tool from the toolbox.

2. Change the foreground color in the toolbox to **red**.

3. From the options bar, type in the number of sides you want the polygon to have. For this project, choose **5**.

4. Make sure that Create a New Shape Layer is selected.

5. Select a style.

6. Click the down arrow next on the options bar to see the polygon options. Check the **Star** choice. See Figure 8-5.

Figure 8-5: Drawing a star using the Polygon tool

7. Drag the mouse to draw the polygon.

8. Use the Move tool with Auto Select Layer chosen in the options bar to move the star to the correct place in the file.

9. To add a picture to the star, choose **File>Open** and open the file that contains the photo to add.

10. Use the Crop tool and the Image>Resize command to crop and resize the image so that it will fit on the star.

11. Choose **Select>All** then **Edit>Copy** with the file open that contains the edited photo.

12. Select the file that contains the star and choose **Edit>Paste**. The picture will be added to the new file. Use the Move tool to position the photo in the center of the star. In other chapters we learn how to smooth the edges of the photo, use blending modes, and perform other editing tasks.

13. Add text if desired; text is detailed in depth in the next chapter.

14. Use **File>Save As** to save the file if desired.

Practice drawing other polygons too, and experiment with various numbers of sizes. From the polygon options, uncheck Star. Experiment drawing polygons again, and draw at least an octagon, pentagon, and a triangle or square.

Line Tool

The Line tool allows you to draw straight lines using the mouse. The Line tool is located with the other Shape tools and draws vector-based lines. (You can toggle through the Shape tools using Shift+U.)

The Line tool is pretty intuitive; just choose it from the toolbox and click and drag on the canvas to draw the line. Each time you draw a line and let go of the mouse button, a new layer is created. This is true of the other shapes too.

As with other tools, Style and Color can be selected from the options bar, and there are options for drawing the lines. You can hold down the Shift key while drawing to draw straight lines without any effort at all (and guaranteeing that only lines at 45 and 90 degree angles are drawn no matter how erratically you move the mouse!). Let go of the Shift key to draw straight lines at any degree angle. Finally, you can set geometric options to add arrows to the lines and to set the length and width of the arrowheads as a percentage of the weight of the line.

Practice using the Line tool by working through the following exercise:

1. Open a new file. Choose RGB, 1024 x 768, and a white background.

2. Choose the **Line** tool from the toolbox.

3. From the options bar, change the color to **red**.

4. Without holding down the Shift key, draw three separate lines and create a triangle.

5. The line width is not set as with other painting tools; it is set from the weight area of the options bar. Change the weight of the line from 1 px to 5 px by typing in **5 px** and pressing **Enter**, and draw a new line.

 Caution!

When changing the weight, make sure to type in the letters px after the number, or the weight will default to inches.

6. Change the weight again from 5 px to **10 px** and draw a new line.

7. Change the weight to **5 in.** and draw a new line. Try **10 in.** Change the line back to **1 px**.

You can also specify that you want arrowheads added to the lines. To draw arrowheads on the beginning or end of a line, click the down arrow on the options bar and place a check in start and end and draw a new line. The arrowheads will be placed appropriately. The size of the arrowheads are proportional to the width of the line by default, but this can also be changed by typing in new values in the arrowhead pop-up dialog box.

Custom Shape Tool

Finally, custom shapes can be added. Custom shapes are vector-based clip art that come with Photoshop. It isn't any clip art collection you'll want to write home about, and you'll definitely need your own library of clip art if you plan to do much design work with Photoshop, but it is certainly a start.

To see all of the available custom shapes available in Photoshop:

1. Choose the **Custom Shape** tool from the toolbox.
2. Click on the down arrow in the options bar to see the pop-up palette that contains the shapes.
3. Click the right arrow in this palette to see the additional options.
4. Choose **All** and click **OK** when prompted. See Figure 8-6.

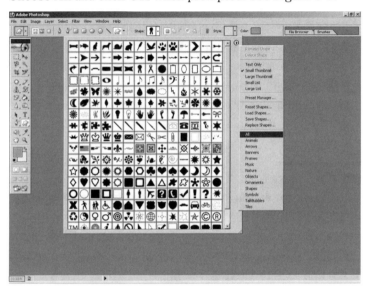

Figure 8-6: Locating the custom shapes from the options bar

Because the shapes are vector-based, they can be resized, moved, and manipulated on the page without distortion. In the next project, we combine what you've learned so far about shapes with some new tools for adding custom shapes.

 Tip:

When looking for a clip art collection of you own for purchase, make sure it's vector-based and preferably in EPS (Encapsulated PostScript) file format.

Project 8-3: Creating a Personalized Tag

In this project we use the Shape tools to create personalized luggage tags for a graphics company. The artwork can then be printed on items with sublimation techniques, by screen printing, or by using a heat transfer machine.

The steps detailed here can be modified and applied to create a personalized golf bag tag, key chain tag, company nametag, school ID card, desk nameplate, trophy plate, license plate holder, plaque, coaster, or even a print for a clipboard or mouse pad.

1. Use **File>Open** to create a new file using RGB color and a white background. Choose 5 inches by 7 inches from the preset size option.

2. Choose **Image>Rotate Canvas>90 Degrees CCW**. This is closely proportional to the size of most luggage tag blanks and gives us room to work. You'll reduce it later to fit on the luggage tag blank.

3. Configure the foreground color green and the background color white from the toolbox.

4. Choose the **Rectangle** tool and draw a large rectangle on the canvas.

5. Choose the **Rounded Rectangle** tool and draw a rounded rectangle inside the larger one. From the options bar, choose **white** for the new shape.

6. Choose the **Line** tool. Configure the weight as **3 px** from the options bar.

7. Draw lines above and below the rounded rectangle, staying inside the regular rectangle.

 Tip:

Use View>Rulers to help you align your artwork.

8. Select the **Custom Shape** tool from the toolbox. Make sure all of the available shapes are loaded from the additional options in the options bar and Custom Shape palette.

9. Select a custom shape from the Custom Shape pop-up palette in the options bar by double-clicking on it.

10. Click and drag in the image to place the shape on the canvas. Size the shape appropriately. Choose **Edit>Undo** to erase any errors.

11. Add four custom shapes, one in each corner. Figure 8-7 shows how this might look.

12. Select the **Move** tool to reposition the shapes if necessary.

13. Add text. (If you aren't sure how to do that, wait until the next chapter!)

14. Crop the image as desired.

15. Choose **Image>Image Size**. Resize the image to fit the blank substrate you'll be printing on. Because blank luggage tags for sublimation are usually 3 inches by 1.75 inches, that's what size I chose. Leave the resolution at 300 pixels/inch for now.

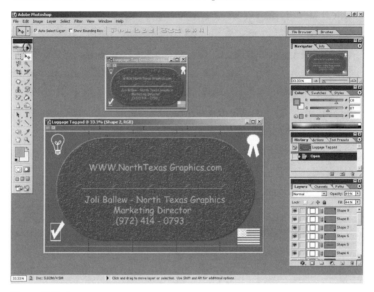

Figure 8-7: Luggage tag project

In this example, I've modified the shapes a little by choosing them from the Layers palette and performing some modifications on their styles. I've also added text and color. This file is located in the Chapter 8 folder of the companion CD under Luggage Tag.psd. You can open this file and look at the layers if you want or experiment with the colors or text. We discuss how to apply these additional effects and styles later in this book, but hopefully, your luggage tag looked kind of like mine!

Summary

In this chapter you learned how to locate and use the Shape tools, including rectangles, ellipses, lines, and custom shapes. Adding text was also introduced as a means to create actual artwork but is detailed in full in the next chapter. In the last project, creating a luggage tag was explained, incorporating all of the information in the chapter. This project can be adapted to create ID tags, mouse pads, key tags, and other items.

Chapter 9

Working with Text and Numbers

No matter what you do as a graphic artist, whether it is screen printing, embroidery, sublimation, sign making, heat transfer, or especially engraving and similar fields, you'll create and print type and numbers more often than anything else. In almost every job, there's the aspect of type. Type (also referred to as text) tells who the company or person is, what team they play for, or what they're promoting. You'll print a lot of text! You can count on doing many numbers too—on backs of jerseys, yard signs, and sports uniforms. For this reason, in this chapter we discuss all there is to know about type and Photoshop.

In order to be successful in what you do, you have to know how to use the Type tools well enough that you could create text in your sleep. This includes using the Horizontal and Vertical Type tools, the Type Mask tools, and setting options from the options bar. At some point, you'll probably also need to work with Chinese, Japanese, and/or Korean type too. Once the type has been added (and while adding it), it will need to be edited. Editing includes, but is not limited to, changing the font's size, color, orientation, justification, kerning, leading, and warping.

There are concepts such as rasterizing, converting to shapes, fractional character widths, and working with multiple type layers that you'll also need to understand, as well as how to do things with text such as mold it to a shape or add a text effect. We discuss all of these in this chapter.

Adding Text

Besides the obvious reasons to add text, such as getting the company name and phone number on a T-shirt, tote bag, or hat, text can be used to add spice to the design as well. Although the purpose of this chapter is to explain how to *use* text, choosing the right font and color and how you choose to place the text on the page is equally important. The Samples folder that installed with Photoshop 7.0 has some good examples of how text can be added and is well worth a look.

 Tip:

Go to a souvenir shop, a beach shop, or a tourist attraction and take a look at what is printed on the shirts and totes that they're selling. Notice how and where text is added to get a feel for what sells and why.

Using the Horizontal and Vertical Type Tools

The Type tools are located on the toolbox and are the eighth tool down on the right side. There are four: the Horizontal Type tool, the Vertical Type tool, the Horizontal Type Mask tool, and the Vertical Type Mask tool. These can be seen in Figure 9-1.

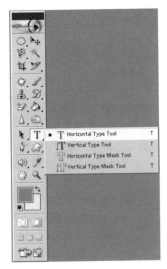

The Type tools can be selected by pressing the T on the keyboard to access the tool that's showing on the toolbox or Shift+T to toggle through the four available tools. The Horizontal Type tool types on the page horizontally and the Vertical Type tool types vertically.

Figure 9-1: The Type tools

Tip:

You can switch from horizontal to vertical after the text is added. I think it's easier to type horizontally first, check spelling, grammar, and capitalization, and then switch to vertical.

Each time you choose, use, and commit your work with the Type tool in the manner described in this section, a new layer is created. This type layer lies "on top of" the other layers in your image so that it can be seen and edited independently of the others. (You wouldn't want to change the color of the text and have that color affect the image or file you are adding text to!) When adding text you can set the font, font size, color, and more. These things can also be edited after the text has been added and even after changes have been made to other layers in the image. In the following example, you'll learn to add horizontal text (which is virtually the same process as adding vertical text) and change the type's attributes while working. Later, in the "Editing Type" section, we discuss editing the text after it's already been added.

To add horizontal text to a file and choose a font, font color, and font size and set other basic attributes, perform the following steps (later you'll use this knowledge in a project to create a design for a client):

1. For this exercise, choose **File>New** and create a file that is RGB color, 1024 x 768, and has a white background. You could follow these same steps to add text to *any* image or file or to a new file with a transparent background. When creating artwork for burning screens, you'll want to choose the transparent background. For now, we choose a white background until we get the hang of adding and manipulating text.

2. Choose **Window>Workspace>Reset Palette Locations** to configure the palettes to their default state.

3. Click and hold on the **Type** tool in the toolbox and choose **Horizontal Type** tool (you can also right-click). Notice that the options bar changes. Figure 9-2 shows the options bar, a file with some text added, the Type tool chosen in the toolbox, and more.

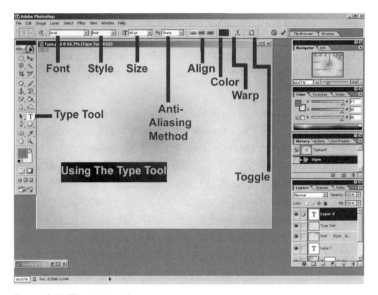

Figure 9-2: The options bar

4. Click with the mouse in the top-left corner of the new canvas. Wait a second or two until the line appears that signifies text is ready to be added. The flashing horizontal line is the same size as the type when it is added. In my experience, the type's default size is generally too small. From the options bar, click the down arrow by the font size to change the font size to 48 pt.

5. Type in your name or your company's name. The text is added using the settings in the options bar. Notice in the Layers palette that a new layer has been added, and the History palette has a new level.

6. From the options bar, click the down arrow for the font, and choose another font. Repeat step 5 and continue to experiment with different fonts. See Figure 9-3. Press **Enter** when reaching the end of the canvas so the letters don't fall off the page! Pressing Enter also keeps the text in the same layer (which is good for right now).

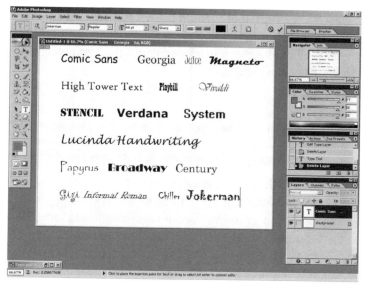

Figure 9-3: Experimenting with fonts

7. When changing the font you can also choose a font style. Common styles are Bold, Regular, and Italic, although different fonts offer different style options, including Roman and Faux Bold. Click the down arrow to change the font style before typing it.

8. The color of the text is changed from the options bar as well. Click on the colored square in the options bar to bring up the Color Picker. Note that changing the color doesn't change text that's already been added; it only changes the color of text that is going to be added. The same is true of styles and font size.

 Tip:

Choose the color, font, size, and other attributes before you start to type. It's easier to do it right the first time than it is to go back and do it over!

9. Click the check mark on the options bar to commit your text to the page. All of the text that you've added so far should be on a single layer, and this layer will have a name applied to it in the Layers palette based on the first few words of text that you added (see Figure 9-3). Once you've committed the text, the next time you add text you'll be adding another layer.

10. Choose the **Type** tool again (if it isn't still chosen) and add another line of text. Notice in the Layers palette that a new layer has been added. Click the check mark to commit the text and notice that the layer has been named.

Tip:

Click the Commit button often while working on a complex file with lots of text. This will allow you to create separate layers for different lines of text. Having the text as different layers makes it easier to edit and manipulate the text later.

This example walked you through the most basic aspects of adding text, and you learned skills that you'll need for the upcoming projects. There are many other things to learn about text though, and most likely you won't get the text exactly right the first time you add it. In the "Editing Type" section, we discuss correcting these problems by moving the text, changing orientation, changing color, rotating, and more. For now, the objective is to get you familiar with the four Type tools. If you have a few more minutes, work through the steps in the above exercise with the Vertical Type tool.

Note:

This is the easiest way to add type to an image or file. However, you can click and drag with the mouse to create a "bounding box" for the text prior to typing if you like. This process will be introduced briefly in the section "Typing in Paragraph Form."

Using the Type Mask Tools

With the Horizontal and Vertical Type Mask tools, you can create a selection in the form of typed letters. These selections can be moved, copied, or filled with color just like any other selection can. Type selections are best created on a normal image layer and not a type layer, since the type is created from the underlying image. Figure 9-4 shows type that has been created from various images.

Figure 9-4: Using the Type Mask tools

To create text from an underlying image, perform the following steps:

1. Open the files **Potatoes.psd** and **Sunflower.psd** from the Chapter 9 folder on the companion CD.

2. Open a new file using **File>New** with RGB color and 1024 x 768.

3. Position all three files on the page, as shown in Figure 9-5. Do this by dragging from the title bars to position them in the workspace so that all three can be seen. I've removed all of the palettes too by closing them from the Window menu.

Figure 9-5: Opening the files

4. Click the title bar of the Potatoes.psd file to make it active.

5. Choose the **Horizontal Type Mask** tool from the toolbox.

6. Click inside the Potatoes.psd file and type the word **Potatoes**. (A reddish mask will appear over the image—that's normal.)

7. After typing the word Potatoes, use the mouse to highlight the text by dragging the cursor over it. The type will have a blue cast over it when selected.

8. From the options bar, change the font, font size, and font style as desired.

9. With the type still selected, position the cursor outside the selected area and stop when the cursor changes from the type cursor to an arrow. Click and drag to position the text over the correct area of the picture that contains the potatoes.

10. Click the **Commit** (check mark) button on the options bar.

11. Choose **Edit > Copy** from the menu bar.

12. Click on the title bar of the new, blank file to make that file the active file.

13. Choose **Edit > Paste** to paste the selection onto the new file.

14. Select the **Move** tool from the toolbox and click on the word **Potatoes** in the new file. Drag to position the word appropriately.

15. Click on the title bar of the Sunflower.psd file.

16. Choose the **Vertical Type Mask** tool in the toolbox.

17. Click on the top of the largest sunflower.

18. Change the font size to **50** in the options bar.

19. Type the word **Sunflower** over the sunflower in the picture.

20. Use the mouse to select the word after typing it and drag it to the correct position on the image using the arrow cursor. (The cursor will change to the arrow cursor for moving the text if you position it just outside of the selected text box.)

21. Change the font and size again as desired.

22. Click the **Commit** button in the options bar.

23. Choose **Edit>Copy** from the menu bar.

24. Click on the title bar of the new file to make that file the active file.

25. Choose **Edit>Paste** to paste the selection onto the new file.

26. Select the **Move** tool from the toolbox and click on the word **Sunflower** in the new file. Drag to position the word appropriately. Click once to apply the change.

27. Choose **Layer>New Fill Layer>Solid Color**. Click **OK** when prompted to add the layer.

28. From the Color Picker dialog box, choose a background color for the layer.

As you might have surmised, this can be quite useful in creating artwork for clients who do something specific—like growing potatoes! Try taking some digital photos of a few apples, oranges, bananas, and grapes, and cut out the words to make a virtual fruit basket, or if a client's products are easily recognizable (like a tie-dye manufacturer), try creating a new logo for them.

Project 9-1: Using the Type Mask Tools to Remove an Area of Type in an Image

The Type Mask tools can be used in other ways as well. Besides cutting out text to be added to another image like the image in Figure 9-4, the exact opposite can be done by removing an area of the original image.

Perform the following steps:

1. Open the file **Water.psd** from the Chapter 9 folder on the companion CD. Set the background color to white in the toolbox.

2. Select the **Horizontal Type Mask** tool from the toolbox.

3. Change the font size to **60** point and the font type to **Papyrus**.

4. Position the cursor at the far left of the image, and type in the word **Fish**.

5. Select the type with the mouse and position it in the center of the image. Click the **Commit** button on the options bar.

6. Choose **Edit>Cut**. This removes the text from the page.

7. Use the Crop tool to finish the logo. See Figure 9-6.

Figure 9-6: Another use for the Type Mask tools

Additional Options from the Options Bar

There are several options from the options bar that haven't been addressed yet. Warping, aligning, anti-aliasing, and changing the text's orientation are certainly important options. These can be set prior to typing in the text or after, but if you do this after typing in the text, you'll generally have to select the text first with the mouse or at least select the type layer from the Layers palette. This process varies depending on the option chosen.

Warping

Warping allows you to configure the type so it isn't simply added to the document in a straight horizontal or vertical line. Although you can curve the text around a shape (as detailed in a later project in this chapter), warping the text is much faster and often fits the bill.

 Caution!

You cannot use the warp effects on any type that uses Faux Bold formatting or fonts that do not have outline data, such as bitmap fonts.

Type can be warped into many different shapes and there are many warp options. These include an arc, wave, bulge, shell, flag, fish, rise, fisheye, inflate, squeeze, and twist. For each, sliders are available to edit the warp using its bend type and its horizontal and vertical distribution. In the next set of steps, we create some horizontal type and warp it to produce a logo.

1. Open the file **Water.psd** from the Chapter 9 folder on the companion CD.

2. Select the **Horizontal Type** tool from the toolbox. (You can also do this with the type mask tools as well.)

3. Change the font size to **60** point and the font type to **Papyrus**. Type in the word **Fish**.

4. Select the type with the mouse and position it in the center of the image. Leave the text selected when finished.

5. Click the warp text icon on the options bar. It is a curved T. The Warp Text dialog box will appear.

 Note:

At this point, the text does not have to be actually selected—only the type layer. However, selecting the text allows you to more effectively see the changes made by warping and is thus a better choice here.

6. Click the down arrow in the Style window and select the fish style.

7. Drag the Warp Text dialog box (using its title bar) so you can see the effect on the text clearly.

8. Move the sliders for the bend and horizontal and vertical distribution as desired. Select both horizontal and vertical while experimenting. Click **OK** in the Warp Text dialog box when you have what you want.

9. If you are happy with the text, click the **Commit** button on the options bar. If you are not, click the warp text icon again and change it.

Warping can also be achieved using Layer>Type>Warp Text. In some cases you won't have the option to choose the orientation in which you want the warp to occur (vertically or horizontally). In warp styles like Inflate and Fisheye, these choices will be grayed out, since the warp would be the same if it were horizontal or vertical.

 Tip:
To warp text enough to really distort it, choose the last warp option, Twist.

Aligning

Aligning is another option from the options bar and is used to left align text, center text, or right align text. These work the same way that align options work in your word processing program, and simply align text as desired. To align the text, select it and click the appropriate alignment option, or set the option prior to typing.

Changing the Text's Orientation

There's a little icon to the left of the font family and to the right of the Tool Preset Picker on the options bar that allows you to quickly change between the Horizontal and Vertical Type tools. It's a capital T with two arrows, one pointing down and one pointing right. Click this when you want to change from the Horizontal Type tool to the Vertical Type tool (or vice versa) or to change the orientation of the text on the selected type layer. Just type in some text using the Horizontal Type tool, and then click this icon to change the text's orientation to vertical. It's very easy!

Anti-Aliasing

Anti-aliasing lets you produce smooth corners, edges, and curves by partially filling in the outline of a letter (and font) with color. This allows the text to blend smoothly into the background. Type that isn't anti-aliased can have jagged edges—the bane of screen printers everywhere! To avoid this, always use anti-aliasing options.

Anti-aliasing does have its downside though. When anti-aliasing is used, additional colors are created to assist in blending the edges of the text. This is not desirable for web designers who need to keep colors to a minimum, and it might not be desirable for all graphic work either. I've personally never had a problem in my screen print shop, but that isn't to say that a problem might not crop up here and there. My suggestion is to always use anti-aliasing and choose an option from the following list that most closely matches what you'd like to do. Remember, you lose sharpness of text at each point in the process—printing the film or vellum, exposing the screen, printing ink on the material, and drying the material—so I'd suggest keeping it as sharp as possible.

There are five options for anti-aliasing text:

- **None**: No anti-aliasing applied
- **Sharp**: To make type appear the sharpest possible
- **Crisp**: To make type appear somewhat sharp
- **Strong**: To make type appear heavier
- **Smooth**: To make type appear smoother

These anti-aliasing options can be set before adding the type by selecting the appropriate one from the options bar, or they can be chosen from the Layer>Type options. Figure 9-7 shows two capital Bs. The B on the left has no anti-aliasing applied; the B on the right has sharp anti-aliasing applied. Notice how much smoother the edges of the second B are. This can greatly improve the look of the text, not only on the written page, but also on a screen. As you know, better screens make better prints!

Figure 9-7: Anti-aliasing example

Working with Chinese, Japanese, and Korean Type

Photoshop offers additional type options for printers who need to use Chinese, Japanese, and Korean type. These types are often referred to as double-byte character fonts and are quite a bit different from our English-language characters. If you need to use these types of characters, you'll have to enable it in Preferences first.

To enable Chinese, Japanese, and Korean type:

1. Choose **Edit>Preferences>General** (or **Photoshop>Prefer-ences>General** for Mac OS X) to open up the Preferences dialog box.

2. Place a check in **Show Asian Text Options**.

3. Make sure that Show Text Names in English is also checked if you want the names to be shown in English.

Of course, you'll have to be set up to type in these languages too, which can involve changing the regional options that are set up on your computer to include Japanese, Korean, and Chinese and configuring keyboard input locales. You'll most likely have to have your operating system's CD handy too and probably have to restart your computer once you've made the changes.

Typing in Paragraph Form

Occasionally, you'll use Photoshop to type words in paragraph form. I generally use a desktop publishing program for such work, but for full-color brochures and similar items, you might prefer to use Photoshop. Typing in paragraph form is the same as typing in only a few words, except you can use the mouse before typing to create a "bounding box" for the type. This bounding box can be rotated, skewed, and resized quite easily too, making it the perfect solution for groups of words that need to be rotated, resized, or otherwise manipulated.

To type in paragraph form:

1. Select the **Horizontal** or **Vertical Type** tool.

2. Click and drag with the mouse to create a box where you'll add the type. This box can be set to specific dimensions for width and height by holding down the Alt key (PC) or the Option key (Mac) while dragging. (This can be quite useful if you need to create a file or section that meets certain size specifications.)

3. Set the type options in the options bar as you would when adding regular type.

4. Enter the text as desired. Press **Enter** to start a new paragraph in the box.

5. When finished, rotate or resize the box as desired using its handles (square boxes around the bounding box). Click the **Commit** button when finished. Once the text is committed, the bounding box can again be resized, skewed, or rotated.

 Tip:

I suggest using bounding boxes for text only if you have a paragraph or more to write or if you want to skew, resize, or rotate the words. Bounding boxes complicate the editing procedure (in my opinion) and are harder to learn initially than simply adding text, as described earlier. For simple logos, a bounding box isn't usually necessary.

Point Type vs. Paragraph Type

Point type and paragraph type are two different ways to specify how characters will act within the text's bounding box. When using point type, each line of text that you add is independent of the other lines; it does not wrap to the next line. If you run out of space in the work area, the letters that don't fit on the page won't show.

When using paragraph type, all of the letters typed in wrap to new lines based on the size of the bounding box. Using this option, paragraphs of text can be entered, and if more space is required, the bounding box can simply be resized.

Paragraph type can be changed back to point type using Layer> Type>Convert to Point Text and back again using Layer>Type>Convert to Paragraph Text.

 Tip:

When converting from paragraph type to point type, you might get a warning about some of the text being deleted; if you do, click Cancel. Then, make sure you can see all of the text on the screen and continue. You will have to select the Move tool and resize the bounding box until you can see all of the text. Once this is done, continue with the conversion.

Editing Type

After text has been added and committed, you will probably need to edit it. This can include moving it to another area of the page, changing the font color, size, style, orientation, and more. Text can also be rotated, converted to shapes for further manipulation, and rasterized so it can be treated as a normal layer instead of a text layer.

Moving Type

There are several ways to move text once it's been added. The easiest way is to choose the Type tool from the toolbox and click on the text in the page. This automatically selects the appropriate type layer. With the layer selected, move the cursor outside of the type until the cursor becomes an arrow. Click and drag with the mouse to move the text. (This doesn't work if you're using a bounding box; for that, commit the type and use the Move tool.)

You can also select the text to move by dragging the cursor over the text to select it and then continue as before by dragging (again, this doesn't work with a bounding box). If you have multiple text layers, you can also select the type layer from the Layers palette first, and then click inside of the text to move it.

Finally, you can select the Move tool from the toolbox and click on the type layer to move the text. Make sure that Auto Select Layer is chosen from the options bar. This works for all added text.

Changing Font Color, Style, and Size

To edit the font color, style, or size after text has been added and committed, choose the Type tool and select the text to change by dragging the mouse over it. With the text selected, make the appropriate changes in the options bar. Unlike moving text, the text actually has to be selected to apply these changes; placing the cursor on the text or its layer won't do.

Changing Orientation

To change the orientation of the text, first select the Type tool and then select the text, either with the mouse or by placing the Type cursor in the text itself. Then click the change text orientation icon on the options bar. Like moving text, a text's orientation can be changed by simply placing the cursor on the text layer and does not require selecting the text with the mouse.

Working with Multiple Type Layers

When creating a file that has lots of text, you'll want to add that text to the page in multiple layers. Doing so allows you to move each line or bit of type independently of the others. If you type in all of the text as a single layer, only committing the text one time after it's all been added, then any attempt at moving *any* of the text will result in moving *all* of the text. If lines of text are added one at a time and committed, each line of text will be on its own layer and can be moved independently.

After working with text for a while, you'll learn when and why to add multiple layers. I use single layers for text that I know will stay together in the design (like words on a business card) and multiple layers when I know specific words and lines of text will need to be realigned once the design is ready to be finalized, like when words are both above and below a piece of clip art.

Layer > Type > Convert to Shape

Changing type to a shape allows you to edit the type as if it were a shape. Shapes can have styles applied to them, so changing text to a shape allows you to add styles to your text. Some of the styles that you might apply are drop shadow, inner shadow, bevel, and emboss. The process allows you to add clean, sharp, and well-defined design elements to text, which can be used to spice up otherwise dull type in a design.

 Note:

You can't change type to a shape if it doesn't have outline data, as with bitmap fonts, and characters in the text can't be edited. When using Convert to Shape, Photoshop sees the text as an object, not text.

To apply a style to text by changing it to a shape first, perform the following steps:

1. Use the Type tool to add some text to a new document. Make sure the font is large so that you can see how the style is applied.

2. Choose **Layer > Type > Convert to Shape**. Notice an outline is placed around the text.

3. Locate this layer in the Layers palette. There are two items shown. One is the layer thumbnail, and the other is the vector mask thumbnail. If you hold the cursor over each thumbnail, you can see which is which. It is this vector mask that allows you to create a style for the text. Double-click on the vector mask thumbnail.

 Tip:

If you double-click on the layer name instead of the vector mask, Photoshop will think you want to rename the layer and will place a cursor in the layer name area. If this happens, double-click again (only this time on the vector mask thumbnail). Alternately, if you double-click on the layer thumbnail, the Color Picker will appear. If this happens, close the Color Picker and try again.

4. Double-clicking on the vector mask thumbnail opens the Layer Style dialog box, shown in Figure 9-8. Position the dialog box so you can see the text in the file; it will show a preview of your changes as you apply them.

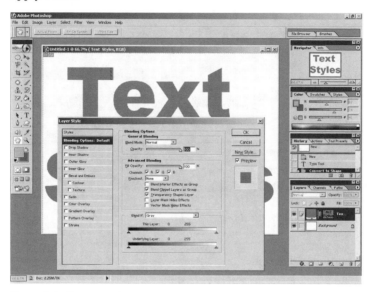

Figure 9-8: The Layer Style dialog box

5. Place a check mark in the **Drop Shadow** check box. Check **Inner Shadow** next.

6. Check **Inner Glow** and **Outer Glow**, and experiment by unchecking and checking other boxes. Texture is a really nice effect.

7. With the style applied, click **OK**. Notice in the Layers palette that the styles chosen are listed. These styles can be changed at any time by double-clicking again and adding or removing styles and effects.

Rotating Type

Type can be rotated in a couple of ways. To rotate all of the text on the page, use Select>All and choose Image>Rotate Canvas. This rotates the entire canvas. Text can also be rotated from horizontal type to vertical type from the options bar. However, the option to rotate vertical text is the most useful, as is shown in Figure 9-9.

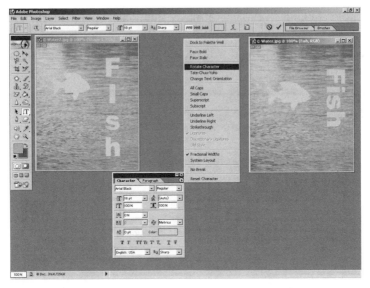

Figure 9-9: Rotating vertical text

To rotate vertical text:

1. Type in some vertical text to a file.

2. With the type layer selected (active), open the **Character** palette using Window>Character.

3. Click the right arrow in the Character palette to see the additional options. Uncheck **Rotate Character**, as shown in Figure 9-9.

4. Click the **Commit** button in the options bar.

5. With the Type tool still selected, click inside the text and position the text appropriately.

Text added using a bounding box can be rotated easily too. This is a good option if you need to rotate a word or text an odd number of degrees. After creating the bounding box and typing in a few words or a paragraph, move the mouse outside the box until it changes to a two-headed curved arrow. Click and drag to rotate the box. Click the Commit button to see the result.

Fractional Character Widths

By default, all type that you add to an image is added in fractional character widths. This means that the spacing between the characters can vary, depending on the size of the type and the font and style. This is generally the best way to add type and makes for great readability, but for really small type, it can cause letters to run together during the printing process. If you've ever gotten an order from a client who wants the team roster on the back of a shirt, you know that type running together can be a huge problem. Printing the type using low mesh screens doesn't help either.

If you find yourself in a situation where you are using small type (less than 12 points or so), you can turn off fractional character widths. Doing so configures the type on the page so that it is added in pixel increments instead of fractional widths. To turn off fractional character widths, uncheck it from the additional options in the Character palette.

Checking Spelling

Before moving any further, especially to a point where you are ready to rasterize a layer (covered next), be sure to check the spelling. To check spelling in a type layer, make sure the layer is selected (to spell check the entire layer), or highlight a group of words (to spell check a specific sentence), or place the cursor in the middle of a specific word (to spell check only that word) and choose Edit>Check Spelling. If a misspelled word is found, select the appropriate ignore or change options.

Rasterizing Type Layers

Type is vector data. Vector data is computed mathematically, and the object or type is defined by its geometric shape. Type, shapes, and vector masks are all considered vector data. Raster data is defined by its colors and pixels and is not defined mathematically. Digital pictures are raster data. Some tools in Photoshop can only be applied to raster data or raster images. Since type is vector data, using these raster tools on type requires you to convert the type to raster data. Performing this conversion is called *rasterizing*.

Once the type is rasterized, it can no longer be edited as type. Photoshop will no longer consider it text—to Photoshop, it's the same as a picture from your digital camera. So, after adding your text and positioning it just right, editing it for style, color, and size, and checking spelling, grammar, and capitalization, you can rasterize the type. Keep in mind that you don't have to rasterize the type if you don't want to, but you'll have to rasterize it if you want to use certain commands and tools, such as filters and painting tools. Rasterizing the text changes it from a text layer to a normal layer. Text can be rasterized from Layer>Rasterize, but generally my layers get rasterized when I see the notice shown in Figure 9-10.

Figure 9-10: Rasterizing a text layer

Once the text is rasterized, you can further edit the type. Tools you can use include the Paint Bucket tool, the Magic Wand tool, the Blur, Sharpen, and Smudge tools, the Dodge, Burn, and Sponge tools, and filters. All of the painting tools can be used too, as well as many others. Don't worry, you'll be prompted if you try to use a tool and the layer needs to be rasterized! There's no need to memorize what can be used where.

Text Palettes

There are two text-based palettes and you'll use them often. They are the Character palette and the Paragraph palette. As you might guess, the Character palette is available to edit and modify how individual characters look on the page, while the Paragraph palette is used to edit and modify how paragraphs should look on the page.

The Character Palette

You can adjust character options from the Character palette. This palette can be opened from the options bar (it's the last icon and toggles on and off both the Character and Paragraph palettes) or from Window>Character. Figure 9-11 shows the Character and Paragraph palettes, which have been opened from the options bar and separated. When you first open either one, they'll be docked together in a single palette.

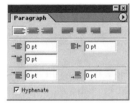 

Figure 9-11: The Paragraph and Character palettes

Using the Character palette, you can accurately adjust how your typed characters will look on the page. There are several items in this palette that will be quite useful to you. The following list gives a brief description of each option, listed in the order they're shown in the palette, starting from the top left and moving right. You can see the names of each by hovering the mouse over each item as well, which will be useful if you are using a different version of Photoshop other than 7.0.

- **Font Family:** Select a font by its name.
- **Font Style:** Select the font's style, usually Bold, Italic, Regular, Roman, etc.
- **Font Size:** Select a font size or type in a specific size.
- **Leading:** Leading is the amount of space between lines of text in a paragraph.
- **Kerning:** Kerning determines how much of a gap to have between specific letter pairs. Letter pairs like AV and Ky often seem out of sync with the other letters in text because of how the sides of the letter pairs line up with each other. Kerning can be used to add to or diminish the space to remove this natural occurrence.

- **Tracking**: Tracking keeps equal amounts of space across an entire range of letters, such as in a paragraph.

- **Vertically Scale**: This is used to specify the proportion between height and width of the type. This can be used to compress type or expand it.

- **Horizontally Scale**: This is used to specify the proportion between height and width of the type. This can be used to compress type or expand it.

- **Baseline Shift**: Baseline Shift is used to specify how much the text deviates from its normal baseline.

- **Color**: This changes the color of the text.

- **Font Options**: These include Faux Bold, Faux Italic, All Caps, Small Caps, Superscript, Subscript, Underline, and Strikethrough.

- **Language Options**: Choose a language.

- **Anti-Aliasing**: Apply or remove anti-aliasing (detailed earlier).

All of these can be changed by clicking the down arrow, typing in a new value, or clicking on the icon.

Working with the Character Palette

The following list explains how to apply various Character palette options.

- To apply kerning, click with the Type tool between the two letters for which you want to set kerning. In the Character palette, type a positive number to move characters away from each other or type in a negative number to move characters together. You can also select a number from the drop-down list. Metric allows you to use the automatic kerning of the selected font.

- To apply leading, highlight the text with the Type tool. Type in a new number or choose one from the list. Larger numbers increase the space between lines, and smaller numbers decrease it.

- To apply tracking, highlight the text using the Type tool. Choose a new number from the list or type in a number of your own. Smaller numbers decrease the gap between letters, and larger numbers increase it.

■ To apply baseline shift, highlight the letters to shift using the Type tool. Type in a positive number to elevate the letters, or type in a negative number to lower them.

Experiment with the other options as well, including underlining, bolding, and using superscripts and subscripts. Many of these changes can also be made from the options bar, so you can use whichever feels the most comfortable.

The Paragraph Palette

The Paragraph palette is used to set options that apply to entire paragraphs of text, such as indentation, alignment, and spacing between lines of type. Using the Paragraph palette is similar to using the Character palette, and the palette can be opened using the toggle on the options bar or from Window>Paragraph.

To use the Paragraph palette, select the paragraph that you want to format by clicking once inside of it, choosing it from the Layers palette, or highlighting it using the mouse and Type tool. Then choose the appropriate action from the Paragraph palette.

The following list details the items found in the Paragraph palette, which is shown with the Character palette in Figure 9.11. Use your mouse to hover over each item in the palette to see what each is called while reading through the following:

■ **Align Text**: Aligns the text to the right, center, or left, and leaves the other edges of the text unaligned (for vertical text it is top, center, and bottom).

■ **Justify Text**: Justifies all lines of text in the paragraph and leaves the last line justified either left, center, right (for vertical text it is top, center, and bottom), or force-justified.

■ **Indenting Text**: Left indent indents a paragraph from the left edge of the paragraph, right from the right edge, and first line to only indent the first line of the paragraph.

■ **Adding Space Before or After a Paragraph**: Sets how much space should be above and below each paragraph.

■ **Hypenate**: Defines if hypenation should be permitted in the paragraph.

Use these tools to format how you want your paragraphs to look prior to typing them, and save a little time! To change any of these options, simply click on them or the down arrow to make the appropriate choice.

Molding Text to Fit an Underlying Shape

One of the most common text applications is to mold the text to fit a shape like a semicircle or arc. Of course, it's easier to simply warp the text to create such an effect, but sometimes it's hard to get the text exactly the way you want it, and there are limitations with the warp commands. For instance, you can't use the warp commands to place text around a circle or in the form of a semicircle without distorting the text a little. In the next two projects we discuss creating text that takes on many forms, first by applying the warp commands with more precise results and then by creating text around a circle.

Project 9-2: Creating a Logo Using Curved Lettering

Think of a client or company who has recently asked you for a logo or artwork. Let's start simple, with, say, the local baseball team.

1. Reset the palettes using **Window>Workspace>Reset Palette Locations**.

2. Reset the foreground and background colors to black and white, respectively by clicking on the small black and white icons representing foreground and background color in the toolbox.

3. Type in the first word of the team name onto a new RGB canvas using the Type tool. Configure the font, size, and other attributes as desired.

4. With the Type tool still selected, click on the **Warp** tool in the options bar.

5. Choose **Arc** and change the bend to create the desired effect. For the first word, make the bend a positive number. Commit the change when complete.

6. Add the second word to the logo and choose to warp again. This time, create a negative bend by moving the slider to a negative number.

7. Add a number to the middle of the two warped words. See Figure 9-12.

Figure 9-12: Warping text

You can probably see the problem with this immediately; the letters became distorted. Most people are not going to be happy with this type of design. Perform these steps again with the Arc Upper and Arc Lower warp options. To do this, just click inside the existing warp text layer and choose to warp again. The Arch warp also gives a better effect and might work for a client. For true molding of text to a circle or semicircle, work through the next project.

Project 9-3: Creating Text around a Circle

Follow these steps exactly to learn the trick to creating text around a circle!

1. Reset the palettes using **Window>Workspace>Reset Palette Locations**.

2. Reset the foreground and background colors to black and white, respectively, in the toolbox.

3. Create a new file using **File>New** and choose **RGB Color** and a transparent background. Make the width and height of the new file 800 pixels.

4. Choose **View>Rulers** and verify that View>Snap to Guides has a check mark by it.

5. Choose **View>New Guide** and check **Horizontal**. Set the position to **5**.

6. Choose **View>New Guide** and check **Vertical**. Set the position to **5**. See Figure 9-13.

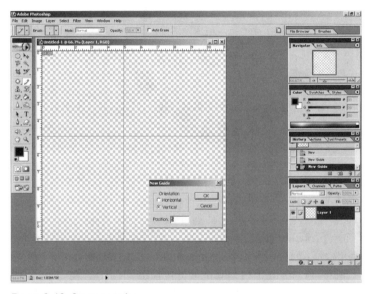

Figure 9-13: Setting guides

7. Select the **Type** tool and add your text. Use any font and size. For best results, choose a font with good readability, like Arial or Times New Roman.

8. Commit the text. Choose **Layer>Rasterize>Type**.

9. Click the **Move** tool.

10. Choose **Filter>Distort>Polar Coordinates**. Verify that Rectangle to Polar is selected. Click **OK**.

11. Use the Move tool to reposition the text. Use **Edit>Transform> Rotate** to reposition the text too. Experiment with the other Edit>Transform tools to get exactly what you want.

The text might still look distorted, depending on the size and font chosen. You can decrease the likelihood that this happens by taking some precautions prior to applying the Distort filter:

■ Change the tracking in the Character palette to increase the amount of space between characters. Depending on the font, choose between 100 and 300.

■ Use **Image>Rotate Canvas>180 degrees** to have the text read around the top instead of the bottom.

■ Choose **Edit>Transform>Scale** before distorting to increase the size of the lettering to make up for the stretching that will seem to occur.

■ Choose **Edit>Free Transform** after distorting to further manipulate the image, including rotating it to a desired position.

■ Instead of applying Filter>Distort>Polar Coordinates, try **Filter> Distort>Ripple**, **Wave**, **Zig Zag**, and others. You can create lots of interesting text shapes using these tools.

It takes a little practice to get these text-molded-to-shape actions down. The more experimenting you do though, the more you discover!

Using the Actions Palette to Add Text Effects

The Actions palette has many text effects already configured, is easily accessible, and is simple to use. To open the Actions palette, choose Window>Actions. You can add the preconfigured text effects by playing a selected action. To see an action in "action," perform the following steps:

1. Type in some text to a new document.

2. Open the Actions palette using **Window>Actions**.

3. Make sure that Text Effects are listed, as shown in Figure 9-14.

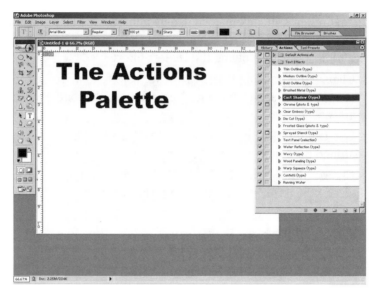

Figure 9-14: Playing actions

4. In the Actions palette, click on **Cast Shadow (type),** as shown in Figure 9-14.

5. From the bottom of the Actions palette, hover the mouse over the icons to locate the Play button. Click **Play.**

6. Click on the **History** palette and move the slide up to **Type** tool to remove the effect. Notice that several steps were taken, and many effects were added.

7. Click on the **Actions** palette again. Try other effects like Die Cut, Sprayed Stencil, and Wood Paneling. Keep in mind that these effects will be placed on top of the effects already added, so continue to undo using the History palette to see the real effect.

8. From the History palette, click on **Snapshot 1** to return to the original state of the text.

You can create your own actions by recording specific steps required to obtain an effect. This isn't the place for that lesson though, but there are multiple help files available on the subject using Help>Photoshop Help and searching. Just type in "Action Palette."

Working with Numbers

To create numbers in Photoshop, just use the keyboard to type them in as you would any text. Then, highlight the numbers and choose different fonts to find the one that you want. Figure 9.15 shows some examples. Adding numbers is done exactly the same way as adding text.

Figure 9.15: Adding numbers is just like adding text

Printing Numbers

There are several ways to work with numbers, and if you print a lot of them you might want to invest in a numbering press. These presses have screens on them that are permanently set up, so it's easy to screen print numbers when necessary. The drawback of these presses is that a client might want a specific "style" of number. Numbers are like fonts, and they can be printed in as many different ways. (Take a look at the numbers on the football jerseys of professional teams; each team has a different "style" of number.) I don't screen print numbers because I don't get a huge call for that, but if you do, creating screens and saving them for those jobs is best. When I get a job requiring numbers, I use the heat transfer machine.

Summary

In this chapter you learned practically everything there is to know about adding text in Photoshop. Adding text is probably the thing you'll do most often, as it is necessary to denote a team name, company name, product, or business. In Photoshop, you can choose from several Type tools, including vertical and horizontal options. Type masks can be used to create type from an underlying image or to remove pixels from the image in the form of type. The options bar offers several ways to configure the text, and text can be molded to fit different shapes, even a circle. Filters and warp options can be further used to manipulate text and together offer an unlimited number of options.

Chapter 10

Erasing

There are three Eraser tools in the toolbox: the Eraser tool, the Background Eraser tool, and the Magic Eraser tool. Each tool does something different, although all do some sort of erasing, of course! They're located in the toolbox, sixth down on the left. You can also access them by pressing E on the keyboard or Shift+E to toggle through all three of them. Two other items, the Auto Erase option and the History Brush tool, can also be used to erase and are included in this chapter.

Before we get too deep into erasing, let's make sure that you understand a couple of things. First, the Eraser tools either erase to "transparency" or to the background color or, in the case of the Magic Eraser, erase pixels of similar color. Erasing to transparency means that they erase completely, all the way to nothing. When you erase to transparency, you erase all the way to the checkered background, which means there's nothing on the page where you've erased. This is great for screen printers because we can erase parts of an image that we don't want on the screen. When erasing to the background color, the eraser works to erase to whatever the background color is in an image.

The Eraser tools aren't just for correcting mistakes or erasing parts of an image you don't want though; you can also use the Eraser tools to apply effects and correct flaws in an image or design. For instance, you can use the Magic Eraser tool to erase pixels of similar color on a layer and erase to a background image layer such as a photo. In this chapter, we discuss all of these tools, tips, and tricks!

The Eraser Tool

The Eraser tool is the most basic of erasers. To use this tool, simply click and drag, kind of like using a pencil eraser. If you are working on a normal layer, and there's nothing underneath where you are erasing, it erases to transparency. If you are working on the background layer or a layer with locked transparency, it'll erase to the background color. If you are working on a file with multiple layers, the Eraser tool erases items on the selected layer and will not erase anything from the area underneath on other layers. In the following project, we do each of these kinds of erasing.

Project 10-1: Using the Eraser Tool to Create a Sign or Logo

In this project, we discuss how to use the Eraser tool and learn what happens when you use the tool on a file that has one layer as well as one with multiple layers. We start with a single photo of a plate with a fish on it. This picture came from a client who wanted it in a new logo for a sign she needed printed for her storefront. We use the Eraser tool to erase to transparency, and then we move the fish to another file, which creates a new file with two layers. We clean up the image by using the Eraser tool again. By the time you work through this project, you'll be an expert on the Eraser tool!

1. Open the file **Plate.jpg** from the Chapter 10 folder on the companion CD.

2. Open the Layers palette using **Window>Layers**. Notice in the Layers palette that the layer is locked and is named Background.

3. Choose the **Eraser** tool from the toolbox.

4. From the foreground and background color area of the toolbox, click the black and white squares to change the colors to their default colors of black and white. Remember, when erasing on a background layer or a locked layer, the eraser will erase to the background color.

5. From the options bar, click the down arrow next to the brush and reset the brush library through the additional options in this palette. Click **OK**.

6. Choose Brush number **13**.

7. Verify that the mode is Brush, that opacity is 100 percent, and that flow is at 100 percent. Change these if they are not, using their drop-down lists.

8. Click and drag inside the fish's eye to erase the color and the eye. The colors in the eye will be replaced with white. Change the opacity to **50** percent, and then do the same with the fish's lips.

9. Double-click on the background layer in the Layers palette. In the New Layer dialog box, click **OK**. The layer is now changed from a locked background layer to a normal layer. Doing so will allow us to use the Eraser tool and erase to transparency instead of to the background color.

10. With the Eraser tool still chosen, change the opacity back to **100** percent.

11. Click and drag outside the fish to erase the blue part of the plate. Notice now that the eraser erases to transparency, not to the background color of white. Continue dragging and erasing until the only thing left on the image is the fish. Try to erase only the plate, not the wall behind it. You'll erase the wall in the next few steps.

12. From the toolbox, choose the **Magic Eraser** tool.

13. Make sure the tolerance is set to 32 in the options bar and Contiguous is checked (there will be more on this later), and click once above the plate. Notice that erasing is done much faster than with the Eraser tool.

14. Click with the Magic Eraser tool a few more times to get rid of all of the color that is outside the fish. See Figure 10-1.

15. Use the Eraser tool one more time to do any touching up. The final result is shown in Figure 10-1.

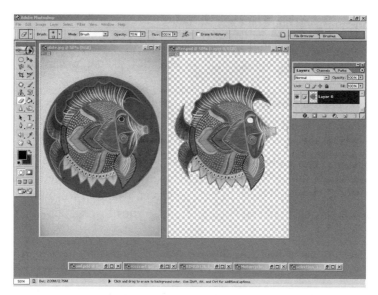

Figure 10.1: Using the Eraser tool

There's nothing in the image now except the fish. This fish can now be moved or pasted into another file and have any background applied to it. The background might be an image or a picture of a fish tank, or it could be left transparent to be placed on a storefront window, T-shirt, or tote. Whatever the case, using the Eraser tool is a great way to get rid of unwanted areas of an image.

Just for kicks (and there is more on this later too) select the History Brush tool from the toolbox. It's the fifth tool down the right side, or you can use Shift+Y to toggle to it. Using a small brush, like Brush 13, click and drag over the eye you turned white earlier. The eye reappears! This is because the History Brush acts like another sort of eraser; it erases what you've done to an image and returns it to its original state.

Now, let's actually apply what we've done by moving this fish to another file.

1. With the fish file open that you've been working on, open the **Palm.jpg** file from the Chapter 10 folder on the companion CD. (If you did not work through the previous exercise, the file FishCutout.psd is available from the Chapter 10 folder on the CD.

2. Resize the files so both can be seen.

3. Click on the title bar of the fish file to make the file the active file.

4. Choose the **Move** tool from the toolbox.

5. Click on the fish and drag it to the Palm.jpg picture.

6. Choose the **Eraser** tool again and clean up the fish you've added by removing any parts of the background you didn't get the first time.

7. From the Layers palette, right-click on **Layer 1** and choose **Duplicate Layer.** Click **OK** in the Duplicate Layer dialog box.

8. Select the **Move** tool and click and drag the original fish. You'll drag its copy. Drag the fish to another area of the image.

9. Use the Eraser tool again to clean up the image of the new fish.

10. Add text to finish it out. See Figure 10-2.

Figure 10-2:
Moving the image
to a new file

You could also add a couple of lines with the Pencil tool using a square brush to simulate a fish tank, as well as different text. Now, instead of having a single picture of a plate with a fish on it, I've got a sign or T-shirt design for a fish shop! The final copy of this file is entitled Fish Final.psd on the CD in the Chapter 10 folder.

Project 10-2: Using the Eraser to Clean Up a Client's JPEG Image

The Eraser tool can be used on JPEGs and GIFs that you receive from clients to clean up a file, remove unwanted areas, or even replace text. Often, a client will come into our shop with a JPEG of a file they used last year (with another print shop), and they want the same thing this year only with different text and/or other artwork. Although you would think that a single-layered image such as this would be difficult to edit, there's a neat little trick you can do with the Eraser tool that, once learned, will become one of your favorite editing tools.

 Note:

The problem with JPEGs is that Photoshop and other programs look at it the same way as a photograph or scanned image. You can't open a JPEG, click on the Type tool, and change the text; it just doesn't work that way. You'll get a lot of JPEGs because they e-mail easily and fit on floppy disks.

When working on a file made up of specific colors, you can use the Eyedropper to match that color as the background color and then use the Eraser tool to "erase" *to* that color. Doing so allows you to remove items in an image that you don't want, even if it's a single-layer image. Figure 10-3 shows a before and after example. Keep in mind that this is a single-layered JPEG image from a client, and this client wants to remove the ribbon from the design and change the year. If you didn't know this trick, you'd have to recreate the image from scratch, since cropping would be too difficult for this file.

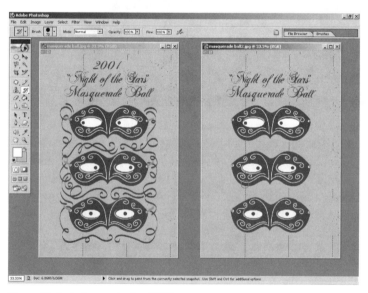

Figure 10-3: Before and after JPEG

To perform this trick on this file and files that are similar:

1. Open the file **Masquerade Ball.jpg** from the Chapter 10 folder on the CD that accompanies this book.

2. In the toolbox, click on the background color. The Color Picker will appear.

3. Move the mouse outside the Color Picker dialog box and click on the green in the image. This will change the background color to the color in the image.

4. Click **OK** in the Color Picker dialog box.

5. Choose the **Eraser** tool.

6. Pick a brush from the options bar for erasing.

7. Click and drag to erase the date and the ribbons. It will erase to the new background color, which essentially removes the extraneous data. (Now you can add the new year!)

This trick can be used on photographs too. For instance, consider a photo of a person standing on a beach with grass sticking up around them. You can use this same trick to match the sand's color and erase the grass. It's a great way to touch up a photo.

The Background Eraser Tool

The Background Eraser tool is also available and erases to either transparency or the background color, the same way the Eraser tool does. The Background Eraser has some additional options though. The Background Eraser can be configured to sense edges of high contrast, such as a figure, animal, person, etc.—perhaps a person standing in front of a scene or background of high contrast. Using this tool, you can remove the background to transparency so that you can place the person or object in another file or in front of another background. (You could even put your brother's head on the president's body if you wanted!) The Background Eraser tool also ignores any locked transparency settings on a layer, making it easier to perform erasures.

Words You Need to Know

There are a few new words you'll see when using this tool, and you'll see these same words again when you use brushes for other applications. You can view all of these by choosing the Background Eraser tool and looking at the options bar. Click the Brush Preset Picker to see the brush options (the first seven items listed here).

- **Diameter:** Controls the size of the brush and can be set using the slider or by typing in a number.

- **Hardness:** Controls a brush's hard center and can be set using the slider or by typing in a number. Hardness can be compared to using a pencil by pressing hard to create a darker and more forceful print; lower this number for a softer effect.

- **Spacing:** Controls the distance between the brush strokes when using a brush. Increasing the spacing creates a skipping effect, while decreasing the spacing creates less of a skipping effect (or none if set to 0).

- **Angle:** Controls the angle of the brush stroke. Angling creates a calligraphic look.

- **Roundness:** Controls how round the stroke will be. A setting of 100 percent creates a circular brush stroke; 0 percent creates a linear brush stroke.

- **Size:** Controls how size should be configured if using a tablet or stylus wheel for drawing. The default is set to Off.

- **Tolerance:** Controls how the tolerance should be set for drawing when using a pressure-sensitive digitizing tablet.

From the options bar:

- **Limits Discontiguous:** Use this setting to erase the sampled color whenever it appears under the brush while you drag, whether or not they are connected or next to each other.

- **Limits Contiguous:** Use this setting to erase the sampled color whenever it appears under the brush while you drag, only if the colors are connected to each other.

- **Limits Find Edges:** Use this setting to erase the sampled color under the brush while you drag and preserve the edges of any other image or item in the area where erasing is occurring.

- **Tolerance:** The default setting works in many cases. Tolerance allows you to set how you want the eraser to erase and how much to erase while dragging. Lower the number to decrease the number of colors that will be erased or when colors are similar; increase the number to erase a broader number of colors or when colors are dissimilar.

- **Protect Foreground Color:** If you do not want to erase any area of the image that contains the foreground color, check this box.

- **Sampling Continuous:** Select this to erase colors that are sampled as you drag. The sampling color will change as you drag over various colors.

- **Sampling Once:** Select to erase colors that match only the first place you click. This erases only the color that was sampled when you first click on the image and will not continuously sample while dragging.

- **Sampling Background Swatch:** Select to erase only colors that match the background color.

With these new words added to your vocabulary, you're ready to do some erasing!

Using the Background Eraser

To use the Background Eraser tool, perform the following steps (you can use the Masquerade Ball.jpg file if you want):

1. In the Layers palette, click on the layer that contains the items you want to erase. If there is only one layer, this isn't necessary.

2. Select the **Background Eraser** tool.

3. Click on the Brush sample in the options bar and configure the settings to define what type of brush you'd like to erase with. See the list in the previous section for a description of each option.

4. Choose a Limits mode for erasing. Experiment with the various options.

5. Choose a Tolerance level and experiment with different options.

6. Choose a Sampling option and experiment with different options.

As you can see, erasing using this tool is the same as erasing with the Eraser tool, except there are more options. You can erase to a specified color using a sample of the image itself, or you can erase continuously. Tolerance can be set, as can brush size and limits. This is a very powerful tool. Be sure to work through the above example and try all of the options, so you have a full understanding of what each of the words and options mean.

The Magic Eraser Tool

The Magic Eraser tool doesn't work by clicking and dragging as the other two Eraser tools do. This tool works with a single click of the mouse. The Magic Eraser tool erases color based on a sample taken where you click and acts like the Paint Bucket tool. It can be used to edit both large and small areas of color with only a single click.

The Magic Eraser tool works best when there are highly contrasting edges in an image. When erasing on a background layer or a layer with locked transparency, erasing is done down to the background color. Otherwise, the eraser erases to transparency.

1. Open the file **Fish Final.psd** from the Chapter 10 folder on the companion CD.

2. Click on the **Magic Eraser** tool.

3. Open the Layers palette using **Window>Layers**.

4. Click on the **Background** layer in the Layers palette to choose it.

5. Choose the **Magic Eraser** tool from the toolbox.

6. Verify in the options bar (and change if necessary) that the Tolerance is set to **32**, **Anti-aliased** is checked, **Contiguous** is checked, **Use All Layers** is not checked, and Opacity is set to **100** percent.

7. Click inside the image on the blue part that represents the water. There are four areas to click to get rid of all of the water. When finished, the image should look like what's shown in Figure 10-4.

Figure 10-4:
Using the Magic
Eraser

8. You could put a frame around this now using the Custom Shape tool and then use the image on a blue coffee mug, blue T-shirt, blue tote bag, etc., letting the color of the ware take over as the color of the water.

You'll discover many uses for all of these Eraser tools if you practice with them a while and on different files. If you don't have any files yet, practice on the sample files that come with Adobe Photoshop.

The Auto Erase Option

The Auto Erase option is available with the Pencil tool and allows you to paint the background color over areas of the image that contain the foreground color. In order to color or erase the foreground color using the background color though, you must click first on an area of the image that contains the foreground color before dragging. If you click and drag on an area that doesn't contain the foreground color, you'll draw with the foreground color (which is the default behavior). This option only works when using the Pencil tool to click and drag over the foreground color in an image.

To use the Auto Erase option:

1. Open the file **Masquerade Ball.jpg** from the Chapter 10 folder on the companion CD.

2. Click the foreground color in the toolbox.

3. With the Color Picker dialog box open, use the Eyedropper (automatically available) to click on the green part of the image. Click **OK**, and the foreground color in the toolbox will change to this color.

4. Click the background color in the toolbox.

5. With the Color Picker dialog box open, use the Eyedropper again to click on and choose the darker purple in the image. Click **OK** in the Color Picker to change the background color to this shade of purple.

6. Choose the **Pencil** tool from the toolbox or toggle to it using Shift+B.

7. In the options bar, reset the brushes from the Brush drop-down palette and additional options.

8. Choose **Brush 29, Flowing Stars.** Change the Master Diameter to **50.** Then click outside the palette to return to the file.

9. Place a check in the **Auto Erase** check box on the options bar.

10. Click once in the green area of the file to place purple stars. Click and hold to place multiple stars.

11. Click once in a purple area of the file to place green stars. Click and hold to place multiple stars.

12. Remove the check in the Auto Erase option and repeat steps 10 and 11. Notice the difference. When using Auto Erase, you print background color on foreground color and foreground color on background color.

13. Recheck the **Auto Erase** option, and choose **Brush 45** from the Brush options.

14. Click on the green and drag purple.

15. Click on the purple to drag green and erase a mask from the image. You can drag green over the image until you unclick and click again on a green part of the image, which will cause the pencil to draw in purple. (Leave this file open and in its current state for the next exercise.)

While this takes some getting used to, you'll find that you can correct mistakes easily by checking this option, especially if you are doing black on white artwork, which is common for screen printers and graphic artists. Remember, you can always use the History palette or the Edit>Undo commands to undo mistakes also.

The History Brush

The History Brush is one of my favorite tools. It works to erase what you've added to an image using data stored in its history (in the form of a snapshot). The History Brush erases by restoring the source data or the data that was underneath what you've added. If you've used the Clone Stamp tool already, it's kind of like that.

To see how the History Brush works, let's continue with the open file Masquerade Ball.jpg from the last exercise:

1. Click on the **History Brush** in the toolbox, or use Shift+Y or Y on the keyboard to choose the tool.

2. Choose **Brush 55, Wet Sponge,** from the Brush options in the options bar. Verify that Opacity and Fill are at **100** percent.

3. Click and drag over the mask you deleted and over some of the stars. Notice that the file reverts to its original state. You might have to click and drag over specific areas several times to get it back all the way.

 Note:

The History Brush won't erase areas of a JPEG image, GIF image, or any other image that is static (or scanned) and not altered; it will only work to return parts of an image (or the entire image) to an earlier state.

Summary

There are many ways to erase; there's the Eraser tool, the Background Eraser tool, the Magic Eraser tool, the Auto Erase option, and the History Brush. Each of these tools offers their own unique ways of erasing, and each is used differently.

The Eraser tool and the Background Eraser tool work while clicking and dragging with the mouse and erase to the background color or to transparency, depending on the image. The Magic Eraser erases while clicking once, and it uses the options set in the options bar to decide how much and what to erase determined by the pixels clicked on. The Auto

Erase option erases the background and foreground colors while using the Pencil tool. The History Brush erases things you've added to the file and reverts an area to its original state based on snapshots in the history.

Chapter 11

Working with Colors—An Introduction

This chapter contains a mishmash of introductory color concepts and color tools that you'll draw on when using Photoshop 7.0. You are probably already familiar with a few of these tools, such as setting the foreground and background colors in the toolbox, using the Eyedropper, and viewing the Info palette. In this chapter, I expand on these tools and introduce others. The Color Sampler needs to be introduced, as does the Curves tool. Each can be used to configure or set color in an image.

Color modes and models are introduced here too, as well as basic information about spot color, indexed color, and process color. Much of the information in this chapter is more textbook related and less hands-on, but it is certainly worth the read. This basic information sets the stage for more complicated concepts later in the book, including spot, index, and process color separations, working with color channels, and outputting from Photoshop.

Foreground and Background Colors

If you worked though Project 3-1, you're familiar with setting the foreground and background colors in the toolbox, as well as the Color palette. I won't repeat these steps here, so if you missed that part, you should go back now and work through it. What *does* need more introducing are the Eyedropper, the Color Sampler, and the Info palette, all of which have a lot to do with setting and configuring foreground and background colors.

The Eyedropper

The Eyedropper is used when setting the foreground and background colors using the Color Picker, as well as the Color palette. As you've probably experienced, you can have any tool selected, click on the foreground color in the toolbox to bring up the Color Picker, and move the mouse on the screen and have the Eyedropper magically appear. You don't even have to choose it from the toolbox. What you might not know about the Eyedropper though is that you can use it to sample color from anywhere on your computer screen (not just the active image or file) simply by holding down the Alt key while dragging.

You can also specify how you want the Eyedropper to sample color. By default, it's set to Point Sample. That means that the color it picks up is the color of the pixel you click on. The sample can be changed to two other options: 3 x 3 Average and 5 x 5 Average. These sample sizes take the average color of the pixels in a 3 x 3 or 5 x 5 area underneath the Eyedropper's pointer.

To use the Eyedropper to select a foreground or background color, change the sample size, and/or choose a color not in the active image, perform the following steps:

1. Open the file **TDaddy.psd** from the Chapter 11 folder on the companion CD.

2. Choose **Window>Workspace>Reset Palette Locations**.

3. In the Color palette, click on the foreground color. The Color Picker will open.

4. Move the mouse over the image. The cursor will become the Eyedropper. Click on the white fluorescent part of the sign.

5. Repeat step 4 to set the background color to the fluorescent red in the image.

 Note:

To perform the first five steps, the Eyedropper did not need to be specifically chosen.

6. Click on the Eyedropper tool in the toolbox. It's the tenth tool down on the right, above the Zoom tool and below the Shape tools. This tool is selected in Figure 11-1.

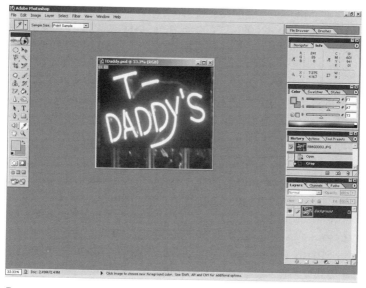

Figure 11-1: The Eyedropper tool

7. Click on the **Info** palette's tab, as shown in Figure 11-1.
8. Move the cursor around on the image and notice that the color values change in this palette (there is more on this later). You'll see exclamation points when the color you are pointing to is out of the color gamut's printable range. If you tried to screen this, you'd have a hard time reproducing these colors!

 Note:

I chose this file because many of the colors are out of printable range.

9. Click once to change the foreground color. Notice the change is made in the Color palette as well as the toolbox.

10. Move the cursor outside the active image's area. Notice that the cursor is no longer an eyedropper.

11. Move the cursor back over the active image and press and hold the Alt key.

12. While still holding the Alt key and with the mouse still positioned over the active image, click the left mouse button and hold it down and drag. Don't click once and drag; you must hold down the left mouse button and the Alt key together while dragging. As you drag, the foreground color changes, and you can drag to anywhere on the screen, including the taskbar, desktop, or any other opened file from any other program that's running and viewable. (You might have to resize Photoshop's window to see the desktop and other files.) Release the mouse button to select the color.

13. Finally, you can change how you want the pixels to be selected by changing the Sample Size in the options bar.

Having the ability to sample color from anywhere in the image or on the screen has several advantages. First, you can match a client's color exactly from Photoshop or any other open application like Arts & Letters or Corel or from any other open Adobe application. You can match exactly any color anywhere on your computer screen, including the colors used in the Microsoft Windows logo, Linux logo, or Macintosh logo. Matching color is not only useful in getting the right color for a new file but can be quite useful in matching colors so that the Eraser tools can be used. The Eraser tools can be applied to remove unwanted parts of images by painting over these parts with the foreground color. If the colors match exactly, you can even "erase" parts of JPEG, GIF, or other "unalterable" one-layered images.

 Note:

In Chapter 14, "Acquiring Files from Scanners," we use the Info palette to determine if the pure white you think you see on your monitor after scanning is actually pure white—and the same with pure black. Chances are good that your scanner isn't perfect, and the Info palette can be used to determine how far off it actually is.

The Color Sampler

The Color Sampler tool is located with the Eyedropper in the options bar. This tool lets you take a snapshot of up to four color samples in an image and lists them in the Info palette. This is useful when you need to compare one color to the next or when you need to see the changes in colors after applying image transformations.

To use the Color Sampler:

1. Open an image and choose the **Color Sampler** tool from the toolbox. (It is probably hidden under the Eyedropper.)

2. Click on the **Info** palette tab. (Choose **Window>Info** if this palette isn't open.)

3. Choose a sampling option from the options bar.

4. Click up to four times in the image. See a sample result in Figure 11-2.

Figure 11-2: The Info palette with four color samples

Note:

In addition to the four color identities in the Info palette, there are also four markings on the image itself.

You can now open up an adjustment dialog box, such as Image>Adjustments>Brightness/Contrast or Image>Adjustments>Curves, to apply color correction while previewing what it will do to the four color samples that you've taken using the Info palette. This allows you to see what changes are being made to what color and how drastically it changes the numbers. This is useful if you need to stay in a specific color range or meet specific color requirements. The concept of colors and color ranges can get fairly complex and is further defined later in this chapter, but for now, just understand that combining these tools with the Eyedropper can be very helpful when working with colors and performing color-matching tasks.

 Note:

The numbers you see in the Info palette are the color's precise color values. Numbers are used to represent each color in the color mode and define the color. In the "Color Modes and Models" section, we learn more about this.

Final Notes about the Color Sampler

A few last-minute items about the Color Sampler:

- When using the Color Sampler, you can still use the Zoom tool. Even though the icon changes, the colors still register when you move the cursor.

- You can still use the scroll bars.

- Use Shift+Click to add a color sample while an adjustment color dialog box is open.

- Click and drag on a sample in the image to move it.

- To remove a color sample from an image, drag it off the screen or hold down the Alt key and click on it with the mouse.

- Click Clear in the options bar to remove all color samples.

- To toggle between showing the color samples in an image and not showing them, choose View>Extras. A checkmark shows them; not having a checkmark removes them from view.

The Info Palette

The Info palette offers information about the colors in an image and is activated by moving the mouse pointer over a color. It doesn't matter what tool you're using either; you can see what color values are in an image with the Move tool, Type tool, Zoom tool, or any other tool.

The information given in this palette about the colors can be used to see if the colors in the image are in the printable gamut of colors for the mode of colors selected. An exclamation point next to a number indicates that it is out of the color gamut for that color mode. This information is very important to screen printers and artists who work with sublimation and heat transfers, as colors out of the gamut are going to be difficult to match, display, and print correctly.

 Note:

When you convert an image to CMYK for printing, Photoshop will automatically bring all colors into the CMYK color gamut. However, you'll want to correct these issues as best you can while working in RGB and before converting. Additionally, any adjustments made after the conversion to CMYK can bring the colors out of the gamut again. Be careful!

The Info palette can be configured to offer colors for different color modes. As a screen printer, you'll mostly be working with RGB (Red, Green, and Blue) and CMYK (Cyan, Magenta, Yellow, and Black) for both working with and outputting a file, respectively. As luck would have it, these are the defaults in the Info palette! You'll want to leave these settings like they are for now. Like anything though, this can be changed, and several other options can be chosen for either the first or second printout in the palette:

- Actual color
- Proof color
- Grayscale
- RGB
- Web color
- HSB color
- CMYK color
- Lab color
- Total ink
- Opacity

Each of these items could have a chapter or two devoted to them, and many of the items listed here are beyond what you really *need* to know. (You probably won't ever be concerned with web color, lab color, and several of the other options in this list.) Therefore, let's move on, keeping in mind that these modes can be changed in the Info palette; we come back to the color modes important to your work in a minute.

Units can also be set to pixels, inches, centimeters, millimeters, points, picas, and percents. To change the order of what is listed in the

Info palette or change the color mode(s) shown, click the right arrow in the Info palette to bring up the additional options, and choose Palette Options. In the Info Options dialog box, make the correct choices from the drop-down lists for First Color Readout—Mode, Second Color Readout—Mode, and Mouse Coordinates—Ruler Units. See Figure 11-3.

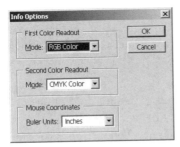

Figure 11-3: The Info Options dialog box

The Info Palette Isn't Just for Colors Anymore!

While this is a little off the mark for a chapter titled "Working with Colors—An Introduction," it's a good place to list a few other things that you can do with the Info palette. You might have noticed that you get numbers for x and y when you move the mouse with certain tools; these are the x and y coordinates of the point that you're hovering over. Sometimes you also get numbers for W and H, or width and height of a selection.

Here's a complete list:

- When using any Marquee tool, consult the Info palette for information on the width and height of the rectangle or ellipse you are drawing, as well as the pointer's location on the x- and y-axes.

- When using the Zoom tool, consult the Info palette for information on the width and height of the marquee as you drag to zoom.

- When using the Crop tool, consult the Info palette for information on the width, height, and angle rotation of the cropping marquee.

- When moving a selection, consult the Info palette for the x and y coordinates of the starting location and how much x and y have been moved (DX) and (DY), as well as angle and distance. This information is updated as you drag.

- When using the Line, Pen, or Gradient tools, consult the Info palette for the x and y coordinates of the starting location and how much x and y have been moved (DX) and (DY), as well as angle and distance. This information is updated as you drag.

■ When using transform commands, such as Edit>Transform>Skew (or Scale, Rotate, Distort, and Perspective), consult the Info palette for information about the skew, rotation angle, and width and height.

In my personalized screen-printer-based workspace (created in Chapter 5), I have the Info palette configured to open each time (you should too). The Info palette offers lots of information about colors and color modes and allows me to see values for colors in my files. I can see immediately if any colors are out of the RGB or CMYK color gamut, and I can see samples of colors in different color modes. In the next few sections we discuss several of the color modes and color models given in the bulleted list shown earlier, and you should understand a little more about why this is an important palette.

Color Modes and Models

Color models are established models for creating and reproducing color. It's sort of like a set of rules that define color. There are many color models, including RGB, CMYK, HSB (hue, saturation, and brightness), indexed, and more. As a screen printer, you'll mainly be concerned with RGB and CMYK color modes, although using indexed color can be useful as well, depending on your needs.

You choose to work with a specific color mode, and choosing a mode determines the color model. When you create a new file using File> New, you get to select the mode; when you get a file from a client, they've selected the mode. While the terms "mode" and "model" are almost interchangeable, they aren't exactly the same. Remember, a *model* is a set of rules; *mode* is a choice you make and determines the color model applied.

As you explored the Info palette, you saw that the numbers in the Info palette changed as you moved the mouse pointer over different areas of color. These numbers define the color scientifically. For instance, when working in RGB mode, all of the 16.7 million colors that can be created are all made by mixing three colors: red, green, and blue. A bright blue might have very little red, very little green, and lots and lots of blue.

The colors for each can range from 0 to 255, with 0 representing a low intensity and instance of the color, and 255 a lot of it.

Note:

When all of the numbers are set to 0, the resulting color is pure black; when all of the numbers are set to 255, the resulting color is pure white.

As mentioned earlier, you'll be working in RGB mode most of the time. That's the default color mode of your computer monitor, so it makes the most sense, although there are plenty of other reasons. (That's also why it's important to calibrate your monitor, as detailed in Chapter 5.) CMYK color mode is important to understand too, since that's what mode you'll use when outputting data to paper. Printers use the CMYK model when producing color output. When separating colors for process color prints, you'll convert your RGB mode image to CMYK mode for process color separation and output.

RGB Mode

Photoshop's default color mode is RGB, as is your monitor. As a screen printer, you should always work in RGB mode. Once the file is ready for printing, you'll convert it to CMYK, tweak the CMYK channels, and configure how the file should print. Make sure that you're finished working on the file before converting it though, since conversions to CMYK will cause some deterioration of color.

RGB mode is best for several reasons; for instance, it has fewer channels than CMYK and is thus less memory-intensive, and RGB color spaces aren't dependent on inks like CMYK modes are. When converting from RGB to CMYK on your computer, you are telling it to configure the CMYK mode after your own settings too, such as dot gain and the type of ink you want to use. (You configured these in the "System Calibration" section in Chapter 5.)

Converting an RGB mode image to a CMYK image creates a color separation in the Channels palette.

Caution!

If a client gives you a file in CMYK mode or another mode, change it to RGB before working on it, or ask them to.

CMYK Mode

The CMYK mode assigns colors to pixels in percentages that are determined by the process inks that you'll be using (and have configured in the Color Settings). There are four colors or components (cyan, magenta, yellow, and black), and color value percentages range from 0 to 100 percent. For instance, a teal color might have 51 percent cyan, 4 percent magenta, 19 percent yellow, and 0 percent black. You can see these numbers in the Info palette. All zeroes produce a pure white. Note that this is different from the RGB mode, where all zeroes result in black.

When converting from RGB to CMYK, Photoshop looks back to the settings configured in Edit>Color Settings. (In Color Settings you can configure and have applied to the CMYK file the ink type and brand, dot gain percentage, ink limits, etc.) During the conversion, these settings are applied to the file. This is why you need to convert any file given to you to RGB, work on it in that mode, and then do the conversion to CMYK on your own computer.

Note:

There are approximately 100 pages dedicated to CMYK color separations in Part V of this book; remember, this is just an introduction.

Additional Modes

There are other modes, and some of them are introduced briefly here:

- **Grayscale:** This mode uses up to 256 shades of gray (or black). Every pixel in the image is defined by its brightness values from 0 to 255 or its percentage of black ink coverage (0 to 100 percent). Grayscale images are the bane of every screen printer new to the field, as grayscale images won't produce good spot color films, and clients seem to love sending them in this format!

- **HSB:** This mode uses a color's hue, saturation, and brightness to define it. Hue is defined by its location on the color wheel and is denoted by a number from 0 to 360 degrees. Saturation is the purity and strength of the color and is defined by the percentage of gray in the image (0 to 100 percent). Brightness is how light or dark a color is and is defined by a percentage (0 percent is black and 100 percent is white).

■ **Indexed Color:** This mode uses 1 to 256 colors. You can convert an RGB image to an indexed color image, and Photoshop will look at the colors and convert them to the colors available in the indexed color model. Indexed color can be used for web images but is used in screen printing as well. Screen printers can use indexing to color separate an image using only a few colors, and those colors can be hand picked.

 Note:

You can switch between color modes using the Image>Mode menu choices.

Introduction to Spot Color

Spot color images are those images that can be printed using a limited number of colors and also have a limited number of colors in the design. Generally, spot color prints are the easiest kind of images to both screen print and color separate. Most of the logos that you've seen in this book up to this point have been spot color designs. Spot color prints are not photorealistic like process color prints; spot color images are created using text, clip art, and color. Figure 11-4 shows a true spot color design.

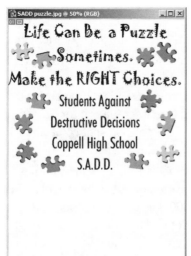

Figure 11-4: Spot color print

In Figure 11-4, the puzzle pieces are different colors and the writing is black. Each puzzle piece has a black outline, so in this spot color design, the colors touch. If you're new to screen printing, you'll probably be more comfortable with designs whose colors don't touch (since the calibration of the press isn't such a big deal), so you might want to remove this part of the design after you print out the color separations (or before). As you progress, you'll become more comfortable with designs where colors touch and even fade into one another.

True spot color images (those whose colors do not fade into each other or contain highlights or shadows) can be printed using premixed inks. Each spot color requires that a screen be created specifically for that color and a plate on the press for printing it. Figure 11-5 shows an example of what the printout for the true spot color design in Figure 11-4 might look like. This design would require four to six screens, depending on how many colors you wanted in the design; three of the screens are shown here.

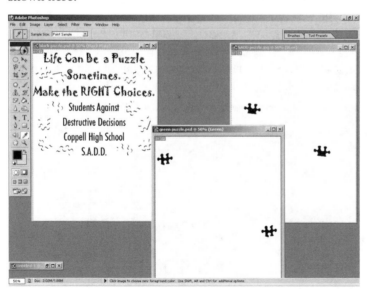

Figure 11-5: Spot color prints

You'll create lots of true spot color designs as you build your business (and certainly lots of them after). In our shop, 60 percent of our work is this type of spot color prints for baseball teams, school teams or clubs, churches, family reunions, and more. Many of our clients only want a single color on a shirt, which is the least expensive way to go, and this type of design only requires one screen.

 Note:

While "true" spot color designs can be printed without halftones, as shown in Figure 11-5, spot color images that have highlights or whose colors fade into one another will require halftone screens and a different process. There will be much more on the different types of spot color processes in Chapter 22.

Introduction to Indexed Color

Indexed color is used often to create graphics for the World Wide Web. There, the fewer colors an image has, the faster it can be downloaded to a viewer's computer. Fast is the key in Internet talk. Indexed color is popular among screen printers too, since fewer colors can mean less work for the screen printer. Of course, you can't create millions of colors like you can with RGB or CMYK, so it isn't always the best solution. However, for designs that have a limited number of colors, indexed color can work quite well. Figure 11-6 shows an image that could be indexed.

Figure 11-6: Indexed color image

Indexed color images can contain up to 256 colors and are created (converted to indexed color) from RGB images. You can choose how many of these 256 to use, and you can pick as few as two. I usually choose four and make adjustments after seeing the result. (We discuss how to do this in Chapter 24.) During the conversion, Photoshop looks at all of the colors in the RGB design and figures out how to create those colors using only the colors you specified or the available 256 colors. This obviously creates some deterioration in the image, but if the image only has a few colors to begin with, you probably won't notice.

 Tip:

When working with an image that only has a few colors (say, fewer than 50 or so), try indexing. If you have a four-station press, choose the four main colors you feel are in the image when performing the color separation. You'll be surprised what you can create from just four colors!

Introduction to Process Color

Process color is used when you want to print photorealistic prints. Process color printing requires that you create unique halftone screens, one for each of the CMYK channels and additional screens as needed for an underbase, spot colors, or highlights. (We discuss how to do this in Chapter 23.) Halftones are really just dots that control how much ink should be put in a particular part of the image. For instance, if one screen has small dots for the black ink and another screen has large dots for the yellow ink, the resulting color will be a medium to light yellow when the inks are both placed on the substrate. You can see the percentages of CMYK in a color using the Info palette.

Figure 11-7 shows a print that would require process color. I got the zebra picture from the Photoshop 6.0 program files and added some text and a border; if you upgraded from 6.0 to 7.0, you'll have that same picture too.

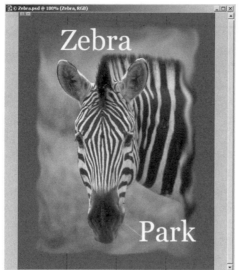

Figure 11-7: Process color image

Because the colors put on the material depend on the dot size on the screen, the importance of controlling the dot becomes a major issue. If you have a specific color that should have 30 percent ink density and the dot gain inherent to printing causes that dot density to be 40 percent, the color isn't going to be what you expect.

 Caution!

You need a PostScript printer to print halftone screens.

So the obvious object with process color printing is to somehow create films and screens that will actually take into effect these dot gains and other issues with inks, such as what brand you use, what types of screens you use, and other items, so that you get the correct colors once the image is printed. Photoshop can do this and is an excellent program to use. Creating CMYK art takes time and practice though and lots of knowledge and experience. Part V of this book is dedicated to this art.

Introduction to the Curves Dialog Box

You'll use the Curves dialog box quite a bit when correcting color. Although you could use Image>Adjustments and pick an automatic adjustment or use the Image>Adjustments>Levels option to set highlights, midtones, and shadows, using the Curves dialog box allows you to control your color changes precisely and from the entire tonal spectrum. The Curves tool also allows you to preview changes as you make them, as well as view the changes to the ink values in the Info palette at the same time.

The Curves dialog box will seem a little complicated though, and it takes a little getting used to. The best way to understand what happens when using the Curves dialog box is to work through some examples. Work through steps 1 to 4 to open a file and position the palettes so that you can see them correctly.

1. Open the file **Peppers.jpg** from the Samples folder in Photoshop 7.0's Program Files folder, under Samples.

2. Open the Info palette and verify (change if necessary) that the first print list shows the color values for RGB and the second for CMYK. Position the Info palette so that you can see the image and the palette.

3. Open the Channels palette using **Window>Channel**. See Figure 11-8 for positioning options.

4. Open the Curves dialog box using **Image>Adjustments>Curves** or **Ctrl+M** on the keyboard.

Figure 11-8: Using the Curves dialog box

With the correct palettes open and the Curves dialog box available, let's take a look at some of the items in it and what they're used for. Feel free to experiment as you read through these options.

- **Horizontal axis and vertical axis:** The horizontal axis represents the original color and intensity of the pixels; these are called input levels. The vertical axis represents the new color values, or the output levels. These axes are separated into 25 percent increments, as denoted by the lines. You can change these markings to 10 percent increments by holding down the Alt key and clicking inside the dialog box. See Figure 11-9.

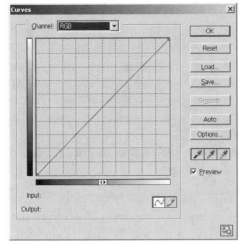

Figure 11-9: The Curves dialog box

- **Diagonal line:** The diagonal line represents the default color levels for the image. Before changes are made to the image, the input levels and output levels are the same. As you move the diagonal line, the input and output levels change. Moving the line up increases the output levels, giving them a higher intensity; moving the line down decreases the output level, giving the colors a lower intensity. The opposite is true of input levels. (Verify that your Curves dialog box is configured as mine is; the blackest parts of both the x- and y-axes should be at the bottom left. Change by clicking the arrows in the x-axis if needed.)

- **Input and Output:** The input and output values are shown based on the color model being used. For RGB, the values range from 0 to 255; for CMYK they range from 0 to 100 percent.

- **Save:** The Save button allows you to save a curve for future use. For instance, if your scanner's white isn't really white, you can correct it using a curve and apply that curve to each scan that you do. You can also create a curve for a specific client's artwork, or a specific type of paper or film.

- **Load:** The Load button allows you to load previously saved curves. This saves time when you use the same curve often.

- **Auto:** The Auto button automatically sets the color the way you have it set in the Auto Corrections dialog box.

There are a few other things to know before we get started. The grid represents a gradual change in grayscale color. The bottom left of the grid in the Curves dialog box represents all black and the top right all white. The top right side represents highlights, the left shadows, and the middle the midtones. This is the setup for RGB images; for CMYK, the highlights are on the left and shadows on the right.

With the basic options in your grasp, let's do some adjusting.

Project 11-1: Using the Curves Dialog Box to Prepare an Image for Printing

You can use the Curves tool to fix problems with colors in a photo. With the Peppers.jpg file still open and the palettes configured as shown in Figure 11-8, perform the following tasks to familiarize yourself with the Curves dialog box:

1. From the bottom-left corner, click and drag on the diagonal line to increase the shadows approximately 10 percent. (Use Alt+Click to show the grid in 10 percent increments instead of 25 percent.)

2. From the top-right corner, click and drag on the diagonal line to decrease the highlights approximately 10 percent. Verify that the black parts of the x- and y-axes are at the left-bottom corner, and the white parts are at the top and far right of the axes, as shown in Figure 11-10.

3. Click at the top right of the diagonal line and drag to the left, click in the top quarter of the line and drag upward, click on the bottom quarter of the line and drag down, and click on the bottom left of the line and drag right. This will create an "S" curve. See Figure 11-10.

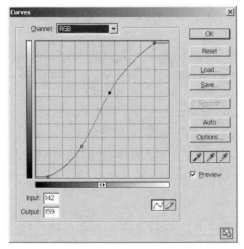

Figure 11-10: Using the Curves dialog box to enhance an image

4. From the Curves dialog box, choose **Red** from the Channel drop-down list.

5. Move the levels in the Curves dialog box to reduce the amount of red in the image. Try dragging from the center first and then experiment with dragging from other areas of the line.

6. Use the mouse to hover over a part of the image; choose one of the red hues. Notice in the Info palette that there are now two numbers separated by a slash. The first is the original color value, and the second is the new color value. These changes will not be applied until you press OK in this dialog box, giving you a moment to decide if the new values are going to meet your needs.

This "S" curve and decreasing the reds in an image is something I do a lot of as a screen printer. The "S" curve can be used to freshen up bad artwork that you've gotten in the form of a JPEG or GIF, and it seems to work well when preparing an image for screening. Photoshop seems to overdo on the reds occasionally, and I find myself reducing that a lot also.

Final Thoughts about the Curves Dialog Box

As you might be able to tell already, the Curves dialog box offers an extremely powerful option for correcting a photo. This works better than the automatic adjustment settings because as a screen printer, you need everything just a little crisper, just a little sharper, and just a little more colorful because of the losses at each stage of the print process.

There are a few other things about curves that you should know before moving on:

■ When you click on the diagonal line, a point is created. This point is fixed unless you click on it and drag. This allows you to configure the line so that specific parts of it can't be moved.

■ You can create up to 14 fixed points.

■ You can delete a fixed point by clicking on it and dragging it off the graph or by selecting it and clicking Delete on the keyboard.

■ You can click on the curve and type in your own input and output values.

■ You can work with various color channels by choosing them from either the Channels palette prior to opening the Curves dialog box or from the drop-down list after.

We revisit the Curves dialog box when we start correcting photos in Chapter 16 and again when we prepare artwork for color separations.

Summary

In this chapter you learned quite a bit about colors and their properties. Tools that were introduced or further expanded on include the Eyedropper tool and the Color Sampler. The Info palette was also introduced and offers a great way to compare colors before and after making changes using an adjustment tool, as well as view out of gamut colors.

Different types of printing were also introduced, including the differences between spot color, indexed color, and process color. Spot color is by far the best place to start if you're new to screen printing and is used for printing jobs requiring one to six colors. For process color you'll use a myriad of premixed inks to print the colors you want, using a screen for each separate color channel. Process color is used for photorealistic images, and color is created using a mixture of four colors: cyan, magenta, yellow, and black. By mixing these colors using halftone screens, thousands of colors can be created. Finally, indexed color is popular and offers a way to choose what colors will be used during the print process and how many colors will be chosen for the 256 available. Photoshop can convert RGB images to indexed color images easily.

Chapter 12

Layer Basics

If you've read this book and worked through the examples up to this point, you probably already have a good idea of what layers are. However, if you've just tuned in and are looking for information about using layers, you probably don't have any idea! With this in mind, I'll start this chapter with a brief introduction of what layers are, followed by how to build an image using layers. While there are literally thousands of references to layers in the Photoshop help files describing everything from creating a new layer to creating clipping groups, what you need to know most is how to use layers to create designs.

As you learn to create artwork by building layers, you'll incorporate everything you know so far and learn how to use the selection tools to add images to layers, cut and paste, feather images so they blend into the new layer, use the Layers palette, and create edges and backgrounds. In addition, you'll learn to change the order of layers, create new layers, show and hide layers, use the Move tool to manipulate images on layers, use styles and effects to add emphasis to text, transform the image using Scale, Skew, and other options, use the History palette, flatten the image, and prepare it for output. Whew—this chapter really brings it all together!

What Are Layers?

If you've ever played with paper dolls or given a presentation using transparencies on an overhead projector, you've worked with layered objects. If you've ever dressed warmly for winter, you've worn layers too. Layers are items that lay on top of one another and can be manipulated independently. In the case of clothing, you can decide what color of coat to wear and if and when you want to take it off. Your overall "look" will change, depending on which of the layers of clothing you have on. It is the same with transparencies; one transparency can be added on top of another to change the overall picture on the overhead projector.

You can do the same thing and more with layers in a Photoshop image. For instance, you can open a file of a sunset (layer 1), add a picture of a motorcycle or a car (layer 2), type in some text (layer 3), add a pretty girl on the side (layer 4), and you've got a cool design for a shirt!

Viewing Layers in the Layers Palette

The Layers palette is where you'll find information about the layers in an image. A digital picture will only have one layer, as you've seen throughout this book. Images that you build will have multiple layers. To see an image that has multiple layers, show and hide the layers, and view the Layers palette, work through this first example.

1. Open Photoshop 7.0 and reset the palette locations to the default using **Window>Workspace>Reset Palette Locations**.

2. Open the file **Morning Glass.psd** from the Samples folder for Photoshop 7.0, located on your hard drive under **Programs>Adobe**.

3. Drag the Layers palette and expand it, as shown in Figure 12-1, so that you can see all of the layers listed.

4. Notice how many layers are included in this image. Click on the eye icons in this palette to hide all of the layers, except for the layer named Layer 1. Clicking on the eye icon hides the layer, and clicking again shows it. Hide and show multiple layers to see how the image has been built. (If you hide all of the layers, there will be nothing but a transparent background showing.)

5. Close the file; do not save the changes.

Figure 12-1: Viewing the Layers palette

Create a New Layer

New layers can be created that are empty, have a fill such as a solid color or a gradient, have a background, or even have a pattern. Duplicate layers can also be created. Adjustment layers can be created also, and they allow you to make changes to a layer without actually having to commit them to the underlying pixels in the image until you're ready. Some of these tasks can be performed from the additional options arrow in the Layers palette, but all can be performed from the Layer menu. You'll be adding layers in this chapter using these options. Sometimes, layers are added automatically. The Type tool automatically adds a layer, as do the Shape tools. New layers can also be created by selecting an object and choosing Layer>New>Layer Via Copy or Layer Via Cut.

Order of Layers

When creating new layers, the newest layer is placed on top of the existing layers (so you can see it and work with it), but the order of the layers can be changed in the Layers palette. Figure 12-2 shows an image with three layers: a blue background, two lines, and a fish. In the first example, the layers are in the order they were created; in the second, the fish and lines layers are switched.

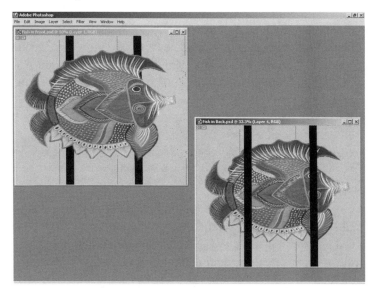

Figure 12-2: Layer adjustments

To change the order of layers, you only have to click and drag the layer in the Layers palette to its correct place in the layer order. Moving a file up the Layers palette will place it on top of the other layers; moving the layer down the list puts it underneath other layers. While working through this chapter, you'll learn how to manipulate layers in this fashion, as well as perform many other tasks.

Additional Options

In the additional options of the Layers palette are options to add a new layer or duplicate layer as mentioned earlier, but there are other options to delete a layer, delete hidden layers, link layers, set a layer's properties, and merge and flatten layers. These options are available from other menus too, but I think it's easiest to work with them from here. You can change how the thumbnails are viewed in the Layers palette by selecting Palette Options from the additional options.

Chapter Project: Building an Image Using Layers

Okay, we're ready to start creating some artwork! First, we need an image, then a background, and then some text. Of course, we'll spice all of this up a bit too, with some neat tips and tricks that you'll learn about styles and effects. Once the artwork is complete, we'll prepare it for output by converting it to CMYK.

 Tip:

Work through the rest of this project and chapter step by step for best results; each builds on the other, and the tips and tricks that you'll learn are embedded in the steps.

To start any new design using layers, you first need a picture that serves as the main focus. I'm going to create a design for a T-shirt for the Dallas Zoo using a picture of a zebra as the focus. You might use a photo of a motorcycle and create a design for a bike shop or a picture of a cedar chest for a logo for a consignment shop. (You might also decide to just follow along using the same file that I choose.) So, before we start, decide on what it is that you'd like to create and locate or take a picture to serve as the focus for it.

Using the Selection Tools

The picture I will use as an example throughout this project is from the Photoshop 6.0 Samples folder on my computer. If you upgraded from Photoshop 6.0 to Photoshop 7.0, you have this file; it is called Zebra.psd. If you don't have this one, you can use the Eagle.psd file from the Samples folder in the Photoshop 7.0 folder. If you plan to use your own picture, make sure the picture or design is in RGB mode by opening it in Photoshop and seeing what is listed in the title bar of the image. If the image you want to use is CMYK or another format, go to Image>Mode> RGB Color and convert it.

 Caution!

If you are using a photo that someone else took, make sure you've acquired the rights to use it! For example, you can't use the Microsoft logo on your own business card without the proper permissions.

With the picture open that will serve as the focus of your design, let's use the selection tools to create a layer from it:

1. Zoom in on the object if necessary so that you can distinguish the object from its background clearly. You're going to trace around the object, so make sure you can see what you want to trace around.

2. With the image open, select the **Lasso** tool from the toolbox. This tool was introduced briefly in Chapter 1 and is the second tool down on the left side. The keyboard shortcut is L or Shift+L. From the options bar, change Feather to **10 px** and be sure Anti-Aliasing is checked. See the sidebar on feathering later in this section.

3. Trace around the object using the mouse by holding down the left mouse key and dragging. If you accidentally let up on the mouse or mess up, choose **Edit>Undo Lasso Tool** and start again. (There is much more on these selection tools in Chapter 16.)

4. Completely trace around the selection. You'll have to trace completely around the object to make the Lasso tool work and end exactly where you started. This means you'll have to run up the far-right side of the image. Once finished, you'll see the "marching ants" around the selected area. See Figure 12-3.

5. Open the Layers palette if it isn't already open.

6. With the marching ants area still selected, choose **Layer>New> Layer Via Copy**. Notice the new layer in the Layers palette and that both layers are showing (they both have eye icons next to them).

Figure 12-3: Using the Lasso tool

7. Hide the background layer by clicking on the eye icon in the Layers palette. Figure 12-4 shows what your image should look like. (Of course, you may have a different picture!)

8. Choose the **Move** tool from the toolbox and move the image as desired on the layer.

9. Use the **Eraser** tools to clean up areas around the image. Use the **History Brush** to "unerase" any areas with errors.

10. To undo any number of steps, use the **Edit>Undo** commands or open the History palette and use the sliders.

Figure 12-4: Using the Layers palette

With the image's focus created, use File>Save As to save the image. Create a new name for the file that is indicative of its state. I'll name mine Zebra Head.psd.

> **Feathering**
>
> Feathering can be used with the Marquee tool or any of the Lasso tools. Feathering softens the edges of a selection to help them blend into their new layers better than they would with a hard edge. Feathering causes images to appear blurry though and might not always be appropriate. You won't see any effect of feathering until you cut, copy, move, or fill a selection.

Creating Backgrounds

Now the design needs a background. The background will be used to fill in behind the focus image of the logo and, in the case of the zebra head, can be anything ranging from a solid background to a picture. For this example, let's choose a picture; in the next section, you can choose a background.

1. Make sure the first image (from the previous example) is still open. Open a new file that contains the photo you'd like to serve as the background image, or open the background image that I'm using from the Chapter 12 folder of the CD (**Palm.jpg**). See Figure 12-5.

2. Click on the new image that contains the background picture and look at the Layers palette. You'll see that this picture contains only one layer.

3. Click on this layer from the Layers palette. Drag this layer to the center of the first image. See Figure 12-5.

Figure 12-5: Opening two images and dragging a layer from one to the other

4. The new layer is now placed on top of the original image, hiding it from view. From the Layers palette, locate this new layer in the first image; it is the topmost layer. Click and drag the layer in the Layers palette down one spot. See Figure 12-6 for the layer's new location in the list.

 Tip:

You can also use the Layer>Arrange options to move layers to the front or back of an image.

5. Click on the **Move** tool in the toolbox, check **Auto Select Layer** in the options bar, and position the background layer appropriately. See Figure 12-6. Do the same with the focus image (zebra head in this case).

Figure 12-6: Positioning the two layers using the Move tool

6. Use **File>Save As** to save this file under a new name, such as Zebra Head with Background.psd. You can close the file you used to drag over the background.

You might encounter problems when performing steps 4 and 5 because of the difference in image size and resolution of the two files. You have a couple of choices if this happens: You can use the History palette to undo a few steps, resize the image that will serve as the background, and drag it over again; or you can use the Transform tools (detailed later) to scale the image so it will fit better against the background.

Other Types of Backgrounds

If you don't want a picture in the background, you can choose a solid color, gradient, or pattern. This would make for a simpler print and is quite easy to do.

To create a new layer background that is a solid color, pattern, or gradient:

1. Open the first saved file that contains only the focus image (in my case, Zebra Head.psd). Use the **Edit>Undo** command or the History palette to return to the Layer Via Copy state. (This state is shown in Figure 12-4.)

2. For a solid background, choose **Layer>New Fill Layer>Solid Color** and click **OK** in the New Layer dialog box. (You could also choose Gradient or Pattern, but for now, just choose a solid color.)

3. In the resulting Color Picker dialog box, choose a color. Click **OK**.

4. From the Layers palette, drag this new layer down one spot to place it behind the existing layer.

5. Choose **Layer>Change Layer Content** from the menu bar. Select **Gradient**.

6. Experiment with the Gradient Fill dialog box if desired. A preview will be shown as you make changes. Click **OK** when done. (Gradients are detailed in Chapter 20.)

7. Repeat step 5 and choose **Pattern**. Experiment with the available patterns. Click **OK** when done.

8. Use the History palette to undo any number of steps, or use Layer> Change Layer Content to select the background you want. Figure 12-7 shows an example of a pattern background—Yellow Mums. (I'm not going to keep it this way though!)

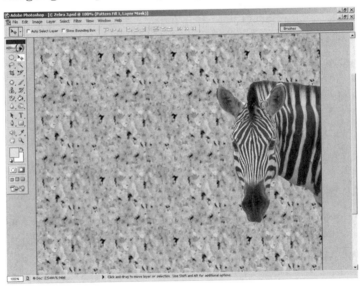

Figure 12-7: Using a pattern background

With the background and focus image selected, you're now ready to transform the image, add text, and add some finishing touches.

Tip:
Use File>Revert to revert quickly to the state that the image was in the last time it was saved.

Transforming Layer Images

If the focus image in your layer isn't the right size or needs a little adjusting other than moving it around, you can transform that layer's object using the Edit>Transform tools. There are several:

- **Scale:** Enlarge or reduce an image's size horizontally, vertically, or both.
- **Rotate:** Rotate an object around its center point. The center point can be changed.
- **Skew:** Slant an image vertically or horizontally.
- **Distort:** Move an image in any direction at all.
- **Perspective:** Apply perspective to an image.

When using the Transform tools, you can push or pull from handles that appear around the object. Look at Figure 12-8. You can use these handles to resize, distort, skew, rotate, or apply perspective to an object.

Figure 12-8: Using the Transform tools

Now you try it:

1. With your design open, click on the focus object's layer in the Layers palette. In Figure 12-8, notice that the layer with the zebra cutout is selected. This should be the topmost layer in the Layers palette.

2. Choose **Edit > Transform > Scale** and resize the image by pushing in or pulling from the corner handles. Click the check mark on the options bar to commit the changes.

3. Choose **Edit > Transform > Rotate** if you want to rotate the image. Rotate the image by placing the cursor just outside the corner handle. When it becomes a two-headed curved arrow, click and drag. Click the check mark on the options bar to commit the changes.

4. Choose **Edit > Transform > Skew** if you want to slant the image. Use the corner handles to perform the skew. Click the check mark on the options bar to commit the changes.

5. Choose **Edit > Transform > Distort** to distort the image. Pull or push from any handle to get the desired effect. Click the check mark on the options bar to commit the changes.

6. Choose **Edit > Transform > Perspective** to give perspective to the image. Pull or push from any handle to get the desired effect. Click the check mark on the options bar to commit the changes.

I used the Scale, Skew, and Perspective commands to make the zebra in my picture appear to be looking at me from inside the photograph. You can get almost any effect you want using these tools and make things seem closer or farther way. You can see the changes in Figure 12-9 in the following section.

Adding Text

The next step is to add some text to the image. As you can see, in this section we start with just plain old text and enhance it with styles and/or text effects. If you need a refresher on adding text, refer to Chapter 9.

With your working file still open, click on the Type tool. Type in some words that are appropriate for your design. I'll type in "Dallas Zoo." For now, keep the text on a single layer so that you can apply styles and text effects to the type on the image only once. Choose a font, font size, and font color that will work for your design.

Tip:

As you progress, you'll probably want to add text on several different layers so that the text lines and/or words can be edited independently.

With the text added, notice the new layer in the Layers palette. This layer can be manipulated like other layers have before; they can be moved up or down the Layers list so that they appear either in front of or behind any other layer. In Figure 12-9, the text is behind the zebra.

Before continuing, make sure that the objects in your image are positioned where you want them. To move the type, select the type layer from the Layers palette, select the type and use the mouse to move it, or choose the Move tool and move it like any other object. To move the focus object, click on the layer that contains that object in the Layers palette, choose the Move tool from the toolbox,

Figure 12-9: Adding text

and move the focus object appropriately. You might even want to move the background so that the text shows up better (if the background is a picture).

 Tip:

If you have Auto Select Layer checked in the options bar, the layers will be selected automatically.

Adding Styles and Blending Options

Text will only convey words if you don't do anything to it. To make the text part of the design and have it convey a message, you need to enhance it. One way to enhance text is to apply a blending option or style to it. To experiment with both, find one that fits your design:

1. Double-click on the type layer in the Layers palette. (If you double-click on the name of the layer, Photoshop will think you want to rename the layer; just click on the layer, not the name.)

2. The Layer Style dialog box appears. Here, you can add some nice effects to your text.

3. Place a check mark next to **Drop Shadow**; then click on it so that it's selected (it will turn a blue color). If you don't click on it, you won't be able to access the options for it. See Figure 12-10. Drop Shadow and the options underneath are Blending Options.

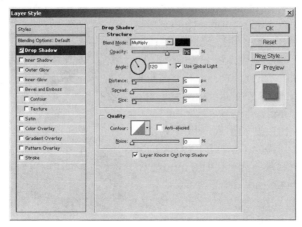

Figure 12-10: The Layer Style dialog box

4. Position the dialog box by dragging on the title bar so that you can see both the dialog box and the text in your image.

5. With Drop Shadow selected and checked, select a color for the shadow, set the angle for the shadow, configure the distance, spread, and size of the shadow, and configure any other options.

6. Uncheck **Drop Shadow** and check and select **Inner Shadow**. Experiment with these options.

7. In reality, you'd continue in this manner until you found a style that fits your design. Otherwise, you'd simply click **Cancel**. For experimentation's sake, remove all of the check marks, and let's apply a style.

8. With the text back to its original state, click on the word **Styles** in the Layer Style dialog box. It's the first one at the top of the list on the left. The available styles will appear in the dialog box.

9. Click on the different styles to see what it does to your text. Experiment for a little longer, leave the Layer Style dialog box open, and continue in the next section to apply some text effects.

Adding Text Effects

Besides styles, you can also add text effects to an image. Continuing from the previous exercise:

10. From the additional options in the Layer Style dialog box, choose **Text Effects**, and click **OK** when prompted. See Figure 12-11.

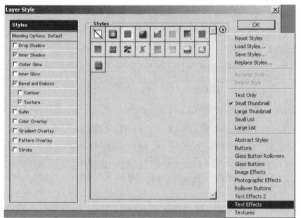

Figure 12-11: Locating the Text Effects in the Layer Style dialog box

11. Work through the different text effects until you see something you like. You can also add Text Effects 2 from the additional options for others.

12. If you want to work on the text without any background, hide the additional layers.

13. You can combine both styles and blending options as desired. Once you've got the look you want, click **OK**.

You'll see the text effects I chose in Figure 12-12. Keep in mind that you'll probably never view all of the available combinations and that you can combine both styles and blending options. The possibilities are endless. Also, remember that you can edit the styles applied at any time by double-clicking on the layer again from the Layers palette (there will be a cursive "f" there to click on).

Now let's finish up the design by working on the edges. Simply placing a rectangular image on a shirt or tote bag would look kind of unfinished, and it would also stretch out of shape after a washing or two. With the image almost finished, let's increase the canvas size and add some edge effects.

Increasing the Canvas Size

When you work with an image, you only have enough room in the image space to work on the image and no space outside of it. This can be remedied by increasing the canvas size. Increasing the canvas size allows you more room to work.

To increase the canvas size:

1. Choose **Image>Canvas Size**.

2. In the Canvas Size dialog box, read what the original canvas size is, and then type in numbers for the new canvas size.

3. If you want to change the anchor for the additional canvas space, click on one of the arrows.

4. The canvas is enlarged with the background color, a transparent background, or the background image (if it's larger than the original), depending on what you've got going on with your image. Save the file with the appropriate name as before.

You might have to use the Crop tool to get the image and canvas size just right. The object is simply to create a little working space around the image.

Creating Edges

Let's finish off the edges of our new design by using a variety of tools. You'll have to experiment with several to get the effect you want, and I'll walk you through a few suggestions here. Creating edges around an image allows you to remove the hard edge of the rectangular image by distorting it in some way or painting over it.

1. Choose **Layer 2** in the Layers palette; this is the layer with the background on it (a picture, fill, or gradient). Depending on what you've done to the layers, it might be called a Normal layer or something else. Choose the layer that contains the background for your image.

2. Change the foreground color to white in the toolbox. (You might want to experiment with other colors too, such as the color you've chosen for your text or a color in your focus image.)

3. Choose the **Brush** tool from the toolbox and click on the airbrush icon in the options bar.

4. Choose a soft round brush, like **Brush 100**, and change the Flow to **75** percent in the options bar. Spray around the outside edges of the image.

5. Try other brushes and colors too, increasing and decreasing opacity, flow, and brush size. Use the History palette to erase any mistakes. Figure 12-12 shows an example of what an edge might look like.

6. Undo the brush strokes.

7. Choose the **Smudge** tool from the toolbox. Work around the edges using this tool to create an edge effect. Experiment with various brushes and modes.

8. Experiment with the Blur tool, choosing different modes and strengths.

Figure 12-12: Creating an edge

The best way to get to know what each tool can do for you is to experiment. If possible, work through this exercise several times, choosing different settings for the tools each time.

Flattening Layers

With the design finished, you'll now want to color separate it and print it out. So far, you've been working in RGB mode. However, you can't color separate an image while it's in RGB mode; it must be converted to CMYK first. To convert it to CMYK, the image must be flattened. Flattening an image combines all of the layers together in a single layer.

Flattening a layer is a simple process, but before you do it, make sure the image looks the way you want it to. To make sure there aren't any extraneous parts to the image that need to be cropped, use File>Print with Preview. You should see only the image in the Preview window, not any extra backgrounds or too much white space. If you do, go back and crop the image appropriately. Click Cancel in the Print dialog box.

From the Layers palette, click the additional options and choose Flatten Image, or flatten the image using Layer>Flatten Image. If you have any hidden layers, you'll be prompted to discard them; if so, click Yes. Notice in the Layers palette that there is only a single layer.

Preparing for Output

Although you can print a single copy of your RGB design to send the client for approval, you won't print color separations in RGB mode. To convert an image to CMYK, choose Image>Mode>CMYK Color.

With that done, you can now look at the CMYK channels in the Channels palette. This palette is generally grouped with the Layers palette, as it looks similar to it, but it is completely different. You can remove the eyes to hide or show the different color channels and get an idea as to what each plate on the screen will look like. As you are aware, Part V of this book is dedicated to performing and working with color separations.

Summary

In this chapter you learned how to use layers and the Layers palette to create and build images for clients. This chapter combined everything that you have learned thus far in the book and enabled you to create a composite design that could be used for a client.

Building an image using layers incorporated many aspects of the Layers palette and the Layer menu. In this chapter you learned how to use the selection tools to add images to layers, how to cut and paste, what feathering is, how the Layers palette is used, and how to finish off a design using edges and backgrounds. In addition, you learned how to change the order of layers, create new layers, show and hide layers, use the Move tool to manipulate images on layers, use styles and effects to add emphasis to text, transform the image using Scale, Skew, and other options, use the History palette, flatten the image, and prepare it for output.

This completes Part II of the book. In Part III, we discuss how to acquire files that are already created, including those from floppy disks, scanners, and cameras, as well as how to enhance images, such as photographs given to you by clients, and when and if you should use heat transfers.

Part III
Working with Client Files

Chapter 13

Acquiring Files from Disks

Your clients will bring artwork files to your shop in many forms, including files on floppy disks, on CDs, on zip disks, and even via e-mail. In order to work with these files, you have to know not only how to open them, but how to get them into Photoshop in a form that's best suited for editing.

In addition to getting the files *into* Photoshop, you have to make sure you don't contract any viruses while opening them. No, this doesn't mean you have to wash your hands before handling the disk; it means you need to have updated virus protection installed on your computer!

Other issues, including file types and resolutions, also factor into how you'll use a client's file (if it's usable at all). If a client sends you a photograph saved as a GIF file for instance, you'll most likely have to return it to the client with instructions on how to resave it and send it as a JPEG or EPS file.

Finally, you can use Photoshop to work with files among multiple users and computers. This is a really neat feature if multiple people in your art department work on the same files and have different talents.

Whatever the case is in your shop, you'll get files from clients on disks and work with files e-mailed to you that you can save to your own hard disk. In this chapter, we discuss how to deal with all of these issues.

When a Client Brings a Floppy, Zip, or Compact Disk

When a client walks in the door with his or her own disk in hand, I always get a little shiver down my spine. It's more like a premonition actually because there are so many problems associated with client-created artwork that I'm bound to run into a few each time. While it is possible to "train" return clients to bring in what you want and need, getting what you need the first time isn't the norm.

The first problem involves computer viruses. A client who wants the Nike Swoosh on a hat or jacket and can't understand why I won't print it is a close second. Scanning is another problem because a scan usually has a gray tint to it, is difficult to work with, and is usually not at the resolution I need. (I've gotten scans of artwork where images were glued or taped to the original page before the scan!)

Other problems include getting artwork in proprietary formats, like the GED files output by Arts & Letters. Of course, this isn't a problem if you have Arts & Letters installed (which I do) or whatever program they built their design in, and if this is the case, you can open it and change it to whatever you want. Working in the client's native program and exporting the file yourself lets you have more control.

Virus Protection

The best way to protect your computer from viruses is to purchase and install an anti-virus program. There are several manufacturers, including Norton and McAfee. These programs aren't very expensive and can be purchased on the web. You can configure the software to download all of the virus updates weekly, monthly, or even daily, providing continual protection. When a client comes in with a disk, you should scan it using this software. It only takes a minute and is quite easy to do. Just follow your software's instructions.

Another way to prevent viruses in your shop and on your network is isolation. Keep one computer off of the network and use it for opening client's files. From there, the file can be scanned for viruses and evaluated for other problems.

Proprietary File Formats

Many clients create their own artwork using an art program they have at home or in the office, and many of these programs save files by default in a proprietary file format. Proprietary means that the file can only be opened in the program in which it was created, such as Arts & Letters' GED files, Adobe Photoshop's PSD files, Paint Shop Pro's PSP files, CorelDRAW's CDR, and other file formats. If the client has saved the file in one of these proprietary formats, you'll only be able to open it in the program in which it was created.

If you get a file format that you can't open, you have a couple of choices: Either purchase and install the program (if you have a lot of money), or return the file to the client and ask them to use their program's File>Export command to export the file to a floppy as an EPS file. They can also export the file as a JPEG, GIF, TIFF, or other format, as long as it's a common format that all computers recognize, although EPS is best.

 Note:

Common file formats are detailed in the section "File Types and Limitations" later in this chapter.

Scanned Artwork

If a client scans their hand-drawn artwork, puts it on a disk, and either brings it in or e-mails it, it might or might not be usable. In our shop, we generally average about half and half. Some clients have great scanners that make good scans; they scan in RGB, save as a TIFF file, and scan at an appropriate resolution. Others scan at a low resolution, in grayscale, or with a poorly calibrated scanner, making the scan unusable.

If you receive a scan from a client, open it up and see how it looks on screen. If the background looks gray or muddy, you'll most likely have to ask for the original artwork and scan it yourself. If the scan looks good on screen, you might be able to use it without a problem.

In general though, it's best to either get the artwork electronically, where the work is created on the computer or comes from a digital camera, or do your own scanning using the original artwork.

Resolution by the Inch

Resolution is a number, a ratio specifically, that is used to represent how many pixels, dots, or lines per inch an image has during image creation, during printing of halftone screens, and when describing the output capabilities of a printer, respectively. You'll want to have your clients provide artwork to you in resolutions that you can work with, and you'll want to print at optimal resolutions as well.

 Note:

In the following sections, I define the terms as they relate to raster images, which are the images you'll use most of the time in Photoshop. Vector-based images are defined mathematically and thus have a set resolution. Text is vector based in Photoshop, but most of what you do will not be.

Pixels Per Inch

Images such as photos are made up of pixels, which are small squares that contain color. An image's resolution is determined by how many pixels there are in the image per inch. Image resolution is a ratio of *pixels per inch;* the more pixels you squeeze into each inch of the image, the higher the resolution. Higher resolution means a better quality image.

When clients bring you artwork, ask for the artwork to be at least 300 pixels per inch. This guarantees that the image will be of a high enough resolution for you to work with it properly. If the customer only has a lower resolution image, they have to understand that the print is going to look a little jagged or soft around the hard edges and might not produce a really good print.

To see the resolution of an image that's already in Photoshop, use Image>Image Size, as shown in Figure 13-1.

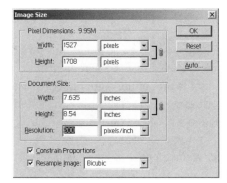

Figure 13-1: The Image Size dialog box

Pixels per inch are used to describe the quality of digital photos, some computer-generated artwork, computer monitor resolutions, and scanner settings. Sometimes, people use the terms "pixels per inch" and "dots per inch" interchangeably; I do not do that in this book. In Figure 13-1, notice the highlighted section is pixels per inch.

Dots Per Inch

Another resolution term is *dots per inch* (dpi). Dpi describes how many dots per inch can be printed on the page and is a measure of how good a printer is. Generally, printers can print many more dots per inch than the pixels per inch that need to be printed. For instance, a 1440 x 1440 dpi printer can be used to print a 200 or 300 ppi image with excellent accuracy, and for many screen printers, this is quite sufficient.

Lines Per Inch

Lines per inch (lpi) is another type of resolution that you'll use often. Lpi is a term used by offset printers, screen printers, and other graphic artists to describe how many lines or dots per inch will be in a halftone screen. Screen printers generally output their images at 55 to 65 lines per inch, depending on the type of print process (spot or process) and other factors, such as the type of screen used and its mesh count and the type of ink used.

 Caution!

Pixels per inch is the term I've used thus far, but the settings can be changed to pixels per centimeter too. For now, always make sure that you're working with pixels per inch. That is the standard.

What to Ask For

If a client calls beforehand and asks you for specific guidelines for artwork, you should have those guidelines ready. For a screen printer, getting perfect artwork from a client is one of life's greatest pleasures. You'll find that larger companies that have screen printing work done often have been properly trained and will offer you "camera-ready" artwork. This work is ready to go!

Here are a few guidelines that you can post on your web site. Try to get your clients to get as many of these right as possible that apply to them. For instance, if they can send the file in 300 ppi as a Photoshop file, the battle is half won!

 Note:

While I see ppi and dpi as completely different, some clients will use the terms interchangeably. You might want to use ppi or dpi in this list, so you don't confuse anyone.

These guidelines have worked for our company quite well:

- File resolution should be at 300 ppi (dpi) for any process color work. If the design is intricate with small logos or italic lettering, send it at 400 ppi. Send artwork actual size.

- If you can send a Photoshop (PSD) file, please do. Otherwise, send in the following order of most to least preferable: editable EPS, TIFF, high-quality JPEG. If you've created the work in Corel, send as PSD or EPS.

- Spot color artwork should be sent at 300 dpi if printed and 300 ppi if electronic. Send artwork actual size.

- All artwork sent via e-mail must be sent as an attachment.

- Grayscale images must be sent at 300 ppi or dpi. Grayscale images can only be printed in one color.

- Send files in RGB mode; we'll convert to CMYK.

- We accept artwork on floppy disks, zip disks, and CD-ROMs. They will be returned. Please write the name of the file(s) on the front of the disk.

- Specify any Pantone colors if applicable.

- We accept Macintosh and PC files.
- Scanned images should be at least 1200 ppi (dpi) or better.

As you spend more time as a screen printer, you'll come up with rules of your own. If you get big enough, you can require that your clients bring camera-ready artwork already on film and ready for print. For those of you with smaller shops and those just starting, you should probably start by taking just about anything and working up!

✖ **Caution!**

Be sure to tell clients who bring low-quality JPEGs that the image you'll try to create on the shirt isn't going to be exactly perfect. Low-quality JPEGs can't really be improved that much, and the client should be made aware of that.

Switching to RGB

As you are by now aware, it is best to work in RGB mode. If a file comes to you in another mode, convert it to RGB first. When doing a scan, scan in RGB mode too. There's also no harm in asking the client to rescan something in RGB mode at a higher resolution or asking them to convert their GED file to EPS so you can open it.

Opening the File

There are several ways to open a file, and in Chapter 6 you learned about using the File Browser for that purpose. The File Browser is an excellent way to open files, but there are several others.

The File > Open Command

The File>Open command opens the Open dialog box with which you are already familiar. It's your operating system's dialog box and allows you to browse your computer's hard drive for the file you want. Figure 13-2 shows this dialog box.

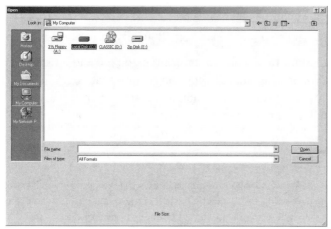

Figure 13-2: The Open dialog box

This figure shows a sample Open dialog box on a PC running Windows 2000 Server. Your dialog box will look similar. To locate any file, click the down arrow in the Look In window and select the appropriate drive and then folder. As you can see in the figure, I've browsed to My Computer, where I can access the floppy drive, the hard disk, the CD drive, and the zip drive.

The File > Open As Command

Use the File > Open As command when you want to open a file in a specific format. This won't always work, and the file might not open. I don't usually use this command, but it never hurts to experiment. See the "File Types and Limitations" section later for more information about different types of files and their advantages and disadvantages.

The File > Open As command brings up a dialog box that's similar to the Open dialog box shown in Figure 13-2. The only difference is that at the bottom of the dialog box there are choices as to what file type you want to use. There are Photoshop file types, of course, but also BMP, TIFF, GIF, EPS, DCS, and others.

The File > Open Recent Command

This command shows a list of your most recently opened files. The default is 10, but this number can be changed using Edit > Preferences > File Handling and can show as many as 30 files. To open a recently viewed file, simply choose it from the list.

The File > Import Command

This command lets you import files from a scanner or digital camera and import PDF images, annotations, and WIA support. PDF (Portable Document Format) is the primary file format for Adobe Illustrator and Adobe Acrobat. When importing PDF files, you can choose from a list of them, import all of the files, or go to a specific file number.

You can also import from a digital camera, although I've never had much luck with this. Photoshop thinks most cameras should be installed on a COM port, when in reality they're installed mostly on USB and Fire Wire ports. If, however, you are lucky enough to have a recognized camera and hold your breath just right, you might be able to get it to work.

Annotations are recorded messages attached to artwork by the creator or editor. These recordings can be imported using this command.

WIA support is available only on Microsoft Windows ME or XP and helps the operating system, the camera and scanner, and Photoshop work together to import images from scanners and cameras. If you haven't had any luck with the File > Import commands, this might work for you. Even then, you might have problems. For the best solutions for obtaining images from cameras and scanners, refer to Chapters 14 and 15.

Working with E-mailed Artwork

Getting artwork via e-mail is becoming more common these days since there are so many people online and designing their own artwork. As with files on disks, you must ensure that you scan all of your e-mail attachments before opening them by using some sort of anti-virus software. With that out of the way, you have three options for the file:

- Open it
- Save it to disk
- Save attachments

Opening the file will give you a quick look at the image, and you'll most likely be able to determine by looking at it if the file will work. You can then send a reply stating that you received the e-mail and the file will or will not work and for what reasons.

To open the file, you simply need to click on the name of the file in the attachment list and choose Open It from the resulting dialog box, as shown in Figure 13-3. (Some files will open automatically.) If, after viewing the file you deem it satisfactory (it's a valid file type, has nice resolution, is virus-free, etc.), you can save it to your hard disk.

Figure 13-3: The Open Attachment Warning dialog box

Opening Attachments

The file will open in the program that your system is configured to use. If you want to quickly open the file just for viewing though, you might not want to wait the two or three minutes it takes Photoshop 7.0 to open; you might want to view it in a different program that loads faster. To change the default program that opens specific files on a PC with a Windows operating system, first open Windows Explorer. Then go to Tools>Folder Options>File Types, select a file type (like JPEG), and click the Change button. Choose a program from the list.

Saving the File

There are two (sometimes three) ways to save a file. Occasionally, in the case of Word documents and similar files, the file opens automatically when you click on it, and you can save the file to the hard drive from inside the program in which it opens. This doesn't happen too often; usually you'll get an Open Attachment Warning dialog box (Figure 13-3) that prompts you to choose to either open the file or save it to disk. It's best to open the file and then save it to the hard disk using the program's

File>Save As command. (I'm assuming of course that you have your virus protection software set to scan all incoming files.) If you choose Save It to Disk, it might save as an e-mail attachment that Photoshop won't recognize.

With the file saved to the computer's hard disk, you can now open the file in Photoshop (if the file wasn't opened there already!).

Acquiring a File from a Workgroup

If your computers are networked together as a workgroup and/or if you are part of a corporate domain, you can share files across computers. This means that in any size shop or company, files can be shared on a local drive or a domain server, and all users can access that file and perform editing on it.

Figure 13-4 shows two computers that are near me on my network, one of which belongs to the lead artist. I can easily browse her hard drive to access, open, and view the latest work done on any file and even add my own touches to it. If you work in a networked environment, consider setting up something like this. If you are still carrying floppies from one computer to the next, you should really, really, look into it!

Figure 13-4: Accessing files on other computers

File Types and Limitations

So what file types should you ask for and what file types are the best to work with? Well, in Photoshop, the best type of file to work with is a Photoshop PSD file. If your clients have Photoshop and submit their artwork in it, that's your best bet. However, in most cases, that's usually not what happens.

There are *many* file types, some of which are proprietary for specific programs but others that are universal like EPS, BMP, TIFF, JPEG, and GIF. Photoshop can be used to open many file types.

Figure 13-5 shows the File>Open dialog box and several of the options for opening files. While I won't go into explaining all of these, I will explain the ones you'll want to work with most and those your clients will give you often.

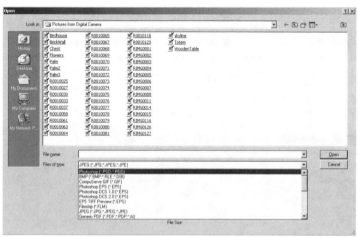

Figure 13-5: Using the Open dialog box to see various file types

PSD Files

Photoshop files you create that are raster-based and contain layers and channels are automatically saved as this type of file. The image's resolution and spot color channels are also saved, as is image bit depth. If you want to save the file in any other format, you'll have to flatten it first. PSD files save information about the file, including its layers and channels, so that those items can be continually edited. (As you know, once an image is flattened and saved as another file type, this information is gone.) PSD files can be created in CorelDRAW as well.

EPS Files

EPS files are Encapsulated PostScript files and contain both raster- and vector-based images. EPS files can be edited in Adobe Illustrator as well as Photoshop, and some EPS files from third-party clip art companies can be edited in other programs, such as CorelDRAW and Arts & Letters.

EPS files can be created in any color space and any image bit depth. EPS is a good file format to receive from a client and for saving. Printing an EPS file requires a PostScript printer. EPS does not support alpha channels.

EPS DCS2 Files

EPS DCS2 files are variations of EPS files. DCS stands for Desktop Color Separated file. This file type allows you to save color separations as CMYK files. The DCS2 format also allows you to export images containing spot channels, which regular EPS doesn't support. To print DCS files, you must have a PostScript printer.

BMP Files

BMP files are bitmap files, which are pixel-based files usually considered standard Microsoft Windows files. Bitmap files only support RGB color spaces and 1, 4, 8, or 24 bits per channel. This is quite low channel support, making bitmap images unsuitable and rarely chosen for Photoshop file work. Bitmap images are best used for PC buttons and icons or for creating images in low-end art programs.

TIFF Files

TIFF files are Tagged Image File Format files (also called TIF files) that are widely used in graphic design. TIFF files are raster based and support almost all color spaces. TIFF files can be compressed using a lossless compress scheme, making them better for saving than JPEG files.

TIFF files are generally used to transfer files from one application like Photoshop to other graphic applications. Practically all desktop publishing programs support it. If a file created in Photoshop is saved as a TIFF and opened again in Photoshop, layers are preserved; if the file is transferred to another application, the layers are lost.

JPEG Files

This is the type of file I get most often from clients because it's small in size and e-mails easily. JPEGs are best suited for saving photographs or images with lots of colors. Most people are familiar with JPEG, and they understand that it is a universal file format.

JPEG stands for Joint Photographic Experts Group and is sometimes also written as JPG. JPEG files are lossy, meaning that because they are compressed, they lose detail. When the file is changed from a JPEG to another format, those compressed or lost pixels must be reconstructed. This usually results in jagged edges in the design. Designs used for T-shirts and other material lose detail in every step of the process, so it's best to stay away from JPEG files when possible. The JPEG file format supports RGB, CMYK, and grayscale color models.

✖ **Caution!**

Each time you open, edit, and close a JPEG file, the file is recompressed, so there's always more and more data loss.

GIF Files

GIF stands for Graphics Interchange Format and is generally used for files that are considered line art or have only a few colors. GIF images are good for images containing less than 256 colors, so they're not good for photographs. GIF file format supports grayscale and RGB color spaces. This format can be used for indexed color spaces as well, although it isn't a common Photoshop working file format.

PDF Files

PDF stands for Portable Document Format and is used mainly for documents. PDF file format preserves fonts, page layout, and other document information and can be imported into Photoshop for editing.

PDF files are platform independent, meaning almost any computer OS can be used when opening them. PDF files are not used in Photoshop for creating artwork.

Summary

In this chapter you learned about obtaining files from disks; these included hard disks, floppy disks, CDs, zip disks, and even a client's hard disk via e-mail or workgroup.

There are several issues that need to be considered when using work from a client's disk or work that's already created. First, viruses can wreak havoc on a computer system, so you must always be prepared to scan artwork or disks that clients give you. Second, make sure the image is of a usable resolution or inform the client of the possibility of image deterioration.

With the image at hand, the file can be opened several ways. The File menu offers several, including Open, Open As, and Import. While opening the file and after working with it, file formats come into play. Common file formats are PSD, EPS, TIFF, JPEG, GIF, and PDF. When possible, ask the client to give you a Photoshop file.

Chapter 14

Acquiring Files from Scanners

Scanning files seems like an easy task; just place some artwork on the scanner and press the scan button. In reality, it isn't quite that simple. To get the most out of your scanner, you'll need to calibrate it properly, verify that white is really white and black is really black, and understand the file formats, resolutions, and scan settings, as well as the drawbacks of using scanners to acquire files versus other types of file acquisition.

I begin the chapter with some scanner terminology. Following that, we go through the steps for calibrating and setting up the scanner. You'll want to spend the time now to do this, even if you've been using your scanner for a while and think everything is set up properly. Installing the scanner using the defaults, scanning with the defaults, and outputting with the defaults just won't do for a professional artist (especially a screen printer!).

Once the scanner is properly set up, we do a few tests to verify that the scanner is scanning properly and configure a curve for the scanner if it is not (which is very likely). With that done, you can then begin scanning client files with confidence.

Understanding Scanner Terminology

When you scan an image, several words pop out at you immediately since you generally have to make selections from the software screen before scanning. Some of the options that you'll come across include Color Mode, Resolution, Source, Moiré, and Output Size. Some abbreviations and/or proper names that you'll see include TWAIN, OCR, dpi, and TIFF. While some of these terms are probably familiar to you, others might not be. Take a couple of minutes to browse through the definitions here, so you will understand what your scanner has to offer.

Figure 14-1 shows the dialog box for the Epson 1200U scanner, which has been opened using the File>Import command in Photoshop. Notice the options; these terms are introduced in the next section. Your scanner's software interface might look similar to this.

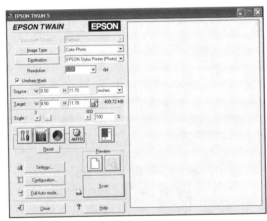

Figure 14-1: Using your scanner's software

Configuration Options

There are several options for configuring the scanner before you perform a scan. When scanning, you should choose RGB mode, since working in RGB is preferable to any other color mode available. In Chapter 11, color modes and models were introduced in depth. Also, ask clients to do their scanning in RGB as well.

Resolution was introduced in the last chapter, and you learned that 300 ppi or dpi is a nice resolution to get from a client. However, 300 dpi for a scanned image sometimes isn't enough. At 300 dpi, the scanner is only putting down 300 dots per inch of image, which is okay for scanning photos but not for line art. Do your line art scans in the highest resolution possible. I always shoot for 1200 dpi with line art, but (depending on the image) the computer can freeze up at that resolution, so I usually wind up with 600 dpi.

Moiré is a word that you see in the configuration options of more expensive scanners. Moiré patterns are unwelcome lines and shapes that run through a scan. If you get moiré patterns when scanning, use a "Descreen" option if one exists, scan the image at twice the final size, and then resize the image as needed and experiment with other settings.

Output Size

When scanning, you can configure the output size. Many times, you'll get a photograph that is 5 x 7 inches, and you'll need to blow it up to 8 x 10 so you can put it on a shirt. This is called *upsampling*. Photoshop doesn't do a really good job of upsampling. When scanning, configure the output size to be the same size that you want to use when printing, and let the scanner do the work of upsampling.

 Tip:

If you are trying to get rid of moiré patterns, it's best to create a scan at twice the size of what you'd like the output to be and then downsize in Photoshop.

Finally, Sharpen, Blur, and similar options are best left up to Photoshop, so refrain from using the settings in the scanner's software interface. The Source is the scanner itself, so if you have more than one scanner, make sure you've chosen the right one.

Abbreviations and Proper Names

Some abbreviations and/or proper names that you'll need to familiarize yourself with include TWAIN, OCR, and TIFF. You know about TIFF files from the last chapter. When scanning, if you have to save before opening in Photoshop, this is the file type to choose. If you are using the File> Import command to scan a file directly into Photoshop, this won't be an issue.

TWAIN is a proper name that is often followed by the words "Compliant Driver" or "Compliant Application." TWAIN-compliant hardware, such as scanners, allows you to use your scanner to scan an image from various applications that are also TWAIN compliant. (This is what makes the File>Import command work.) Other hardware can be TWAIN compliant too, such as digital cameras and virtual devices, which explains why some digital cameras, scanners, and similar hardware work from inside Photoshop and others don't.

OCR stands for Optical Character Recognition and is a technology that allows text to be scanned and then recognized by word processing programs.

Configuring the Scanner

As mentioned earlier, you shouldn't just plug in the scanner, install it, and accept the defaults. (While the defaults might work for the home or office user, they are not set up for screen printers and artists.) Not all scanners are alike either, and some are better than others at producing true scans. In this section, we learn how to calibrate your scanner and find out how good the scanner actually is. Once you know what your scanner's limitations are, you can create a curve in Photoshop to apply to each scan you make so that these limitations are less noticeable and you produce better scans.

Project 14-1: Calibrating the Scanner

Even if you've been using the same scanner for years, perform these steps to calibrate your scanner:

1. Purchase an 11-step gray wedge from a photographic supply store, or get one of these from an offset print supplier. You can create your own step wedge in Photoshop if you trust your printer to output the step wedge with professional accuracy (I don't suggest it). To create your own step wedge, follow the steps in the sidebar on the following page. Figure 14-2 shows an example of a step wedge.

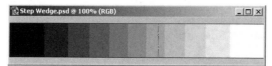

Figure 14-2: Example of a step wedge

Creating Your Own Step Wedge

Although purchasing a step wedge is a far better choice than creating one yourself, instructions for creating your own are listed here. Creating your own step wedge is difficult since you can't guarantee the accuracy of your printer, and a step wedge that isn't accurate will cause numerous problems when calibrating your scanner.

1. Choose **File>New**.

2. Set up the file to be 468 x 60 Web Banner, 300 dpi, and with a white background

3. Set the foreground and background colors to white and black, respectively.

4. Choose the **Gradient** tool from the toolbox and drag across the image in a straight line to apply the gradient.

5. Choose **Image>Adjustments>Posterize**. Choose **11** for Levels. Click **OK**.

6. Use the Info palette to verify that the black areas of the image are all 0,0,0 for the RGB values and all 255,255,255 for the white areas of the image.

7. Print the file using a high-end printer that you know produces consistent, quality output.

2. Place the step wedge into your scanner, choose **File>Import**, and select your scanner from the list. See Figure 14-3.

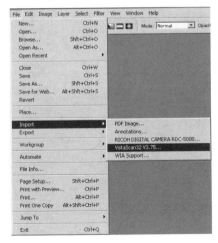

Figure 14-3: Choosing a scanner

3. Use your scanner software's graphical interface that appears, and choose **RGB** color mode and **300** dpi. Uncheck any options to automatically sharpen, blur, or color correct. Click on **Preview** to create a prescan.

4. If available, drag a rectangle around the area to scan.

5. Click the **Scan** button.

6. Choose **File>Save As**. Save to the hard disk as a PSD file. (Any other file type would lose some quality.)

7. Open the **Info** palette.

8. Using this scanned file, use the Eyedropper to see if you still get all 0s for black and all 255s for white. Chances are good that you won't get these numbers, but hopefully they won't be too far off.

Figure 14-4 shows two scans; the bottom scan was produced using a high-quality scanner that cost around $400, and the top scan using a low-end scanner that I purchased for $19 (specifically for the sake of showing this example). In this figure, the top scan is being tested using the Eyedropper and the Info palette. The Eyedropper is testing the last black rectangle. The numbers in the Info palette are showing what is supposed to be pure black (R-0, G-0, B-0); instead it shows R-48, G-54, and B-42. You can also see in the top scan that the first three or four steps all look the same color. This is not a good scan. You can see in this image how different the scan quality is between the two scanners.

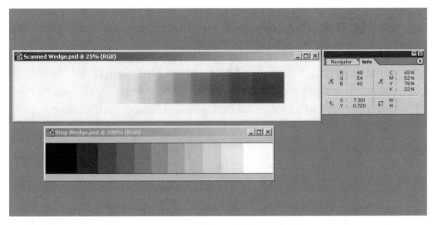

Figure 14-4: A poor-quality scan compared to a high-quality scan

So Now What?

So what does it mean if after you use your scanner to scan the step wedge, you don't get dead white and dead black? It only means that your scanner isn't scanning perfectly, and most scanners don't. (It could also mean you spent $19 on a scanner!)

You can be a little off and still consider your output a pretty good scan. Perhaps on the pure white in the scanned step wedge you get the numbers R-239, G-255, and B-254. That's pretty close to all 255s, but what the numbers are telling you is that you'll probably get a blue/green cast to all of your scans, since the red is low. Your scanner will perform this way each time you use it. The same is true of the pure black. Although it may look black to you, the numbers might say R-20, G-40, and B-20. This isn't black, and even though you can't tell with the naked eye, you will certainly encounter problems during printing.

In order to compensate for these deficiencies, you need to create a curve using the Image>Adjustments>Curves command. That's detailed next.

Creating a Curve

Now that you understand that your scanner has limitations, you can compensate for those limitations by creating a tonal curve for the scanner, saving it, and applying it after every scan. Doing so will repair problems that your scanner has added to a scanned image, and remove any unwanted colorcasting.

To create a curve for your scanner:

1. Look at the dead white numbers in the last step of Project 14-1.

2. Decide what type of colorcast will most likely be placed on your scans. For instance, if the numbers for green and blue are close to 255 and the red number is way off, you'll get a bluish cast to the scans since red will be lacking. If the numbers for red and green are okay, but the number for blue is way off, your image will lack blues and be too red or green.

3. Open the Curves dialog box using **Image>Adjustments>Curves**, or use Ctrl+M.

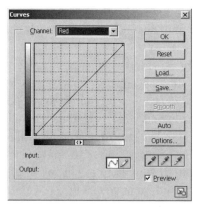

Figure 14-5: Using the Curves dialog box

4. Open the Info palette.

5. In the Curves dialog box, choose a channel to change. For instance, if the scan has a red cast, choose red and adjust the curve. Perform the same steps for the other channels. You can even try adjusting the RGB channels together by choosing RGB from the Channel window. The object is to get the numbers as close to perfect as possible (all 0s and all 255s).

Tip:

This takes a little practice and you might not get it perfect right away. Don't get discouraged. Remember, you're trying to get rid of any colorcast or tint that your scanner applies. This can be done with the Curves tool; it just takes time.

6. Between adjustments, use the Eyedropper tool to see the before and after numbers for the pure white that you are testing. (The first number in the Info palette is the "before" number, and the second is "after.") You can perform the same functions on pure black as well.

7. Once you've gotten the numbers close to 0s and 255s, click **Save**.

8. Save the curve as **Scanner Calibration**.

9. You can test what you've done by rescanning the step wedge, applying the curve, and retesting the colors. You might have to do this a few times to get the scanner functioning just right. The next time you scan, apply the saved curve to the scanned image.

Hopefully, your scanner is a nice piece of equipment and you didn't have to do too much calibrating and tonal curve reworking. If you did happen to find out that your $19 scanner is a dud, you are at least aware of the problems and can adapt your work accordingly. (This might involve purchasing a newer and better scanner too!)

Tips for Scanning a Photo or Line Art

If you worked through the calibrating exercise, you have already used the scanner. Chances are, you've already scanned other items as well. In this section, I won't go through all of those steps again, but I will summarize what you've learned so far, including some tips and tricks and what you should do each time you scan.

■ Make sure the scanner glass is clean at all times and the top shuts all the way.

■ Use File>Import to select your scanner so that you can scan directly into Photoshop.

- Scan photos at 300 dpi. If you get moiré patterns, try 200 dpi.

- Use a "Descreen" option if one exists and scan the image at twice the final size if you get moiré patterns.

- Scan line art at 1200 dpi. If the computer freezes up, switch to 600 dpi.

- Preview the scan first, and then drag a rectangle around the part you want to scan. This will take less RAM than scanning the entire space if it isn't needed.

- Select RGB color mode.

- Choose the type of image from the Image Type choices (black and white, line art, color photo, black and white photo, etc.)

- Set the output size to the size you want the image to be. It is better to have the scanner upsample the artwork than it is to have Photoshop upsample it.

- Save the file immediately after the scan. Choose PSD.

- Apply your saved curve after the scan has been saved.

- Crop any excess from the scan using the Crop tool.

With the image scanned and saved, you can begin working with the image.

What if File>Import Doesn't Work?

There's a slim chance that the File>Import command won't work with your scanner. If this is the case, you'll need to use your scanner's software to scan, save the scan to the hard disk, and open it in Photoshop. To do this:

1. Open the software that came with the scanner.

2. Choose **File>Select Source** (or something similar) and choose the scanner from the list.

3. Choose **File>Acquire** (or something similar) and scan the image as detailed earlier using the tips listed above.

4. Save the file as a TIFF to your hard drive.

5. Open Photoshop and choose **File>Open As**.

6. Browse to the location of the saved file and click on it.

7. Open the file as a PSD file if possible. If not, open as a TIFF.

Project 14-2: Scanning and Enhancing the Scanned Image

In this project we scan a photo using the correct settings, use the tips and tricks mentioned earlier, and save the image to the hard disk. With the image saved, we then learn to enhance the image using Photoshop's built-in scanning improvements.

1. Choose a photograph to scan and place it on the scanner. Close the cover.

2. Choose **File>Import** and choose the scanner.

3. Using your scanner software's graphical interface that appears, choose **RGB** color mode at **300** dpi. Choose **Color Photograph** from the list, and uncheck any items that will automatically sharpen, blur, or create color. Click on **Preview** to create a prescan.

4. Drag a rectangle around the area to scan.

5. Configure the output size so that the scan created is the size of the file that you want to work with. Sometimes, this requires typing in an actual size, such as 8 x 10 inches; other times you need to choose 150 percent, 200 percent, or 300 percent to increase the size.

6. Click the **Scan** button. After the scan is complete, you might have to press Exit or Close in the scanner's software interface.

7. Choose **File>Save As**. Save to the hard disk as a PSD file. (Any other file type would lose some quality.)

8. Crop the image if needed using the Crop tool from the toolbox.

9. Choose **Image>Adjustments>Curves** and click on the **Load** button.

10. Browse to the scanner calibration that you created earlier. Once located, click **Load** and then **OK**.

11. Choose **Filter>Sharpen>Unsharp Mask**. This allows you to sharpen the image for screen printing. As you know, the image loses sharpness at every step of the screen printing process, so sharpening the image almost to the point of "oversharpness" is a good idea. (I made up this word.) Check and uncheck the preview box to see before and after shots. Click **OK**. Figure 14-6 shows the Unsharp Mask dialog box as well as an image that I've scanned.

Note:

Figure 14-6 shows two images, one of a raw scan and the other with improvements made using the Unsharp Mask command. The Info palette is showing too, and the colors for the white in the image show R-243, G-255, and B-255. I can see from this that the image will still have a bluish/green tint to it, and my scanner calibration needs to be adjusted and/or I need to apply the Curves tool to remedy this problem before printing.

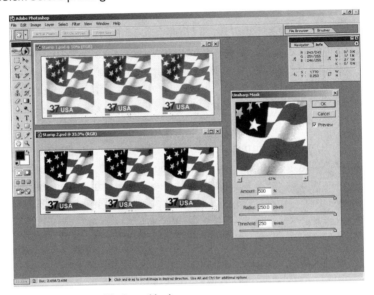

Figure 14-6: Using Unsharp Mask

12. Open the Info palette if it isn't open. If any part of the image is supposed to be pure white or pure black, use the Eyedropper to check the color values. If necessary, use **Image>Adjustments>Curves** to remedy any tonal problems.

13. Use **Image>Adjustments>Hue Saturation** to increase saturation; you'll lose saturation when you screen. Increase it enough to see the slight changes but not to the point of overdoing it.

14. Add any edge effects, as detailed in Chapter 12.

15. Add text as detailed in Chapters 9 and 12.

16. Save the file.

The steps above will pretty much work for any scan you need to do. Remember, increase the resolution for line art.

Pixelation, File Size, and Other Drawbacks

As you've probably already surmised, scanning can have its drawbacks. The color can be off, the scan can have a colorcast or moiré patterns in it, the file size can be huge, and working with scanned images can slow down the computer to the point of freezing it up. A good scanner can cost hundreds (or thousands) of dollars as well, but working with an inexpensive scanner is sometimes more trouble than it's worth. If given a choice to work with scanned images or computer-generated images, it's almost always best to go with computer-generated images.

That being the case, tell your clients that you'd rather them give you artwork on a disk or via e-mail instead of a printout or physical photograph that you'll have to scan. Chances are fair that you can get photos in digital form (from a digital camera) instead of a picture developed at the local photography store. In addition, any line art designs they want printed will come to you in an electronic format, eliminating problems associated with scanning line art at a high resolution. Of course, there's always the chance that they'll scan the image themselves; if they do, make sure to ask for the original artwork along with the file.

Solutions

Here are several other common scanning problems and some workaround solutions:

- **The file is extremely large:** Crop the scanned images and scan at lower resolutions. Work in PSD file format, save the final as a compressed TIFF, and e-mail as a JPEG. Delete scanned files that you don't need anymore from your hard drive.

- **The computer is slow:** Scan at lower resolutions, scan using the right image type (black and white, color photo, line art), close unneeded open programs while scanning, and add more RAM to your computer. Use Edit>Purge>All to free up RAM only *after* the image has been saved to the hard drive.

- **The colors don't look right**: Calibrate your monitor as well as your scanner (see Chapter 5). You won't see the right image color on the screen if your monitor is calibrated incorrectly. Create curves for your scanner and load them after every scan.

- **The image is pixelated**: Use a higher resolution or get a better scanner.

- **The scanned image has lost a lot of quality and detail**: Use unsharp masking on every image to be screen printed, increase saturation settings, and apply curves.

Summary

In this chapter you learned all about scanning images. You learned how important it is to calibrate your scanner and test it to see what (if any) colorcasts or other problems it creates during the scan. These problems, once identified, can be corrected using the Curves tool in the Image> Adjustments menu.

In this chapter you also learned some tips and tricks for scanning images, such as what resolution to use, how to upsample an image, and why you should crop images after scanning. You also learned how to enhance an image after scanning it, using saturation, curves, unsharp masking, and other adjustment options.

Chapter 15

Acquiring Files from Digital Cameras

Depending on the work you do as a screen printer or graphic artist, you may or may not use digital pictures. For instance, if you are mainly a spot color screen printer with a two- or four-station manual press, you won't have the capability to print digital photographs with much accuracy. However, if you have a process color shop, create signs or business cards, or use heat transfer machines to put photographs on specialty T-shirts, then digital photography is quite important to your work.

In this chapter, I begin by offering several ways to obtain a digital picture from a camera, including from inside Photoshop and by using the camera's own software. Following that, I detail how to use the Batch Rename command to rename multiple files at once. Creating a contact sheet is also covered, as is resizing an image in a couple of different ways. File information can be added to photographs as well, including captions and copyright information. Finally, I'll encourage you to create your own digital library of stock photographs of animals, backgrounds, and other scenes, which can then be used to create artwork of your own.

So, even if you don't work much with photos, you should probably skim the chapter anyway, at least to learn about contact sheets and image sizes. Who knows, you might even decide to purchase a digital camera!

Acquiring the Photo

There are several ways to acquire photos from a digital camera, and as you learned in Chapter 6, the File Browser is one of them. I won't repeat that information here, but it is certainly a good way to get a photograph into Photoshop. Other ways include the File>Import command, the File>Open command, and the File>Import>WIA Support command (if you are running Windows ME or XP). Of course, you can also use the camera's own software package; you can decide which way you like best after reading the chapter.

✖ **Caution!**

You *must* have your camera turned on, connected properly to your PC, and on its PC setting for any of the following open commands to work.

File>Import

The File>Import command can be used to open your digital camera and view the pictures on it. Figure 15-1 shows this choice, and Figure 15-2 shows the resulting dialog box for choosing the camera.

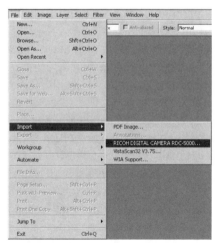

Figure 15-1: Using File>Import and choosing a camera

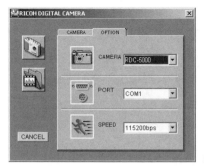

Figure 15-2: The Camera dialog box

From the Camera dialog box, choose the port to which the camera is attached and the speed at which to transfer data. From the Camera tab, choose Card or Memory to configure from where to get the picture. Problems can occur when Photoshop looks for your camera on a COM port when it's really connected to a USB or other type of port. If this problem occurs, install the latest drivers for your camera as well as any operating system updates. This might solve the problem. After connecting to the camera, you can select the picture(s) that you want to display.

 Tip:

If your camera is an older model, you won't be able to use the File>Import command. If this is the case, use the File Browser or the File>Open command, or try the File>Import>WIA Support options.

File>Open

File>Open almost always works, since Photoshop sees most digital cameras as additional drives. Just use the Open dialog box to browse to the camera or its associated drive. In Figure 15-3, notice in the Open window that the drive I've browsed to is the G drive, and the folder is named 100Ricoh. This is the drive of the memory card; F is the drive of the camera's internal memory.

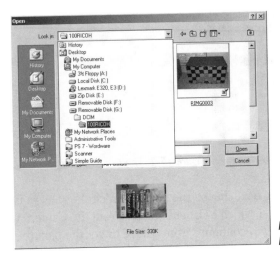

Figure 15-3: Using the File > Open command

Once you've located the file, simply double-click on it to open it.

File > Import > WIA Support

If the File > Import > <your camera name> command didn't work, you can try File > Import > WIA Support if you're using Windows ME or Windows XP. WIA Support is Windows Image Acquisition and allows your digital camera, scanner, Photoshop, and Windows XP or ME to work together to acquire images.

To use WIA Support:

1. Choose **File > Import > WIA Support**.
2. Choose a destination folder for saving your acquired files, such as My Pictures or a subfolder that you've created.
3. Place a check in **Open Acquired Image** and click **Start**.
4. Select the camera to acquire images from.
5. Choose the images to import.
6. Click **Get Picture**.

If you are running Windows ME or Windows XP and this doesn't work for you, try downloading and installing the latest drivers for your camera, as well as the latest service packs and patches from Microsoft.

Using the Camera's Software or Your Operating System

If all else fails, you can use your camera's software package to open your digital pictures and then save them to your hard drive for opening later in Photoshop. Just locate the software in the Programs list or folder, double-click on it, and use it to access your camera. When saving the pictures to your hard drive, save in the best format possible so you'll retain as much image quality as possible.

Troubleshooting

If none of the previous options work and you can't obtain pictures from your camera, try the following troubleshooting tips:

- Make sure the camera is turned on.
- Verify that the camera has power by either plugging it into a different outlet or adding fresh batteries. A light should be on.
- Verify that the camera is connected properly to the PC, both at the PC and at the camera. Reset connections.
- Verify that the USB, COM, or serial port is working by plugging another piece of hardware into it.
- Make sure the camera is set to its PC setting, not a setting for taking photos, deleting photos, or to set up the camera.
- Log on to the manufacturer's web site and download the newest drivers.
- Download the latest patches and service packs for your PC.
- Always use proper shutdown techniques to avoid the error message shown in Figure 15-4.

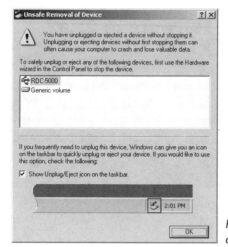

Figure 15-4: A message about incorrect camera removal

Using the Batch Rename Command

The Batch Rename command is available from the File Browser's additional options. Digital cameras automatically name their pictures in succession and often need to be renamed in groups as they're copied to the hard drive. This can be done using the Batch Rename command.

Renaming Multiple Files

When you've taken multiple pictures using a digital camera and copied or imported them to your hard drive, they'll have names that were assigned to them by your digital camera. It would be a painstaking process to rename all of these files one by one. With the Batch Rename command, you can rename them all in a single move.

To use the Batch Rename command to rename multiple files at once:

1. Amass all of the files to be processed into a single folder. This folder can be a folder you create and move files to, or it can be a folder that contains pictures from your digital camera.

2. Open the File Browser using **File>Browse**.

3. Locate the folder that contains the images to rename.

4. Make sure no images are selected and the images to rename are showing. See Figure 15-5.

5. Click on the arrow to bring up the additional options shown in Figure 15-5.

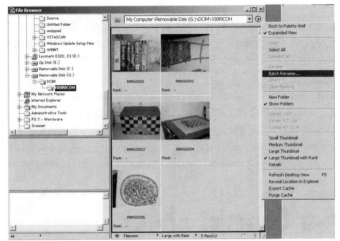

Figure 15-5: Locating Batch Rename

6. Choose **Batch Rename** from the list.

7. In the Batch Rename dialog box, choose to either rename the files and store them in the same folder or rename the files and store them in a different folder. See the top of Figure 15-6.

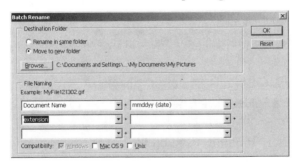

Figure 15-6: The Batch Rename dialog box

8. If you choose to rename and store in a different folder, click the **Browse** button to locate and choose the new folder. In Figure 15-6, the new folder is the My Pictures folder on my hard drive.

9. In the File Naming area of the dialog box, choose a naming convention. Make sure that the extension is *last*. You must have something chosen that's different about each file so that the files aren't written on top of the previous ones.

10. If you want the files to be compatible with other operating systems, place the appropriate check marks in the boxes.

11. Click **OK**. You'll be prompted if the naming convention that you've chosen isn't acceptable; if that happens, redo as necessary. You'll see the changes in the same folder, or you can browse to the new folder to see the newly named files.

✖ **Caution!**

If you choose to rename the files and store them in another folder, the files will now be in two places on the hard drive, the original folder with their original names and the new folder with the new names. If you have limited hard drive space, this could pose a problem. Rename in the same folder when you can.

Create a Contact Sheet

A contact sheet is a sheet that contains thumbnails of images. Contact sheets can be used to catalog images on your computer, in your digital library, and for your library of logos and designs, or to offer choices for different photos or logos to clients. You can automatically create a contact sheet using the File>Automate>Contact Sheet II command.

To create a contact sheet:

1. Place all of the images that you want on the contact sheet in a single folder.

2. Choose **File>Automate>Contact Sheet II**.

3. Under Source Folder, click **Choose** or **Browse** to locate the images to place on the contact sheet.

4. Place a check in **Include All Subfolders** if the folder you've selected contains subfolders that contain images you'd also like to add to the sheet.

5. Configure the dimension for the thumbnails; 4 inches by 6 inches is good for creating a library.

6. Choose a resolution and mode, and check **Flatten All Layers**. (Unchecking Flatten All Layers will produce a contact sheet where each image and caption is on a separate layer.)

7. Specify layout options and check to use the file name as the caption. Choose a font if desired. See Figure 15-7.

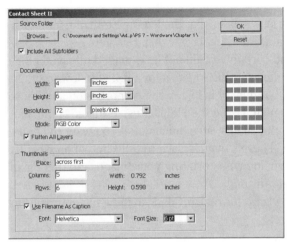

Figure 15-7: Creating a contact sheet

8. Click **OK**.
9. With the contact sheet created, you can now print or save, as with any other file.

Resize an Image

Many digital cameras take *huge* pictures, and when saving them in Photoshop's PSD format, they can take up a lot of hard drive space. If you're good with your camera, you can configure the size of photos it takes before it even gets to Photoshop. If you like the current settings or are unable to change them, you'll want to resize them in Photoshop.

You've probably already used the Image>Image Size command in previous chapters, but there's a better way if you're new to image resizing—the Help>Resize Image command.

Help>Resize Image

The Sunflower.psd file shown in Figure 15-8 is 5.8 MB. To get a feel for how big this file is, consider that the average e-mail user's inbox can hold up to 2 MB of data. Anything larger than this gets rejected. 5.8 MB then is quite large and certainly could not be e-mailed or saved efficiently.

Saving this file as a JPEG instead of a PSD file lowers its file size to just over 1 MB, but quality is lost in the compression and it's hard to judge just how much. Using the Help>Resize Image command, you can decide the size, the quality, how much detail you want to keep or lose, and much more. There's even a place to tell Photoshop what halftone screen you'll be using when printing your image, and there's an option of 65 lpi for screen printing!

To use this wizard for resizing and saving a file optimally, follow the instructions here:

1. Open the file **Sunflower.psd** from the Chapter 15 folder on the CD that comes with this book or any other large file that you have handy.

2. Choose **Help>Resize Image**. Your screen should look like Figure 15-8.

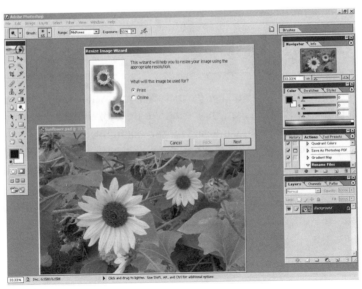

Figure 15-8: Sunflower.psd and the Resize Image Wizard

3. Choose **Online** and click **Next**. Even though we aren't saving the file for online use, it's still a great way to optimally resize and save a file.

4. Type in the size that you'd like your image to be. Click **Preview** to see it. Notice that the width and height are locked to preserve proportion. Click **Next**.

5. Click **Finish**.

To use this wizard for resizing and printing the file optimally, follow these instructions:

1. Open the file **Sunflower.psd** from the Chapter 15 folder on the CD that comes with this book or any other large file that you have handy.

2. Choose **Help>Resize Image**. Your screen should look like Figure 15-8.

3. Choose **Print** and click **Next**.

4. Choose the size that you'd like the image to be. It's best to resize down; Photoshop doesn't do a really good job of upsampling. If you need the file to be larger, either request it larger, scan it in at the appropriate size, or configure your camera to take bigger pictures. Click **Next**.

5. Select the appropriate lpi to which you'll be outputting. If it's for an art book, choose 200 or greater; for screen printing, choose **65**. Click **Next**.

6. Use the slider in the next window to preview file sizes compared to quality settings. Choose a setting that meets your needs. Click **Next** and then **Finish**.

As mentioned in the steps, if you have to upsample or if you are trying to add pixels to the image by increasing the quality, you might not get the desired results. Photoshop is really good at throwing away pixels that aren't needed when image size or quality is lessened, but when increasing image size or quality, Photoshop has to make up pixels and place them where it deems appropriate. This does not always produce quality images.

Adding File Information

Photos belong to the person who created them. You can't just find a photo that you like, perhaps one used for Windows wallpaper, and put it on a shirt or use it as a background without the proper permissions. Artwork can be protected by copyright. You can protect your own artwork by adding some personal file information to it, including captions, keywords, origins, credits, and categories. This information can be used not only to protect the photo from copyright infringement but also for cataloging the data in clip art or photo libraries.

 Note:

On Windows operating systems, file information can be added to TIFF, JPEG, PDF, and EPS formats; on Macs you can use any format.

File > File Info

Figure 15-9 shows the File Info dialog box, which can be opened using File > File Info. This screen shot shows the General section, although there are others: Keywords, Categories, Origin, and EXIF. I've typed in some information about the title, author, copyright status, and more.

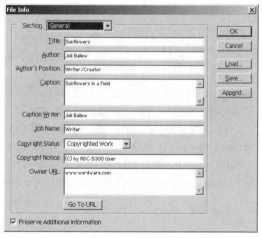

Figure 15-9: Using the File Info dialog box

View the options for each section by opening the File Info dialog box and choosing each of the different sections. To apply any items to a photo, open the photo or image and type in the information here. The information will stay with the photo and can be accessed each time the file is opened.

General

You can enter title, author, caption, copyright information, and a URL. If you select Copyrighted Work, a small copyright symbol will appear on the title bar of the image when it is opened. If you add a caption to the image and want to print it out, click the Caption button in the Print dialog box prior to printing.

Keywords

When cataloging images for libraries, configure keywords so those images can be found quickly. For instance, in the Sunflower.psd image, I use flowers, sunflowers, flower, yellow flowers, and others. This way, when a user searches my library for a yellow flower, this one will come up as a choice.

Categories

You can enter an Associated Press code. These are three-letter codes that allow you to put an image into a particular category. For more information, visit www.ap.org.

Origin

Origin details the record of the image. This includes dates, credits, and more.

EXIF

EXIF displays information acquired from your digital camera, including the date the image was taken, file format, file size, f-stop, whether a flash was used, and similar information. Information differs from camera to camera.

Note:

File information can be saved, loaded, and appended from the File Info dialog box.

Create Your Own Digital Camera Library

I've taken many pictures, including pictures of animals, scenes, mountains, forests, oceans, and (my favorite) golf courses, using my digital camera. This way, when a client wants a new logo or design, I have plenty to choose from in my personal digital camera library. Instead of having to purchase stock art or libraries of photographs and the rights to use them, I can just use my own. Browse through the images on the CD, and you'll see many of the photos that I took. I encourage you to do the same.

Summary

In this chapter you learned all about digital cameras, how to acquire pictures from them, and how to rename them. You also learned how to create a contact sheet, use the Batch Rename command, and resize an image.

Chapter 16

Working with Photos and Making Selections

Working with photos comes down to two different areas of skill—getting the color right and making selections. Getting the color right is the first task, and Photoshop offers many ways to do that. There are several automatic color adjustments, including Auto Levels, Auto Contrast, and Auto Color. There are also manual adjustments for hue, saturation, brightness, color levels, and more. As mentioned in earlier chapters, the Curves tool is also available and offers the best choice for adjusting images for screening.

The other side of working with photos is making selections. Selections can be made using the Magic Wand tool and the three Lasso tools. Selections can be made for various reasons, but mostly they're made to remove an object from one photo and place it in another, to extract an object from its background, or to remove a selection because it isn't needed in the picture. Figure 16-1 shows a picture of Miss Scarlett before and after using the selection tools to remove her from the photograph. Now, Miss Scarlett can be placed in another photo, on a gift card, or even on a shirt or bag.

Figure 16-1: Working with photos 101

Look at Miss Scarlett now, moved from her grandmother's lap in Texas to the beautiful streets of Seattle, Washington!

Figure 16-2: Working with photos 201

Basic Color Correction

Let's start with some basic color corrections. There are two types: automatic and manual. I usually give the automatic adjustments a shot first if I'm adjusting a photo for personal use, and if I like them, I keep them. For professional work, I do the adjustments myself using manual adjustments.

Using Automatic Adjustments

There are three basic automatic adjustments—Levels, Color, and Contrast. Each can be found under the Image>Adjustments menu and performs adjustments that Photoshop deems necessary based on the pixels in your image. Sometimes it guesses right, and sometimes it doesn't!

Auto Levels

The Auto Levels command sets highlights and shadows in an image by defining a black point and a white point based on the majority of colors in the image and the lightest and darkest points. With the black and white points set, it configures the intermediate colors accordingly. This command works well for photos that generally have good color distribution and perhaps only a small amount of colorcast. It doesn't work well with images that have a variety of color problems or those images whose contrasting colors are vague.

Using the Auto Levels command is as simple as choosing Image> Adjustments>Auto Levels. If the result is unsatisfactory, choose Edit> Undo Auto Levels.

Auto Color

The Auto Color command adjusts the contrast and color of an image differently than Auto Levels. Auto Color adjusts the colors by searching the image for shadows, midtones, and highlights instead of basing those adjustments on the histogram settings.

To see if Auto Color can enhance your image, choose Image>Adjustments>Auto Color. If the result is unsatisfactory, choose Edit>Undo Auto Color.

Auto Contrast

The Auto Contrast command adjusts the contrast of an image and does not repair color-related problems, such as colorcasts. By enhancing the contrast of the image, whites appear whiter and blacks appear blacker, and everything in between changes accordingly. Using Auto Contrast works well with images that have many midtones and can increase the amount of contrast between like-colored items in an image.

To see if Auto Contrast can enhance your image, choose Image> Adjustments>Auto Contrast. If the result is unsatisfactory, choose Edit>Undo Auto Contrast.

Variations

Finally, the Variations window offers different ways to view an image and suggestions for viewing it differently. Figure 16-3 shows the Variations window, opened using Image>Adjustments>Variations.

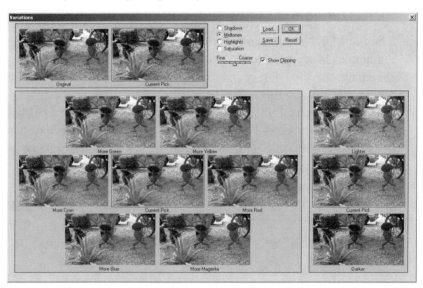

Figure 16-3: The Variations window

Note:

If the image has multiple layers, make sure the layers on which you want to view the variations are chosen in the Layers palette.

In Figure 16-3, the picture is displayed in various formats, including options for More Magenta, More Yellow, More Green, More Cyan, More Red, and More Blue. You also have choices to make the changes using midtones, highlights, and shadows and to work with the image's saturation. Experiment with this when you correct photos.

Using Manual Adjustments

Usually, manual adjustments, which leave everything up to you, are a better choice than using automatic adjustments. You get to decide how to increase or decrease not only the levels, color, and contrast, but also the individual balance of colors in the image (RGB or CMYK). Performing these changes yourself gives you complete control. These options are all available from the Image>Adjustments menu.

✖ Caution!

Make sure your monitor is calibrated if you plan to make these changes without consulting the Info palette and checking the numbers. What you think you see on the screen and what will be printed can be two entirely different things!

Brightness/Contrast

The Brightness/Contrast manual adjustment lets you make changes to the image by making changes to every pixel in the image equally. By changing the brightness and contrast, you can make changes to the entire image using the sliders in the dialog box. You can't make changes using this adjustment if you're working with individual channels; therefore, I don't use it much for tweaking an image for screen printing. However, it is useful for low-end prints, personal photos, and images that are not critical to your work.

Hue/Saturation

The Image>Adjustments>Hue/Saturation command allows you to change the hue, saturation, and lightness of an image by using the available sliders. See Figure 16-4. By checking the Colorize box, you can also add color to a grayscale image that's been converted to RGB.

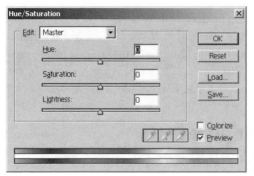

Figure 16-4: The Hue/Saturation dialog box

Project 16-1: Colorizing an Image

You can colorize a grayscale image easily using the Hue/Saturation command.

1. Open the file **Ranch House.jpg** from the Samples folder in the Photoshop program files.

2. Change the mode from grayscale to **RGB** with the **Image>Mode> RGB Color** command.

3. Choose **Image>Adjustments>Hue/Saturation**.

4. Place a check in the **Colorize** box.

5. Move the Hue slider slowly up the scale, noticing how the color changes in the image. (Make sure Preview is checked if you aren't seeing any changes.)

6. Move the Saturation slider to increase or decrease the applied color's saturation.

7. Adjust the Lightness slider. Click **OK**.

8. Close the file using **File>Close**. Choose **No** and do not save the changes.

Project 16-2: Making a Sunny Picture Look Cloudy Using Saturation, and Readying a Picture for Screening

Saturation almost always needs to be increased some when screen printing, and this is usually done in conjunction with applying the Curves tool and before converting to CMYK. Increasing the saturation of an image helps the image to not look so "flat" when printed. To see how a color image can be changed using the Saturation tool, let's change an image from sunny to cloudy using only a single slider:

1. Open the file **Dune.tif** from the Samples folder in the Photoshop program files.

2. Select **Image > Adjustments > Hue/Saturation.**

3. Slowly move the Saturation slider to the right. Notice how the entire image changes and the image becomes more saturated with color. You'll want to move up this slider to ready the image for screening, since color and detail will be lost during the print process. (+ 55 is a good number for this picture.)

4. Slowly move the Saturation slider to the left. Notice that color is removed from the image, and the otherwise sunny picture begins to look cloudy. (Try –38.)

5. Click **Cancel** and close the file. Do not save the changes.

You should almost always adjust (increase) the saturation before converting to CMYK and color separating artwork for screening. Doing so will enhance the final output, as saturation is lost during the print process. In addition to increasing saturation, increase the sharpness too; this will be discussed shortly.

Color Balance

Color Balance is the last of the manual adjustments from the Image > Adjusments menu. It changes the color balance of the entire image. I shy away from this manual adjustment myself and prefer the Curves tool instead. However, this command can be used for general color correction in an image or for correcting color in a selection. The Color Balance dialog box, shown in Figure 16-5, allows you to change the color balance of various channels of color in the image (CMYK or RGB).

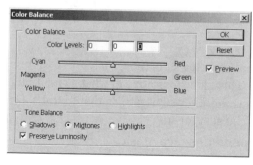

Figure 16-5: The Color Balance dialog box

To experiment with color balance, open any photo or image, choose Image>Adjustments>Color Balance, and move the sliders accordingly. Combining this information with the information in the Info palette, you can move the sliders to a correct and usable color balance. By moving these sliders, you can also remove or add color tints from an image.

 Note:

The Color Balance dialog box can be used with selections also. Later in this chapter we learn how to make selections, and with a selection made, you can apply color correction only to the selected part of the image.

Unsharp Mask

You'll want to sharpen each image before printing, and this can be done using Filter>Sharpen>Unsharp Mask. Increasing the values in this dialog box makes the edges, pixels, and colors in the image sharper (they'll stand out more), so when you lose sharpness during the print process, the final product will look similar to the original.

When using unsharp masking, start off with settings of 150 percent for Amount (specifies how much to increase the pixels' contrast from the original), 1 for Radius (specifies the radius of the region to change the sharpness for), and 5 or 6 for Threshold (specifies how different the sharpened pixels must be from their surrounding pixels before they are considered edge pixels). If the original is extremely poor in quality, try upping the Amount to 400 to 500 percent and 8 or 10 for the Threshold.

 Caution!

Images that are screen printed get darker and softer during the print process. At each step, sharpness is lost. Therefore, be generous and aggressive when sharpening an image or increasing saturation.

To use Unsharp Mask:

1. Open the file **FishFinalCopy.jpg** from the Chapter 16 folder on the companion CD-ROM. This file is indicative of what a client might give you for a sign, shirt, or other substrate, in that first it's a JPEG and second it needs to be sharpened.

2. Choose **Filter>Sharpen>Unsharp Mask**.

3. In the Unsharp Mask dialog box, make sure the **Preview** box is checked. Then move the sliders as follows:

   ■ Change Amount to **150** percent

   ■ Change Radius to **1**

   ■ Change Threshold to **5**

   See Figure 16-6.

4. Look at the picture while unchecking and rechecking the Preview box to see the difference. The additional sharpness enhances the picture. Click **OK** when done.

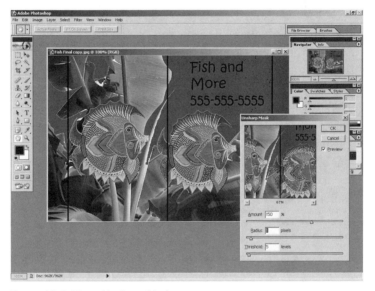

Figure 16-6: Using Unsharp Mask

When you get to the point in sharpening when the image looks grainy or too sharp, step back a level or two. Try not to get a halo effect on the image; if you do, reduce the levels a little. You'll use this command on almost all images for screen printing.

The Curves Tool Revisited

As I mentioned earlier, the Curves tool is my favorite and is great when working with photos. Curves can be used to perform all of the adjustments mentioned earlier, including adjusting highlights, midtones, and shadows, increasing brightness and contrast, and correcting color. By combining this tool and the options from the Image>Adjustments menu, with practice you can correct almost any photograph.

Project 16-3: The Basics—Readying an Image for Color Separation and Screening

In order to get a photograph ready for screening, you need to prepare it by using and applying Unsharp Mask, adjusting tone curves, and adjusting the brightness, contrast, hue, and saturation. Although each photo or image is different, here are some basic steps to follow to get you into a good habit of using and applying the available correction tools:

1. Open the file **CosmosPeppers.psd** from the Chapter 16 folder on the companion CD-ROM. This is a photograph of artwork created by our artist here at North Texas Graphics. She would like this artwork colorized and placed on a tote bag to promote her proposed art gallery.

✎ **Note:**

The quality here is indicative of the quality you might get as a screen printer. The image is flat, doesn't have enough contrast, and has other issues that will make screening the image complicated.

2. Notice that there is a fine rectangular line around the image, and it shows in the top-left of the image. Use the Eyedropper tool to sample the color of the background. Use either the Paint Bucket tool or the Brush tool to clean up the background.

3. Apply unsharp masking to the image using **Filter>Sharpen> Unsharp Mask**. This image needs a lot of sharpening. Change Amount to **290** percent and Threshold to **8**. Leave Radius at 1. To see the before and after, check and uncheck the **Preview** box. See Figure 16-7. Click **OK**.

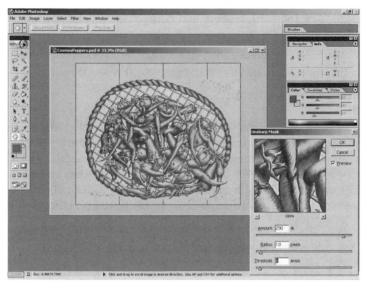

Figure 16-7: Readying an image for screening

4. Select **Image>Adjustments>Hue/Saturation**. Move the Saturation slider to **+35**. Click **OK**. (Remember, you'll lose saturation when scanning and printing, and when the ink hits the shirt.)

5. Use **Image>Adjustments>Curves** to open the Curves dialog box. This particular artwork is flat, so position the curve so that it looks like the one shown in Figure 16-8. This is an "S" curve and enhances this image (as it does with similar flat images).

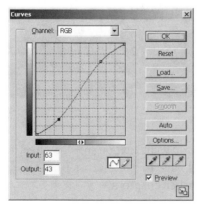

Figure 16-8: Applying an "S" curve

6. Click on the **Red, Green,** and **Blue** channels and position the curve accordingly. Changing the red channel will only affect the red in the image, green affects only green, and blue affects only blue. Configure the curves to suit your artistic tastes. Press **OK.**

 Tip:

As you get more comfortable here, combine this step with the Info palette and Eyedropper to see if the colors that you are using are in the CMYK gamut. Although Photoshop automatically brings all colors into the color gamut when converting from RGB to CMYK, it's best to try to bring all colors into the gamut before converting. There is more on this in Chapter 23. Out of gamut colors are represented by an exclamation point in the Info palette (see Chapter 11).

7. You can continue to tweak the image indefinitely; however, one must decide when enough is enough! Save your new file as **PeppersII.psd.**

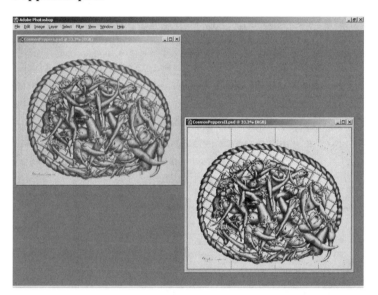

Figure 16-9: Before and after

Of course, your client will probably want text or an edge effect to go along with their design, so you'll have to continue on from here. These topics have been discussed in earlier chapters.

 Note:

Image>Adjustments>Selective Color is also an important tool, but it is very complex. You'll learn about this option in Chapter 26.

The Magic Wand

Let's move on to selections. Having the ability to select an area or an object in Photoshop is quite powerful, and allows you to manipulate images and objects like you've never experienced with other art programs. Using selections, you can remove an object (like Miss Scarlett in Figure 16-1) from an image and place that object elsewhere or erase it completely and fill it with the background color in the toolbox. One way to select an object is to use the Magic Wand.

The Magic Wand tool is available from the toolbox and is the second tool down on the right side. Pressing the W key on the keyboard also accesses this tool. The Magic Wand tool lets you select a consistently colored area of color without having to trace its outline. The options in the options bar let you change the tolerance and color range and allow you to add to or subtract from a selection already made.

Understanding the Options in the Options Bar

If you haven't read the book from start to finish, you might not understand what the terms in the options bar mean. Here's a quick review:

- **New Selection:** When this icon is chosen, the selection created is a new selection. This is the default.
- **Add to Selection:** When this icon is chosen, the selections created using the Magic Wand tool are added to the previously selected items.
- **Subtract from Selection:** When this icon is chosen, the selection that is made using the Magic Wand tool is removed from the current selection.

- **Intersect with Selection**: Selects the intersection of the selected sections.

- **Tolerance**: Sets the tolerance level of the selection. 32 is the default. Lower levels create more tolerance so smaller areas of color are selected; higher numbers create less tolerance so that larger areas of color are chosen.

- **Anti-aliased**: Check this box to create smooth edges in your selection. This allows you to soften the edges of a selection. This isn't noticeable until you paste the selection into another image.

- **Contiguous**: Check this box to select colors in the tolerance level that are adjacent to each other. Uncheck it to select all pixels in the image having the selected color.

- **Use All Layers**: Check this box to select colors in all of the layers that match the desired color. Uncheck it to work only on the active layer.

Use these options to fine-tune what you would like to select in the image.

✖ Caution!

You cannot use the Magic Wand tool to create selections while the image is in Bitmap mode. This should not be a problem, since most screen printing and graphic work is done in RGB mode. You can switch from Bitmap mode to RGB mode using the Image>Mode menu choices.

Using the Magic Wand Tool

To use the Magic Wand tool to make a selection and erase that selection leaving only the background color underneath:

1. Open the file **PeppersII.psd**. This is the file you used in the last project and is also on the companion CD.

2. Select the **Magic Wand** tool from the toolbox.

3. Change the background color in the toolbox to green.

4. Verify that the tolerance level is set to 32, New Selection is chosen, and Anti-aliased is checked. Click once inside one of the small squares in the basket. It will automatically be selected.

5. Fill that square with the background color by hitting the **Delete** key on the keyboard.

6. Repeat these steps with red, green, and white to change the entire look of the basket.

7. Change the tolerance level to **50** and select **Add to Selection** (the second icon on the options bar).

8. Change the background color to yellow using the toolbox and the Color Picker.

9. Click once on an area of yellow pepper. Click again on the same pepper to add to that selection. Press the **Delete** key on the keyboard to change the pepper to yellow.

 Note:

If the automatic selection is too large, use Select>Deselect to deselect the Magic Wand's selection, lower the tolerance level, and try again. (Ctrl+D also works.)

10. Continue in this manner to change the picture from a drawing to a painting and give the artwork a more spot color look. These brighter colors will print better, will show up better, and can enhance the image.

Figure 16-10 shows an example of some work in progress. Notice the background has been changed also, and the image is looking less and less like a drawing and more and more like a painting.

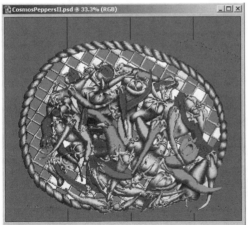

Figure 16-10: Using the Magic Wand tool

Other Uses for the Magic Wand Tool

Besides using the Delete key to erase a selection made with the Magic Wand tool, there are several other ways to work with a selection. The selection can be copied and pasted into another image or the same one, moved, edited using many of the Image>Adjustments commands, and more.

To see how a selection made with the Magic Wand can be cut and edited for color, perform the following exercise. Other selection tasks, such as Cut, Copy, and Paste, are detailed in the "Using the Lasso Tools" section that follows.

1. Open the file **Eagle.psd** from the Samples folder in Adobe's Program files folder.

2. Using the Magic Wand tool, set Tolerance at **32**, and with Contiguous and Anti-aliased checked, click in the green area of the image.

3. Choose **Edit>Cut** to remove it from the image. You can now put any background behind the eagle if desired by creating a new layer and placing it behind the eagle. See Figure 16-11.

Figure 16-11: Selecting a background to remove and replace

4. From the Layers palette (Window>Layers), click on **Layer 1**. This is the layer with the eagle and no background.

5. With the Magic Wand tool still selected, change Tolerance to **50** and make sure that Contiguous is checked.

6. Click inside the eagle's beak to select it.

7. Choose **Image>Adjustments>Curve**. Configure an "S" curve to lighten the eagle's beak. Use the Info palette to view the CMYK and RGB values. Click **OK**. (You can also use the other Image>Adjustments options, such as Color Balance, Hue/Saturation, Brightness/Contrast, and the automatic adjustments.)

8. Choose **Select>Deselect**. Close the picture without saving.

Using the Magic Wand to automatically make selections based on color can be a very powerful and valuable asset when working with images and client artwork. Making a selection in this manner can help you remove items of similar color from an image, remove backgrounds from an image, place selections into other files, and more. The selections made using this tool are color based. In the next section, you'll learn how to make selections manually using the Lasso tools and the mouse. The basic Lasso tool makes selections that are not based on color but rather on where you draw using the mouse.

Using the Lasso Tools

Another way to make a selection in an image is to use the Lasso tools. These tools are great for removing unwanted objects from a picture or separating the main object from its background. Many times, a client will bring in a photo or a logo with extraneous information attached to it that needs to be removed. For instance, a client might bring in a picture of a motorcycle that was taken in front of a house, and they want you to put that motorcycle on a black shirt with a different background (a beach, highway, nightclub, etc.). To achieve these tasks, you'll use the Lasso tools.

The Lasso Tool

The first of the three Lasso tools is simply called the Lasso tool. It is located second from the top on the left side of the toolbox or by pressing L on the keyboard. The Lasso tool lets you draw straight edges and free-hand lines around an object and thus create a selection, which can then be edited in a number of ways.

The Lasso Tool Options

When the Lasso tool is chosen, there are several options in the options bar. Before we get into the nuts and bolts of using it though, you should understand what the terms mean. There are some that are common to other Selection tools of course, such as New Selection, Add to Selection, Subtract from Selection, and Select an Area Intersected by Other Selections. Anti-aliased is also available and should be checked under most circumstances. Feather is an option that you might be unfamiliar with.

Feathering

Feathering is similar to anti-aliasing in that they are both used to soften the edges of a selection. Both are used with Cut, Copy, and Paste, and the results of both are only seen after the Cut, Copy, and/or Paste are performed. Anti-aliasing only changes the pixels on the edge of the selection and thus causes no detail loss. Feathering blurs the edges of the selection so they fit better into the new image, but in doing so, it makes the image harder to print on a T-shirt.

The amount of feathering that you can configure is a number between 1 and 250, and these numbers represent pixels. You'll have to experiment with both and see what works best for the artwork at hand. Generally, I shy away from feathering since it leaves a halo effect around the selection, but if you keep the numbers lower than 5 or so, it will most likely be okay for screening. Figure 16-12 shows an example.

Figure 16-12: Feathering

Caution!

Any time you configure loss of detail and blurring on purpose, you are heading in the wrong direction when it comes to screen printing. Use feathering wisely, stick with anti-aliasing, and always do a test print! You can see from the figure that printing the first flower would yield a sharper print over the other two.

Project 16-4: Using the Lasso Tool to Extract an Image

To use the Lasso tool to extract the flower, as shown in Figure 16-12, perform the following steps.

1. Open the file **Flower.psd** from the Chapter 16 folder on the companion CD.

2. Use the **Image>Adjustments** options to tweak the image and correct its color.

3. Crop the image if desired, but be sure to leave the large flower intact and in the picture.

> **Using the Crop Tool**
>
> Although the Crop tool has been mentioned in passing several times, you might not know exactly how it works. To use the Crop tool, simply choose it from the toolbox, click and drag in the image to choose what to keep, and click the check in the options bar.

4. Use the **Zoom** tool to zoom in on the large flower.

5. Select the **Lasso** tool from the toolbox, making sure that Anti-aliased is checked and Feather is set to 0.

6. Click, hold, and drag the mouse around the flower. Don't let go, or you'll have to start over! After tracing around the flower and ending where you started, let go of the mouse. You'll see "marching ants" around the flower, as shown in Figure 16-13.

Figure 16-13:
Marching ants

7. Choose **Edit>Copy**.

8. Choose **File>New**. Choose **5 x 7**, **RGB Color**, and a **white** background.

9. Choose **Edit>Paste**.

10. Drag the new file to an area of the screen so that both files and the selection can be seen. Click on the Flower.psd file's title bar to make it active. Notice the marching ants again.

11. Choose the **Move** tool from the toolbox.

12. Click on the selection of the flower in the Flower.psd file and drag it to the new file. Notice the flower is copied to that file.

13. In the new file, use the Move tool to move the flower around the page.

14. With the new file active, open the Layers palette (**Window> Layers**). Notice that each selection added has created an additional layer. In the options bar, check **Auto Select Layer**. Use the Move tool to move the first pasted flower around on the page.

This technique can be used to copy almost any image from a file. Remember that there are other options though; the Magic Wand could have been used to perform this same task. When using the Magic Wand, just continue to click on the image and change the tolerance until the entire image is selected.

After copying the image to a new file, you can add a background and use Arrange>Send to Back to apply it, and you can add gradients, fills, etc. Additionally, selections can be copied into the same file as a new layer using New>Layer>Layer Via Copy. The new layer is placed directly over the selection and can be moved using the Move tool by clicking and dragging. Figure 16-14 shows the Flower.psd file with several copies of the selection added and moved. Notice in the Layers palette the number of copies that have been applied.

Figure 16-14: Using New>Layer>Layer Via Copy

There are other Lasso tools too. Next, I discuss the Magnetic Lasso tool and the Polygonal Lasso tool.

The Magnetic Lasso Tool

The Magnetic Lasso tool can also be used when making selections. It is best used with selections that stand out from their backgrounds, since the Magnetic Lasso snaps to the outline of the image based on the contrast between the selection you are trying to make and what's outside or behind it.

The Magnetic Lasso tool uses "fastening points," which are similar to handles you might have seen in other programs. These fastening points are created each time you click with the mouse and each time Photoshop feels it's necessary as you trace around an object. As you move the pointer, the active segment snaps to the area that you're tracing.

Options in the Options Bar

There are several new options in the options bar, as well as some familiar ones. Anti-aliased and Feather are available and were detailed in the previous section. The selection icons are still there too, so you can create a new selection, add to, subtract from, or choose the intersecting part of a selection. There are a few others:

- **Width:** The default width is 10 pixels, which means that the Magnetic Lasso will only look within 10 pixels from the pointer for an edge. This can be raised or lowered depending on the distance from the edge of the selection where you'd like Photoshop to look.

- **Edge Contrast:** The default edge contrast is 10 percent, and the number can be between 1 percent and 100 percent. A higher number will only detect edges that contrast sharply with their backgrounds, meaning that the contrast between the object and its background must be severe. A lower number detects lower contrast areas. Set this accordingly.

- **Frequency:** The frequency is 57 by default. Frequency defines how often Photoshop will put down a fastening point. The higher the number, the more points; the lower the number, the fewer points. Here, a higher number is generally better for screen printers, since the trace is done more quickly and accurately than with a lower number.

- **Pen Pressure:** If you are using a stylus tablet, check this box if you want to take into effect the pressure you put on the tablet. The more pressure, the smaller the edge width.

☑ **Tip:**

Take a look at your image and the selection you want to cut out. If the edges contrast highly and are well-defined, use a high width and high edge contrast. If the selection and the background are similar in contrast and color, do the opposite.

Using the Magnetic Lasso Tool

To use the Magnetic Lasso tool and switch between other Lasso tools:

1. Open a file that contains an object that you'd like to trace. You can use the Flower.psd file if you don't have one available.

2. Select the **Magnetic Lasso** tool from the toolbox. If you've been working through this chapter, it'll be hidden, so you'll need to hold down the Lasso tool icon to select it.

3. Configure the options in the options bar.

4. Click in the image where you'd like to start tracing.

5. Move the mouse along the edge of the selection to trace. Double-click when you've made your way around the object. The object is selected.

You can click once to add a fastening point manually, use the Delete key to erase the last segment(s) drawn, and use the Enter or Return key to close the border after making the selection. You can also switch between Lasso tools by pressing the Alt key (Option key on a Mac) and dragging to use the Lasso tool or the Polygonal Lasso tool (detailed next). With the selection made, you can perform tasks with the selection, as detailed in the two previous sections.

The Polygonal Lasso Tool

This tool draws straight segments by default and is applied by clicking and dragging. This is quite useful if you need to trace around something that is polygonal, such as the birdhouse in Figure 16-15. (The file, Birdhouse.jpg, is available in the Chapter 16 folder on the companion CD.)

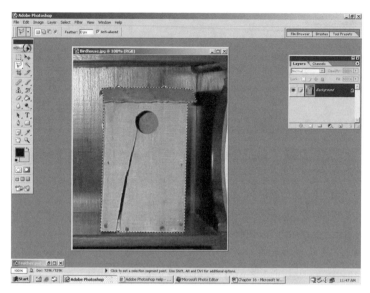

Figure 16-15: Using the Polygonal Lasso tool

To use this tool, click on the area to start tracing, drag, and click again where you'd like the straight line to end. Continue in this manner to completely trace around the object. You can hold down the Alt or Option key to draw freehand if you'd like also. As with the other tools, the Delete key can be used to delete the last segment drawn.

Summary

In this chapter you learned all about photos. In essence, there are two tasks; the first is to color correct the photo, and the second is to make selections in a photo.

Color correction can be done automatically or manually. For personal work, the automatic adjustments are fine. For professional work though, you should learn how to use the manual adjustments, such as the Curves tool.

Selections can be made using the Magic Wand tool or any of the Lasso tools. By making selections, you can remove parts of an image, copy and paste the selection to another image, and extract an object from an image for use with another background.

Chapter 17

Heat Transfers and Sublimation

Photoshop can be used in your business in ways other than preparing artwork for screen printing. You can also use Photoshop to create and output artwork for heat transfers and sublimation. There will be instances in your business where creating a heat transfer will be more cost-effective than screening an item, and you can use sublimation to expand the business in ways that you might not have thought of. Both are pretty inexpensive to get into and well worth the time, effort, and money.

Heat Transfers

Heat transfers, also called digital transfers, can be output by Photoshop and your inkjet, laser, thermal-wax, or microdry printer. Heat transfers are great for small-run jobs and specialty prints such as shirts with a team photo or a single shirt for a birthday party. Having the ability to print these short-run jobs almost guarantees your customer will return to you when a larger job arises.

Heat transfers can also be used when names, numbers, one-of-a-kind artwork, artwork with many different colors, artwork with gradients, multicolors, and process color, and short runs are desired. With a heat transfer, there are no screens to burn, and you (should) get what you see on your computer screen. Heat transfers can be used on mouse pads, can coolers, puzzles, tote bags, and similar products and are quite easy to produce in Photoshop. The downside of heat transfers is that they can currently only be applied to light-colored fabrics.

Caution!

Make sure the screen is calibrated, you use the Info palette, and you are using a good printer, or what you see might not be what you get!

Heat transfer presses can be purchased for as little as $400, and you can probably use your existing printer. Specialty papers aren't too expensive either, so getting into digital transfers can be quite affordable.

How Photoshop Plays a Role

Because heat transfers come right out of the printer on a single sheet of paper ready for application, anything that you create or acquire for artwork for any client can be applied to a shirt. This is simple too; there's no need to color separate the artwork!

Using Photoshop to print out an image for a heat transfer (usually) requires that you reverse the image. This is necessary because the transfer printout is placed face-down on the shirt before the heat is applied. Some artwork won't require this reversing; photos, clip art, and images that do not include numbers or lettering are examples. However, most artwork will require reversing, as the image in the following example shows.

Project 17-1: Preparing an Image for Heat Transfer

To reverse an image in Photoshop and prepare it for the heat transfer machine:

1. Open or create the image in Photoshop and do any tweaking needed to bring the colors into the color gamut and printable color range. You can work through this example by using the file Green Puzzle.psd from the Chapter 17 folder on the companion CD.

2. Choose **Image>Rotate Canvas>Flip Canvas Horizontal**. Once the image has been reversed, you can decide if you want the background of the image to be printed or not. In the case of photos, this won't be an issue, but for spot color images like the Green Puzzle.psd file shown in Figure 17-1, you'll probably want to remove the background.

3. To remove the background of an image, choose the **Magic Eraser** tool from the toolbox. Uncheck **Contiguous** in the options bar so that all of the background will be removed, even the background behind and inside the letters. Click on the blue background. Figure 17-1 shows two images; the second has been reversed and the background has been removed.

4. Print the heat transfer as directed by your printer and paper's instructions and by using the settings detailed in Chapter 30 of this book.

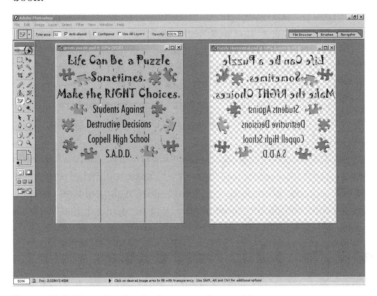

Figure 17-1: Preparing for the heat transfer machine

Heat transfers are a lifesaver when artwork like this comes into the shop, especially if the client only wants a dozen or so shirts. Instead of color separating the artwork, creating film, burning screens, lining them up on the press, and printing the shirts, all you have to do is flip and print, turn on the heat transfer machine, and go!

Sublimation

While heat transfers are used only for substrates, such as clothing, tote bags, and mouse pads, sublimation is a technology that can be used on these items and more. By expanding into sublimation, you can offer your clients items such as coffee mugs, clipboards, dry erase boards, picture frames, plaques, TV trays, wine stoppers, license plate holders, name tags, luggage tags, key chains, magnets, and more. As with the heat transfer technology, the move into sublimation is fairly inexpensive (complete packages start at around $1,500).

To get into sublimation, you'll need a printer that can accept sublimation inks, the inks themselves, a press that will hold the type of material that you want to print, and the materials you want to print on. You'll also need to purchase specialty paper that can accept and transfer the ink from the printer to the item being printed. Oh, and you can use Photoshop!

Sublimation inks adhere to the substrate when heated, and the dyes are absorbed into polyester and acrylic materials where they form permanent images. Sublimation dyes work on light-colored objects as heat transfers do, which limits what they can be printed on.

How Photoshop Plays a Role

As with heat transfers, you'll need to flip the image horizontally before printing the image for sublimation. You'll also want to crop the image so that it will fit on the substrate. For instance, the area on a coffee mug only lends itself to a 3 by 4 inch print, while a license plate holder will need to have its design printed around the edge of a rectangle that is the plate's exact size. Plates and clocks will need artwork created in a circle, although the paper and its image can be cut accordingly after printing.

Here are some tips for creating artwork for sublimation:

■ For rectangular prints, such as those used on coffee mugs, clipboards, mouse pads, and plaques, use the Crop tool to crop around the image and/or use the Image>Image Size command or the Help>Resize Image Wizard to reduce or enlarge the image appropriately.

- Use Image>Canvas Size to add extra room around the image. This can be used to make cropping easier or to add a border or edge.

- To create an odd-shaped print, such as a polygon, circle, or hand-drawn shape, use any Lasso tool to draw around the object that you want to crop, choose Edit>Copy, open a new file, and use Edit>Paste. An example is shown in Figure 17-2. (You can then add a border, soften the edges using the Blur or Smudge tools, or cut out the print manually after it's printed.)

Figure 17-2: Cropping manually

- Because the image won't be screen printed, feel free to add artistic touches using distortion filters, sketch filters, and brush stroke filters. These filters make screen printing an item almost impossible, but with sublimation (and heat transfers) this isn't an issue.

- Use the Image>Adjustments command to improve the image before printing.

✖ Caution!

Using the Resize command to make an image larger will cause pixelation and reduce the clarity of the image. Remember, you can always make the image smaller, but the opposite isn't always true.

To sell your new sublimation items to clients, bring it up as they place their order. I have found that clients will often order a dozen coffee cups if told they're available. Usually, they go with the same logo that I'm putting on their shirts too. The artwork is already there and available and usually only requires resizing. Not only is the order now larger, but another person can spread the news about the diversity of your business!

Summary

In this chapter you learned about heat transfers and sublimation. Heat transfers are great for short-run orders and specialty orders, such as team photos, one-of-a-kind shirts, or a few tote bags for display. Sublimation is great for applying artwork to coffee mugs, clipboards, and similar items. Adding both to a screen printing business is inexpensive and can enhance sales. Photoshop can be used to output for both technologies.

Part IV
More Tools

Chapter 18

Cloning and Correction Tools

There are several tools that you'll use quite often in your work as a graphic artist. The Clone Stamp and Pattern Stamp tools are two of them. These are powerful tools than can be used with photos, spot color, or process color work and images. These tools are a must when you need to clone or repair a part of an image, but they can be used to enhance an image as well. For instance, the Clone Stamp tool can be used to remove a part of an image, including large unwanted items, small blemishes from a person's face, and even scratches in an old photo. The Pattern Stamp tool can be used to "paint" a pattern for use as a background, edge, or border. You can even use your client's logo for the pattern!

The Healing Brush and the Patch tools are similar, as these are also used for correcting imperfections in photos and other artwork. The Healing Brush tool is used mainly for retouching images in a Clone-Stamp-Tool kind of way and can be used to remove scratches, dust, dirt, dents, nicks, and similar flaws in photos. The Patch tool allows you to select a problem area in a photo and patch over it with an area containing similar attributes. This allows you to patch over (in essence, remove) problem areas of photos.

The Clone Stamp Tool

The Clone Stamp tool allows you to take a sample of an image, called a source point, and use that point for painting. The source point is selected by holding down the Alt key and clicking with the mouse at the same time. The diameter of the source point is determined by the brush size selected in the options bar.

As you paint, the source point moves with you. This enables you to clone a specific part of an image, down to the finest detail. To see how the Clone Stamp is used to clone parts of an image, look back to Project 4-1. In that example, the Flower.psd file is used, and the sunflower in the image is cloned several times. To use the Clone Stamp to remove unwanted parts of an image, work through Project 18-1.

Project 18-1: Using the Clone Stamp Tool to Remove Unwanted Objects from an Image

In this project, you'll learn how to use the Clone Stamp tool to remove unwanted objects from an image. Take a look at Figure 18-1. Using the Clone Stamp tool, you can remove the coasters from inside the wooden bowl. The same technique used in this example can be applied to remove unwanted items from other artwork as well, including blemishes on a person's face or even a car from a driveway.

Figure 18-1: Using the Clone Stamp tool

1. Open the file **WoodenTable.jpg** from the Chapter 18 folder on the companion CD.

2. Locate the **Clone Stamp** tool in the toolbox; it's the fifth one down on the left side.

3. From the options bar, click on the down arrow next to Brush to open the Brush pop-up palette. Click the right arrow and choose **Reset All Brushes** from the list. Click **OK**.

4. Choose brush number **65**. Make sure **Aligned** is checked in the options bar. (Checking Aligned allows the sampling point to move as you move the mouse.)

5. Hold down the **Alt** key and position the mouse in the top-left corner of the bowl. The cursor will change to a bull's-eye. Click once with the mouse to make this area be the sampling point. Let go of both the Alt key and the mouse.

6. Click and drag the cursor over the coasters in the bowl. Notice that the sampling point moves as you brush over the coasters. If the sampling point (denoted by a + sign) is positioned over the white background or another coaster, you'll need to start again with a new sampling point. If this happens, repeat step 5 and choose a new

sampling point inside the bowl. Continue in this manner until all of the coasters are covered over. See Figure 18-2.

 Tip:

As you get to the right side of the picture, change to a smaller brush and take new sampling points often.

Figure 18-2: The end result

You can also use the Clone Stamp tool between files. Figure 18-3 shows two open files. The first file is from Photoshop 6.0's Samples folder (you have it if you upgraded from Photoshop 6 to Photoshop 7). The second file is a new file that I created. In this figure, you can see the plus sign in the first picture indicating the sampling point and the circle in the new file indicating where the cloning is occurring.

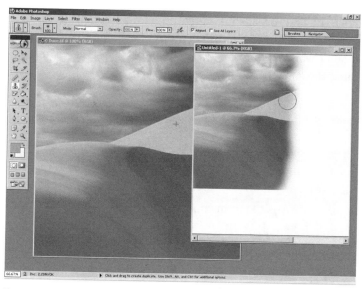

Figure 18-3: Cloning between files

The Options Bar

Besides choosing a brush, you can set other options in the options bar. Most of these options have been detailed in other chapters of this book, such as Mode, Opacity, and Use All Layers. They work similarly here. Some options that you might not be familiar with are Flow, Aligned, and the Airbrush tool.

- **Flow:** Specifies how quickly the paint is applied with the brush. Combined with the Airbrush, this option can be used to brush over an image for effect, correct errors, or hide imperfections.

- **Aligned:** By default, this option is checked. When checked, the sampling point moves with you each time, even if you release the mouse button while painting. Uncheck this option to apply the Clone Stamp tool using the initial sampling point each time you stop and resume painting. With Aligned unchecked, the sampling point will move with you until you let go of the mouse. When you click again, the sampling point reverts to its original starting point.

- **Airbrush**: The Airbrush is a great tool for screen printers, as it allows you to clone and airbrush areas of a picture, cover up areas you don't want, or draw and write text "graffiti style." This can be done in the same file or between files.

Tips

Here are some things to keep in mind when using the Clone Stamp tool:

- Keep a watchful eye on what you're cloning; by default, the sampling point moves as you move the mouse and can easily get off track.
- Use short strokes to get maximum effect.
- Resample frequently.
- After applying the tool, choose Edit>Fade Clone Stamp to change the opacity and blending mode of the strokes just applied.
- To increase and decrease the brush size while using the tool, press the right bracket (]) and left bracket ([), respectively.
- To quickly access the Clone Stamp tool, use Shift+S.
- To reset the options bar to its default settings, click on the clone stamp icon at the far right of the options bar, click the right arrow in the pop-up palette to access the additional options, and choose Reset Tool.

The Pattern Stamp Tool

Unlike the Clone Stamp tool, you won't work with a source point with the Pattern Stamp tool. Instead, you'll choose or load a pattern to copy, and you'll lay down this pattern as you drag across the image. In a few words, the Pattern Stamp tool lets you paint with a pattern.

The Options Bar

The options bar has options similar to the Clone Stamp tool, including brushes for determining the size of the paint stroke, mode, opacity, flow, and aligned. There are two new ones—the Pattern pop-up palette and the Impressionist check box.

Note:

Aligned is checked by default and enables each stroke to use the same offset each time, so the pattern will match as you draw.

Patterns

The Pattern pop-up palette offers many predefined patterns. You can choose any of these patterns for painting, enabling you to create your own backgrounds and even your own artwork. For instance, a grass pattern could be created and painted around an object to act as a background for a landscaper's business card, logo, or similar item. The same pattern could also be used to fill in around an object, as shown in Figure 18-4.

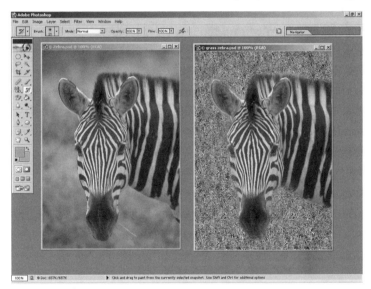

Figure 18-4: Painting around an object with a pattern

Patterns can also be used to create a border around a rectangular (or other shaped) piece of artwork. Creating edges and borders is a common task for screen printers. Generally, a client brings in a rectangular photograph that he wants screened, but without a border, the screen print looks unfinished and unprofessional.

Project 18-2: Creating a Border Using an Existing Pattern

Let's take a look back to some artwork that we worked on in Chapter 16. This artwork definitely needs a border before the final print can be considered complete.

1. Open the file **CosmosPeppersII.psd** from the Chapter 18 folder on the companion CD.

2. Change the foreground and background colors to their defaults of white and black in the toolbox.

3. Choose **Image>Canvas Size** to increase the size of the canvas. Change the width to **21** inches and the height to **18** inches. Maximize the file by clicking the large square in the top-right corner of the file.

4. Select the **Pattern Stamp** tool from the toolbox.

5. From the option bar, choose Brush number **100** (Soft Round 100 Pixels).

6. Click the down arrow next to Pattern to open the pop-up palette for the available patterns.

7. From the additional options in the pop-up palette, select **Reset Patterns**.

8. Choose the blue pattern called **Woven**.

9. Change Opacity and Flow in the options bar to **75** percent.

10. Open the Brushes palette using **Window>Brushes**.

11. Place a check in the **Airbrush** option.

 Tip:

Notice that using the Airbrush is like spray painting with a can of paint. The longer you hold down the mouse in a single area, the more paint is applied.

12. Paint a border around the edges of the canvas.

13. Crop the image appropriately.

14. Choose the **Smudge** tool from the toolbox and work around the image to soften the edges. See the final result in Figure 18-5. Save this file as **CosmosPeppersIII.psd**.

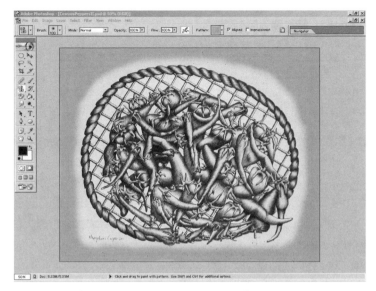

Figure 18-5: Creating a border with the Pattern Stamp tool

There are many other ways to enhance this border. Experiment with other patterns, change the options in the options bar, check and uncheck the options in the Brushes palette, etc. With practice, you'll be able to create any border you want!

The Impressionist Check Box

The Impressionist brush can be used to give an impressionist "feel" to the pattern that you are painting. Impressionist artists like Monet made this type of artwork popular, and you can apply this look to your artwork too.

Open the file CosmosPeppersII.psd again, and apply some other patterns. This time, apply the chosen pattern to the top of the image with Impressionist unchecked, and apply the same pattern to the bottom of the image with Impressionist checked. You'll quickly be able to tell the difference.

 Tip:

Choose a pattern with a visible repetitive pattern and strong colors and lines for the best effect.

Matching Patterns

Of course, you can create your own pattern too. This pattern can be a client's logo, or a picture, text, numbers, shapes, etc. In the next project, we learn how to create a pattern using a client's name, save that pattern, and then paint with the pattern to create a new design for that client.

Project 18-3: Creating Your Own Pattern Using a Name and Logo

Think of one of your favorite clients—one that's been with you from the beginning, and that you have already created a logo for. I'll use Rowlett Golf for this example, but you can use any client name that you'd like.

1. Type in the name of the client, as shown in Figure 18-6.

2. Select the type using the Rectangular Marquee tool, also shown in Figure 18-6.

3. Choose **Edit > Define Pattern**.

4. Name the pattern after the client's company name. Click **OK**.

5. Minimize this file, and then open the file that contains the existing client logo. The file should have a transparent background for best results. See Figure 18-7.

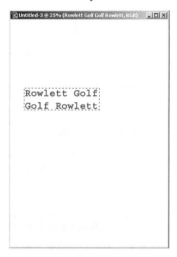

Figure 18-6: Create your own pattern with the Pattern Stamp tool

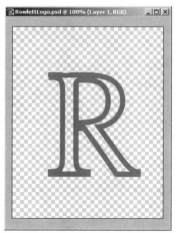

Figure 18-7: Open the existing logo for the client

6. Select the **Pattern Stamp** tool.

7. Choose **Layer>New>Layer**. Name the Layer **text layer**. Select **None** for Color, **Normal** for Mode, and **100** percent for Opacity. Click **OK**. (You'll now have at least two layers in your image, depending on the original composition.)

8. Select a brush size. Use a hard round brush.

9. Set the Opacity and Fill; this is entirely subjective. I'll leave both at 100 percent.

10. From the Pattern pop-up choices, choose the new pattern that you created in steps 3 and 4.

11. Paint over the logo with the pattern until the canvas is filled with the logo. You won't be able to see the original logo while painting.

 Tip:

You might run into problems when painting with the pattern when the pattern is entirely too big or too small for the image. If this happens, return to step 1, increase or decrease the font size, and start again. (This usually happens when the resolution size of the two files are different.)

12. If you want to change the opacity or mode of the layer at this time, choose **Edit>Fade Pattern Stamp**. The resulting dialog box allows you to increase or decrease opacity and change the mode. You won't have this choice after performing another step.

13. Choose **Layer>Arrange>Send to Back**.

14. If necessary, fill in the original logo so the words don't show through, as shown in Figure 18-8. (You'll have to make sure that this layer is chosen first in the Layers palette.)

If the opacity of the newly added layer isn't what you wanted, you can change it and other attributes from the Layers palette. To do this, open the Layers palette using Window>Layers and double-click on the patterned layer. The Layer Style dialog box will appear as shown in Figure 18-9. Here,

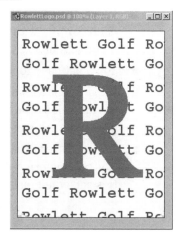

Figure 18-8: The final product

you can change almost anything about the layer. (This dialog box was detailed earlier in the book.)

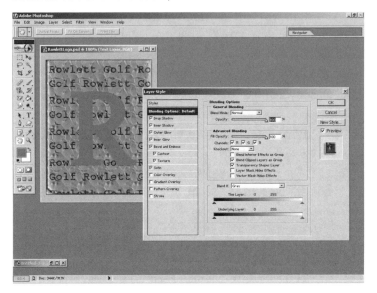

Figure 18-9: Applying styles and modes and changing opacity

Tips

When using the Pattern Stamp tool, consider these useful tips:

- Check the Impressionist box if you want the pattern to look like it's been covered with water and to give it an impressionist feel. Experiment with different brushes.

- You don't have to use text as a pattern; you can use the logo itself.

- Experiment with all of the patterns available. Light and busy patterns are difficult to use when text is involved. Less busy and more neutral patterns work well with most anything.

- After a pattern has been applied, select its layer and choose Edit>Transform>Rotate to rotate the patterned layer. Sometimes, this adds the finishing touches!

■ When you define a pattern that you've created, it is placed in the Pattern pop-up palette. However, if you reinstall Photoshop, load a new palette using the Replace option, or delete your preferences, you'll lose them. If you've created a pattern that you want to save indefinitely, use the Preset Manager (Edit>Preset Manager). Choose Patterns and then Save Set. Save the set outside of the Photoshop folders for safekeeping.

So that's it for the Clone Stamp and Pattern Stamp tools. As you can see, they are quite powerful and can be used in a number of ways. Just remember that to save a pattern, you must first select it with the Marquee tools!

The Healing Brush

Adobe has really outdone themselves with the Healing Brush, especially if you're into scanning and retouching those old photos of yourself as a kid or relatives long gone. It works like the Clone Stamp tool, so there really isn't anything that new to introduce, except that it works better than the Clone Stamp tool on photos because it takes into account the amount of light in the original picture as well as the texture of the picture itself. Using the Healing Brush, you can remove dirt, wrinkles, blemishes, and other unwanted items from a person's face and anything else that the Clone Stamp tool can do.

Figure 18-10 shows a before and after of a family photo. For correction, I used the automatic adjustments in the Image menu, cropped the image, and used the Healing Brush to remove dirt from the walls and the scratches in the photo. You can see the Healing Brush in use in the photograph on the right.

Figure 18-10: Using the Healing Brush

Because it's basically the same as the Clone Stamp, I won't spend too much time detailing how to use it. However, there are a few extra options in the options bar that should be noted. For instance, the Brush pop-up palette is different from other Brush pop-up palettes you've already seen. There are several options:

- **Diameter**: Controls the size of the brush. Enter a number or use the slider.

- **Angle**: Controls the angle of the brush. Enter a number to have the stroke paint at an angle to give a calligraphic look.

- **Hardness**: Controls how hard the brush edges are. 100 percent is a hard brush, and lower numbers create softer brushes. Use the slider or type in a number.

- **Spacing**: Controls how much paint is used. Paint is applied in dots. Higher numbers increase the amount of space, and lower numbers decrease it. Use the slider or type in a number.

- **Roundness**: Specifies how round the brush is. 100 percent is round, 0 percent is linear. Type in a number to configure this option.

- **Pen Pressure**: Configure this option if you have a graphic stylus tablet.

In the Mode drop-down list, there are several options. One option is Replace. Use this mode when you want to preserve the noise, film, grain, lighting, and other aspects of the image.

Tips

When using the Healing Brush tool on photographs, consider the following:

- As with the Clone Stamp tool, sample often.
- Use the Healing Brush to give "facelifts" to yourself and others by removing wrinkles and lines.
- Experiment with various blending modes.
- You can also use the Healing Brush with a pattern.
- If sampling from one image to another, the images must be in the same color mode. One exception to this is if one of the images is grayscale.
- Use the Zoom tool to zoom in on an area of an image prior to working.

When finished with the Healing Brush tool, save the image with another name. Although you might like the new look of the photograph, your client might not. Always keep the original intact.

The Patch Tool

The last tool detailed in this chapter is the Patch tool. The Patch tool lets you select an area that is a "problem area" in the image and lets you patch over it with an area in the image that matches it closely. Take a look at Figure 18-11.

Figure 18-11: Problem areas

The problem area in this picture is the sticker. There are three of these on the oranges. Using the Patch tool, these areas can be removed (or patched over).

1. Open the file **Oranges.jpg** from the companion CD; it's in the Chapter 18 folder and shown in Figure 18-11.

2. Choose the **Patch** tool from the toolbox. The cursor will change to a symbol that looks like a piece of a patchwork quilt.

3. Click the **Source** button in the options bar.

4. Use the Patch tool to drag around the sticker on the topmost orange. Use **Edit>Undo Patch** tool if you need to reselect.

5. Position the mouse in the center of the selection and drag the selection to the orange underneath and to the right of the top orange. The object is to drag the selection to another area that most closely matches the area that you're trying to patch in color, texture, shadow, and lighting.

6. Click once outside the selection to remove the marching ants. See Figure 18-12.

Figure 18-12: Removing problem areas

Notice in this figure that I've also removed a few blemishes as well as the remaining stickers. Because the other two stickers were on the edge of the orange, I used the Clone Stamp tool for those areas. This same technique can be used with other kinds of artwork, including spot color logos and process color artwork.

 Tip:

Use the Marquee tools to make a selection inside the bowl of oranges and use Edit>Define Pattern to save the pattern as Oranges. You can then use this pattern for other artwork.

Destination

You might also have noticed the Destination option in the options bar. This offers another way to use the Patch tool. When Destination is selected instead of Source, the selection you make with the tool is from a "good" area of the photo, and this "good" area is then dragged to cover up the "problem" area. Using the Oranges.jpg file:

1. Choose the **Patch** tool.
2. Select **Destination** from the options bar.
3. Draw a circle around an area that does *not* contain a sticker.
4. Drag the selection over the area with the sticker to cover it up.

The problem with working in this manner is that you have to guess how large the problem area is, instead of simply circling the problem area using the Source option. This method is usually more difficult.

Summary

In this chapter you learned about four commonly used tools for the print shop: the Clone Stamp, the Pattern Stamp, the Healing Brush, and the Patch tool. Each tool has a specific purpose, but by combining them you can create some really nice effects and do some major image restoration. For a screen printer, this can mean having the ability to create borders and edges and correct photos before they're printed on the substrate. For other graphic artists, it means you can make your subjects look younger by removing lines and wrinkles and giving pseudo facelifts, and remove problem areas from photographs before printing them.

Chapter 19

Working with Third-Party Clip Art

Clip art is defined as non-photographic graphic images that can be either vector or bitmap in form. Images in clip art collections are generally categorized by type, such as animals, vehicles, monuments, people, borders, edges, etc. These images can be edited, colored, and resized, as required by the user. Figure 19-1 shows an example of a piece of clip art. This particular image is from the Arts & Letters Corporation and is located on their Classic Clip Art Collection CD, available at www.arts-letters.com.

Figure 19-1: Clip art

Caution!

Most clip art carries some sort of copyright restriction, so you'll need to read the small print carefully before using purchased artwork commercially or professionally (as I'm doing here). This will be addressed later in this chapter.

In this chapter, you'll learn different ways of acquiring clip art, how to open clip art in Photoshop, and how to edit it. These edited clip art images can then become the basis for a new logo or artwork for a client. Since Photoshop 7.0 doesn't come with any clip art of its own, you'll have to acquire some clip art from a third-party manufacturer to follow along with the examples in this chapter.

 Note:

Photoshop 7.0 does come with the Custom Shape tool, which offers several vector-based images that could be considered clip art, although technically Adobe calls them shapes. For more information on these custom shapes, refer to Chapter 8, "Using the Shape Tools."

Obtaining Clip Art

Clip art collections can be purchased, and clip art can also be downloaded from the Internet for free. There are numerous sites on the Internet that offer clip art subscriptions as well, where a specific amount of clip art can be accessed each month or clip art is delivered to you via e-mail each day or each week.

 Note:

If you plan to do a lot of work with third-party clip art, you should consider using another program in addition to Photoshop. These programs are better suited than Photoshop for working with clip art. However, this doesn't mean you can't use Photoshop for your clip art work; it only means that other programs can offer more functionality and be easier to use.

Purchase from a Computer Store

Clip art comes in all shapes and sizes; there are clip art programs for as little as $9.99, while larger collections can sell for well over $1,000. I have several clip art collections in my shop, including MasterClips 500,000 Click Art image collection, several collections from Arts & Letters, and several collections from DRT Artworks, as well as a few of the cheesier $9.99 collections.

When purchasing a collection from a store, make sure the files are in Encapsulated PostScript file format. EPS file formats are the industry standard nowadays for clip art, but you might run into another format if you purchase an older collection, so be aware.

 Tip:

When purchasing software, always verify that your computer meets the minimum requirements, usually printed on the side or back of the box.

Get Clip Art Free from the Web

You can also get clip art free from the Internet. Sites offering free clip art can be located by typing "Free Clip Art" into your web browser. At the time this book was published, a search yielded over 100,000 hits.

 Tip:

A good site for beginners is www.clip-art.com. Once there, choose All Free Original Clipart. From the left side of the page, choose a category. As the introductory page says, there's no registration, no pop-ups, no misleading links, and no registration forms.

Downloading the Clip Art

Once at a site that offers free clip art (and be careful, sometimes it is suddenly not free once you're at the site), browse until you find the piece of clip art that you want. Once located, if there is a download button:

1. Click the **Download** button next to the image.

2. The file will either open up automatically or you'll get a dialog box that says Save. If the file opens up automatically, choose **File>Save** and save the file to the appropriate folder on the hard drive. If a dialog box appears, click **Save** and save the file to the appropriate folder on the hard drive. Notice the file format when saving. Save as an EPS if possible, followed by GIF, TIFF, or JPEG.

If there isn't a download button:

1. Right-click on the image and choose **Save Image As** or **Save Picture As**.

2. Name and save the picture.

When searching for clip art on the Internet, you'll obviously begin by finding something that matches your current needs. Second to that though, try to locate the clip art as an EPS file. You might not find it in this form though, as much free clip art is in GIF, JPEG, or another file format, but it doesn't hurt to look. Additionally, you'll notice that the artwork, once opened, probably isn't in RGB color mode either; it is most likely in indexed color mode or CMYK. That's no big deal though because changing from one color mode to the other is painless in Photoshop and can be converted using the Image>Mode commands.

 Caution!

If a free clip art web site asks you to register using your e-mail address and you're averse to spam, go to another site. Chances are good that they'll be passing your e-mail address around before you even get one image downloaded!

Clip Art Subscriptions

Clip art subscriptions can be purchased from various web sites, including www.ArtToday.com (with 1.5 million images) and www.GifArt.com (with 25,000 images). Of course, there are thousands of other sites too; these are just a few that I found while quickly surfing the web. ClipArt.com boasts 2.5 million downloadable images! At www.ClipArt.com, subscriptions range from $7.95 a month to $149, depending on the plan you choose (at least at the time this book was published), and these prices seem to be competitive for what you get. At www.GifArt.com, prices run about $50 per year or, if you subscribe monthly, around $10.

How to Use Clip Art

When creating a spot color logo or any other design for a client, you have several options. You can use an image or artwork that the client gives you, you can draw or create something from scratch, you can create an image using layers, or you can build something starting with a piece of clip art. Building a logo or design starting with a piece of clip art is the topic of the next few sections and is a great way to build spot color (one- to four-color) logos for clients quickly.

 Tip:

I almost always prefer to build from scratch; this way I have the correct resolution, I can create the new image as a PSD file, I can color separate easily, and I maintain ownership of the artwork.

Project 19-1: Building a Spot Color Logo from Clip Art

Clients come to the shop all the time asking me to create a logo for their new business, band, club, or group. They want a one- or two-color design for the logo so that their shirts, business cards, and other paraphernalia can be produced inexpensively. (A two-color T-shirt at our shop runs about $7, which is just about right for their budget.) Creating a logo for this type of client almost always begins with clip art.

In this project, we create a new logo for a client. It could be for a school's chess club, a teenager's new lawn mowing service, the local rock band (they'll probably want black shirts with white printing), someone's 40th birthday, or a family reunion, just to name a few. In this example, we create a logo for a kid's museum, and the logo will have limited colors and clip art.

1. Place the CD that accompanies this book in the CD drive.

2. Choose **File>Open** and browse to this drive, usually D: or E:.

3. In the Files of Type window, select **Photoshop EPS (.eps)**; this is the same choice that you'll make when working with clip art collections that you purchase. Double-click on the file **Cc131075.eps** to open it.

✎ **Note:**

Special thanks to Fred Schoeller from Arts & Letters (www.arts-letters.com) for letting me use his clip art in this chapter and on the CD-ROM. This clip art is from the Arts & Letters Classic Clip Art collection.

4. From the Rasterize Generic EPS Format dialog box, shown in Figure 19-2, change the mode to **RBG Color.**

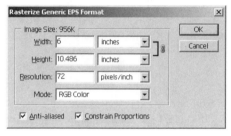

Figure 19-2: The Rasterize Generic EPS Format dialog box

5. From this same dialog box, change the width and height to **6** and **10** inches, respectively. (They'll automatically produce the right adjustments from there.) This adjustment will open the file larger than how it was originally saved.

6. Check **Anti-aliased** and click **OK**. The clip art is now open and ready for editing.

7. Using **Image>Canvas Size**, increase the canvas size to 10 by 14. Click **OK**.

8. Change the foreground color to blue in the toolbox.

9. Select the **Paint Bucket** tool. Use this tool to change the color of the dress to blue. Click in each section to change the color of that section. Change the color of the platform as well.

10. Choose **Edit>Transform>Scale**. Use the corner handles to resize the image and make it smaller. Click and drag to move the image.

☑ **Tip:**

Notice the other Transform options—Skew, Rotate, Distort, and Perspective. These can also be used with clip art.

11. Use the **Type** tool to add text to the image. (You'll have to agree to apply the transformation in step 10 before continuing; click **Apply** in the dialog box.)

12. Open the Layers palette (**Window>Layers**). Select **Layer 1**.

13. Select the **Magic Eraser** tool from the toolbox. Click once in the top portion of the tool that the person is holding. Click again on the second part to make this tool transparent. See Figure 19-3.

Figure 19-3: Creating a spot color logo

This logo is now ready for color separation and spot or indexed color printing. You can further reduce the number of colors if desired using various tools. The design can also be enhanced for process color printing. Backgrounds, gradients, borders, etc., can be added using layers. As an example:

14. Choose **New>New Fill Layer>Gradient** and click **OK**.

15. Choose a **Radial** gradient.

16. Choose **Layer>Arrange> Send to Back**.

17. Add or create a border if desired. In Figure 19-4 I used a soft brush with the Airbrush option checked, and then I used the Smudge tool to work around the edges. The smudging is in progress in this image.

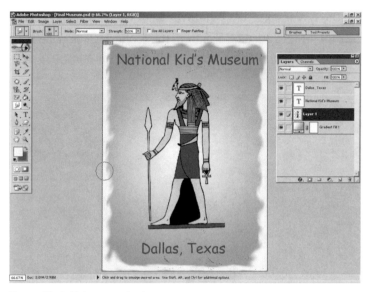

Figure 19-4: Enhancing the logo

 Note:

If the clip art has a background, which this one does not, you can remove it with the Magic Eraser tool. Using the Magic Eraser tool, click once on the white background. Depending on the design, you might want to uncheck Contiguous from the options bar so that the background behind the clip art is transparent as well.

Besides what we've done in this project, you can also add styles to the image, including bevel, emboss, and others. Experiment to your heart's content with this design and apply what you've learned to clip art of your own.

Using the File > Place Command

The File>Place command can be used to "place" or put files in another image. Doing so also creates a new layer. Items that can be placed into other images are PDF files, Illustrator files, and EPS files.

Once the file has been placed into an existing file, it will have a bounding box around it for resizing. The Transform options can also be used, including Scale, Rotate, and Skew. You can cancel any placed image using the Esc key or accept it using the check mark in the options bar.

Once the file has been placed, resized, and accepted, you can use the Paint Bucket and similar tools to edit it. However, you still cannot perform as many edits as you could in a more functional program like CorelDRAW, Adobe Illustrator, or Arts & Letters. You cannot edit the vector data itself.

With the logo you created in Project 19-1, use the File > Place command to add the original image again. Resize it so that it fits appropriately and use the Paint Bucket to edit the image. You can then use Layer > Duplicate Layer to create a copy of the placed artwork and move a copy of it to another location. See Figure 19-5.

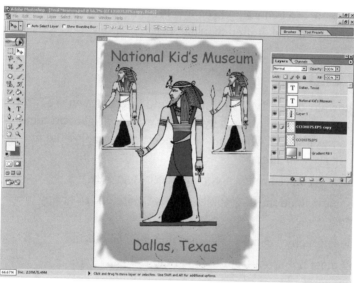

Figure 19-5: Adding placed artwork

Stock Photos

While stock photos aren't considered clip art, they are used similarly. You can purchase stock images the same way you purchase clip art, both through the Internet or from a computer store. These stock images can then be used like clip art to build designs from scratch.

These photos are often used as a background for process color artwork, such as the kind you see on concert T-shirts, motorcycle T-shirts, etc. These photos can be of seascapes, landscapes, skyscapes, and often animals. Consider purchasing, along with a collection of clip art, a collection of stock images too.

What about Copyrights?

If you are going to use or incorporate images that someone else has created, such as a photo, piece of clip art, or a combination of both, you'll need to understand about copyrighting. Copyrights are created to protect the creator or artist from unlicensed use of their artwork and from having others profit from something he or she spent time creating. If you want to use the artwork professionally or commercially, you'll have to pay the creator for the rights to do that. When you purchase clip art (or stock photos), there are generally three levels of copyrights: royalty free, rights protected, and limited distribution.

Free Clip Art

When downloading artwork for free on the Internet, you are rarely given the rights to use it commercially. The artwork is "rights protected." Here's an example of what you can expect when reading the fine print on a free clip art web site:

■ These graphics are for non-commercial use only.

■ Do not include these graphics on a web site, a CD, or any other media.

■ These graphics cannot be redistributed in any form.

■ You must not profit from these graphics in any way.

■ These graphics are for personal use only.

■ If you want to use this clip art for profit, you must purchase it from us.

As you can see from this list, you're not going to be able to use this clip art on an object that you plan to sell for profit.

Purchased Clip Art

When you purchase a clip art collection or artwork from the Internet, you'll get certain rights for reproduction. This is generally royalty free artwork. Here are a few examples of what you'll see when reading the fine print:

- You must have written consent to include this artwork in any other software program, such as a game, publishing program, or office program.

- This artwork can be modified and reproduced for print or publishing. However, you cannot resell the clip art itself, either modified or unmodified in any form.

- When using a service company for output, you can make a single copy of the artwork for their use. The copy must be deleted from their system after the job is complete.

Basically, you can (for the most part) modify and reproduce purchased clip art for use on T-shirts or any other printing or publishing medium, for profit, with no maximums. However, you should read the fine print on your particular software, as some have limited rights.

Limited Distribution Artwork

Limited distribution artwork can be distributed only under specific circumstances. If your artwork has a limited distribution clause, you'll probably have rights similar to these:

- Catalogs—up to 500
- Postcards—up to 300
- General packaging—up to 500
- Newspapers—up to 1,000
- Stationery—up to 1,000
- Promotional goods—up to 1,000

Depending on the size of the run, you might be able to use this limited distribution artwork, which is usually much cheaper than royalty free artwork.

Summary

In this chapter you learned all about clip art. You learned where to get clip art for free and how to purchase it. Clip art subscriptions were also introduced. The chapter project walked you through creating your own spot color logo from a piece of clip art and how to use the File>Place command to add clip art to an existing image. Finally, copyrights were introduced, including royalty free, limited distribution, and rights protected types.

Chapter 20

Special Effects

Special effects can be applied and used to enhance artwork in many different ways. The most effective way to apply a special effect to an image is with filters and blending modes, although sometimes a gradient can be used to achieve the desired effect.

Filters can be used to prepare an image for printing, as shown with the Filter>Sharpen>Unsharp Mask command in previous chapters. You'll use this filter quite a bit. Filters can also be used to extract an image from its background to assist in separating an object from the rest of the image. However, most filters are used to add artistic touches to an image (for instance, taking a plain photograph or piece of artwork and making it look as if it's been created using watercolor, oil, or colored pencil instead).

Blending modes are used to specify how a layer's pixels will blend with the underlying pixels in the image. Changing the blending mode changes how the image is put together and thus how it looks. Blending modes can be used to create wonderful special effects.

The Gradient tool can also be used to create effects, although these are usually less drastic than using filters or blending modes. In this chapter, we discuss all of the ways that you can create special effects. You're going to be surprised at how many effects Photoshop offers!

Using Filters

Before we get started, open up any file in Photoshop and browse through the options from the Filter menu. Figure 20-1 shows the clip art used in the last chapter with the artistic filter Neon Glow applied. Notice how many artistic filters there are; browse through the other filters to see just how many other filters are available.

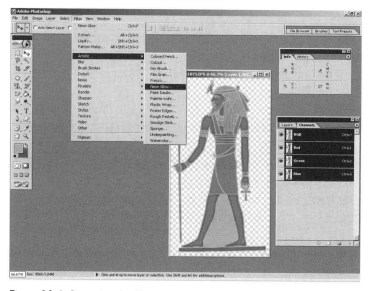

Figure 20-1: Browsing the filters

As you can see, there are a hundred or so filters available, and most allow you to configure how the filter should be applied, thus offering thousands of options. The artistic filters are my favorite, so let's start there.

Artistic Filters

Artistic filters enable you to take a regular photograph or image and give it a hand-drawn feel. These filters are especially good for artwork created for a fine arts facility, museum, art show, county fair, and similar clients.

Instead of simply reading an explanation of what the artistic filter Cutout does vs. the artistic filter Film Grain, it is infinitely better for you to work through each yourself. To experiment and get a feel for what each can do:

1. Open the file **Downtown.jpg** from the Chapter 20 folder on the companion CD. The client would like something "artsy" done with the photograph of the white building in the back.

2. Verify that Image>Mode is set to RGB Color. (It is of course, but this is a good habit to get into; several filters won't work unless you're in RGB mode.)

3. Choose **Filter>Artistic>Colored Pencil**.

4. In the Colored Pencil dialog box, notice there are options for Pencil Width, Stroke Pressure, and Paper Brightness, as well as a minus and plus sign for zooming in and out. Use the minus sign to zoom out to 25 percent.

5. Experiment by moving the sliders. Click **OK** when finished to apply the colored pencil.

6. Choose **Edit>Undo Colored Pencil**.

 Note:

When working with filters, remember that they are cumulative; this means that if you apply one, then another, then another, the image will have all three filters applied, not just the last one.

7. Choose **Filter>Artistic>Cutout**. Again, use the Zoom tools and sliders to see the effect on the image. Click **OK** when finished.

8. Repeat these steps with the remaining artistic filters.

As you can see, these filters can be used to create real artwork! A little text, a border, and some lighting, and you've got yourself a design that can be used on a tote bag, coffee mug, or T-shirt.

 Note:

If you're still confused as to what exactly each filter is doing as it works its magic, consult the Photoshop Help files and search for Artistic Filters. Each is explained in detail.

Figure 20-2 shows a before and after shot of the same photograph. Watercolor is one of my favorite filters and can be used in a variety of instances.

Figure 20-2: Watercolor effects

Other Filters

Besides the filters and effects that make an image or photograph look artsy, there are plenty more that distort and disrupt the image. It's up to you to work through the different filters to see what each can do; working through each here in multiple examples would not be effective time- or space-wise. The following sections briefly summarize the remaining filters. If possible, open a file and work through each as you read along, keeping in mind that almost all of these filters have dialog boxes that open similarly to the dialog boxes shown in the "Artistic Filters" section and are used similarly.

 Note:

Filters can be applied to entire layers or selections. To apply a filter to a selection, use the Marquee tools to select it first.

Blur

Blur filters soften the selection or layer by blurring the edges. This is a good tool for retouching photographs but is not so great for screen printed artwork. Several Blur options can give nice effects though, including Radial Blur and Motion Blur. Both give the image a sense of movement and can be just the right touch for a picture of a car, runner, or sports figure.

 Tip:

Combine the Radial Blur filter with other filters for a different type of movement effect. For instance, use the Render filter to create a background pattern for an image and then apply Radial Blur to give it a special effect.

Brush Strokes

Brush stroke filters are like the artistic filters; they give an artistic look and feel to the artwork. The filters can be used to give a brushed look, including angled strokes, crosshatch, ink outlines, sprayed strokes, and more. Be careful not to overdo this effect; more is not necessarily better!

Distort

Distort filters do exactly that—they distort the image. While there are too many to list, options include Ripple, Twirl, Wave, and Diffuse Glow. Experiment with these filters to see what each does. Figure 20-3 shows an example of the Twirl distort filter. Notice that as with the artistic filters, a dialog box appears where the effect can be configured.

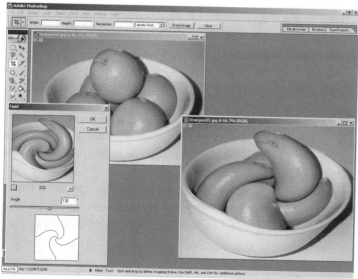

Figure 20-3: Using Distort filters

Note:

As with the other filters, the dialog box is pretty intuitive. Click inside the window to adjust the amount of distortion for this one, and use the – and + signs for zooming.

Noise

Noise adds or removes noise, or static, in a picture. Noise consists of random pixels, and adding it is useful when you need to apply random pixels for a special effect. I can't think of any reason why you'd want to add noise to an image, unless you've got a picture of a TV set and want to make it look like it's broken, but I'm sure there's a reason out there somewhere!

On the flip side, reducing noise is generally helpful, and the Despeckle and Dust & Scratches options can be used to reduce noise in an image. Be careful if you plan to screen print the image though; the Dust and Scratches options can significantly blur the image and might not be useful.

Pixelate

Pixelated images are generally bad news, but if you're looking for an effect that will cause it, look no further. The Color Halftone filter takes each channel of color, divides the image into rectangles, and then replaces them with circles, similar to halftone screens. Crystallize uses polygonal shapes, Facet uses block shapes, and Mosaic uses square blocks. The other filters in this category do similar distortions.

Render

Render filters can be used to create 3D shapes, cloud patterns, refraction patterns, and light reflections in an image. The patterns that can be created can be used as special effect backgrounds.

To create a background using a cloud pattern for instance, start with a new canvas and choose Filter>Render>Clouds. A cloud pattern will fill the area using the foreground and background colors in the toolbox. You can then apply other filters, such as Filter>Blur>Radial Blur or Filter> Distort>Ocean Ripple for more effect.

Lighting effects let you create effects on RGB images using various lighting styles. Using the Lighting Effects dialog box shown in Figure 20-4, you can create light from any direction, choose a spotlight, use directional or omni light, configure intensity and focus, and more.

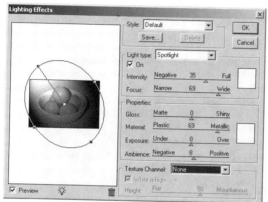

Figure 20-4: The Lighting Effects dialog box

 Note:

Remember, you can apply filters to selections too, not just entire layers.

Sharpen

You've already been introduced to the Unsharp Mask command, and there are other Sharpen tools as well. Sharpening an image results in clearer edges, a less blurry image, and clarity improvement. Most images can be sharpened quite a bit prior to screen printing them and should be used generously.

 Tip:

Sharpen filters can be used to repair blurry photographs! They can also be used after selecting a part of an image that's blurry to sharpen only the object that was in motion as you snapped the picture.

Sketch

These filters add texture to an image and can be used like the artistic and brush strokes filters. Examples of sketch filters include Chalk and Charcoal, Conte Crayon, Graphic Pen, Photocopy, Plaster, Torn Edges, and Water Paper.

Stylize

These filters produce a painted or impressionistic effect by increasing the contrast in the image. Figure 20-5 shows before and after pictures of the OrangesII.jpg file. The filter applied is Filter>Stylize>Glowing Edges. I use this filter quite a bit for creating images for printing on black shirts—concert shirts, motorcycle shirts, etc.

Figure 20-5: Using the Stylize filters

If you'd like to experiment with this, open the OrangesII.jpg file from the Chapter 20 folder on the companion CD, and apply the filter. While you're at it, try the Extrude, Solarize, and Wind commands.

Texture

Texture filters add texture to an image to make it look like you could reach out and touch it and actually feel the texture that you've applied. Texture options include Craquelure, which gives the image a cracked look, Grain, Mosaic Tiles, Patchwork, Stained Glass, and Texturizer. Stained Glass is a nice one to try if you need to create a logo for a church, while Mosaic Tiles might work for a handyman.

Other, Video, and Digimarc Filters

The Other filter options let you create your own filters to use to modify masks, make color adjustments, and offset a selection in an image. The filters you create can also be saved for later use. Video filters are used for creating artwork for video or TV. Digimarc filters embed copyright information into an image using a watermark. These topics are beyond the scope of this chapter and book.

Extract

Extract lets you remove an object or objects from an image and works when other options don't (like the Background Eraser tool or the Magic Eraser tool). With the Extract option, you can trace around an image to select it for removal using a large highlighter-type pen, fill that area with color, and extract it from the image.

To use the Extract tool:

1. Open an image that contains an object to extract. From the Layers palette, select the layer that you want to work with.

2. Try to erase the background using the Magic Eraser tool or the Background Eraser tool. If this doesn't work, undo this attempt and continue with the next steps.

3. Choose **Layer>Duplicate Layer** to create a copy of the layer. You can see the duplicate layer in the Layers palette.

4. To work only in a selected area, use the Marquee tools to select an area. Notice that there is an area selected in Figure 20-6. This is optional.

5. Choose **Filter>Extract**. You'll see a dialog box similar to the one shown in Figure 20-6.

6. Configure the options for Brush Size, Highlight, and Fill as you would with any other dialog box. The Highlight color is the color that you'll see when you trace around an image; Fill is the color that will be used to define the extracted object. The Brush Size defines the tip of the tracing brush.

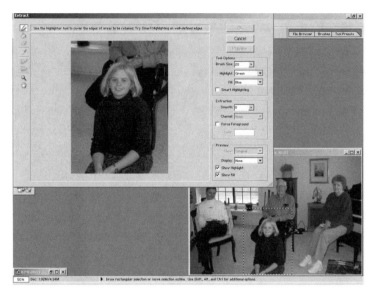

Figure 20-6: Using the Extract command

7. If the edge that you want to trace around contrasts highly with its background, check **Smart Highlighting**.

8. Use the Zoom tools in the Extract dialog box to zoom in on the object, and press the **Alt** key to zoom back out. Use the Hand tool to view other parts of the image while zoomed in.

9. Select the **Highlighter** tool. Use the mouse to trace completely around the image and create a closed shape. See Figure 20-7.

Tips for Tracing

■ When tracing around an object, position the brush so that you get a little of the background and a little of the object itself.

■ If possible, draw completely around the object and enclose it by connecting the beginning and ending points.

■ Use a larger brush for tracing around hair or other wispy edges. Use a smaller brush for more defined areas.

■ Use the Eraser tool in the dialog box to erase a highlight drawn incorrectly. Use Alt+Backspace on a PC to erase the entire highlight, or use Option+Delete on a Mac.

---

10. Once the object has been traced around completely, select the **Fill** tool from the left side of the Extract dialog box and fill the area by clicking once inside it. See Figure 20-7.

 Tip:

To remove a fill, click again in the filled area with the Fill tool.

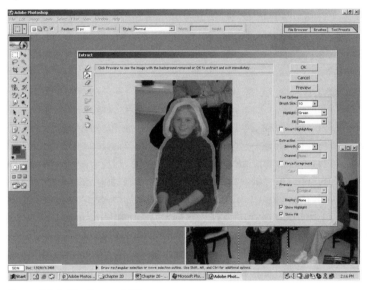

Figure 20-7: Tracing and filling

11. Click **Preview**. If the preview doesn't yield the results you want and you want to start over, change the Preview Show window in the Extract dialog box from Extracted to **Original**. Then choose **Alt+Backspace** on a PC to erase the entire highlight, or use **Option+Delete** on a Mac.

12. If the extraction is off to a good start, you can edit it. Simply repeat the steps above.

13. Locate the Clean Up tool and the Edge Touch Up tools in the Extract dialog box. Use these tools to touch up the extraction.

14. To see how the object would look against a different background, select a choice in the Preview area of the Extract dialog box. Under Display, choose None, Black Matte, Gray Matte, White Matte, Other, or Mask.

15. Click **OK** in the Extract dialog box when you are finished.

16. From the Layers palette, remove the eye icon from the original image layer so that only the duplicate layer is showing. You'll see your extraction. (If you did not create a duplicate layer, this step isn't necessary.)

17. Use **Edit>Fade Extract** to add the final touches to the image.

While using the Filter>Extract tool is a bit more complex than using the Lasso or Eraser tools, it's also much more functional. Practice makes perfect, so practice away!

Liquify

Liquify is a fun tool for making a mess of things. Beyond that, it's usefulness lies in the ability to create awesome borders and special effects. Use this filter to turn any piece of artwork into a gooey, liquid-looking mess of colors, or use the colors as an edge for a rectangular design. To experiment with the Liquify filter, open the file Trunk.jpg from the Chapter 20 folder on the companion CD (it's very colorful and perfect for this project), choose Filter>Liquify, and follow along here:

1. In the Liquify dialog box shown in Figure 20-8, choose the **Twirl Clockwise** tool. You can select it from the left side of the Liquify dialog box or press R on the keyboard.

2. Choose a brush size in the Liquify dialog box that is approximately the size of one of the squares in the trunk. Position the mouse over a rectangular part of the trunk where red meets gold. Click and hold to apply the twirl effect. See Figure 20-8.

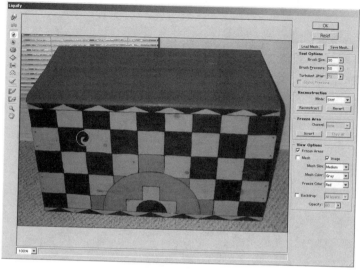

Figure 20-8: The Liquify dialog box

3. Select the **Twirl Counterclockwise** tool and repeat step 2.

4. Select the **Pucker** tool and repeat again. You'll have to drag this tool to get the desired effect.

5. Work your way through the rest of the tools.

6. Click **Reconstruct** to revert the image to its original, or click **OK** to accept the changes. See Figure 20-9.

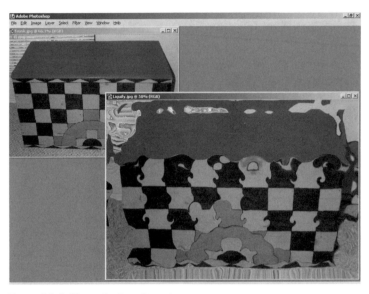

Figure 20-9: Using the Liquify tool

As with other tools and dialog boxes, the Liquify dialog box offers the Hand tool and Zoom tool. There are other options though, such as Mesh. Mesh puts up a grid so you can keep track of your distortions. When this is checked, you can deselect Image to hide the image if desired. You can also show only the active layer in the dialog box by deselecting Add Backdrop (Backdrop on a Mac). However, only the active layer is actually distorted.

Experiment with this tool to create borders and edges for photos that you need to blend into shirts and other items. With practice, you can make the object look like it's moving as well. After applying a filter, try Edit>Fade <filter> to see the effects that can be created after the transition. Use your imagination!

The Fade Command

The Fade command appears in the Edit menu after a filter has been applied and allows you to change the blending options for that filter. The Fade command also appears after using a painting tool or an eraser or after making a color adjustment. The Fade dialog box has two options, one to change the opacity and another to change the blending mode.

The Fade command can be used on a single layer, a selection, or an entire image. To work on a layer, choose that layer from the Layers palette before applying the filter and working with Edit>Fade. To use it on a selection, make the selection, apply the filter, and then use the Fade command to edit the selection. The Fade command can only be used immediately after applying a filter, eraser, painting tool, or color adjustment.

Blending Modes

A layer's blending mode determines how the layer's colored pixels will mix (relate) with the underlying pixels in the image. By default, there is no blending of layers, but by choosing and applying a blending mode, you can change this. When the blending mode is changed, the order of the image's composition is changed too. Blending modes are generally used to create special effects, like adding soft light or hard light, or changing the color, saturation, hue, luminosity, or other attributes of how the layers can be combined.

 Caution!

Remember to work in RGB mode. Some blends and filters won't work in indexed color mode, lab mode, or CMYK mode.

Blending Mode Options

As with understanding filters, the best way to understand exactly what blending modes do to an image or layer is to work through each type using the same file. By doing so, you can see exactly how the layers interact with different blending mode options. In this section, I briefly describe what each blending mode does, and in the next section, you can apply the different modes to an image.

Note:

Blends can be between two layers, a layer and a selection, or a layer and what is being painted on that layer with a tool such as a painting or erasing tool. You'll run across blending mode options often after painting or editing an image.

- **Normal:** Called Threshold when using bitmap or indexed color mode instead of RGB mode, this mode is the default. The blend is natural, and no distortion of pixels is added. The pixels added to the image simply replace the underlying pixels.

- **Dissolve:** Randomly distributes foreground pixels throughout the layer or selected area and often gives a textured look to the image

- **Behind:** This mode can only be used on layers, and only transparent pixels on a layer are changed. It's similar to painting on the back side of a sheet of acetate on which a design has been painted previously on the front.

- **Clear:** Like the Behind mode, this can only be used on layers. This mode changes opaque pixels to transparent and can be used with the Paint Bucket tool, the Paintbrush tool, the Pencil tool, and the Fill and Stroke commands. This can only be used on layers that are not locked.

- **Darken:** This mode changes pixels that are lighter than the foreground color. Pixels that are the same color or darker aren't changed.

- **Multiply:** Like the Darken mode, the Multiply mode darkens the image. This is good for creating shadows, as it combines the existing pixels with the foreground color in the toolbox when painting or editing.

- **Color Burn:** Increases the contrast by darkening the colors on the bottom layer of the image. If the layer is white, no change occurs.

- **Linear Burn:** The target layer's colors are blended with the bottom layer's colors to decrease the brightness of the image. As with Color Burn, no change occurs if the target layer is white.

- **Lighten:** Looks at both the original color and the blend color and chooses the lightest color as the result color. If a pixel is darker than the blend color, it is replaced.

- **Screen:** Produces a bleached look by blending the inverse of the blend color and the original colors of the pixels in the image

- **Color Dodge:** Decreases the contrast of the layers in the image by brightening the original colors in the image

- **Linear Dodge:** Increases the brightness in the layers in the image by brightening the original colors in the image

- **Overlay:** Good for creating ghost-like images and effects, this mode either multiplies or screens the colors, depending on the original colors in the image. The original color and the blend color are mixed.

- **Soft Light:** Applies a soft light to the image, which can either brighten or darken the image, depending on the original colors in the image. If the image is light, the image is lightened similar to a dodge; if the image is dark, the image is darkened similar to a burn.

- **Hard Light:** Applies a hard light to the image, based on its original color. It is similar to the Soft Light mode and is useful for creating shadows.

- **Vivid Light:** Burns or dodges the original color and the blend color, depending on the darkness or lightness of the image. Lighter images have their contrast decreased; darker images have their contrast increased.

- **Linear Light:** Similar to Vivid Light, except the brightness is changed instead of the contrast

- **Pin Light:** Replaces the original colors in the image based on its blend color. The math is complicated, but the result is not. Generally, this mode doesn't produce anything usable (as far as I can tell).

- **Difference:** Compares the blend color with the original color and determines which is brighter. With that information, either the blend color is subtracted from the original color or the original color is subtracted from the base color. Blending with black produces no change.

- **Exclusion:** Creates an effect similar to Difference mode, but with less contrast in the resulting colors

- **Hue:** Combines the luminance and saturation of the original color with the hue of the blend color

- **Saturation:** Combines the luminance and hue of the original color with the saturation of the blend color

- **Color:** Combines the luminance of the original color with the hue and saturation of the blend color

- **Luminosity:** Combines the hue and saturation of the original color with the luminance of the blend color

Applying a Blending Mode to a Layer

To understand what all of this means, open the file Blending Modes.psd from the Chapter 20 folder on the companion CD. It has several layers that will be perfect for applying and understanding what blending modes do.

Note:

This file was created in a matter of minutes if you'd like to recreate it. First, use the Magnetic Lasso to trace around the bowl of oranges in the OrangesII.jpg file, and then copy the bowl of oranges to the clipboard. Create a new file, add a background, and paste the oranges in. Add a background and text.

1. With the Blending Modes.psd file open, select **Window > Layer** to open the Layers palette.

2. In the Layers palette, select the **Oranges** layer by clicking on it once. See Figure 20-10. (Notice that you can now select any tool to work on this layer if desired; choose the **Move** tool to move the bowl of oranges around on the image.)

Figure 20-10: Choosing the layer

3. Double-click in the Layers palette on the Oranges layer to open the Layer Style dialog box. Locate the Blend Mode window in the Blending Options section and click the down arrow to see the options. See Figure 20-11.

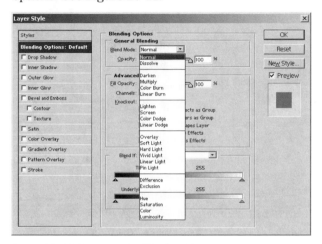

Figure 20-11: Locating the Blending Options

4. Make sure **Preview** is checked, move the Layer Style dialog box so you can see it and the image, and choose the blending mode **Dissolve**.

5. Repeat step 4 with the other blending modes. Luminosity gives a nice effect for this image.

6. Work back through the blending modes that you liked, and this time, change the opacity settings and experiment with the Blending Options on the left side of the dialog box. Click on the option to choose it and configure additional settings.

If, after finding the perfect blending mode, you want to save it for future use, you can. Simply click the New Style button in the Layer Style dialog box and name your creation. It will then be available the next time you need it.

You can also work with the blending mode of the patterned layer. To do this, you must change the order of layers in the Layers palette. Figure 20-12 shows the order of the layers in the Blending Mode.psd file. Change it to what is shown in Figure 20-13 by dragging the Blue Pattern Background layer up one position. Now, double-click on the Blue Pattern

Background layer to open up its Layer Style dialog box. Work through the blending modes again with this layer.

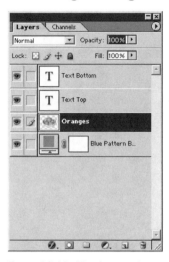

Figure 20-12: Blending mode order

Figure 20-13: Changing the blending mode order

Using the Gradient Tool

The Gradient tool can also be used to add an effect to a layer or image. Gradients are gradual blends of multiple colors and can be radial, linear, angle, reflected, or diamond shaped. Gradients can be used as backgrounds for all kinds of artwork, including artwork for T-shirts, bags, or even business cards.

 Tip:

If you look around your neighborhood at the signs created for businesses, you'll see many gradients. In particular, look for tanning salon signs, beauty parlors, and billboards.

Types of Gradients

There are five types of gradients. Figure 20-14 shows them all—radial, linear, angle, reflected, and diamond. Notice that the colors fade together in each.

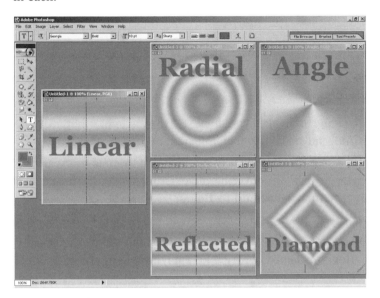

Figure 20-14: Gradient types

Figure 20-14 shows the defaults for the chosen gradients, but these can be changed. For instance, the radius of the circle can be changed when using a radial gradient, so the circle of colors is larger or smaller. The other gradient types have similar options.

Applying a Gradient

To apply a gradient, perform the following steps:

1. Choose a layer to apply the gradient to from the Layers palette, select an area to apply the gradient to using one of the selection tools, or choose **Layer>New>Layer** to create a new, independent layer on which to apply the gradient.

2. Choose **Layer>New Fill Layer>Gradient** to create a new gradient layer. Click **OK** in the New Layer dialog box.

3. In the Gradient Fill dialog box, shown in Figure 20-15, choose a desired color scheme by clicking the down arrow in the Gradient window.

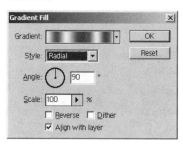

Figure 20-15: The Gradient Fill dialog box

4. Choose the style of the gradient, set the angle or other attributes as desired, and click **OK** when finished.

5. If this is not the only layer in the image, if there is transparency in the image, or if it is covering the existing data in the image, choose **Layer > Arrange > Send to Back**.

You can also change the opacity of the gradients once applied by selecting the gradient layer in the Layers palette and then sliding the Opacity slider. Often, this is just the trick for applying a light gradient for color or effect.

Tips for Good Special Effects

Finally, when creating special effects, keep the following things in mind:

- Don't overdo it. Many special effects can be used with minimal settings.

- The artistic Dry Brush filter reduces the colors in the image and softens the edges at the same time. This makes screening the image easier and allows for mistakes with alignment of the screens.

- Using filters can be memory intensive. When experimenting, consider applying the filter to only a part of the image if the computer seems to respond excessively slow.

- Use the Purge command before applying filters to free up memory space.

- To quickly apply a particular filter again, choose it from the top of the Filter list of commands. You won't get the dialog box when using this command option.

- Use the filter Stylize>Wind to make an object look like it's moving.

- When working with gradients, check Dither for smoother transitions.

- Special effects can be applied to create edges and borders for rectangular images that will be printed on T-shirts and other material.

- Use filters and gradients to create backgrounds for an image.

- Learn about masks. Using masks to create selection areas helps you gain control over transitions and effects.

- Use filters and special effects to cover up flaws in an image.

Summary

In this chapter you learned to apply filters and blends, use blending modes, and create and apply gradients. Each of these Photoshop elements can be used to create special effects, cover up flaws in an image, or create artistic-looking images.

Chapter 21

Pens, Paths, and Masks

Paths are shapes that you create, and they can be open or closed. Paths are created using the Pen tools. There are two Pen tools available: the Pen tool and the Freeform Pen tool. The Freeform Pen tool can be converted into the Magnetic Pen tool using the options bar for a total of three distinct tool options. The Magnetic Pen tool snaps to the edges of an image, making tracing around an image easy. These tools allow you to create intricate selections by tracing around an object's defined edges or drawing freehand to create a particular shape. The selections created from this tracing or drawing can then be saved and edited for future use.

Vector masks can be created from paths, and these masks can be used to mask (or hide) part of a layer; they can be edited by configuring styles or adding special effects, or they can be used to reveal specific areas of a layer. Vector masks are created with the Pen and Shape tools.

Layer masks can be used to obscure entire layers and layer sets. By using masks, you can apply special effects without actually affecting any of the original data on that layer. After you've found the perfect effect, you can then apply the changes. The changes can also be discarded. Layer masks are created using the painting and selection tools.

Using the Pen Tools

The Pen tools (Pen and Freeform Pen) can be used in two ways: as drawing tools or as selection tools. The Pen tools are used to draw straight or curved lines called paths. The Pen tools can also be used to create elaborate selections by tracing around an object's interior or exterior. These paths can then be saved, filled, and edited. When editing a path, you can add points to the path (called anchor points), remove points, reuse the selection, and convert straight lines to curves and vice versa.

What Is a Path?

A *path* is a shape that you create by drawing with the Pen or Freeform Pen tools. Paths can be open or closed; closed means they meet at the beginning and the end to form a closed and complete shape, such as a circle, while open means they do not meet but form distinct shapes, such as an S. In order for a path to be printed, it must be filled or stroked. If the path is not, it is simply a vector object that does not contain any bitmap pixels.

Options Bar Choices

When you choose a Pen tool, the options bar changes to reflect your choice. (The Pen tools are located ninth down on the left side of the toolbox.) From left to right, the options bar contains these options:

- **Tool Preset Picker**: Contains preset tools such as Lasso, Crop, and various brushes

- **Shape layers icon**: Choose this to create a shape layer instead of a path. When this is selected, the shape is automatically filled with the foreground color (whose attributes can be changed after it's filled). The shape's outline is stored as a vector mask linked to the shape layer.

- **Paths icon**: Choose this to create a work path. These paths are stored in the Paths palette until they are deleted or saved, and they are temporary. A new path will delete an old path unless it has been saved. By default, paths are not filled with color.

- **Fill pixels icon**: Allows you to adjust the fill properties using opacity and mode
- **Pen tool**: Selects the Pen tool
- **Freeform Pen tool**: Selects the Freeform Pen tool

The remaining options bar icons change depending on what has been selected above. Choices can include adding to or subtracting from a selection, blending mode, color, opacity, style, and more.

Drawing a Path

Paths are one of the more complicated areas of Photoshop, so this tutorial in drawing paths is pretty basic (as is the entire chapter). Once you've learned your way around these tools, you can expand your horizons with practice and the Photoshop Help files, which are extremely complete in this area. Here are the basics:

1. Open the Paths palette using **Window>Paths**. Here, you can see the paths as you draw them. Open the Layers palette using **Window>Layers**.

2. Open a new file using **File>New**, and choose **1024 x 768**, **white** background, and **RGB Color** mode.

3. Select the **Pen** tool.

4. In the options bar, select the **Paths** option, click the down arrow next to the custom shape icon to verify that Rubber Band is *not* checked, verify that Auto Add/Delete is checked, and select **Add to Path Area**. See Figure 21-1.

Figure 21-1: Preparing to draw a path

5. Click once with the Pen tool inside the new file. Click a second time in another area of the file to create a straight line. Notice the temporary work path created in the Paths palette.

Note:

The squares at the beginning and end of the line are called anchor points. The filled anchor point is the last one drawn (the active anchor point).

6. Click on the **Pen** tool again to tell Photoshop that you are finished drawing this particular path. (If you don't, the next click will be associated with this line.)

7. Double-click the work path in the Paths palette to open the Save Path dialog box. Name the path and click **OK**. (If you don't save the path, it'll be deleted if you deselect it and start drawing a new path, and the old one will be replaced.)

8. Repeat step 5, and this time create a triangle by drawing three lines and connecting the third line back to its starting point. (Consider using View>Show>Grid so that you can create a true triangle.)

9. Do not deselect the paths by clicking in the Paths palette; you can use this triangle in the next section. If you do deselect the paths, you'll notice that those paths will be deleted.

You can also draw curves using the Pen tools. You'll learn about that shortly.

Editing (Adjusting) a Path

Paths can be adjusted by moving them using the Direct Selection tool from the toolbox. The Direct Selection tool is located above the Pen tool and is hidden under the Path Selection tool. To move the line segment created in step 5 in the previous example, choose this tool, click on the line, and drag. The Direct Selection tool can also be used to drag an anchor point to change the shape of the triangle created in step 8 above.

 Tip:

When using the Pen tool, you can switch to the Direct Selection tool by holding down the Ctrl key on a PC or the Cmd key on a Mac.

To see how this works, draw a triangle with the Pen tool. Select the Direct Selection tool, click on the triangle, and drag. You can drag from one of its sides or from any anchor point.

Multiple Segments, Closed Paths, and Curves

Of course, using paths rarely involves drawing only straight lines and triangles, so in this section, we delve a little deeper into how to use the Pen tool. In this section, we learn to draw multiple segments, stroke paths, fill paths, draw a curved path, and create separate work paths.

1. Open the Paths palette using **Window > Paths**. Here, you can see the paths as you draw them. Open the Layers palette using **Window > Layers**.

2. Open a new file using **File > New**, and choose **1024 x 768, white** background, and **RGB Color** mode.

3. Select the **Pen** tool.

4. In the options bar, select the **Paths** option (the second icon), click the down arrow next to the custom shape icon to verify that Rubber Band is *not* checked, verify that Auto Add/Delete is checked, and select **Add to Path Area**.

5. Click with the mouse ten times in various places on the blank file to draw a series of connected line segments. Double-click on this path in the Paths palette and save it as **Connected Segments**.

 Tip:

When drawing, you can always use Edit > Undo to remove the last added segment. Choose View > Show > Grid if a grid is needed.

6. Choose the **Direct Selection** tool and experiment with moving various segments of the path.

7. With the Direct Selection tool still selected, hold down the **Alt** key on a PC or the **Option** key on a Mac and click on the path with the mouse. Let go of both. Drag the path to a new area. To make a copy of the entire path, hold down the **Alt** or **Option** key while dragging.

8. To stroke a path (which adds pixels to the image and thus makes it a part of the image and printable), select the **Brush** tool from the toolbox and choose a brush that you'd like to use to paint over the path. Select a foreground color from the toolbox as well.

9. Select the **Direct Selection** tool. Make sure the path is chosen in the Paths palette, and from the additional options in that palette, choose **Stroke Subpath** (or **Stroke Path**). See Figure 21-2. Select the **Brush** tool from the Stroke Path dialog box and click **OK**.

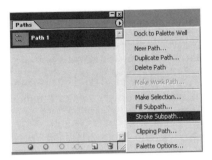

Figure 21-2: Stroking a path

10. You can also fill a path from the additional options. Choose **Fill Subpath** (or **Fill Path**), and the path will be filled with the color configured as the foreground color in the toolbox.

 Tip:

From the additional options in the Paths palette, choose New Path, and create a polygon or other closed shape using the Pen tool. Use Fill Path to fill the new triangle with color.

11. To draw a curved segment using the Pen tool, choose **New Path** from the Paths palette's additional options first or create a new file. You can also delete existing paths in the image by right-clicking on them in the Paths palette and choosing Delete Path. (Notice that you can also create duplicate paths here too, among other things.)

12. Click with the mouse to create a starting point, continue to hold the mouse button down, and drag upward. You'll see a line extend above and below the starting point, as shown in Figure 21-3. Let go of the mouse.

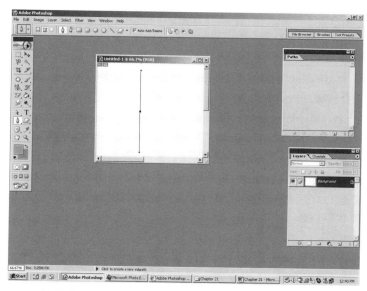

Figure 21-3: Drawing a curve, step 12

13. Position the cursor parallel to the starting point in step 12, approximately an inch or so to the right of it. Repeat step 12. Notice before
letting go of the mouse that the shape of the curve can be changed.
See the result in Figure 21-4.

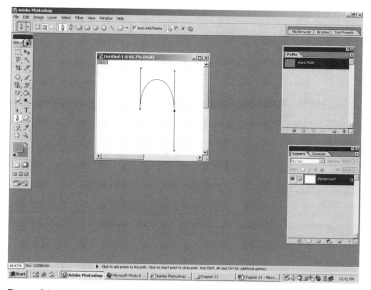

Figure 21-4: Drawing a curve, step 13

14. Repeat step 13 to create a third line and thus a second curve. Click the **Pen** tool to see the S that you've created.

15. Click on the line again. Notice that the anchor points are in view again. Click on the first point that you created in step 12 to create a closed figure 8 shape.

16. Save the path, apply fills and strokes to it, and practice editing it with the Direct Selection tool. You can fill and stroke different areas by clicking on them first. Experiment as time allows.

So, those are the basics! As you can probably tell from this introduction, you can create extremely intricate designs using the Pen tool, but it'll take practice!

Converting Paths to Selection Borders, Adding and Subtracting Anchor Points, and Other Important Features

Once the path has been created and saved, there are several things that you can do with it. For instance, you can add or subtract anchor points. Adding anchor points gives you more room to edit the path that's been drawn, but too many can make the path choppy. To add an anchor point to an existing path, click Add Anchor Point from the Pen tools icon in the toolbox. Note that it is a hidden option. You can subtract anchor points in the same manner.

Once a path has been finalized, you can make a selection border from the path (if it is a closed path). This border can then be treated like any other selection and added to, subtracted from, or combined with other selection data. To make a path a selection border, make sure the path is closed, and select the path in the Paths palette. Next, hold down the Ctrl key on a PC or the Cmd key on a Mac, and click once on the thumbnail image in the Paths palette. The path now becomes a selection.

☑ Tip:

If you want to specify settings for the selection, choose Make Selection from the additional options in the Paths palette. Creating a selection in this manner allows you to choose feathering options, anti-aliasing, and selection choices.

Here are some other interesting facts:

- Any selection that is made with any selection tool can be turned into a work path by clicking the Make Work Path button at the bottom of the Paths palette or in the additional options, and the Tolerance can also be configured.

- Paths that are saved with the image are available the next time the image is opened.

- The Convert Point tool, a hidden tool in the Pen tool section of the toolbox, can be used to change a smooth point (like that on a curve) to a corner point (like that on a rectangle or square). Clicking and dragging with the tool achieves this. Practice makes perfect!

- The size of the thumbnail in the Paths palette can be changed using the additional options in the Paths palette.

- The Freeform Pen tool lets you draw freehand. Place a check in the Magnetic box to have the Pen tool snap to the high-contrast areas of the image.

- When using the Freeform Pen tool with Magnetic checked, you can set options for width, contrast, frequency, and pen pressure.

Freeform Pen and Magnetic Option

Make sure you experiment briefly with the Freeform Pen and the Magnetic option before leaving this section. Open the file Fish.jpg from the Chapter 21 folder on the companion CD. Choose the Freeform Pen tool and attempt tracing around the fish. Next, check the Magnetic option and trace again. Figure 21-5 shows a final trace. The path has been stroked so you can see it in this screen shot.

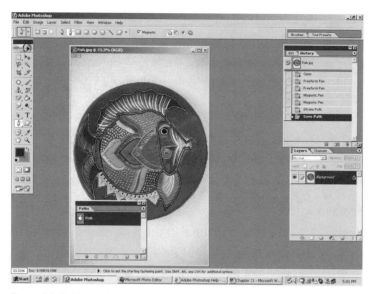

Figure 21-5: Using the Magnetic Pen option

While tracing around an object using the Magnetic Pen tool is much easier than using the Pen tool to draw curves around an object, the output is not as good. With the Pen tool, you can create a semicircle with only two anchor points, making the curve extremely smooth. Tracing around the same semicircle using the Magnetic Pen tool creates multiple anchor points, creating a less smooth path.

 Note:

There's much more you can learn about paths. In fact, the Photoshop Help files are filled with information. This section has offered only a brief introduction to these powerful tools.

What Are Masks?

There are two types of masks—layer masks and vector masks. Both control which parts of an image or layer will be hidden or revealed, and the masks can have special effects and styles applied to them. Once you're sure of the effects that you want to add, you can then apply them. This allows you to see what the changes will look like before actually changing any pixels in the image itself. Layer masks are created with the painting and selection tools; vector masks are created with the Pen and Shape tools.

In the Layers palette, the masks that you create are shown as thumbnails inside the appropriate layer. A vector mask's thumbnail image is the path that you've created using the Pen tool. A layer mask's thumbnail is a rectangle with a black background that represents the grayscale channel created when you add the layer mask. You can create a vector mask that shows or hides an entire layer and shows the contents of a shape, or you can create an inverted mask, where the entire page is colored and the shape is knocked out of the image.

 Note:

When you use the Pen tool and create a new shape layer, the new path appears automatically as a vector mask in the Paths palette.

Using Vector Masks

Let's look at the different ways that a vector mask can be used, created, and/or edited:

- Add a vector mask that shows or hides an entire layer
- Add a vector mask that shows only the content inside the shape that has been created by a path
- Edit a vector mask that is already created
- Remove, disable, or enable a vector mask
- Convert a vector mask to a layer mask (rasterize the vector data)

1. To add a vector mask that hides or shows an entire layer, select the layer from the Layer palette that you want to add the vector mask to. Choose **Layer>Add Vector Mask>Hide All** or **Reveal All**. (If these are grayed out, make a copy of the layer first.)

2. To add a vector mask that shows the contents of a shape, select the layer to apply the mask to in the Layers palette, select the path from the Paths palette, and choose **Layer>Add Vector Mask>Current Path**.

3. To edit a vector mask, click the vector mask thumbnail in either the Layer or Paths palettes. Edit the mask using the Shape or Pen tools.

4. To delete a vector mask, select it and choose **Layer>Delete Vector Mask**.

5. To enable or disable a vector mask, select it and then choose **Layer>Enable Vector Mask** or **Layer>Disable Vector Mask**.

6. To convert a vector mask to a layer mask, choose **Layer> Rasterize>Vector Mask**.

Using Layer Masks

A layer mask is represented in the Layers palette as a rectangle with a black background and the shape of the selection in white or gray. Layer masks can be used to hide or reveal entire layers or selections on layers. The black part of the layer mask (in the mask's thumbnail in the Layers palette) is hidden.

To create a Layer mask that hides or reveals an entire layer:

1. Make sure no selection is currently active, and select the layer to mask in the Layers palette.

2. Choose **Layer>Add Layer Mask>Reveal All** to reveal the entire layer or **Layer>Add Layer Mask>Hide All** to hide the entire layer.

To create a layer mask that hides or reveals a selection only:

3. Select the layer you add the mask to in the Layers palette.

4. Make the selection for the mask using a selection tool.

5. Choose **Layer>Add Layer Mask** and either **Reveal Selection** or **Hide Selection**. Only the selection will be hidden or shown, and this selection can be edited independently of the other parts of the image.

To work with layer masks that have been created:

6. Select the layer in the Layers palette that contains the mask you wish to edit. Click once on the layer mask thumbnail to make it active.

7. Select an editing or painting tool.

8. Paint with white to subtract from the image, black to add to it, and gray to partially hide the layer. You can switch to using the foreground and background colors in the toolbox and revert to the original black and white there too.

9. When complete, you can either apply or discard the mask by holding down the Shift key and clicking once on the mask in the Layers palette. A red X indicates that the mask is discarded.

Using layer masks allows you to separate and control specific parts of an image by producing a stencil of a selection. This stencil can be altered but the area around it is protected from change. These selections can then be saved for later use by saving the mask in an alpha channel. This is briefly detailed next.

A Little about Alpha Channels

You can save a selection as an alpha channel mask. Saving the selection as a mask will allow you to keep your work for later use. Alpha channels are storage areas for data, like selections. When selections are saved as a mask, this channel is created automatically; to save a selection manually, open the Channels palette and click on the save selection as channel icon.

You can open the Channels palette using Window>Channels. With the selection active in the image, click the save selection as channel icon. A new channel appears called Alpha 1, which can be renamed. These alpha channels can be deleted, added, and edited using the painting and editing tools, and opacity and other mask options can be set. Alpha channels can be converted to spot color channels for spot color separations.

Once the mask has been saved as a channel, you can paint with white to erase part of the mask, black to add to the mask, or gray to apply opacity to the mask. There is more on alpha channels in the next chapter, "Spot Color Separations."

Summary

In this chapter you learned a little about paths and how to draw curves as well as straight lines. To create paths, you used the Pen tools. You learned to fill and stroke paths and how to save them for later use. You learned that paths can be useful for tracing around objects that would be harder to deal with using other tools, and the paths can be saved as selections for various other applications and purposes.

Vector masks and layer masks were also introduced. These can be used to control what parts of a layer will be hidden or revealed. The masks can have special effects applied or they can be inverted for more effect and usefulness. Paths, layer masks, and vector masks are a quite powerful and complex feature of Photoshop. This chapter introduced only the basics, but with this knowledge you are well on your way to uncovering the magnificent power of these tools.

Part V
Color
Separations

Chapter 22

Spot Color Separations

Of all of the types of color separations that you can perform in Photoshop, spot color separations are the easiest. You'll use spot color separations when there are only a few colors in the artwork, and they are distinct. Spot color artwork usually contains 12 or fewer distinct colors. The fewer the better though, since each color must be chosen and separated manually.

Spot color separations where the colors fade into one another or have highlights or shading must be printed with halftones output by a PostScript printer. *True* spot color images can be printed using an inkjet or laser printer and film or vellum without halftones. True spot color images are those whose colors are few and distinct and do not fade into one another or have highlights. If you print T-shirts using a four- or six-station press to print true spot color, remember that you can print only as many colors as you have stations on the press.

Besides allowing you to color separate different types of spot color images, Photoshop also makes it easy to *create* spot color artwork, thus allowing you more options when creating artwork for clients. Creating your own artwork for clients can be both profitable and rewarding and can help you expand your business by allowing you the ability to offer art services.

Building Your Own Design

Photoshop makes it easy to create your own design from hand-drawn line art. If you have line art that you've drawn or artwork that a client has drawn, you can scan an image as line art at 600 dpi and fill the areas of the image with the color. As detailed in previous chapters, the Paint Bucket can be used to fill any area with color, brushes can be used to add highlights, and the Magic Wand can be used to select areas in the scanned line art quickly for other editing tasks.

✖ Caution!

You can't fill a bitmap image with color using the Paint Bucket, so you'll have to convert it to RGB first. Use Image>Mode>Grayscale and Image>Mode>RGB to convert.

You can also use Photoshop to open or scan a client's colored spot color images and separate them in-house. Often, a client will bring in a floppy disk with a logo or design on it and want you to print it on a shirt. Photoshop allows you to work with these types of files too. Finally, you can use clip art and text to create designs.

True spot color designs are ideal for local sports teams, staff shirts, family reunions, school choirs and bands, police and fire departments, and any other group or organization looking for a fast, inexpensive, and effective design stating who they are. Figure 22-1 shows some examples.

Figure 22-1: True spot color designs

 Tip:

Practice creating spot color designs in Photoshop; my clients are always amazed when I import some clip art, add some text, and say "Do you like this?" They almost always do.

Prepare Photoshop

Before performing any kind of color separations, make sure your monitor, printers, and scanners are calibrated, along with any other equipment that offers calibration options. Also, check the Edit>Color Settings to verify that the settings there are appropriate for the ink, mesh, dot gain, color working space, and other options. These were covered in Chapter 5. Figure 22-2 shows the settings that I configured regarding my shop, ink, and equipment; yours might be different. If in doubt, return to Chapter 5 and work through the projects.

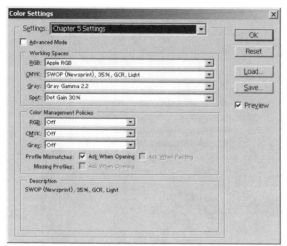

Figure 22-2: The Color Settings dialog box

Note:

Depending on your system, you might configure your color settings to include an Apple RGB working space, a specific ink brand, specific settings for manual and automatic presses, and dot gain of 35 percent for CMYK and 30 percent for spot color.

Prepare the Image

You'll get images in many forms, some of which were discussed in Chapters 13, 14, and 15. Images that you'll get from clients can be from digital cameras, floppy disks, or CDs, or they can be on hard copy and need to be scanned. The following offers a brief compendium of the information covered in those chapters but is by no means a complete account:

- If you have to scan a colored, spot color image, scan it at 225 to 250 dpi or greater.
- If scanning black and white line art, scan at 600 dpi.
- Scan the image at 100 percent, unless you need it to be larger than the image given to you, in which case you should upsample it on the scanner by choosing 150 percent or so.
- Turn off anti-aliasing if the file size is too large.

- Always scan as RGB mode.

- If prompted about an Embedded Profile Mismatch when opening a file, choose Convert Document's Color to the Working Space and click OK.

- If the file is a Corel or Illustrator file, export it as 225 dpi with anti-aliasing turned off.

With the image now showing on the screen, save the image. If this were a photograph, you'd most likely need to perform some additional adjustments. With spot colors though, there isn't much to do. You can delete areas of the image if they aren't needed using the Clone Stamp tool to paint over the unwanted part with the color of the background, or you can erase backgrounds that you don't want using the Magic Eraser. You can also select areas using the Magic Wand to perform edits as well.

Figure 22-3 shows two images. The image on the left is from a client who wants this design printed on a green shirt. The background in the picture is green. The background isn't needed in the actual print and needs to be removed. Clicking once on the background with the Magic Eraser tool removes the background.

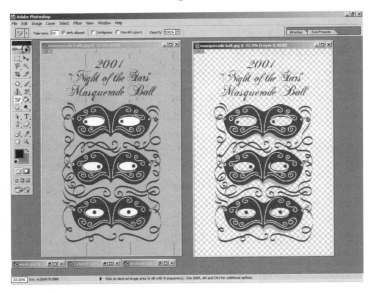

Figure 22-3: Preparing an image

✎ **Note:**

Once the image is complete and ready for printing, save the image.

About Pantone Colors

When you perform a spot color separation, you can match the colors in the image with the closest Pantone color. Pantone colors are industry standard colors that are represented by names and numbers. Clients will occasionally give you a specific Pantone color number to use, and you can purchase inks based on specific Pantone colors.

The Pantone Matching System (PMS) is an ideal way to ensure true colors when you print. Pantone colors include Pantone Yellow, Pantone Red, Pantone Purple, etc., and various shades in between with names like PMS251 and PMS262. Keep in mind that the color of the shirt or substrate can have an effect on the final color once the ink has set, so always perform test prints if perfect color is an important issue.

Alpha Channels

When performing spot color separations, you'll work with RGB channels and alpha channels. Channels and alpha channels are represented in the Channels palette, which is shown in Figure 22-4.

In Figure 22-4, the composite channel (the first channel) and each of the three channels for Red, Green, and Blue are selected. The RGB channels are in grayscale and created automatically when a file is opened. You will create additional channels called alpha channels to specify the plates for printing spot color images.

Figure 22-4: The Channels palette

Getting to Know the Channels Palette

To familiarize yourself with the Channels palette, open any RGB file and then open the Channels palette using Window>Channels. Familiarize yourself with the Channels palette by doing the following:

■ If the channel in the Channels palette is blue (as are the channels shown in Figure 22-4), the channel is active. By default, all channels are selected. You can select a single channel by clicking on it in the palette. To select all of the channels again, select the composite channel (the topmost channel).

■ When adjustments are made to an active channel, the adjustments are applied only to that channel. For instance, if you select only the Red channel and use Image>Adjustments>Curves to adjust the image, the changes are only applied to that channel. Figure 22-5 shows the Channels palette with only the Red channel active and the Curves dialog box with the Red channel listed at the top.

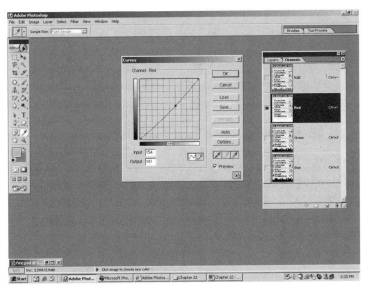

Figure 22-5: Selecting channels

- Remove the eye icons from channels to remove them from view.

- When printing separations, use the eye icon in the alpha channels that you'll create to tell Photoshop which channels to print. There are no alpha channels in Figure 22-5.

- Change how you preview the channels from the additional options in the Channels palette. In Figures 22-4 and 22-5, I've chosen the largest options.

That's it! Let's get busy color separating.

Performing Spot Color Separations

There are several ways to color separate a two- or three-color spot color image like the ones shown earlier in Figure 22-1. However, most images aren't just two or three colors, and recreating the image or performing color separations by hiding colors or using other tricks is not very efficient! There is a specific way to perform spot color separations in Photoshop that will work for all spot color images; this is the task at hand. In Project 22-1, we work with a simple, two-color separation and learn the basics. This process can be used to perform spot color separations on images with more colors simply by repeating the steps listed here.

Project 22-1: Performing a Spot Color Separation

To perform a basic, two-color spot separation, follow these steps:

1. Open the file **Fire.psd** from the Chapter 22 folder on the companion CD.

2. Open the Channels palette using **Window>Channels**.

3. Choose **Select>Color Range**. In the Color Range dialog box, make sure the Select window is set to **Sampled Colors**, Invert is checked, and Selection Preview is **None**. Let's use the Eyedropper tool, also selected in this dialog box. See Figure 22-6.

Figure 22-6: The Color Range dialog box settings

4. Use the cursor (an Eyedropper) to click on the red part of the image.

5. Adjust the Fuzziness slider to pull the amount of color you want. Because the image is only red and black, you can move the slider most of the way to the right. You want to select all of the red, but you don't want the edges to be too hard (170 or so is a good value for this image). Click **OK**.

6. The red part of the image has been selected. You can see the marching ants around the red in the image. In the bottom of the Channels palette, click the save selection as channel icon; it is a square icon with a circle inside it. A new alpha channel will be created (from the selection), as shown in Figure 22-7.

Figure 22-7: Saving a selection as an alpha channel

7. Hold down the **Ctrl** key on a PC or the **Cmd** key on a Mac and double-click on the new alpha channel. The Channel Options dialog box appears. (The red in this dialog box has nothing to do with the red in the image; it's just a default color for the channel.)

8. As shown in Figure 22-8, select **Spot Color** and change the solidity to **100** percent. (Do not press OK just yet!)

Note:

Solidity values can be between 0 and 100 percent. This option lets you simulate on your computer monitor how solid the printed color will be. Zero percent is used for transparent inks, while 100 percent is used for more solid inks. These settings only affect the on-screen image and do *not* have anything to do with the printed separation.

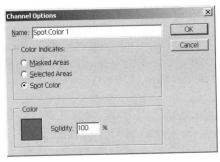

Figure 22-8: The Channel Options dialog box

9. Click on the color square in the Channel Options dialog box to bring up the Color Picker.

10. Use the Eyedropper to click on the foreground color in the toolbox, which is also the color of the red you selected in the image.

11. If you need to match this color with the nearest Pantone color, click **Custom** and choose a Pantone color from the list. The nearest match is selected. Click **OK**. Notice that the name of the channel is changed to the name of this Pantone color.

12. Click **OK** in the Channel Options dialog box.

13. Select the new spot color channel in the Channels dialog box. From the Select menu, choose **Deselect** (or use Ctrl+D).

Note:

Double-click on the alpha channel, now called Spot Color 1, or the name of the Pantone color you selected and rename it to Red Spot Color (if desired). This will help you keep track of what channel is what color.

14. In the Channels palette, select the composite channel. Choose **Select>Color Range.** In the Color Range dialog box make sure the Select window is set to **Sampled Colors**, Invert is checked, and Selection Preview is **None.**

15. Use the cursor (Eyedropper) to click on a black part of the image.

16. Adjust the Fuzziness slider to pull the amount of color you want. Because the image is only red and black, you can move the slider almost all the way to the right (130 is a good number here). Don't slide it so far that the image loses its clarity or pulls too much from the image, but pull it far enough to get all of the black. Click **OK.**

17. The black part of the image has been selected. In the bottom of the Channels palette, click the save selection as channel icon. It is a square icon with a circle inside it.

 Note:

The next few steps differ from the previous steps for working with the red channel to show you another way of working in the Channels palette.

18. Select the channel in the Channels palette, and choose **Select>Deselect** (Ctrl+D). Notice that the spot color is black by default, and the foreground color in the toolbox is black as well. This is because we did not perform the same series of steps as we did earlier (notably, holding down the Ctrl key or the Cmd key when double-clicking on the channel). (Had we performed these steps when working with the red channel, the foreground color would have been black, not red.)

19. Double-click the **Alpha** channel (named Alpha 1) to bring up the Channel Options dialog box shown in Figure 22-8.

20. Select **Spot Color**, and change Solidity to **100** percent. Click on the color square in this dialog box to bring up the Color Picker. Choose black.

21. If you need to match this color with the nearest Pantone color, click **Custom** and choose a Pantone color from the list. Choose **Pantone Black**. Click **OK**. Notice that the name of the channel is changed to the name of this Pantone color.

22. Click **OK** in the Channel Options dialog box. (Rename the channel if desired.)

23. In the Channels palette, use the eye icons to view only the two new alpha channels. Remove the eye icons from the other channels. These are the two channels that you'll use to print out your spot color separations. By creating the red as red in the Channels palette and the black as black, you can see what the image looks like with either selected.

Steps 3 to 13 show one way to separate a spot color from the rest of the image, and steps 14 to 22 show another. Both provide the same result but offer different ways to perform the task. In order to become competent with Photoshop, you should be aware of the different ways that a spot color separation can be achieved.

Project 22-2: Performing a Spot Color Separation on a Five-Color Spot Color Image

The file that we use in this project is an actual file my company received from a client (she's given me permission to use it here). It has five colors (black, green, orange, red, and purple). These colors are distinct and separate, thus making it a perfect candidate for a spot color print. The font used here makes working with the text easy too; it's all jagged around the edges, giving us some wiggle-room with pixelation of the text. This file is similar to what you will receive in your shop and makes a perfect practice project. In this project, we color separate this artwork. We also learn how to clean up the channels using the Brush tool. As mentioned in the last chapter, you can paint with white in a channel to remove information and paint with black to add it.

1. Open the file **SADD Puzzle.jpg** from the Chapter 22 folder on the companion CD. (Clients love their JPEG files, and I receive this type of file often.)

2. Open the Channels palette if it isn't already opened.

3. Choose **Select>Color Range**. In the Color Range dialog box, make sure the Select window is set to **Sampled Colors,** Invert is checked, and Selection Preview is **None.**

4. Use the cursor (an Eyedropper) to click on a black part of the image.

5. Adjust the Fuzziness slider to pull the amount of color you want. A setting of 170 for this particular color collects all of the black text and the outline of the puzzle pieces without collecting any other colors. Click **OK.**

6. The black part of the image has been selected. In the bottom of the Channels palette, click the save selection as channel icon; it is a square icon with a circle inside it.

7. Hold down the **Ctrl** key on a PC or the **Cmd** key on a Mac and double-click on the new alpha channel. The Channel Options dialog box appears. (The red in this dialog box has nothing to do with the red in the image; it's just a default color for the channel.)

8. Select **Spot Color,** and change Solidity to **100** percent.

9. Click on the color square in the Channel Options dialog box to bring up the Color Picker.

10. Use the Eyedropper to click on the foreground color in the toolbox, which is also the color of the black you selected in the image.

11. If you need to match this color with the nearest Pantone color, click **Custom** and choose a Pantone color from the list. The nearest match is selected. Click **OK.** Notice the name of the channel is changed to the name of this Pantone color. (You can also choose a different color from the Color Picker if desired.)

12. Click **OK** in the Channel Options dialog box.

13. Select the new spot color channel in the Channels dialog box. From the Select menu, choose **Deselect** (or Ctrl+D). Figure 22-9 shows how your screen should look at this point.

Note:

If you do not assign a Pantone color to the channels as you create them, name the channels by their actual color. Default names such as Alpha Channel 1 or Spot Color Channel 2 are difficult to work with.

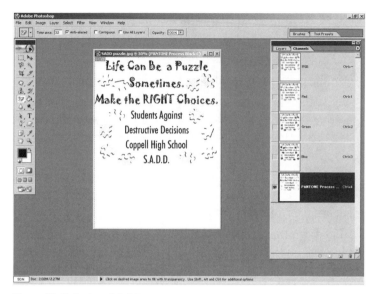

Figure 22-9: Project 22-2 in progress

14. In the Channels palette, select the composite channel (the others are selected automatically).

15. Repeat these steps to create a green spot color channel and then a purple spot color channel.

16. Select the composite channel in the Channels palette.

17. Create the orange channel by following steps 3 to 13. When creating this channel, use a Fuzziness value of 65 (instead of 170) in the Channel Options dialog box so that you do not pick the red puzzle pieces. Any number lower than 65 and you won't pick up all of the orange. (Don't forget to save the selection as a channel.)

18. Notice that after you view the channel, there are shadows of the red puzzle pieces in the channel. Select the **Brush** tool in the toolbox and change the foreground color to white. Brush over the shadows of the unwanted puzzle pieces. See Figure 22-10.

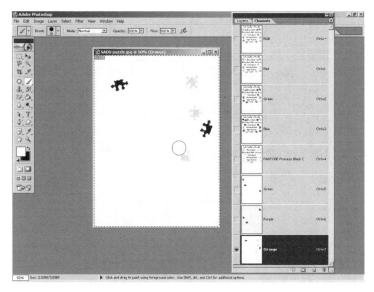

Figure 22-10: Removing unwanted color

19. You might also see that the black can be blacker. Configure the fore-ground color to black and use a small brush to fill in the puzzle pieces where they are not completely black.

 Tip:

The idea of course is to come to a happy medium where you get the channel per-fect the first time, but this isn't always possible. Your choices when tweaking a channel include performing steps 18 and 19 or deleting the channel and starting again.

20. Create the red channel by following steps 3 to 13. When creating this channel, use a Fuzziness value of 55 (instead of 170) in the Channel Options dialog box so that you do not pick the orange puzzle pieces. Any number lower than 55 and you won't pick up all of the red.

21. Notice that after you view the channel, there are shadows of the orange puzzle pieces in the channel. Select the **Brush** tool in the toolbox and change the foreground color to white. Brush over the shadows of the unwanted puzzle pieces. You can use this same tech-nique to complete or darken a puzzle piece as well. Change the fore-ground color to black and use the brush to fill in missing parts of any piece.

22. After the spot color channels have been created for the five colors in the image, deselect everything in the Channels palette except for the Black channel. This channel should be selected and have an eye icon by it. No other channels should be selected or have an eye icon showing.

23. Add the eye icon by the Green channel to show this layer. Add the eye icon by the Purple channel to show this layer.

24. Add the eye icon by the Red and Orange channels.

25. Save the image as a PSD file.

That's it! You've created spot color separations from client artwork in house.

Printing Spot Color Separations

In Part VI of this book, we learn all about printing, but printing spot color separations, such as the two in this chapter, isn't that difficult. These images are true spot color images, and they can be printed using an inkjet printer and vellum (or something similar). This is possible because none of the colors fade into one another, and no gradients are inherent to the image, so you don't need halftones or a PostScript printer. When colors are distinct and separate like the images here, you can create a simple, solid output and create screens easily using the printout. (This is how most shops get started and is the easiest way to get into screen printing.)

To print out a true spot color image like the ones in this chapter using an inkjet printer and vellum:

1. In the Channels palette, denote the pages to print with the eye icon. You only want to print the alpha channels that you created, not the original RGB channels. See Figure 22-11.

2. Choose **File>Print with Preview** to verify that the print will come out the right size. Choose **Scale to Print Media** if desired, or drag the image to the correct size.

Figure 22-11:
Preparing for printing

Caution!

If you increase the image size too much here, you get pixelation around the edges in the image. It's always best to work with and print the image using its actual size, rather than trying to upsample it at the printer.

3. Choose **Print** and select the printer.

4. Click the **Properties** button and configure the ink flow to be heavy and set other options. All of these options are covered in Part VI; this is just an introduction. (Make sure the appropriate paper is in the printer.)

5. Click **OK** and **OK** again. The separation pages will print.

We print out our spot color designs using vellum and on inkjet printers, but there are other options, as detailed in Part VI. You want to lay down the ink with inkjet printers if you're using vellum (or a similar paper) so that you get a solid print for burning the screens.

What If It's Not a "True Spot Color" Image?

If there are highlights, shading, or gradients in the image, you won't be able to use the print process outlined above. You will need to print the separations to a PostScript printer, and you'll need to tell Photoshop which halftone frequency and angle you need. You will also need to configure a dot shape and other information for the color channels that you're printing. This is much more complex than simply printing output to an inkjet printer and is detailed in Part VI of this book.

 Tip:

In addition to images that can be spot color separated, you can also combine spot colors with process colors when necessary.

Summary

In this chapter you learned how to perform color separations on spot color artwork using Photoshop 7.0. You learned first that creating your own spot color design in Photoshop is user friendly, allowing you to scan artwork or create your own from clip art and text. You can also color separate client's artwork that comes to you via e-mail or disk.

With the image in hand, preparing Photoshop is next. Calibrated equipment is a must, as is configuring the color settings to match your inks, equipment, dot gain, etc., to match your shop's setup. You learned about using Pantone colors too, which can be incorporated into the color separation procedure.

Finally, you experimented with two files and learned to color separate a two-color PSD image and a five-color JPEG. Color separating spot color artwork involves creating a selection and saving the selection as a channel. These channels are then selected and printed out as separated artwork.

Chapter 23

Process Color Separations

Process color separations are performed when you have a photorealistic image that needs to be printed on a shirt. Photorealistic images are generally created using actual pictures of things, such as animals, motorcycles, carnival rides (Ferris wheels, roller coasters), rock and roll bands, landscapes, seascapes, moonscapes, sunsets, and mountain scenes.

Color separating an image such as this is called a *process color separation*. Process color separations can only be printed with PostScript printers, so you have to make sure that you have one installed and running if you want to print them out!

Third-Party Color Separation Software

While Photoshop can be used to create superb process color separations, it is generally faster, better, and *much* more effective to perform separations using a color separation plug-in or program. These programs can be expensive though, and usually run about $1,000 (U.S.) for a single-user license. One popular color separation program is FastFilms ($995), produced by Scott Fresner of the U.S. Screen Printing Institute (www.fastfilms.com). If you have the money, I highly recommend it.

Before Starting This Chapter

Before starting this chapter, make sure you've adjusted and calibrated the monitor, the scanner, and any output device to obtain the best results. Verify that the settings configured in the Color Settings dialog boxes are set to match your equipment, inks, press, etc.

As a review, use SWOP (Newsprint) as the default in the Color Settings dialog box, or use the plug-in from your ink manufacturer that has the ink settings and other information preconfigured and select what they advise. Set dot gain to 35 percent for CMYK and 30 percent for spot colors. Verify that you are in Apple RGB working space.

For the separation options, choose GCR for the separation type and set the black ink limit to 85 percent, the total ink limit to 250 percent, and the UCA at 0. If there isn't too much black in the image, set the black generation settings to light. If there's a lot of black in the image, set it to medium. These separation options are set in the Color Settings dialog box by choosing Custom CMYK from the CMYK drop-down list. For more information on these settings, refer to Chapter 5 and the glossary.

Chapter Project Part I: Prepare the Image

There are two places to get a photograph, either from a client as a hard copy or from a personal collection of images. If the photograph comes directly from the client, it is scanned first. If the photograph is part of a stock photography suite that you've purchased or created using a digital camera, those files are already on the hard disk or in the photo library.

In this project, we take an image obtained from a client's digital camera, clean it up, create a border to finish it, and then color separate it. Color separating an image involves converting the RGB image to CMYK, tweaking the colors, and if necessary, adding a spot color channel.

Note:

Working through this process gives you a good feel for what you'll be doing in your own shop. While this chapter might take you an hour or two to complete, once you're familiar with the process, you will be able to perform the tasks detailed here in substantially less time—perhaps half an hour or 15 minutes.

Clean Up the Image

The client in this project has taken a picture of a plate that hangs on her wall. She's going to use the fish that is painted on the plate as a basis for a logo that she wants you to create for her new tropical fish shop. She gives you a copy of the picture on a disk and asks you to create the logo for her. Figure 23-1 shows the before shot (on the left) and what we do in this section to clean it up (on the right).

Figure 23-1: Cleaning up the image

 Note:

You may skip this part of the chapter project and move on to another section if you'd like. The finished files for each section are on the companion CD.

Cleaning up the image involves removing the background of the wall or painting over it, painting with a background color, and then enlarging the canvas.

1. Open the file **Fish Picture.jpg** from the Chapter 23 folder on the companion CD.

2. Choose **Image>Canvas Size**. Change the image size to 18 by 25 inches.

3. Select the **Eyedropper** tool and select the green color of the plate, just behind the fish's back fins.

4. Select the **Paint Bucket** tool, and in the options bar change the Mode to **Normal**, Opacity to **100** percent, and Tolerance to **100**, and verify that Anti-aliased and Contiguous are checked.

5. Click in the newly added part of the canvas, outside the wall area.

6. Select the **Brush** tool from the toolbox.

7. Select the **Hard Round Brush #19** from the Brush palette in the options bar.

8. Paint with this brush around the outside of the fish. Change the brush and brush size as needed to cover over the flaws in the green part of the image.

9. Save the image as **Fish.psd** (a Photoshop PSD file).

Text and Borders

You can add text and borders to finish the logo; however, we save the section on type for later. There are different ways to work with type in a Photoshop image, and it deserves its own section. In this section, let's just add a border.

 Note:

If you want to skip this part of the exercise, the completed file is Fish3.psd on the Chapter 23 folder on the companion CD.

1. Open the file **Fish.psd** from the Chapter 23 folder of the companion CD, or use the file you created in the last exercise. Use the Zoom tools to zoom in or out on the image.

2. Use the **Crop** tool to crop the image so that it forms a more proportional, rectangular shape. Leave enough room for a border. (If

desired, use **Image>Image Size** to increase or decrease the size of the image.) Save the image to the hard drive as **Fish.psd**.

Figure 23-2: The Fish.psd file

3. Choose the **Brush** tool from the toolbox.

4. Set Mode to **Dissolve** and Opacity and Flow to **100** percent. Select the **Airbrush** option.

5. Change the foreground color in the toolbox to white.

6. Open the Brushes palette from the arrow in the options bar. From the additional options, choose **Faux Finish Brushes** and click **OK**.

7. Choose **Sea Sponge 2** and brush number **90**.

8. Paint around the image using this tool. See Figure 23-3. I've added some additional touches with the Grass Brush tool at the bottom of the image. The Grass Brush is available if you choose Reset Brushes from the additional options.

9. Crop the image again if desired and save the image as **Fish2.psd**. (You can see my Fish2.psd in Figure 23-3.)

When you are preparing an image for screen printing, you generally have to perform manual and automatic color adjustments too. These include using Filter>Sharpen>Unsharp Mask to sharpen the image and Image>Adjustments>Hue/Saturation to saturate the image. There are other things too; if you've been skipping around in this book, return to Chapter 16 for other image preparation tasks. Use your knowledge in this area to further prepare the image before moving on. After applying Unsharp Mask and increasing the saturation, resave the file as Fish3.psd.

Figure 23-3 shows Fish2.psd on the left and Fish3.psd on the right. Fish3.psd has had unsharp masking and saturation increases.

Figure 23-3: Preparing the image

 Tip:

This particular image needs lots of unsharp masking and saturation.

Chapter Project Part II: Perform the Separation

Once the image has been readied for print, you can perform the actual separation. The first step in performing a color separation is to change the mode of the image from RGB to CMYK:

1. Open the file **Fish3.psd** from the Chapter 23 folder of the companion CD, or use the file you've created in previous sections.

2. Choose **Image>Mode>CMYK Color.** You'll be prompted to merge the layers *if* you have more than one layer. If this happens, click **Merge**.

3. Open the Channels palette from **Window>Channels.** Now there are four channels of CMYK and a composite channel. See Figure 23-4.

4. Save the file as **Fish4.psd**.

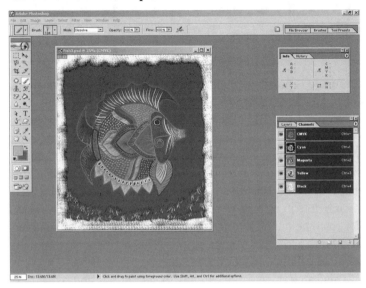

Figure 23-4: Viewing the separations

 Tip:

If your computer has noticeably slowed down, choose Edit>Purge>All to remove information from RAM.

Channels were discussed fully in Chapter 22. If you need to review channels, refer to that chapter. Briefly, channels are the separations of colors C, M, Y, and K. You can change the size of the thumbnails in the channels from the additional options in the Channels palette; showing larger channels is generally better if you only have a few channels. If there's an eye on the channel, the channel is visible on the screen. If the eye icon is removed, it isn't showing. If the channel in the Channels palette is blue (like each channel in Figure 23-4), it is selected. When a channel is selected, you can adjust that channel. To work with a single channel, select only that channel. Viewing the channel and selecting the channel are two different things; this is exactly how the Layers palette works as well.

Chapter Project Part III: Correct Color

Your image is now color separated. Performing this separation is as easy as changing from RGB to CMYK. However, correcting the colors after converting to CMYK is the biggest part of creating a good, usable process color separation. There are several problems that can occur while screen printing using a color separation performed by Photoshop; a big issue is that Photoshop tends to add a little more cyan than you usually need when it creates the separations. This is a problem because printing cyan ink dots in an area that's supposed to print yellow will cause the color to come out all wrong at press time. Even a small amount of cyan (taking into account dot gain, screen tension, mesh size, and ink types) can cause yellow to go green.

This same thing can happen with red. Red is created with CMYK inks by printing yellow and magenta together. If Photoshop adds a few dots of cyan—and those few dots (with dot gain) turn into a hundred dots—the red color you are expecting at press time will be purple after it's printed.

In addition to these types of problems, you might also need to increase the black in the image. This is useful if the image has a lot of black outlines in it, or if it consists of a lot of sharp edges. After looking at the design after the separation, you might also decide to add a spot color channel to it too. Adding a spot color channel allows you to get the pure red, pure yellow, pure black, etc., while at the press.

So, how do you go about correcting these issues? Well, it's trial and error and lots of practice and patience. It's also experimenting with your equipment and inks to get to know them and know what to expect. In the next few sections we learn where to start to access the tools to correct these issues, how to use them, and what the common tasks are.

✖ Caution!

Throughout this project we perform a color separation that is intended for printing on a white shirt. Creating separations for other colors requires additional techniques, as detailed in Chapter 25.

Working with Colors

There are several ways that you can "clean up" the colors in your images before printing out the color separations. You use two main palettes—the Channels palette and the Info palette—and you use two main tools—the Curves tool and the Selective Color tool. Both of these are available from the Image>Adjustments menu choices. Before continuing then, configure your work area to contain the Channels and Info palettes.

 Tip:

If you worked through Chapter 5, you created a workspace named Screen Printer-based. This is available from the Window>Workspace menu and contains everything that you need.

Use the Curves Tool and the Info Palette to Clean Up an Image

Let's experiment with checking and changing the colors in this image using the Curves tool and the Info palette.

1. Open the **Fish4.psd** file that you created in the last section or have obtained from the Chapter 23 folder of the companion CD.

2. Position the Info palette near the image. Click on the **Eyedropper** tool in the toolbox. *Verify that all channels are selected in the Channels palette.*

3. Use the Eyedropper to check the white in the thickest part of the border and see if it's really white; all of the numbers in the Info palette should read 0 percent for the CMYK percentages.

4. Using the Eyedropper, hover over the center of the fish's eye where it is black. Notice the percentages in the Info palette. Mixing the four colors of ink will create the black. (If you wanted to, you could create a black spot color channel.)

5. Using the Eyedropper and watching the numbers in the Info palette, move the Eyedropper over an area of yellow in the image. Choose an area in the fish's bottom fin around the black dots in that area. Look at the numbers in the Info palette and notice how the yellow has some cyan in it. Because Photoshop exaggerates cyans when

creating a separation, you should lower those numbers a bit. In a pure yellow, you should theoretically remove all the cyan.

6. Choose **Image>Adjustments>Curves**. Choose **Cyan** in the Channel drop-down list. The changes you make now will only affect the Cyan channel. Because the other channels are visible in the Channels palette though, you can see the effect of your actions on the entire image.

7. In the Curves dialog box in the bottom left of the grid, pull down the highlights a little, as shown in Figure 23-5. This will reduce the cyan in the image.

8. Use the Info palette to see if you've removed the cyan and gotten the percentages down to 0 percent for (most of) the yellow part of the image. Use the Info palette to look at the before and after numbers for the cyan in the yellow. See Figure 23-5.

✖ **Caution!**

View the composite to see what's happening to the entire image. See Figure 23-5. Although the numbers never lie, reducing the cyan too much can result in a washed-out image. You'll have to use your own judgment.

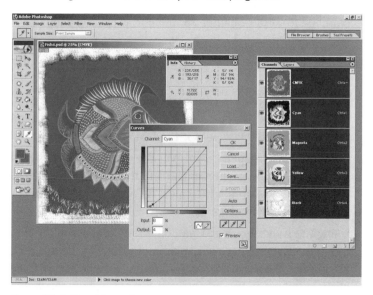

Figure 23-5: Tweaking colors

9. When you've reduced the cyan and verified that the image still looks as it should, click **OK** in the Curves palette. Resave the image as **Fish5.psd**.

You can perform the same operations on the magenta, yellow, and black channels if you feel it's necessary. You'll have to experiment, print, and experiment some more before you really understand the limits of your inks, screens, equipment, and, yes, even Photoshop.

 Tip:

The file Fish4 With Color Adjustment.psd on the companion CD is an example of what your new file with color adjustments might look like.

Use the Selective Color Tool and the Info Palette to Clean Up an Image

You can also use the Selective Color tool to work with specific colors in an image. The Selective Color tool allows you to work with specific colors—red, yellow, green, cyan, blue, magenta, white, neutral, and black.

Let's experiment with checking and changing the colors in this image using the Selective Color tool and the Info palette.

1. Open the file **Fish4.psd** from the companion CD, or use the file you created in the last exercise.

2. Choose **Image>Adjustments>Selective Color**. The Selective Color dialog box appears, as shown in Figure 23-6.

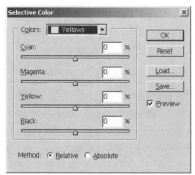

Figure 23-6: The Selective Color
dialog box

3. Choose **Yellows** in the Colors drop-down list.

4. Since yellow shouldn't have any extra cyan in it, move the slider to reduce the cyan in the image. Use the Eyedropper and the Info palette to see the before and after values for Cyan. You can remove virtually all cyan from the yellows in the image. Check and uncheck the Preview box to see the difference. Try not to go overboard; reducing too much cyan can substantially change the look of the image.

5. While still on the yellows, increase the magenta and yellow sliders. Use the Info palette to see the change in the values.

6. Choose **Reds** in the Colors drop-down list. Position the Eyedropper on the fish's lips. Red is made from magenta and yellow. Move the sliders to remove the cyan, and boost magenta and yellow.

7. With the Eyedropper positioned over the fish's lips, view the changes for cyan and other colors using the Info palette. The Info palette should read 0 percent for Cyan in the fish's lips. Use the Preview check box to see the before and after.

8. Choose **Magentas** in the Colors drop-down list. Position the Eyedropper over the fish's eye, where the eyebrow is (supposedly) pure magenta. Notice there is a bit of cyan in there.

9. Use the sliders to reduce the cyan and up the magenta and you get a purer color. Check and uncheck the Preview check box to see the changes. Use your best judgment as to when "enough is enough."

10. Choose other colors in the Selective Color dialog box and view their numbers. You'll learn a lot about how colors are created using the Eyedropper and the Info palette. For instance, green is made from yellow and cyan; thus, when hovering over a green in the image, you'll see higher numbers for these two components.

11. When finished, click **OK**. Save the file again as **Fish5.psd**.

The Selective Color command is a powerful part of Photoshop and allows you to work and adjust colors independently of one another. Understanding what colors are created from what combination of CMYK will help you use this tool more effectively. For practice, open a colorful image and use the Selective Color command, the Eyedropper, and the Info palette to note how specific colors are created.

Chapter Project Part IV: Additional Techniques

When creating process color separations, there are a few other things that you can do besides the actual separation and color correction. Often, a spot color channel is added, especially if you want to bring out a color or there is a lot of a specific color in an image.

Create a Spot Color Channel

If you want or need to, you can create a spot color channel for any process color-separated image. Creating a spot color channel is done the same way as was detailed in Chapter 22. To create a spot color for the image that we're working with in this chapter:

1. Open **Fish4.psd** or **Fish4 With Color Adjustments.psd** from the companion CD, or use the **Fish5.psd** file that you created in this chapter.

2. Choose **Select>Color Range**.

3. Check the **Invert** check box and verify that Selection is checked and **None** is showing in Selection Preview.

4. In the Select window, choose **Sampled Colors**.

5. Use the Eyedropper to click on the fish's red lips in the image. Let's make a spot color channel for the red in this image. See Figure 23-7.

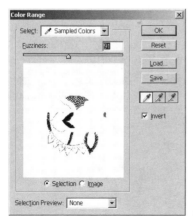

Figure 23-7: Creating a spot color

6. Use the Fuzziness slider to select the red, as shown in Figure 23-7. Click **OK**.

7. At the bottom of the Channels palette, click the save selection as channel icon.

8. Click on the new channel in the Channels palette.

9. Choose **Select>Deselect**. (You might have to clean up the channel some, as detailed in Chapter 22.)

10. Double-click in the **New Alpha** channel to open the Channel Options dialog box.

11. Select the **Spot Color** radio button in the Channel Options dialog box. Change the name to **Red Spot Color** in the Name window, and change Solidity to **30** percent.

12. Click on the color window and choose a red from the Color Picker that matches the red in the image. Click **OK** twice.

13. In the Channels palette, click on the composite channel so that you can see the entire image. All of the channels should have an eye by them, except for the new spot color. Notice how red the reds are in the image.

14. Click in the **Channels** palette to view the red spot color along with these. Click the eye icon to remove it. Notice the difference. When screen printed, this red will show up much better and be more robust.

15. Save the file as **Fish6.psd**.

Color separations like the one we've done in this chapter are for white shirts. Note that the fish images have white in them. The white in the shirt will create the white in the image. If you are going to print this on another color of shirt, you will need to create a white plate (which is like a spot color for the white in the image) so that the white you want will actually be white on the shirt. Chapter 25 introduces you to creating color separations for darker shirts, but for light shirts like off-white, neutral, light tan, gray, etc., the following should work fine.

To create a white plate (also called a negative white plate or white printer):

1. Using the **Fish6.psd** file, duplicate the file using **Image>Duplicate**. Click **OK** to accept the default name.

2. Select the **Magic Wand** from the toolbox. Change Tolerance to **15** and leave Contiguous and Anti-aliased checked.

3. Change the background color in the toolbox to black.

4. To create a mask around the image, click on a white area around the outside of the file to select it.

5. Use the Magic Wand to delete any additional white areas around the edges of the file.

6. Choose **Select>Deselect**. You've created a mask around the image.

7. Choose **Select>Color Range**.

8. Use the Eyedropper to select a white part of the fish. The best area is around the gills and face area.

9. Move the Fuzziness slider so that you pick up the white that you want, without picking up so much that you'll fade out the image. Click **OK**.

10. Click the save selection as channel icon at the bottom of the Channels palette.

11. Choose **Select>Deselect**.

12. Click once on the new channel, and rename it **White**. Change Solidity to **30** percent.

13. Select the **Spot Color** radio button.

14. Use the color square to choose white for the color. Click **OK**.

15. Drag this new white channel to the first version of the file, and drop it there.

16. Close the duplicate file without saving.

17. Place eye icons next to all of the channels in the original file to see the result. Save the file as **Fish7.psd**.

If the file doesn't look as it should, continue on to the next section. There, you can configure the channels in the order that they'll be printed on the press.

View the Final Separation

If you are printing on a light-colored shirt instead of a white shirt, you can simulate the shirt color while viewing the final separation to see how it might look once it's printed. You can also change the order of the channels to help you stack the channels the way you'll print them on the press. These things can't be done in CMYK mode though; you'll have to convert to Multichannel mode.

Caution!

Before changing to Multichannel mode, make sure you're finished with the composite channel. Once it's converted, there will no longer be a composite channel available, and you won't be able to create any more spot colors or white plates.

To convert to Multichannel mode, change the order of the channels, and simulate a T-shirt color:

1. Open the file **Fish6.psd** or **Fish7.psd** that you created in the last section, or open the file from the companion CD.

2. Choose **Image>Mode>Multichannel**. Notice that the composite channel is gone.

3. Notice the file doesn't look as it should.

Tip:

Your file might not look so great your first time through these exercises. Learning to create the right mix of colors takes time. Additionally, monitor calibration, the output device you are using, inks, screens, and other items can interfere with a good output.

4. Rearrange the channels. If you've created a white plate, drag that plate to the top of the list.

5. Place the yellow second, then magenta, then the spot color, then cyan, and then black. You are now previewing in correct print order.

6. In the Channels palette, click the additional options arrow and choose **New Channel**. This new channel will represent the T-shirt color.

7. Name the new channel **Shirt Color.**

8. Click on the color box to bring up the Color Picker. Choose a light shirt color from the Color Picker dialog box.

9. Click **OK** twice.

10. In the Channels palette, drag this new channel to the top of the channel list.

11. Show the eyes in the Channels palette to see all of the channels. By removing the eye icon from the shirt color channel, you can see what happens to the colors in the image.

12. Save your new image.

This ends the introduction to process color separations. The steps are basically the same for any image that you might have, although the actual values and amount of tweaking you do will differ.

 Note:

The image chosen for this chapter was selected for its range of colors, not for its ability to be screen printed easily. Screen printing process color separations takes testing, practice, and familiarity with your equipment and inks. The image might look off when viewed on your monitor or when printed using your equipment.

Working with Vector Type Layers

About the image we've been working with in this chapter—you might have noticed that there isn't any type added. That's because there are two different ways to work with type, and the subject deserves its own section. Type can blend in with the image on a process color print and have type effects applied, such as a drop shadow and gradients, or type can stand on its own away from the image and look and act like a spot color. Type that blends in with the image in a process color print is printed as halftones; type that does not blend and stands on its own can be printed as a vector type layer. Vector type layers are the optimal choice when possible, because they are printed as vector data and are thus much cleaner, less pixelated, and a whole lot easier to screen print than rasterized data.

If you are working with a piece of artwork in which the text blends with the image, just work with the text as you would with any other process color image. You don't have to do anything special. If, however, your type stands alone, as it will in this section, you can configure it so that it prints as vector text.

Add the Type

Let's add some type to the Fish2.psd file and work through the basic separation process again.

1. Open the **Fish2.psd** file from the companion CD.

2. Use **Image>Image Size** to change the size of the image to 504 pixels by 554 pixels. Click **OK**.

3. Use the **Zoom** tool to fit the image on the screen.

4. Choose the **Type** tool from the toolbox.

5. Type in white text, as shown in Figure 23-8. Keep the text separate from the other elements in the image.

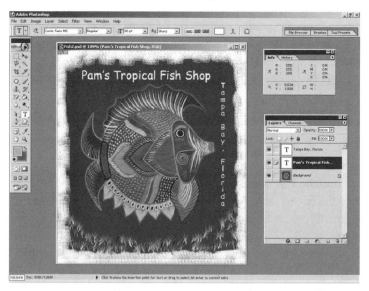

Figure 23-8: Adding type

 Note:

Don't worry that the text looks like it's pixelated here; it'll print out just fine.

Convert to CMYK and Test the Output

Since this job is a process color job, it needs to be converted to CMYK. After adding the type to the RGB mode image:

6. Click on the background layer (only) in the Layers palette and choose **Image>Mode>CMYK Color.**

7. In the dialog box that asks you to flatten the image, choose **Don't Flatten.** You do not want to flatten the type layers; if you do, you won't be able to print them as vector data.

8. Test your printer to make sure that it's set up to print vector-based data. It needs to be a PostScript printer and have the appropriate drivers installed. Choose **File>Print with Preview.**

9. The Print dialog box will appear. Make sure Show More Options is checked and then check **Include Vector Data.** This will allow you to print the vector type layer as vector text. See Figure 23-9.

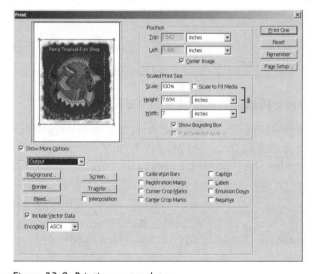

Figure 23-9: Printing vector data

10. If the Include Vector Data option is grayed out, work through the steps in the following sidebar.

Include Vector Data is Grayed Out

If the Include Vector Data option is grayed out, perform the following steps:

1. Verify that steps 1 to 10 were performed correctly.
2. If you get the same result, place the Adobe Photoshop 7.0 CD into the CD-ROM drive and install the Adobe PostScript Driver 4.5 for 9X and 5.2 for NT/2000. (The latter also works on XP.)
3. When prompted, choose your printer from the list of printers. If it isn't listed, choose **Generic PostScript Printer.**
4. When prompted, print a test page and set the generic printer or the printer you chose from the list as the default. Close the installation window once it has completed.
5. Choose **File>Print with Preview** from inside Photoshop. (This step corresponds with step 8 in the example.)
6. In the Print dialog box, choose **Page Setup.**
7. In the Page Setup dialog box, choose **Printer.**
8. Choose the new printer you added. (It should be the default already, but it never hurts to double-check.)
9. Click **OK** twice.
10. Check **Include Vector Data.**

11. To print, click **Print.** To cancel, click **Cancel.**

This is the simplest way to create and print vector type data and layers using Photoshop and a PostScript printer. It gets a little more complicated if you involve the type with a spot color (alpha) channel.

 Note:

You can output the color separations and the file to another program like Adobe Illustrator, Freehand, or Quark and add text to it there if you prefer.

Include the Type in a Spot Color Channel

When using an alpha channel or spot color channel in a process color job, you can configure the type to print out with the spot channel. For instance, if you wanted the type in this image to be red, you can configure it to print out with the red spot color channel that you created earlier. This enables the type to be printed as a spot color, increasing its boldness and clarity while also allowing it to be printed as vector type.

1. Open the file **Fish with Red Spot Color.psd** from the companion CD. It is located in the Chapter 23 folder.

2. Open the Channels palette, and notice there is a red spot color channel already created. In the Layers palette, notice a type layer has been added.

3. Drag the Layers palette away from the Channels palette so that they are separate.

4. Configure the palettes as shown in Figure 23-10. The Background layer should not be selected nor should it have an eye showing. All of the channels should be showing in the Channels palette.

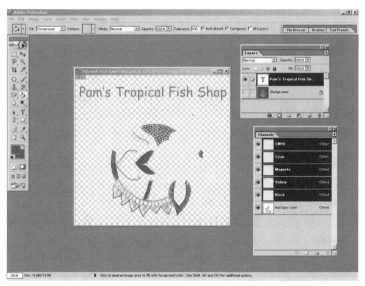

Figure 23-10: Working with spot colors and text

5. Select the type layer in the Layers palette. Using the **Type** tool, highlight the text and change the color of the text to black.

6. Double-click on the **Red Spot Color** channel.

7. In the Spot Channel Options dialog box, click on the color square.

8. Change the color to black. Click **OK** twice.

9. Choose **File>Print with Preview** to see the results.

Use vector type only when the type is separate from the design or image. Don't use vector type if your type has gradients, is part of the design itself, or requires process color to create. Vector type is for simple type.

Note:

To actually print the separation, refer to Chapter 29.

Getting More Help

For more help with creating process color separations and other Photoshop tasks, as well as how to actually screen print a color separation, visit www.screenprinters.net. There, you can access articles, read tips and tricks, and purchase DVDs on how to use Photoshop in a screen printing shop. You can also join e-lists, read screen printing news, join chats, and more.

Summary

In this chapter you were introduced to process color separations. You learned what is required of you and your system before starting a process color separation and how to prepare the image by cleaning it up and adding a border.

Once the print is ready, you learned to perform the separation and tweak the colors. Tweaking the colors is a major part of creating usable color separations and is required to keep color contamination at the press under control. Correcting color involves the Curves tool and the Selective Color tool, as well as the Info and Channels palettes.

With the color separation complete, you learned to create a spot color channel and a white channel. Finally, working with vector type layers was introduced as a way to print type as vector data. This reduces the amount of pixelation that you normally get when working with type in process color prints.

Chapter 24

Indexed Color Separations

So far, you've learned about creating "true" spot color separations, spot color separations with gradations, and process color separations for light-colored shirts. In this chapter we discuss how to perform indexed color separations.

Indexed color separations are best used when you need to print a color image on either a light- or dark-colored shirt and can be used for any type of image. If you're new to indexed color separations and printing though, you'll get better results if the image doesn't consist of too many distinct colors. With indexed color separations, you choose the main colors in the image, and Photoshop tries to recreate the image using only the colors that you select.

Indexed color is easier to screen print than process color because the dots are all the same size. This makes production tasks much easier (vs. printing halftones). The prints look good too; they're bright on all colors of shirts. The downside of printing indexed color is that it can look coarse, grainy, and/or cartoonish and might not look exactly like the original due to the mix of colors you choose. You can decide how you feel about indexed color prints after experimenting a while on your own equipment.

 Note:

Indexed color can use from 1 to 256 colors.

Indexed Color Explained

Indexed color separations are different from spot and process color separations in several ways. With process and spot color with gradations, the shading required of these prints is created using halftone dots that have a pattern and an angle (like an ellipse shape with an angle of 15 degrees, for instance). Index separations use randomly placed square dots, and all of the dots are the same size.

Indexed color separations also use only a limited amount of colors that you choose. Obviously, you'll want these to be the most important colors in the image. This is the reason that indexed color separations work better with limited color images; if you have to create a thousand colors, it's going to be difficult to do that if you only have a four-station press! (On the other hand, I've seen some pretty fantastic ten-color index prints at award shows, but I'm sure it takes quite a bit of practice!)

❌ **Caution!**

If scanning for an index print, scan at 175 to 200 dpi and at the final image size.

Choosing Your Colors

So how will you decide what colors to select? Well, that all depends on the print and how many stations you have on the press. Open the file Eagle.psd from the Programs\Adobe\Photoshop 7.0\Samples folder on your hard drive. It's shown in Figure 24-1. This image consists of many shades of colors, but you can easily see which four or five you'd choose. White, black, orange, and green are obviously the most prominent.

Figure 24-1: Eagle.psd

Now open the file PoolBalls.jpg from the Chapter 24 folder on the companion CD. It is shown in Figure 24-2. The colors to select here would include green, blue, white, purple, orange, black, red, and yellow. If you want to choose fewer colors though, you can let Photoshop try to mix the red and yellow to create the orange or mix the blue and red to create the purple. You'll want to take all of this into consideration before deciding on what colors to choose.

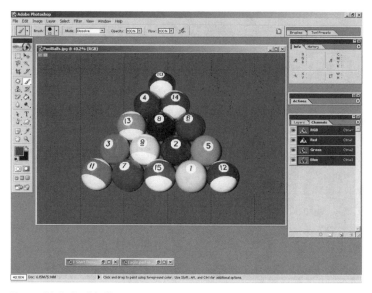

Figure 24-2: Pool balls

Zooming in on Indexing

As mentioned earlier, indexed color separations are printed using square dots, not halftones. Figure 24-3 shows a close-up of the PoolBalls.psd file after it's been indexed. You can see how the print is made up of randomly placed square dots. After zooming back out from this image, the dots are barely noticeable. However, it is these dots that will give the image a grainy look when printed on the shirt, and it is these dots that make printing the shirt at the press easier!

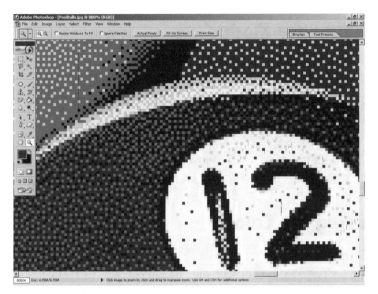

Figure 24-3: Square dots

With an image in mind and the number of colors calculated, you can begin the indexed color separation.

Chapter Project: Perform an Indexed Color Separation

In this project, we work through the steps to create an indexed color separation using the file PoolBalls.jpg. These are the same steps that you take when performing your own indexed color separations with any other image. In this example, we create six colors.

 Tip:

In order to perform indexed color separations, you have to start with an RGB file. RGB mode was discussed in Chapter 11.

Changing the Mode

This process involves several steps, the first of which is to open the file and change the mode.

1. Open the file **PoolBalls.jpg** from the Chapter 24 folder on the companion CD.

2. Open the Info and Channels palettes.

3. Select **Image>Mode** and choose **Indexed Color.** Move the Indexed Color dialog box out of the way so that you can clearly see the image.

Choosing the Colors

With the mode changed, it's time to pick the colors that you'll use.

4. Check **Preserve Exact Colors**, change Amount to **100** percent, and verify that Diffusion is selected.

5. In the Palette drop-down list, choose **Custom** as shown in Figure 24-4.

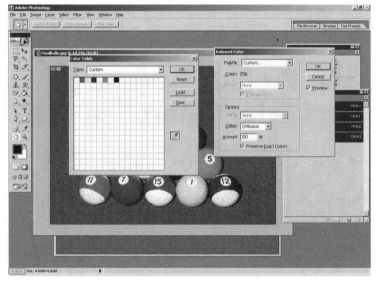

Figure 24-4: The Indexed Color dialog box

6. The Custom choice in the Palette drop-down list opens the Color Table.

7. The colors in the Color Table have nothing to do with the image. Click at the top-left corner of this table and drag down to the bottom right to select all of the boxes; from the Color Picker that comes up, choose white. You can choose white by clicking and dragging off of the top-left edge of the Color Picker window. Click **OK** in the Color Picker dialog box. Click **OK** in that box again. The Color Table is shown in Figure 24-5 with no color selected.

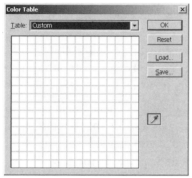

Figure 24-5: The Color Table

8. Position the Color Table so that you can see the image. Click in the first box (in the top-left corner of the Color Table window) to select it. The Color Picker window appears again.

9. Use the Eyedropper to select the yellow in the image. Click **OK** in Color Picker.

10. Click the second box in the Color Table to select it. The Color Picker window appears again.

11. Use the Eyedropper to select the royal blue in the image. Click **OK**.

12. Click the third box in the Color Table to select it. Use the Eyedropper to select the red in the image. Click **OK**.

13. Click the fourth box in the Color Table to select it. Use the Eyedropper to select the teal in the image. This is the background color in the image, the felt on the pool table. Click **OK**.

14. Click the fifth box in the Color Table to select it. Use the Eyedropper to select pure black in Color Picker. Picking up a color here will guarantee it's pure black. Click **OK**.

15. Click the sixth box in the Color Table to select it. Use the Eyedropper to select the pure white in the Color Picker. Picking up white here will guarantee it's pure white. Click **OK**.

16. Click **OK** in the Color Table and the Indexed Color windows.

Looking at the Image

Looking at the image after indexing won't give you the right idea of what it'll look like at press time.

17. The image won't look as you expect it to on the shirt. To see how the image will look on the shirt, choose **Image>Mode>RGB Color**. The pixels won't change, only how you view the image.

18. Select the **Zoom** tool from the toolbox and zoom in on the purple pool ball. Keep zooming until you can see that the purple (which we did not choose, by the way) has been created using blue, red, teal, and bits of white. Right-click and choose **Print Size**.

Creating Channels

Now you have to create channels for each of the colors you chose in the indexing part (steps 1 through 18) so that you can tell Photoshop to print them out. To do this:

19. Create a duplicate of the image using **Image>Duplicate**. Click **OK** to name the file **PoolBallsCopy**.

20. With the duplicate copy active, choose **Image>Image Size**. Uncheck **Resample Image**. Change the height and width to 2 by 3 or so inches. Click **OK**.

21. Position this image in the bottom corner of the workspace, as shown in Figure 24-6. You'll use the image to correctly identify the colors in the image later.

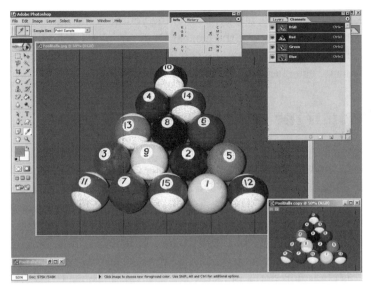

Figure 24-6: Setting up the work area

22. Click on the original file's title bar to make it active. Choose **Select Color Range**.

23. From the Color Range dialog box, use the Eyedropper to choose the yellow in the image. Move the Fuzziness slider so that you pick up the yellow in the yellow balls and some of the yellow you'll need in the orange. Since we're not picking orange as a channel or indexed color, some yellow will have to be included there. (Verify that Sampled Colors is chosen from the Select window, Invert is chosen, Selection is chosen, and Selection Preview is None. This holds true for the rest of this project.) Click **OK**.

24. In the Channels palette, click the save selection as channel icon.

25. In the Channels palette, click once to select the new channel.

26. Choose **Select>Deselect**.

27. Double-click on the new channel. From the Channel Options dialog box, select **Spot Color** and change the Solidity to **10** percent.

28. Click on the color square in the Channel Options dialog box.

29. Drag the Color Picker away from the duplicate file, and choose **Custom**.

30. Use the Eyedropper to click on the yellow in the duplicate image. Click **OK** to choose the closest Pantone color. Click **OK** again. (You might want to change the name of the channel by clicking on its name and changing the name to Yellow.)

Repeat for Each Channel and Color

You'll need to create a channel for each color.

31. In the Channels palette, click on the composite channel so that the image is showing in full color. Choose **Select Color Range**.

32. In the Color Range dialog box, use the Eyedropper to choose the royal blue in the image. Move the Fuzziness slider so that you pick up the blue in the blue balls, plus a little extra. Remember, the purple is created from the blue and the red. (Verify that Sampled Colors is chosen from the Select window, Invert is chosen, Selection is chosen, and Selection Preview is None. This holds true for the rest of this project.) Click **OK**.

33. In the Channels palette, click the save selection as channel icon.

34. In the Channels palette, click once to select the new channel.

35. Choose **Select>Deselect**.

36. Double-click on the new channel. From the Channel Options dialog box, select **Spot Color** and change the Solidity to **10** percent.

37. Click on the color square in the Channel Options dialog box.

38. Drag the Color Picker away from the duplicate file if necessary, and choose **Custom**.

39. Use the Eyedropper to click on the royal blue in the duplicate image. Click **OK** to choose the closest Pantone color. Click **OK** again. (You might want to change the name of the channel by clicking on its name and changing the name to Blue.)

40. In the Channels palette, click on the composite channel so that the image is showing in full color. Choose **Select Color Range**.

41. Repeat these steps for red, teal, black, and white. Figure 24-7 shows the result. To see how the image looks with the colors that you've created, use the eye icons in the Channels palette to show the channels that you've created.

Tip:

As with process color, you can change to multichannel mode to change the order of the channels, add a T-shirt color, and more. Review the end of Chapter 23 for more information on this mode.

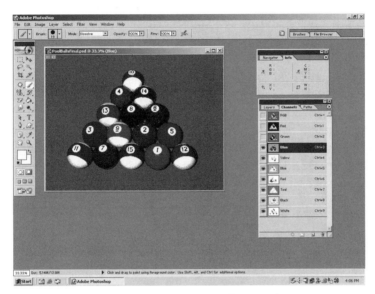

Figure 24-7: Finished product with all channels created

There are two additional files on the companion CD—one called PoolBallsFinal.psd and the other called PoolBallsFinalII.psd. I created both using different colors and techniques. You'll probably get a different result each time you perform an indexed color separation as well.

Now you're ready to print. For information on printing indexed color separations, read Chapter 29, "Printing Color Separations."

Summary

Indexed color separations are great for any image but are easiest to create for images that have less than 100 or so colors. Indexed colors are created either automatically by Photoshop or by the user choosing custom colors. In this chapter, you learned to choose custom colors. With the colors selected and the indexing complete, channels are then created from the selected colors in the same way that spot colors were created in previous chapters.

Indexed artwork is a very easy and forgiving way to screen print multicolor images onto T-shirts. The dots aren't halftone dots like in process prints; instead they're randomly placed square dots. Indexing is a great way to ease your shop into more complicated printing, and Photoshop makes it pretty easy to do.

Chapter 25

Simulated Process Color Separations

Simulated process color separations are created when you want to print a process color print onto a dark-colored shirt. Common images and clients for simulated process color prints include rock bands, fantasy groups, animals, motorcycles, and photographs. As you learned in Chapter 23, process color simulations only work well on light-colored shirts. Creating a separation for a dark shirt is more complex.

Simulated process color differs from true process color because these images are not printed using CMYK inks like regular process prints. These images are printed using "regular" colors like red, black, orange, yellow, blue, white, etc., and are printed with all-purpose inks.

In this chapter, we take an image created for use on a dark shirt, prepare the image, and perform the separations. For simulated process color, this requires creating extra plates including an underbase and highlight white. Keep in mind that this chapter only provides an introduction; screen printers have spent years perfecting this art, and getting good at it will require lots of practice!

 Caution!

Make sure you tell your customers that the print isn't going to look exactly like what they brought in. Since you will be printing on dark shirts using general-purpose inks, the image might be a little muddy and will only be about 75 percent as sharp as the original.

Preparations

Before performing any simulated process color separations, there are a few items that must be reviewed and checked. For instance, make sure after you perform the separations and output them that your printing department can successfully and accurately mix the inks, align the screens, have and use the correct equipment, and have enough stations on their presses to handle the job. If the printing department can't meet these minimal requirements, the print won't come out right at press time.

Additionally, check these items:

- Make sure the image you are working with is at least 150 dpi. Anything between 150 and 200 dpi is reasonable.

- Make sure the image is in RGB mode. If you must scan an image, follow the instructions in Chapter 14; to learn more about RGB mode, refer to Chapter 11.

- Get the image as perfect as possible before separating it.

- Verify that the background in the image is the same color as the shirt. Black backgrounds work great on black shirts. However, if the background of the image is not the same color as the shirt, you'll have to extract the image, place it on a new layer, and create a background layer that *is* the correct color.

- Verify that someone in your shop has experience with process color separations; if they don't, consider purchasing videotapes, attending a class, or visiting another screen print shop for pointers.

 Note:

Although simulated process color is generally reserved for darker shirts, it can be used on lighter ones. However, regular process color is generally easier, so this process is normally not employed under those circumstances. For this chapter, I'll assume we are all working on a dark shirt.

Chapter Project: Simulated Process Color Separations

Creating a simulated process color separation has several steps. You have to create an underbase plate, a white highlight plate, and, of course, the color separations for the ink colors that you've chosen. The following sections in this chapter take you all the way through the process. Figure 25-1 shows an example of the type of image that we work with when creating simulated process prints and is the image I use throughout this chapter.

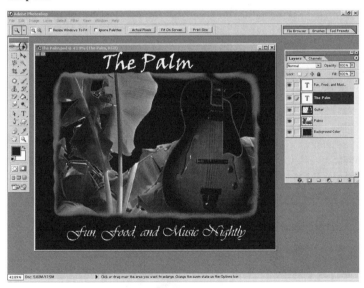

Figure 25-1: Simulated process color example

Create an Underbase Plate

A gray underbase plate (also called a white underbase, an underlay, or simply underbase) is always created for simulated process prints and is used to create the underbase plate. I like to create this plate first.

So, let's begin!

1. Open the file **The Palm - with Layers.psd** from the Chapter 25 folder on the companion CD or open any file from your own library you'd like to experiment with.

2. Select the **Zoom** tool from the toolbox, right-click on the image, and choose **Fit On Screen**.

3. Choose **Layer>Flatten Image** if there are multiple layers in the image you are using. (There are multiple layers in the file used in this example and they must be flattened prior to separating.)

4. Using **Image>Duplicate**, create a duplicate of the image.

5. For the duplicate image, choose **Image>Mode>Grayscale**. Click **OK** to discard color information if prompted.

6. Choose **Image>Adjustments>Invert** to create the gray underbase plate.

7. Open the Info palette using **Window>Info** and use the Eyedropper to verify that the white is white. If there are any other colors in the white part of the image, you'll need to use the Curves tool to get rid of them. Figure 25-2 shows what your workspace should look like.

 Tip:

You can also tweak this from the Curves dialog box by creating an S curve. Doing so will bring out the highlights even more.

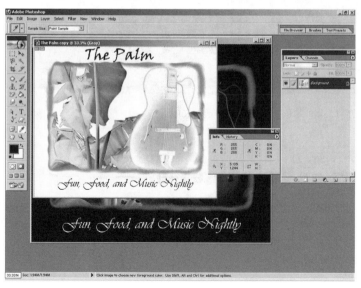

Figure 25-2: Create the gray plate

8. Save this duplicate file as **Underbase Plate**.

So far, so good. That's the first step. Leave these files open as they are, and proceed to the next section.

Create a Highlight White Plate

A highlight white plate is used to bring out the highlights in the image. The image I'm using certainly needs a highlight white plate, and yours likely does too. Highlight white gives the image depth by adding a sense of light.

To create a highlight white plate:

9. Duplicate the Underbase Plate file you created in step 8 of the last exercise. (Use **Image>Duplicate**.)

10. Open the Curves tool using **Image>Adjustments>Curves**. Drag the Curves box away from the image so you can see the entire copy of the underbase plate file.

11. Verify from the Curves dialog box that the x- and y-axis show black in the bottom-left corner and move toward white at the end. If the bottom-left vertex of the grid shows white, click on the arrow in the x-axis to switch them. The Curves dialog box should look like the one shown in Figure 25-3. (Use Alt+click to change the grid marks from large to small or vice versa.)

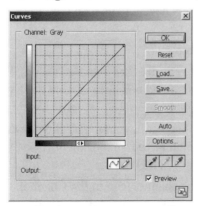

Figure 25-3: The Curves dialog box

12. Click and drag on the handle in the top-right corner and drag it to the left. Drag it approximately one-third of the way across. Use the preview to see how much white you've picked up. You don't want to lose too much detail, but you want to pick up the white highlights.

13. Click **OK** in the Curves dialog box.

14. Save this file as **Highlight White Plate**.

Minimize both of these files. You need them later in this chapter.

Select the Main Colors

With the plates created for the white and underbase plates, you can now concentrate on the various colors in the image. You'll want to look at the image and see what colors are the most prominent first. For this section, we pick the three most prominent colors and create a spot color channel for them. In the palm file, these colors are light green, black, and orange-brown.

Choosing these colors is just like choosing spot colors; hopefully, some of this will look familiar!

To select the first three colors for channel creation:

15. Open the file that you've been working with so far, or open **The Palm.psd** file. Make a decision about the three main colors in the image. For the palm file, let's try black, light green, and orange-brown. Of course, you'll need white too—you might be able to use your white plate, or you might have to actually pull a white spot color, depending on the design.

16. In the Channels palette, verify that the composite channel and the Red, Green, and Blue channels have an eye icon next to them and that they are selected.

17. Choose **Select>Color Range**.

18. In the Color Range dialog box, verify that Sampled Colors, Selection, and None are chosen. Invert should be checked. Use the Eyedropper to click on the black in the image.

19. Move the Fuzziness slider to select how much black you want. This is always a judgment call; you'll have to experiment to see what works best on various prints. Click **OK**.

20. Click on the save selection as channel icon in the Channels palette.

21. Hold down the **Ctrl** key and double-click on the new channel.

22. Rename it **Black**, select **Spot Color**, change Solidity to **5** percent, and click on the color square. Use the Eyedropper to choose black from either the file or the Color Picker. Click **Custom** if you want to

select a specific Pantone color. Click **OK** (click OK twice if you've chosen a Pantone color). Note that if you select a Pantone color, the name Black will be overwritten.

23. Choose **Select>Deselect**.

24. In the Channels palette, make sure that only the composite channel and the Red, Green, and Blue channels have an eye icon next to them and make sure that they are selected.

25. Repeat steps 17 to 23 for the remaining two colors you've designated as main colors in the image. Configure percentages at 5 percent for these colors. You can always change it later if you feel it's necessary.

Don't look at the image with only these three channels yet. You've got a long way to go before your separations will look like the original!

Choose the Remaining Colors

Now comes the hard part. You have to decide what other colors to select and what colors you think you'll need to print with. You also have to weigh this decision with how many stations you have on your press and how many screens you want to burn. The process for doing this is the same as detailed in the last section.

So, decide how many colors you can create and work with successfully. Keep in mind that you'll need an underbase and a highlight white. If you only have a six-station press, you're going to have a pretty hard time making this image (and most likely any simulated process image) work. For the palm file, I have created a pretty good simulated process color separation by pulling these colors:

- Underbase white
- Lemon yellow
- Scarlet red
- Light blue
- Kelly green
- Gray
- Brown
- Highlight white
- Black

Practice as much as possible pulling colors from this file or any other you have in your library. Use the eye icons to view how the colors you've chosen are working out when viewing the image using only these channels. Work with the colors until you have created something that looks similar to the original. As mentioned earlier, this is an art. Creating simulated process color is a time-consuming task, and many of the decisions that you have to make are based on experience, practice, and sometimes educated guessing. Although I can't teach you all of this in only a few pages, I can help you get started on the right track.

Once you feel like you're close, you can create a shirt color and add the highlight white and underbase plates. From there, you can change the order of the plates so they look more like the print does at press time.

Make a Shirt Color Channel

Making a shirt color channel is detailed in Chapter 23. Briefly, in the Channels palette, click the arrow to bring up the additional options, and choose New Channel. Name the new channel Shirt Color. Change the color to black, set Solidity to 100 percent, and drag the shirt color to the top of the list in the Channels palette, just below the Blue channel. Add icons to see how the image looks so far.

Drag the Underbase and White Plate to the Original File

Let's finish up by dragging the underbase and white plates that you created earlier to the new file. Verify that they're all open and available.

1. Position all three files (the underbase plate, the white plate, and the original file that you've been working on) so you can see them on the screen, and verify that you can see the Channels palette.

2. Click the title bar in the Underbase Plate file.

3. Click on the **Gray** channel and drag it to the original file. Drop it there.

4. Close the Underbase Plate file by clicking the **X** in the top-right corner.

5. Click on the title bar in the Highlight White Plate file.

6. Click on the **Gray** channel and drag it to the original file. Drop it there.

7. Close the Highlight White Plate file by clicking the **X** in the top-right corner.

8. Working now with the original file, locate the Alpha 1 channel in the Channel palette and rename it **Underbase Plate**. Change the color in the color square to the color of your underbase ink (white, gray, etc). Set Solidity to **85** percent and choose **Spot Color**. Click **OK**.

9. Locate the Alpha 2 channel in the Channel palette and rename it **White Highlight Plate**. Change the color in the color square to white. Set Solidity to **90** percent, and choose **Spot Color**. Click **OK**.

10. Add the eye icon to both of these new channels and replace the eye icon by all of the other channels except for the composite channel and the original RGB channels listed at the top.

You can continue to tweak these channels endlessly if you so desire. You can delete channels and recreate them. You can double-click on the channels and create a new color for them, or choose a Pantone color. You can remove the eye icon from specific channels to see if the screen is needed or not. You can switch the order of the channels so that you can see how the actual print would look if the inks were added in a specific order. Professionals can spend hours doing such work. At some point, you'll have to know when to say enough is enough, though, and thus balance time and compensation.

View in Print Order

This book isn't about teaching you *how* to screen print, so I'm not going to go into the specifics of print order. You have to read the manuals that come with your inks and get to know your equipment. However, I can tell you how to view the image in the print order that you choose and offer some general guidelines.

In the Channels palette:

1. Remove the eye icon from the composite channel and the original RGB channels. Place an eye icon next to the other channels.

2. Drag the Shirt Color channel to the top of the list, underneath the composite, Red, Green, and Blue default channels.

3. Drag the Underbase Plate channel underneath this.

4. Next, place the whites, yellows, reds, blues, purples, and blacks.

✖ **Caution!**

Understand that professional separators can spend literally hours getting just the right separations, deleting and adding channels, and perfecting their work. Don't be discouraged if your first few attempts aren't that great.

Split the Channels

To send the separations to programs that don't accept DCS 2.0 files, you can split channels to create a separate file for each channel that you've created. When splitting channels, Photoshop renames them and places them on the screen one by one as they're created. With these separate files, you can do a File>Save As command on each file, and then you can send them to the service bureau or import them into another program.

To split the channels, simply click the right arrow in the Channels palette and choose Split Channels. Don't do this until you're sure though; this can't be undone!

 Tip:

If you plan to do a lot of simulated process color separations, consider purchasing a third-party separation plug-in to do them automatically. FastFilms is one of those programs and sells for around $1,000.

Summary

In this chapter you learned the basics for creating a simulated process print for a dark-colored garment. Printing on dark garments means you'll need an underbase plate, a highlight white plate, and additional plates for each color you want to add. Unlike regular process color, simulated process color is printed with general-purpose inks, so when creating the separations, you get to choose what colors you'd like to pull.

This, unfortunately, makes creating simulated process colors pretty difficult, and learning this art takes lots and lots of practice. Work through this chapter with your own artwork and experiment with your own equipment for practice. Before you know it, you'll have it conquered!

Chapter 26

More about Color Separations

In this chapter I discuss a little more about color separations and the theory behind the techniques. While most of this has been touched on in previous chapters, none of these topics have been discussed in depth. Topics covered in this chapter include color gamuts and out of gamut issues, halftones, information on dot gain and loss, selective color correction, Undercolor Removal (UCR) and Gray Component Replacement (GCR), more about the DCS 2.0 file format, and information relative to image resolution, line count, mesh count, and moiré.

Color Gamuts

You'll mainly be working with two color gamuts: RGB and CMYK. Colors on a monitor are produced using the RGB color gamut, meaning that combining red, green, and blue creates all the colors. You scan in RGB, work in RGB, and view in RGB. While in RGB mode, you have access to over 16 million colors. When you're ready to print separations, you convert to CMYK.

CMYK is the color gamut the printer uses. In fact, many printers have four ink cartridges, one for each of these colors. These four colors are put on the page to create the colors printed in the image. In screen printing, these four colors are known as process colors. The number of colors available in CMYK is substantially less than in RGB.

RGB

The RGB color model is a "projected light" model that produces colors by mixing its primary colors and projecting them onto a black screen. The secondary colors, cyan, magenta, and yellow, are produced when these colors overlap. Combining various amounts of red, green, and blue using this projected light produces colors in the same manner that spotlights of red, green, and blue are used to illuminate a stage or in projection TVs. As with stage lights, too much of a good thing washes everything out with white light (producing a white color).

CMYK

CMYK, on the other hand, is referred to as "reflected light." These inks are placed on white paper, completely opposite of the monitor's colors being projected onto a black screen. In contrast to RGB, when too much of the base colors are added, black is the resulting color.

Our world works on the reflected light principle. As the sun shines its white light on something, a part of the color spectrum is absorbed by it. The rest of the light is reflected to our eyes so we can see it. Understanding the theory behind this brings us to the following points:

■ Because too much ink darkens an image, use selective light colors to create a wider spectrum of colors.

■ Magenta absorbs green.

■ Yellow absorbs blue.

■ Cyan absorbs red.

■ Black darkens anything and can also be used to create gray.

A problem obviously occurs when you need to convert RGB to CMYK because the color gamuts are different. Many colors that are in the RGB gamut or range of colors cannot be produced effectively using CMYK. This is where screen printers encounter their most basic problem—reproducing the color they see on their computer monitor.

How Basic Colors are Created from Process Inks

You should know by now that green is created from yellow and cyan, and red is created from yellow and magenta. But what about the other common colors you'll be using? Here's the lowdown:

Table 26-1: How process colors combine to create other colors

Ink Color	Cyan	Magenta	Yellow	Black
Green	100%	-	100%	-
Dark green	100%	-	100%	25%
Red	-	100%	100%	-
Dark red	-	100%	100%	25%
Blue	100%	50%	-	-

Of course, different percentages offer different shades of color, and black can be used to make the color darker. Use the Info palette to compare colors in your image to these and learn what other colors consist of. Understanding these points can help you to know when cyan isn't needed and should be removed, when magenta isn't needed and should be removed, etc.

Out of Gamut

A gamut is the range of colors that a system can print or display. The monitor displays colors in the RGB color gamut. Between RGB and CMYK, RGB offers the largest range of colors. (This makes sense, since we should be able to *see* more colors than we can *print*, not vice versa!) Some colors though, like cyan and yellow, can't be displayed exactly on the monitor, although pretty good renditions are created. When you have colors that can't be viewed properly on the screen, you've got out of gamut issues.

The same thing occurs when you need to print an image using CMYK, and that image's colors are out of gamut and can't be reproduced correctly. They are deemed *outside* of the printable CMYK gamut. Thus, problems occur when trying to view or print colors that are out of the color's gamut.

Photoshop can tell you if the colors are out of gamut for the CMYK working space or for any of the CMYK working plates. However, you won't get accurate results with this unless the monitor and printer are calibrated. After the hardware is calibrated, the color space must also be configured using the Edit>Color Settings command. Many printers now come with color calibration software; make sure you read your printer's documentation carefully and set up the software accordingly.

Viewing Out of Gamut Colors

To see if an image has out of gamut colors, work though the following steps:

1. Open any RGB image file into Photoshop.

2. Choose **View>Proof Setup>Working CMYK**. (You can also choose various plates from the menu choices.)

3. Choose **View>Gamut Warning**.

4. The colors that cannot be reproduced at the printer will show up as gray.

5. Uncheck **View>Gamut Warning** to remove the gray cast.

You can change the color that the out of gamut colors are shown as using Edit>Preferences>Transparency and Gamut if you desire. You can also view out of gamut colors from the Info palette as detailed in previous chapters.

 Note:

When converting from RGB mode to CMYK mode, all colors are brought into gamut during the conversion.

So what do you do if the RGB image is out of the CMYK working space's color gamut? Well, you can simply leave them alone if you want; Photoshop will bring the RGB image into the CMYK color gamut upon conversion. However, you can also choose to tweak the image prior to conversion to bring all colors into the CMYK working space gamut beforehand.

Note:

Technically, Photoshop uses Relative Colorimetric as its standard rendering method. Photoshop will dutifully translate all of the RGB colors that have exact matches to the CMYK color space, and those that don't have exact matches will be translated to their closest four-color equivalent.

If your image has many out of gamut colors, you might try recoloring it a little while still in RGB mode. You might also try Perceptual rendering. Perceptual rendering changes all of the colors in the image to recreate the image in the CMYK gamut. This setting can be changed using Edit>Color Settings, as shown in Figure 26-1.

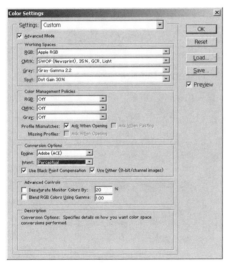

Figure 26-1: The Color Settings dialog box

 Tip:

Remember that an exclamation point is added to the color value in the Info palette when a color is out of gamut.

ICC Profiles

ICC profiles are color space descriptions. ICC stands for and was defined by the International Color Consortium as a cross-platform color standard. Having the ability to cross various platforms allows different hardware to be used to view the same file and allows all viewers to see the file in the same way. PCs and Macs also support ICC profiles, so computer users on different platforms can also benefit. Photoshop is an ICC-compliant application, as is Adobe Illustrator 8 and above and Quark 4 and above, among others.

Photoshop uses a color management module to interpret ICC profiles. As always, having a calibrated monitor is a must. To install or set up an ICC profile, follow the instructions offered by the device or software that includes the profile. Most new high-end printers now come with ICC color profiles.

To install a new (RGB) color profile that you've received with a new sublimation printer, high-end laser printer, scanner, or similar device, copy the ICC profile from the CD or web site to the appropriate folder (sometimes this is done automatically through an installation script):

- For Windows XP—Windows/System32/Spool/Drivers/Color

- For Windows 2000 and Windows 2000 Server—WINNT or WINNT32/System/Spool/Drivers/Color

- For Windows NT—WINNT/System32/Color

- For Windows 98—Windows/System/Color

- Mac OS 9.x—System Folder/ColorSync Profiles

- Mac OS X—Users/Current User/Library/ColorSync

Once the copy is complete:

1. Choose **Edit > Color Settings**.

2. In the RGB window, click the down arrow to locate the newly copied profile. See Figure 26-2.

3. Click **OK**.

After performing these steps, you can see additional options for the profile in the Color Settings window by choosing Custom RGB from the RGB window in the Working Spaces section. Choosing this option brings up the window shown in Figure 26-3. You'll want to follow the

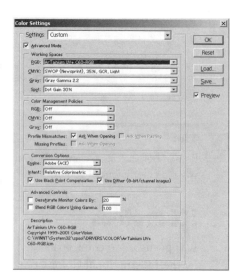

Figure 26-2: Choosing an ICC profile

instructions that come with the machine when changing anything here. This profile was copied from an Epson C60 Sublimation printer.

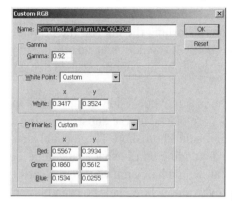

Figure 26-3: Choosing a custom RGB profile

Note:

When using the File>Save As command, you can choose to save the file using its specific ICC profile. Just check ICC Profile before saving.

Halftone Screens

Halftone screens are used to print color separations. For a four-color process separation, you create four halftone screens. Halftone screens must be created so that a combination of colors (CMYK) can be used to print at the press to simulate the colors in the original image. Halftones are dots of a specific shape. For screen printing, we use an ellipse.

Halftones dictate how much of each color goes on the material at press time. Varying how large or small the dots are determines the actual color printed on the shirt. For instance, if a color on a shirt fades from yellow to black, the yellow part of the screen will have more (and larger) dots and put down more yellow ink where needed, and the black will do the same. In between the two colors where the fading occurs, the dots will be configured so that some yellow and some black is applied, giving a fade effect and creating a myriad of in-between colors. Varying the size and number of halftone dots where the fading occurs does this. We learn to define halftone screen attributes in Chapter 29.

Dot Gain and Loss

Dot gain is the result of the paper absorbing the ink and the original dot growing in size. Dot loss is the result of the dot being so small that it doesn't get printed. Both can cause problems, but dot gain is usually a screen printer's main concern.

Consider how printing green is achieved. Yellow and cyan are mixed to produce green, and these inks are placed on the substrate using a screen that you've created from inside Photoshop. There could also be a touch of magenta involved too, depending on the shade, and generally there's no black. So imagine what would happen if you went to print green by way of printing some cyan and yellow, and the cyan plate had tremendous dot gain. This would mean that the correct amount of yellow was applied but way too much cyan was added. The green you are after is not going to turn out the way you want. Making things worse, if the single tiny little dot of magenta gets blown out of proportion and becomes 25 dots, you're sure to get problems at press time.

Correcting Dot Gain Problems

The solution to correcting dot gain problems is complex. First, you must configure dot gain settings in the Color Settings dialog box. For custom CMYK, we set dot gain to 35 percent, since that's what is generally produced. For spot color, we set dot gain to 30 percent. By configuring dot gain here, we are admitting that there will be dot gain and try to compensate for it.

 Tip:

If you are sending out your artwork to a service bureau, call first. Some shops want dot gain set to as low as 20 percent!

Other corrective techniques include using good equipment, high mesh screens, specific films, and high-output printers. You'll need good inks too, firm squeegees, and high-tension screens. Since you can get dot gain at every step of the printing process, you need to make sure that you are working with the best equipment you can afford. It won't matter how good your original print is if you're using a low mesh screen for a high-end print, or if you're printing the output on a $29 printer!

Selective Color Correction Techniques

Selective color correction is a technique used to increase and decrease the amount of process color inks used in both RGB and CMYK images. The Selective Color dialog box shows how much process ink is used to create each primary color in the image. You can increase or decrease the amount of process inks in relation to the other process inks to change a primary color selectively without affecting any of the other primary colors in the image. For instance, you can modify the cyan used to print the green in the image without affecting the cyan used to print the blue in the image.

To use the Selective Color command:

1. Verify that the composite channel is showing in the Channels palette.

2. Choose **Image>Adjustments>Selective Color**.

3. In the Selective Color dialog box, as shown in Figure 26-4, choose the color to modify from the Colors drop-down list.

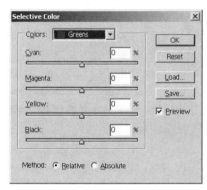

Figure 26-4: The Selective Color dialog box

4. To modify how much red, green, and blue (or cyan, magenta, yellow, and black) make up a specific color in the image, move the sliders appropriately.

5. Compare the changes in the Info palette.

6. In the Selective Color dialog box, check and uncheck **Preview** to view your changes.

You can work with selective color to remove excess cyan from various primary colors where cyan isn't needed. You can also use the Info palette to view the before and after values for both RGB and CMYK values.

Color Settings

Although you were told in Chapter 5 how to configure the color settings in the Color Settings dialog box, you might be a bit confused as to what some of the terms mean. UCR vs. GCR, Black Generation, and similar terms are detailed more fully here.

Undercolor Removal (UCR)

When creating color separations, RGB is translated into CMYK. In theory, the new colors (C, M, and Y) are combined to create the black needed in the image. In reality, however, when mixed together these colors create a muddy brown instead.

Using UCR, the black ink is used to replace cyan, magenta, and yellow in areas with neutral colors like shadows, grays, and white highlights. This uses less ink and is generally used with newsprint and other types of print where dot gain is forgiven easily.

More technically, UCR reduces the amount of C, M, and Y ink in the darkest neutral areas of the image when the colors exceed the specified ink weight configured in Color Settings. Thus, UCR is better suited for newsprint where ink is heavily restricted.

 Note:

The purpose behind UCR is to compensate for printing problems that occur when inks are overprinted.

Gray Component Replacement (GCR)

GCR is an extension of UCR in that it will replace the neutral colors in the image as well as the colored areas with equal amounts of cyan, magenta, and yellow throughout the tonal range of the image. The gray component is replaced with black ink. GCR is a better option for most high-quality print work, thus the reasoning behind choosing it for our CMYK custom settings.

Choosing GCR over UCR allows the colors to be printed easier and cleaner, with less muddying. GCR offers brighter colors and prints than UCR when printing traditional color separations.

Black Generation

This setting, which we configure at light to medium, determines the amount of black ink used in the CMYK separation. This value is used to determine how dense the darkest shadows in the image will appear. By keeping the values at light or medium, you are preventing loss of color intensity in the image at press time.

In addition to setting the Black Generation value, Black Ink Limits and Total Ink Limits can be set. Generally, 75 to 85 percent and 250 to 300 percent, respectively, are good numbers here. As with Black Generation, setting these numbers reduces the problems associated with prints getting darker on the press. Remember, if a small black dot inherently has dot gain, reducing the numbers for black is a good thing.

Undercolor Addition (UCA)

UCA adds cyan, magenta, and yellow where black is present in a photograph or neutral colors in an image. UCA gives density to an image and increases ink coverage. UCA is not generally desirable in offset printing or screen printing and should be set to 0 percent.

DCS 2.0

Desktop Color Separations format is a version of the standard EPS format that lets you save not only the file or image but also its CMYK or Multichannel color separations that you see in the Channels palette. DCS 2.0 allows you to save spot channels too. These files can then be exported to various other graphics programs, and their separations can be printed on PostScript printers.

There are two types of DCS files: version 1.0 and version 2.0.

- DCS 1.0 creates one file for each of the color channels in the CMYK image and one additional channel that can be either a grayscale or a color composite.

- DCS 2.0 saves spot color channels in the image and can also save a color composite channel or a grayscale channel. The color channels can be saved as multiple files (like DCS 1.0) or as a single file. Saving as a single file saves disk space.

When saving a DCS 1.0 or 2.0 file, use File>Save As and choose the version you want from the Format drop-down list. You'll notice that the file extension becomes .eps, as shown in Figure 26-5. Click Save.

Figure 26-5: Saving as a DCS file

You'll then be prompted to make choices, as shown in Figure 26-6, concerning what channels to save, what encoding to use, and whether other items should be included. Each of these are discussed next.

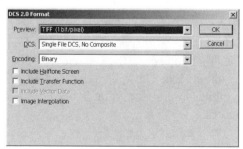

Figure 26-6: DCS/EPS file properties

- **Preview TIFF options**: There are three options: None, 1 bit/pixel, and 8 bits/pixel. Choose 1 bit/pixel for the preview to create a smaller file and 8 bits/pixel if the size of the file is not of concern.

- **DCS options**: There are several options for creating the file. You can choose between a single file and multiple files, color composite or no color composite, and grayscale composite or no grayscale composite. Choose the option that is right for you.

- **Encoding options**: Encoding determines how the data will be sent to the PostScript printer. Choose ASCII if printing from Windows or if you've had problems printing to this device in the past. Choose Binary to produce a smaller file but leave the original file intact or if you are printing from a Mac OS system. Do not choose JPEG if you don't have to. JPEGs compress the file by discarding color information.

- **Include Halftone Screen**: Check this if you want to include a half-tone screen.

- **Include Transfer Function**: Check this if you plan to use the Transfer function to compensate for extra dot gain.

- **Include Vector Data**: Check this if the file has vector data, such as text, that you'd like to save with the file. (If there is no vector data in the file, this option will be grayed out as it is in Figure 26-6.)

- **Image Interpolation**: Check this to anti-alias the printed appearance of a low-resolution image.

DCS 2.0 is supported by several other programs, including Adobe Page-Maker, Adobe Illustrator, and QuarkXPress. If you are preparing an image with spot colors for printing from another application, consider unchecking Include Halftone Screen and select Include Transfer Function.

Resolutions

A big part of successful color separations and screen printing is working with the right resolution. Different types of resolution have been introduced briefly in this book in various chapters and for various hardware and software, but you need a firm grasp on the concept to truly understand the importance of it.

Image Resolution

When an image is printed, an image with a high resolution contains more pixels than a low-resolution image, and the pixels are smaller. Consider this: A 2 inch by 2 inch image with a resolution of 72 dots per inch creates (144 pixels by 144 pixels) 20,736 pixels. The same 2 inch by 2 inch image created and printed at 200 dots per inch creates (400 pixels by 400 pixels) 160,000 pixels. (At 600 dots per inch, this escalates to 1,440,000 pixels.) Because there are more pixels created for the same size image, the image will print out with more detail than a low-resolution image.

This is why low-resolution images get a "pixelated" look. You can actually see the pixels on the page, making low-resolution prints difficult to work with at the press. In contrast, using a resolution too high for the output device or substrate that it is printed on is a waste of resources and time. The object, of course, is to find a happy medium.

 Note:

Image resolution is measured in pixels per inch (ppi).

Printer Resolution

Printers can print in many different resolutions and the resolution quality is generally proportional to the price of the printer. Wide format thermal imagesetters usually print resolutions between 400 dpi and 1200 dpi to 2450 dpi, depending on how much you invest. The technology is always growing though, so you can always expect more in the future. These wide format printers can print directly on the film too, reducing the steps (and thus dot gain) associated with other types of printers.

Laser printers can print various resolutions, but they generally print between 300 dpi and 600 dpi; however, some expensive laser printers print as high as 1200 dpi or more. Inkjet printers usually don't print this high, and the low-end printers average around 300 dpi. You get what you pay for.

 Note:

Printer resolution is measured in dots per inch (dpi).

Screen Resolution and Frequency

Line screen, also called screen ruling, is how many lines of halftone dots appear per linear inch on a printed page, positive or negative. Line screen is measured in lines per inch (lpi). It is limited by the output device and the paper or film you print on. Common settings for screen printers range from 55 lpi to 65 lpi. Newspapers print around 85 lpi and magazines around 133 or 155 lpi.

When thinking about lpi settings, consider this: A 300 to 600 dpi laser printer can usually only print at an lpi of 55 to 65, and better printers get a better lpi. Some screen printers have the ability to print at 85 to 100 lpi, and they get good results with good equipment. Obviously, a higher line frequency will produce sharper images; however, the limitations of the film, paper, printer, and screen, along with various associated costs, make obtaining a high lpi for screen printing unreachable for most of us.

When you print out color separations using Photoshop's Print with Preview command, you can set the frequency of the halftone screens. Figure 26-7 shows the Halftone Screens dialog box.

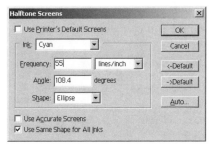

Figure 26-7: Setting screen frequency

Though theories vary, in Chapter 29 we discuss what the most common settings are for the various plates and how to configure them. For most screen printers, an lpi of 55 to 65 is reasonable.

 Note:

Screen (press) resolution is measured in lines per inch (lpi).

Mesh Count

Mesh count is denoted by a number that increases as the fineness of the mesh does. Mesh counts for screen printers generally range between 110 and 205 for plastisol inks, simple spot color prints, and direct prints and 110 to 380 for other types of prints, including process prints. You determine what mesh count you need based on your design and inks.

Choose higher mesh counts for finely detailed designs (305) and lower mesh counts for lower detail designs (110). Process color images are considered on the high end; spot color images are on the low end.

While theories differ, the mesh count of the screen should be two to four times the halftone screen frequency (although some people will say it should be as high as 4.5 times the lpi). Therefore, for a spot color print that is 55 lpi, consider a 110 mesh screen (2X). For a process color print with a limited amount of fine detail printed on an automatic press at 65 dpi, consider a mesh count of 230 (approximately 3X). For a process print at 65 dpi with lots of fine detail, consider a mesh count of 305 (over 4X).

 Tip:

Yellow meshes ensure more exact dot reproduction.

Other things will affect the mesh count you choose, including:

- Screen tension
- Type of ink
- Ink modifications
- Garment type
- Garment color
- Known issues with the printing press, squeegees, and other equipment

 Caution!

Don't let anyone tell you that you have to use a 305 or higher mesh for every job—you don't.

Moiré

Moiré is the unwanted addition of patterns on a print or scan. These patterns are usually caused when two similar repetitive grids are placed on top of one another. Screens and their inherent mesh pattern when combined with the halftone dots and their inherent dot patterns can cause the print to have unwanted lines and patterns. You can also get moiré when you scan an image that has already been halftoned, like a photograph from a magazine. If you can see moiré patterns after scanning, you can be sure you'll see it at the press also.

So what do you do if you get moiré patterns? As with anything, theories abound. Since the patterns are basically caused by the clash of dot patterns though, you'll want to try to avoid it from the beginning. Start with a good print or scan, followed by optimal and tried-and-true settings from the Screen options in the Print with Preview dialog box. Ellipse-shaped halftones seem to work best for screen printing, and setting the screen angles for each screen plays a role too. As with anything, you'll need good equipment. In Chapter 29, we configure your screen frequency and angles in such a way that these patterns are minimized. If you still find yourself getting moiré patterns after configuring optimal settings, you need to troubleshoot your equipment, scanner, printer, and other devices.

 Tip:

Screen printers sometimes find using a higher mesh screen solves the problem of moiré, but there are other issues at work. The threads in the garment can cause problems, as can bad scans, working with the wrong image resolution, and more. Generally, working with or configuring the correct screen angle corrects most problems.

PostScript

You've heard of PostScript printers, but what exactly does the word PostScript imply? PostScript is a page description language for medium- to high-resolution print devices. The language consists of software commands and protocols that allow you to send data (including picture and font information) from your computer to the printer for output.

PostScript is device independent, allowing different computers and printers to communicate independently of platforms.

Device independence means that the image is described without reference to any specific device features, such as printer resolution, so that the same description can be used on any PostScript printer without having to be changed in any way.

Currently there are three versions: PostScript 1, PostScript 2, and PostScript 3. Level 2 has better support for color printing and is widely accepted by applications and printers. The newer version, level 3, has better support for fonts, graphics handling, and speed.

Summary

In this chapter you learned a little more about color separations and the theory behind performing them. Color gamuts, out of gamut colors, and how colors are created were discussed. ICC profiles were introduced too and can be used to calibrate printers and other devices.

Techniques used when screen printing were also covered, including understanding halftones, dot gain and loss, and correcting dot gain problems. Selective color correction was introduced too, and additional information on color setting options was offered.

UCR, GCR, UCA, Black Generation, screen line, and angles were introduced, as well as resolution issues and options. Mesh count, moiré, and other printing pitfalls were discussed also, and PostScript language was introduced.

Part VI
Printing

Chapter 27

Page Setup and Print Dialog Boxes

Photoshop's print dialog boxes are a bit more complex than the print boxes you've seen in word processing programs or other graphics programs. In this chapter we explore the available print dialog boxes and learn what each button does and what each term means. Buttons such as Screen, Transfer, and Bleed are most likely new to you, as are terms such as interpolation and encoding. However, some might seem second nature—background, border, print size, and caption. In this chapter, we discuss all of them.

There are several printing options in the File menu. There's File>Page Setup, File>Print with Preview, File>Print, and File>Print One Copy. The Page Setup option opens the Page Setup dialog box where paper, orientation, and margins can be set and allows access to the printer properties. The Print with Preview choice offers a myriad of choices, as shown in Figure 27-1, and is where we spend most of our time. The Print choice brings up the Print dialog box where the printer and its properties can be configured, where the status of the printer is shown, and the print range and number of copies can be configured. The Print One Copy choice does just that; it prints one copy automatically with no prompts. This choice uses the default printer options and configuration. You'll most often use the Print with Preview choice. This is detailed next.

Note:

You can set default printer properties from the Printers folder on your PC or Mac. On a PC running Windows XP, the printers can be accessed from the Control Panel under Printers and Faxes.

Exploring the Print Dialog Box

You can access the Print dialog box using File>Print with Preview. Figure 27-1 shows this dialog box. This is the command that you'll choose when you want to set up a print job. From here you can access everything, including your printers and a preview of the image. You can also configure options concerning screen frequency and angle, set crop and registration marks, and more.

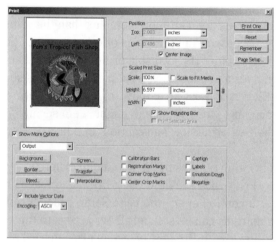

Figure 27-1: The Print dialog box

As you can see, there are many options. In the following section I go over what each of the main options are and what they are used for; in the next section I introduce the additional options that are available by checking the Show More Options check box. (Figure 27-1 shows all of the options, including the additional ones.) You use these options to print out spot, index, and process color separations.

Previewing the Image

Before printing any image or color separation, you'll want to preview the image to make sure it all fits on the page. If it doesn't, you need to enlarge or reduce it to the correct size. The Preview window shows the image or channel as it is printed on the page.

Notice in Figure 27-1 that Show Bounding Box is checked. Checking this option adds a bounding box around the image so it can be resized using the corner handles. I suggest that you not resize the image here though; doing so can cause unwanted distortions. Instead, start with the correct image size when working with an image or, if necessary, enlarge or reduce while scanning or working inside Photoshop. When working inside Photoshop, use the Image>Image Size command to change the size before printing.

To view the Print dialog box and see a preview of an image and a channel and to print them:

1. Open the file **Print.psd** from the Chapter 27 folder on the companion CD.

2. Use the **Zoom** tool to zoom in and resize the image if desired.

3. In the Layers palette, verify that all of the channels are selected and an eye is showing next to each (including the composite channel).

4. Choose **File>Print with Preview**. Your screen should look similar to Figure 27-2. Notice that in the Preview window you can see the entire image. If you print this image as-is, only one page will be printed—the composite print. Choose **Print** or **Cancel**.

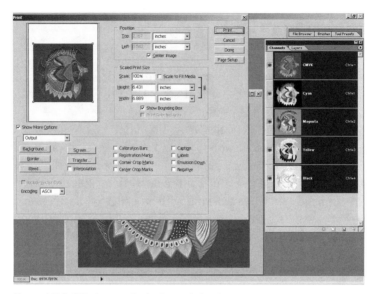

Figure 27-2: Working with the Print dialog box

5. To print a single channel, remove the eye icon from all of the channels in the Channels palette, except the one you want to print.

6. Choose **File>Print with Preview**. Notice in the Preview box that only the specific channel chosen is showing. Choose **Print** or **Cancel**.

 Tip:

You can also click Done if you do not want to print, but you do not want to cancel either. Clicking Done preserves the changes you've made, which will be applied the next time you print.

Position

By default, the image is centered on the page. The image can be positioned anywhere on the page though by unchecking Center Image. Once the box is unchecked, the Top and Left windows are no longer grayed out and any number can be typed in. There are several measurement choices as well—inches, centimeters, millimeters, points, and picas. I prefer to leave the image centered, as the results are usually more accurate than if they had been changed.

Scaled Print Size

The scale determines how large or small the image should be printed in relation to the actual size of the image itself. The default choice of 100 percent prints the page full size. This is the best option. Scale To Fit Media enlarges or reduces the image size to fit the page perfectly. Finally, height and width can be manually set to create any size printout you'd like.

There are two check boxes also. The Show Bounding box places handles on the corners of the image, allowing you to resize the image by dragging from the corners. The Print Selected Area is available if you've used a selection tool to select a specific area of the image prior to opening the Print dialog box. When this box is checked, only the selected area is printed.

 Tip:

If possible, don't resize images with the Print dialog box. Instead, use the Image> Image Size command and uncheck Resample Image. Then use File>Print with Preview to see exactly how the image will fit on the page. It's best to make size adjustments using the Image command rather than from the Print dialog box. Additionally, there are options for enlarging the image using cameras after the image is printed if you have the necessary equipment.

The Print Dialog Box's Additional Options

You can see the additional options in the Print dialog box by checking Show More Options. When you check Show More Options, you'll see what's shown in Figure 27-2. By default, Output is selected. The next several subsections detail what each of these Output options do. In this chapter we discuss what all of the terms and buttons mean; in Chapter 29, we discuss what settings to use for each and when. (Settings differ depending on what type of separation or image you are printing.)

 Tip:

Use Ctrl+P to quickly open the File>Print with Preview option.

The Background Button

The Background button lets you select a color from the Color Picker that will be printed on the page outside the image area. For instance, if you are printing slides for a film projector, you might want the background to be a specific color. See Figure 27-3.

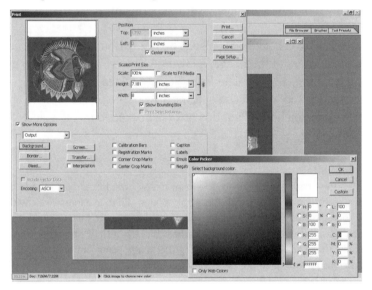

Figure 27-3: Selecting the background color

Using the Print.psd file, for instance, you can create a background color that matches the original background color in the image. Choose File> Print with Preview, click the Background button, and use the mouse to click on and select a color in the image itself (not the preview). Click OK in the Color Picker and the background will be created. You'll see it in the Preview window.

 Tip:

Choose white if you want a white background outside the image.

The Border Button

Use this button to create a border around the image's printed area. The border is black and can be between 0.000 and 0.150 inches. This border is quite small and won't suit all needs. If you really need a border, consider creating the border prior to printing.

 Tip:

A simple border can be created using a square brush and the mouse; just draw around the image. This allows you to create any size border you'd like.

The Bleed Button

Use this button to create crop marks inside (instead of outside) the image. This allows you to trim the image if needed inside the graphic instead of outside of it. You can specify the width of the bleed.

The Screen Button

Use the Screen button to set screen frequency, angle, and dot shape for each of the ink colors (CMYK) in the process print. After selecting the Screen button, you'll see the Halftone Screens dialog box, as shown in Figure 27-4. You need to uncheck Use Printer's Default Screens to choose your own settings.

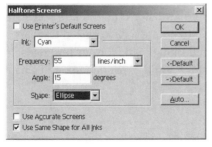

Figure 27-4: The Halftone Screens dialog box

About Screens

When printing process color prints, you use screens to physically transfer the ink onto the shirts and other materials. These screens are created
from printouts that you print from your PostScript printer. These printouts can be created on vellum, film, or similar paper. To create printouts
that will make for good screens, you need to configure how the halftones
will be printed on the paper. Halftones are dots of different sizes that control how much ink of each color (cyan, magenta, yellow, and black) will be
deposited on the substrate.

There are specific guidelines for different types of printers and
presses concerning how the numbers for angle, dot shape, and screen
frequency should be configured. In Chapter 29, specific numbers for different types of printing is discussed; for now, a general overview of the
terms is in order.

The Transfer Button

This button allows you to compensate for dot gain and loss from inside
the Print dialog box. If you've been reading this book from the beginning
though, you probably already know that dot gain is taken into account and
dealt with appropriately when configuring color settings from the Edit
menu.

However, this option comes in handy if you have equipment that isn't
correctly calibrated and you need some extra compensation for dot gain
between the image and the film. The Transfer function lets you specify
up to 13 values along the grayscale to create a customized transfer configuration. This is quite complicated though, and for our purposes, the
CMYK settings configured in Chapter 5 and expanded upon in Chapter
29 will most likely suit your needs.

 Tip:

You can load, save, and use the default transfer functions. For now, stick with the
defaults.

Interpolation

Interpolation is Photoshop's way of figuring out what should be in a specific pixel when enough information isn't given, such as when you resample an image. If you start with a small image and try to double the size, Photoshop has to guess at what's supposed to be in those extra areas. If you take a large image and reduce its size, it has to guess at what to throw away. There are several types of interpolation: bicubic, bilinear, and nearest neighbor.

 Caution!

As you know already, resampling (resizing) an image will cause degradation in image quality. Remember to always start with the correct size so that resampling isn't necessary.

When deciding on what interpolation method to use, consider the following:

- **Nearest Neighbor**: The fastest but least precise method. This produces jagged edges but is sometimes okay for hard-edged illustration files.

- **Bilinear**: The next up the ladder. This creates medium quality resamples.

- **Bicubic**: The best method, but extremely slow. This is the best option.

The default setting is bicubic, but this can be changed using Edit>Preferences>General.

Page Marks

There are three types of page marks: registration marks, corner crop marks, and center crop marks. These marks can be used to align the prints once they have been output.

Registration marks are used for color separations and print marks on the image (bull's-eyes and star targets). Corner crop marks and center crop marks print marks where the image should be trimmed. These marks can also be useful if you are printing out an image for a demonstration using a slide projector, for package design work, or for any other type of work that requires CMYK printouts be aligned exactly.

Caution!

Page marks (and calibration bars) won't print if there isn't enough room on the page!

Calibration Bars

Checking this option prints an 11-step grayscale step wedge moving from 0 percent black to 100 percent black in 10 percent increments. On CMYK color separations, a gradient tint bar is printed on the left of each CMY plate and a progressive color bar is printed on the right. From this, you can find out if your output device needs to be calibrated, thus guaranteeing that all shades are absolute.

Caption

Use this to print a caption with your separations or printout. To add a caption, you must have previously added information about the file in the File Info dialog box. Check this box after creating the file information.

Labels

Use the Labels option to print the file name above the image. This has saved me more than a few times; I'd highly recommend it.

Emulsion Down

Check this box to denote that the paper used is emulsion side down and must be printed the opposite of what is shown on the screen. If this is checked, Photoshop flips the image around so it'll print correctly. You can see the difference when you check it and uncheck it. Check Emulsion Down if you are printing for sublimation or heat transfer, using a special type of film, or something similar.

To see how Emulsion Down works:

1. Open the file **New ight.psd** from the Chapter 27 folder on the companion CD. This file is to be printed using a heat transfer machine, thus the image must be flipped.

2. Choose **File>Print with Preview** to open the Print dialog box.

3. Check **Emulsion Down**. Notice that the image flips. It's now ready for print. See Figure 27-5.

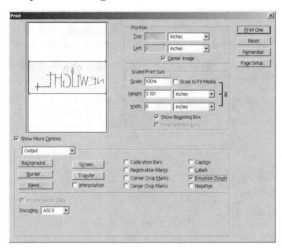

Figure 27-5: Using the Emulsion Down option

❌ **Caution!**

If you check Emulsion Down and then check Reverse Image or a similar command in your printer properties window, you might flip the image twice. If this happens, the image will not print flipped once; it will print as it was originally!

Negative

Use this to print an inverted version of the entire image, including background color and masks. The printout converts the entire image to a negative—but not the preview or on screen version. When printing a negative, white becomes black and black becomes white. You probably won't need this too often in screen printed work.

Include Vector Data

Vector data was introduced in Chapter 23, "Process Color Separations." When there is vector data to print, you can check this box to have it printed as vector data so that it prints out more clearly and with less pixelation. With Include Vector Data checked, vector graphics print at the printer's full resolution, not at the resolution of the image file.

Color Management Options

Although you can print channels a few at a time by selecting them with
the eye icon in the Channels palette and then using File>Print with Preview, you can also print separations by changing the output options in the
Print dialog box from Output to Color Management and then by choosing
the print separations. See Figure 27-6. Choosing this option prints each
color channel as a separate page.

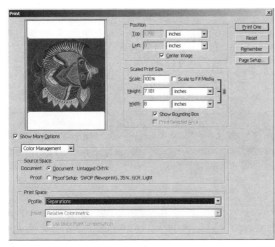

*Figure 27-6: Printing
separations*

✖ Caution!

Make sure you have all of the channels selected in the Channels palette before
using this option.

Although this is a viable option for printing separations, I prefer to use
the Output choice and configure my own settings for screen, frequency,
and angle, and create registration, corner, center marks, and such.

Exploring the Page Setup Dialog Box

The Page Setup dialog box allows you to configure settings for the paper, orientation, and margins and set properties for the printer. There are two ways to access this dialog box: from File>Page Setup and from File> Print with Preview and the Page Setup button. Figure 27-7 shows the Page Setup dialog box for a generic PostScript printer. Your page setup dialog box might look different depending on what type of printer you're using.

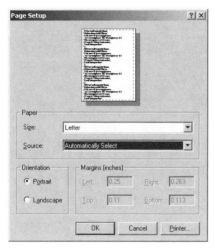

Figure 27-7: The Page Setup dialog box

Paper, Source, Orientation, and Margins

Click the arrow on the Size window to see the choices for sizes of paper that you can put in your printer. You won't be able to select a paper "type" here, like photo paper, premium paper, plain paper, etc., as these options are found under printer preferences; here you can only choose the paper size.

Click the arrow on the window for Source to see the options for different paper feeds; generally there are options for envelope, manual, automatic, and any additional trays that your printer might have.

In Figure 27-7, the orientation is portrait; however, clicking the landscape button prints the image long ways instead of up and down.

If the Margins section is grayed out, margins cannot be set for this particular image, image size, and printer. If they are not grayed out and you wish to configure margins, you can do so by typing in the appropriate numbers for left, right, top, and bottom.

The Printer Button

The Printer button in the Page Setup dialog box brings up an additional Page Setup dialog box, shown in Figure 27-8. From here, you can select and configure the printer of your choice.

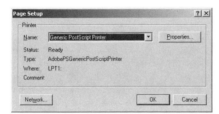

Figure 27-8: Additional page setup options

The Properties button brings up yet another dialog box, one that details the printer's properties.

Printer Properties

Printer properties will differ from one printer to another. Figures 27-9, 27-10, and 27-11 show different printers and their respective printer properties.

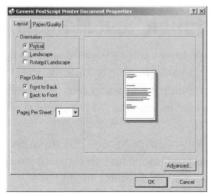

Figure 27-9: Generic PostScript printer properties dialog box

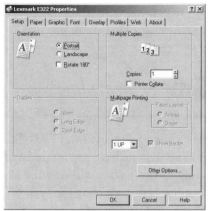

*Figure 27-10: Lexmark E322 printer
properties dialog box*

*Figure 27-11: Epson C60 printer properties dialog
box*

The first printer (in Figure 27-9) is the printer installed using the Post-Script printer driver from the Adobe Photoshop 7.0 CD and will work with Photoshop and your existing PostScript printer. You use this driver and printer if you have trouble enabling vector data or have other problems with your PostScript printer's properties. The second printer (Figure 27-10) is a Lexmark E322 that I purchased and have available for PostScript print work. The third printer (Figure 27-11) is an Epson C60 printer, which I use for printing out sublimation artwork. Sublimation artwork doesn't require color separations and thus doesn't need PostScript capabilities.

Depending on what printer you have available, you'll want to configure the printer properties appropriately. With most printers, you can set options for paper, print quality, print resolution, dithering, ink flow, and more. Consult your printer's documentation to learn more.

The Print Dialog Box

The Print dialog box is available from File>Print and from File>Print with Preview and the Print button. The options here are limited and include choosing a printer and setting its properties, viewing the status of the printer (whether it is ready, offline, etc.), viewing the type of printer it is (PostScript, Generic PostScript, InkJet, etc.), where it is located (LPT1, LPT2, network, etc.), and any comments recorded about the printer. You can also choose the Page Range if you have several pages to print and set the number of copies you want printed. These copies can be collated if desired. See Figure 27-12.

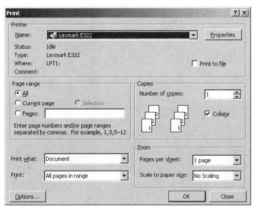

Figure 27-12: The Print dialog box

 Tip:

Your Print dialog box can look different from this one as well. The Print dialog box options differ for different printers and applications.

View>Print Size Command

You can view the image in various ways on the screen. The View>Print Size command offers three ways: Actual Pixels, Fit on Screen, and Print Size. To choose these options, select View>Print Size and then choose the Zoom tool or the Hand tool from the toolbox. From the options bar, select the appropriate choice.

The Actual Pixels option displays the pixels with disregard to the resolution setting of your monitor. For instance, if your monitor is set to 1024 x 768 and the image size is 1456 x 1308 (as is the Print.psd file that we've used in this chapter), then choosing Actual Pixels will give you what you see in Figure 27-13. Using the Actual Size option is a great way to see how others will view the image with different resolutions, and is used often when preparing an image for a web page.

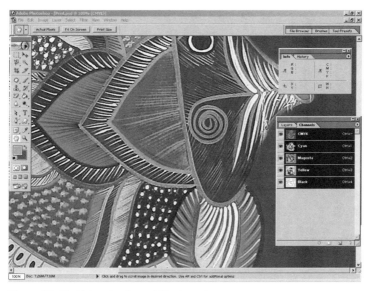

Figure 27-13: Using the Actual Pixels option

Fit on Screen and Print Size are pretty self-explanatory. Choose Fit on Screen to work with the image comfortably; choose Print Size to see exactly how large an image will be when printed.

Summary

In this chapter you learned about the available print dialog boxes and different options for printing. The Print with Preview dialog box is where you'll do most of your configurations and offers options for screens, borders, backgrounds, bleed, transfer, interpolation, and page marks, among other things.

The Page Setup dialog box allows you to configure paper properties such as size, orientation, and margins and also allows access to the printer's properties dialog box.

While this chapter provided an overview of printer terms and options, Chapter 29 details the actual numbers that you use for printing different kinds of images and color separations, including process, spot, index, and more.

Chapter 28

Specialty Papers

In the old days of screen printing, printers created their film positives using a camera, processors, and a little knowledge of chemistry. Darkrooms were required to process the film used to create the screens. This technology has been replaced with newer technology, eliminating the need for screen printers to have a camera and darkroom set up.

These new technologies allow the screen printer to create film positives from laser, PostScript, and inkjet printers. Specialty papers can be used with Photoshop and the color separations created to produce the film required to burn screens.

There are several different options for outputting your work. There's vellum for inkjets and laser printers, polyester-based films, laser acetates for laser printers, films for inkjet printers, and of course service bureaus.

Vellums

Vellum is our choice for printing out positives here at our shop—North Texas Graphics. Vellum is pretty cheap, somewhere between a nickel and a quarter a sheet to produce, and we almost always get a perfect and usable print. Vellum can be purchased for both inkjet and laser printers. Laser vellum is laser printer and dry toner copier safe, and inkjet vellum can be used on inkjet printers as well as large format inkjet plotters.

Problems with Vellum

Vellum isn't for everyone or every job, but it'll certainly work for the simple and non-critical work you do in your shop. There are a few problems with vellum though, including the following:

- **Shrinkage:** Because vellum is paper, it can shrink when it absorbs moisture (ink). This means that for jobs that require real tight registration, it probably won't work. For extremely tight jobs, consider using film.

- **Inconsistency:** You'll see slight differences between brands of vellums and how they work with different printers.

- **Printer problems:** When using vellum, the printer must be able to lay the ink down heavily. If the printer cannot be configured to do this, the vellum will not be usable.

- **Cost of black ink/toner:** The cost of black ink cartridges for inkjet printers can run up to $40 for a desktop printer and up to $500 for replacements for a sublimation printer. The cost of toner cartridges is equally staggering. Laying down the black ink can get expensive after a while.

- **Problems with halftones:** Detailed halftone dots can be lost due to the amount of exposure needed to burn the screen. Lighter dots might be missed. Consider using film if this becomes a problem.

While you can't use vellum for every job, you can use it for almost any spot color job, as well as non-critical process color jobs. Since we get a lot of spot color jobs, we simply separate out the colors, pop the vellum in the printer, and create the screens.

Film and Laser Acetate

Film and laser acetate work better than vellum for critical work and process jobs that require detailed calibration. However, these are more expensive than vellum, which can pose a problem for smaller shops.

Inkjet Films

Inkjet films enable printers to produce high-quality film positives using an inkjet printer and the ink that comes with it. The film comes in various sizes and is clear. It is usually 4 to 5 mm thick and coated to work with various commercial printers. Because it's a film, you don't have to worry about shrinkage like you do with vellum, so it makes for a better choice (although a little more expensive). Films create extremely dense positives, where the black is really black, thus it creates a wonderfully perfect screen.

Depending on the inkjet film you choose, the proof may or may not be waterproof. While some advertisers make this seem like a big deal, it isn't. You don't immerse your films in water at any point, and if you need them to be waterproof for any reason, you can always spray them with a fixative.

Polyester-based Film for Laser Printers

Laser polyester film is heat resistant and dimensionally stable film for laser printers. For screen printing, it makes crisp film positives directly from your desktop computer. Again, this film is more expensive than vellum but creates better output for process color and tight registration and critical work.

Capillary Direct Film

Direct film, also called capillary film, is a clear acetate sheet with a direct emulsion already on it. This stencil is applied to the screen with water. Direct film can be used for screen printing on shirts, but it can also be used for items like car decals for a sports team, political stickers, and similar substrates.

Capillary film has several advantages over older film technologies:

- It's great for long print runs.
- It has good definition and offers easy processing.
- It washes out with cold or hot water.
- It can be removed easily.
- It is consistent.

Laser Acetate

Laser acetate is a film that is a photo sensitized acetate sheet, which is processed through exposure to light. The sheet is printed in a laser printer. Make sure you purchase the right kind of acetate paper for your printer though; some acetate will melt on the rollers of a laser printer and others don't take ink well. The acetate is printed and used to burn the screens.

Service Bureaus

You can always send your artwork out to a service bureau if you can't do it yourself, your print devices aren't large enough, or you need an extremely accurate set of separations for a complex critical job. You'll have to ask the bureau what type of file format it wants, which will most likely be PSD, EPS, or TIFF, and you'll need to find out about any additional requirements before sending. Look for a bureau that will accept your PSD file for best results.

Some things to consider when using a service bureau:

- Be sure to include any fonts that you've used, just in case the bureau needs them.

- Send the file in the appropriate file format and size.

- Send as CMYK, and note what numbers you want for the output of each of the plates (screens, channels). Be sure to specify the line count, dot shape, and frequency.

- Don't compress your files. If they are over 2 MB in size, put them on a disk and mail them instead of sending via e-mail, or call and ask how large of a file you can send. Many e-mail addresses won't accept anything larger than 2 MB.

- Verify that the bureau can use TrueType fonts if you've used them; otherwise use PostScript Type 1 or 2 fonts.

- Include any graphic files linked to the image if necessary.

■ Insist the channels be printed out if sending a PSD file, or split the channels yourself and have each one printed as a separate file.

■ Tell the service bureau you need a film positive.

Keep in mind that the more work you do, the less the bureau has to do. The more the bureau has to do, the more you'll be charged!

Summary

There are multiple options for printing out your color separations, including vellums, films, and outputting to a service bureau. Each has its pros and cons, and understanding these will help you make the correct choice for your output.

Chapter 29

Printing Color Separations

So, you've created your design and are ready to print it out. You've pre-pared the image for printing, whether it is a one- or two-color spot color design, a four- or five-color indexed color design, or a multichannel process color design.

For the spot color and indexed color prints, you've pulled the spot channels and tweaked them. For process prints, you've lightened, saturated, and corrected color contaminations. You've used unsharp masking and done various tweaks on the design, including color correction. You've created the CMYK color separations, created a white printer, underbase, and/or highlight white plate if needed, created spot colors if needed, and you have the channels in the correct print order in the Channels palette. You might have even created a shirt color channel to see how the design will look on a particular color of shirt.

In this chapter, we learn how to print out the images that you've created, including spot color, indexed color, and process color images. There is an overlap in the directions to enable you to jump directly to the section that contains the information you need without having to read the rest of the chapter.

 Note:

In this chapter we work through the print configuration process using files I've included on the companion CD. You have to adapt these settings to match the needs of the files you'll be working with in your own shop.

Double-check the Color Settings

Before we get started with the actual print process, let's verify that the settings in the Color Settings dialog box are correct. These settings should be configured already, but if you didn't start at the beginning of this book and read each chapter in order, they might not be set properly.

 Tip:

If you worked through Chapter 5, you can skip this part.

Work through the following steps to verify that you have the correct settings. These settings should have been configured before converting any RGB image to CMYK, and if they weren't, you'll need to set them and perform the CMYK conversion again. Photoshop uses these settings to perform optimal separations for your equipment and needs.

1. Select **Edit > Color Settings**.

2. In the Working Spaces choices under RGB, choose **Apple RGB**. Yes, you should choose this no matter what, even if you aren't working on a Mac.

 Note:

If you've saved any ink profiles to your hard drive that you've received from your supplier or ink dealer, you can choose Load CMYK, change Files of Type to CMYK setup, and locate the ink values. Click on the file to load these specific ink value numbers.

3. Next, change the CMYK Working Spaces settings to **Custom CMYK**. This will allow you to specify custom ink settings, dot gain settings, and more.

4. In the Custom CMYK dialog box shown in Figure 29-1, rename the custom settings if desired. I prefer to leave the name the way it is, as it is very descriptive and changes as the values change in the Custom Settings dialog box.

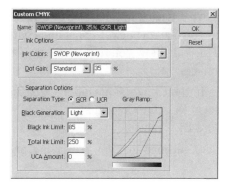

Figure 29-1: Custom CMYK settings

5. From the Ink Colors drop-down list, choose **Custom** if you have specific ink values to input. (Some companies offer a free plug-in for these values that include numbers for their specific product.) If you do not have any custom plug-ins, select another option from the list if it is available and meets your company's specifications. Otherwise, choose **SWOP (Newsprint)** if you aren't sure what to pick. This choice most closely matches standard process colors provided by many ink companies.

6. Continuing in the Custom CMYK dialog box, change the Dot Gain to 35 percent for automatic presses and up to 40 percent for manual presses. Leave the Dot Gain setting at Standard.

7. Change Black Generation to **Light**, Black Ink Limit to **85** percent, and Total Ink Limit to **250** percent. This limits how much ink will print on the paper. Click **OK**.

 Tip:

You'll get different thoughts on these settings; some people will set Total Ink Limit at 240 percent and others at 300 percent. Additionally, Black Ink Limit is sometimes set to 90 percent and Black Generation at Medium. You'll need to experiment with your own presses and equipment; these are simply standard numbers that often work well.

8. In the Separation Type area, GCR is generally the best setting. Choose **GCR** if most of the image is neutral in color and light in most areas; choose **UCR** when the design has lots of black.

9. Leave UCA Amount at 0. Click **OK**.

10. By clicking OK in step 9, we are back in the Color Settings dialog box. From here, click the down arrow next to Spot and configure the dot gain to 30 percent. This will allow you to preview the image with dot gain in a spot color image.

11. Check **Advanced Mode.** In the Conversion Options area, use the Adobe ACE engine, and use Relative Colorimetric. Do not check Desaturate Monitor Colors By.

12. Click **Save.** Name the color settings that you are saving, and click **Save** again.

13. In the Color Settings Comment dialog box, type in **T-Shirt settings** or some other descriptive name. Click **OK** twice.

Photoshop will remember these settings for you. These settings will allow you to get the most out of the program and, as you've seen, even allow you to download ink color values from a supplier and automatically input those into the program's customization settings.

 Caution!

Once again, if you are just making these adjustments to the color settings and you've already performed a CMYK color separation, you'll have to go back and perform that separation again. Photoshop uses these settings to decide how to separate an image. If they're not set up correctly, the separation will not be created correctly.

Printing True Spot Color Separations

True spot color separations are the easiest and most forgiving way to both output the print and to screen print. I define "true" spot color images as those images that consist only of one to eight solid, definable colors and whose colors do not have tints, gradients, or highlights and therefore do not need to be printed with halftones.

These types of images, designs, and logos are great for clients such as sports teams, small businesses, and anyone else interested in buying an inexpensive screen printed shirt. In addition to being a good option for clients, it's a terrific way to start or build a screen printing business and attract clientele.

Note:

You can print true spot color separations on just about any printer at all; it doesn't have to be a PostScript printer because there are no halftones.

To print a spot color design, you'll first need the separations. Figure 29-2 shows a spot color design that consists of four colors—black, green, orange, and purple. These colors have been separated and are shown in the Channels palette. No underbase is needed if the image is to be printed on a light shirt.

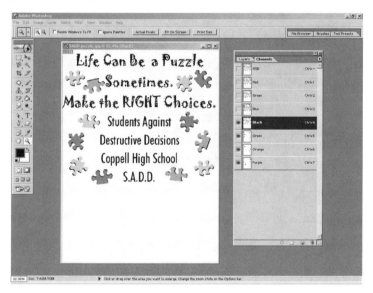

Figure 29-2: Printing out spot color separations

 Note:

If you'd like to experiment with this image, it's on the CD in the Chapter 29 folder and named SADD puzzle.psd.

To print these separations:

1. Verify that you have a PostScript, laser, or inkjet printer available and that this printer can really lay down the ink or toner. (You could use an imagesetter too, although that might be overkill.)

2. In the Channels palette, remove the eye icon from the composite layer and the RGB layers. Place an eye next to each of the spot channels you want to print and select them for good measure. Figure 29-3 shows an example. Although selecting all channels isn't necessary

(as shown in Figure 29-4), some printers might give errors if the channels are not selected. (To select multiple channels, hold down the Shift key while selecting.)

3. Choose **Print with Preview**.

Figure 29-3: Selecting channels to print

Figure 29-4: Selecting channels to print

4. Verify that the print fits in the Preview window.

5. If desired, check **Center Image**, **Scale to Fit Media**, and **Show Bounding Box**.

6. Verify that Show More Options is checked. See Figure 29-5.

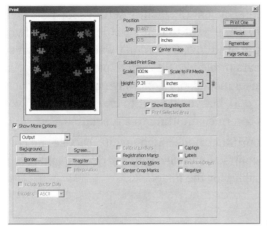

Figure 29-5: More options

7. Because there are no halftones in the image, setting options for Screen and Transfer aren't required. However, you can configure Bleed, Border, or Background options if needed.

8. Click the **Print** button.

9. In the Print dialog box, use the drop-down list to choose the appropriate printer. I'll choose an inkjet printer, as shown in Figure 29-6, although a PostScript printer would do just fine. Notice in Figure 29-6 that the printer understands there are four pages to print; these are the pages that you've chosen to print in the Channels palette.

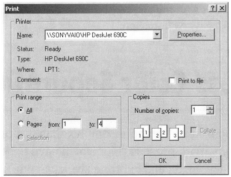

Figure 29-6: Choosing a printer

10. Click the **Properties** button.

11. For an inkjet printer, adjust the quality settings for Best Quality and Black and White. You'll want to really lay down the ink if you are printing on vellum or film, but you don't want to lay down so much that the ink smears or bleeds. Be sure to pick the appropriate paper type and print resolution also. I generally put down as much as possible (600 to 1200 dpi), but you'll want to experiment with your own inks and papers before committing to a resolution.

12. For a PostScript printer, choose high quality, choose the correct paper type, set contrast, increase toner darkness, and configure resolution (if applicable) for the image.

 Tip:

Read your printer's documentation to see how to get the best print possible. Compare this information with what your papers, films, acetates, and vellums suggest.

13. Click **OK** and **OK** again to print.

If the print doesn't come out as desired (for instance if it's pixelated, too light, or the wrong size), you'll have to start over. Read Chapter 22 on spot color separations, Chapter 27 on page setup and the print dialog boxes, and Chapter 28 on specialty papers.

 Tip:

Visit your printer manufacturer's web site and see if there are any ICC profiles available or any tips for working with Photoshop.

Printing Process Color Separations

Printing process separations is a little more complex than printing out solid spot color separations. With process color, you'll have to set screen options, including frequency, angle, and halftone shape, among other things, and you'll need a PostScript printer.

Prepare the Image

Preparing the print is the biggest part of getting a process image ready, and several chapters in this book cover that part of the process. Preparing the image *for the printer* requires you to tell Photoshop and the printer what channels you'd like to print, how large the image should print, and how the page should be set up.

To prepare the image for the printer:

1. Open the file **FishProcess.psd** from the Chapter 29 folder on the companion CD. (This file is provided for this example only; it isn't necessarily ready for the printer and press.)

2. In the Channels palette, place an eye icon next to all of the channels that you want to print. You won't want to print the Shirt Color channel if there is one, and you might only want to print a couple of channels as a test before printing out all of the others. Whatever the case, make the appropriate selections. See Figure 29-7.

Figure 29-7: Selecting the channels to print

> ☑ **Tip:**
> This file is in Multichannel mode, and the print order is correct for most presses.

3. Choose **File>Print with Preview** and verify that the print fits in the Preview window. Click **Cancel**.

4. Choose **File>Page Setup** and verify that Portrait is chosen. Click **OK**.

Output the Image

When you are ready to print, follow the steps listed here:

1. Verify that you have a PostScript printer or imagesetter available.

2. Choose **Print with Preview**.

3. If desired, check **Center Image**, **Scale to Fit Media**, and **Show Bounding Box**.

4. Verify that Show More Options is checked.

5. Because there are halftones in the image, you'll need to set Screen options. Click the **Screen** button.

6. Uncheck **Use Printer's Default Screens**, as shown in Figure 29-8.

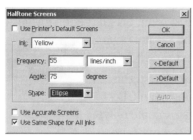

Figure 29-8: The Halftone Screens dialog box

7. Click the down arrow next to Ink, and choose **Underbase**.

8. For Frequency, choose **55** lpi for a manual press and **65** lpi for an automatic press.

 Note:

If you are using a manual press, you might need to set the lpi as low as 25. This is true with all of the ink colors, not just the underbase. You'll have to get to know your equipment.

9. For Angle, type in **15**.

10. For Shape, choose **Ellipse**.

11. Check **Use Same Shape for All Inks**, so Ellipse will be chosen each time.

12. Click the down arrow next to Ink and choose **Yellow**.

13. Set the frequency for either **55** lpi or **65** lpi. Use an angle of **75** and choose **Ellipse**.

 Note:

As mentioned in the sidebar on the following page, you'll get different theories here. At one print shop in our area, the owner sets the Yellow angle to 0.

14. Click the down arrow next to Ink and choose **Magenta**.

15. Set the frequency for either **55** lpi or **65** lpi. Use an angle of **45** and choose **Ellipse**.

Note:

As mentioned in the following sidebar, you'll get different theories here. At one print shop in our area, the owner sets the magenta angle to 75.

16. Click the down arrow next to Ink and choose **Cyan**.

17. Set the frequency for either **55** lpi or **65** lpi. Use an angle of **15** and choose **Ellipse**. (Cyan always seems to be set at 15 degrees, no matter whom you consult!)

18. Click the down arrow next to Ink and choose **Black**.

19. Set the frequency for either **55** lpi or **65** lpi. Use an angle of **75** and choose **Ellipse**.

 Note:

As mentioned in the following sidebar, you'll get different theories here. At one print shop in our area, the owner sets the black angle to 45.

20. Click the down arrow next to Ink and choose **Highlight white**.

21. Set the frequency for either **55** lpi or **65** lpi. Use an angle of **15** and choose **Ellipse**.

 Note:

If you have spot color channels to configure along with the process color channels, you'll need to configure those in the Screen dialog box before closing it. Use the same frequency listed above and 15 to 45 degrees for the angle for each spot channel. Again, you'll need to experiment with your presses, inks, screens, etc.

22. If you are printing to an imagesetter, check **Use Accurate Screens**. Click **OK**. (Be sure to read the following sidebar.)

A Word about lpi, Frequency, and Dot Shape

If you don't agree with the settings that I'm suggesting you configure for your screens, you probably aren't alone. However, these angles, dot shapes, and lpi are what we use at our shop, and they work great for us. They are also the same settings that are suggested by professional screen printers in forums I've visited on the Internet.

Keep in mind though that there are other opinions. I've read articles that state the black plate should always be 45 lpi and the angle set to 25 degrees; I've read articles that say never to use angles of 45 and 90 degrees because you'll get moiré; I've also read articles that say that all spot color halftones should be

printed at 45 lpi—never higher or lower. I've also read that circular dots are
better than elliptical ones, etc., etc., etc. You'll have to decide, but I'm betting
that the settings outlined in this section will work fine for you. If you are new at
this, use the settings I've suggested as defaults and tweak as needed.

23. With the screens configured, place a check mark next to **Calibration
Bars** (if available), **Registration Marks**, and **Labels**. Check any
additional marks as desired. See Figure 29-9.

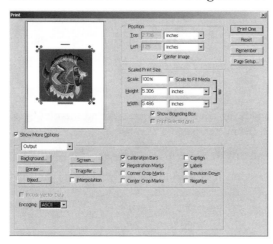

Figure 29-9: Preparing to print

24. Click the **Print** button.

25. In the Print dialog box, use the drop-down list to choose the appropriate PostScript printer or imagesetter. I chose my generic
PostScript printer, whose driver I installed from the Photoshop 7.0
installation CD. This driver is used, and my PostScript printer out-
puts the separations. See Figure 29-10. Notice in the figure that the
printer understands that there are six pages to print; these are the
pages I've chosen to print in the Channels palette.

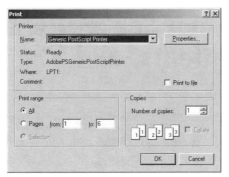

Figure 29-10: Choosing a printer

26. Click the **Properties** button.

27. Configure the settings for the printer. Be sure to pick the appropriate paper type too. I print at 600 to 1200 dpi, but you'll want to experiment with your own inks and papers before committing to a resolution. If applicable, set the contrast, toner darkness, and other attributes.

 Tip:

Read your printer's documentation to see how to get the best print possible. Compare this information with what your papers, films, acetates, and vellums suggest.

28. Click **OK** and **OK** again to print.

If the print doesn't come out as desired (for instance, if it's pixelated, too light, or the wrong size), you'll have to start over or at least reconfigure the image resolution and printer configurations. Read Chapter 23 on process color separations, Chapter 27 on page setup and the print dialog boxes, and Chapter 28 on specialty papers.

 Tip:

If C/15, M/45, Y/75, and K/75 don't work for you, try C/22.5, M/52.5, Y/82.5, and B/82.5. You might get better results with these numbers.

Printing Spot Color Separations with Tints, Gradients, and Highlights

Spot color separations that have tints, gradients, or highlights require they be printed using halftones on a PostScript printer. (In contrast, "true" spot color separations can be output using any printer and do not require halftones.) Since you have to use halftones, you'll have to set the lpi, frequency, and angle in the Screen dialog box in a manner similar to that performed for process color separations. However, because printing spot color images is different at the press and inks are a little different than process color at the press, you'll need different settings.

Printing Spot Colors with Gradients

To print spot color separations that require halftones:

1. Open a file of a spot color image that should be printed with halftones.

2. In the Channels palette, place an eye icon next to all of the channels that you want to print. You won't want to print the Shirt Color channel, and you might only want to print a couple of channels as a test before printing out all of the others. Whatever the case, make the appropriate selections.

3. Verify that you have a PostScript printer or imagesetter available.

4. Choose **Print with Preview**.

5. If desired, check **Center Image**, **Scale to Fit Media**, and **Show Bounding Box**.

6. Verify that Show More Options is checked.

7. Because there are halftones in the image, you'll need to set Screen options. Click the **Screen** button.

8. Uncheck **Use Printer's Default Screens**.

9. Click the down arrow next to Ink, and choose the first channel.

10. For Frequency, choose **25** to **45** lpi (your preference).

11. For Angle, type in **25**.

12. For Shape, choose **Ellipse**.

13. Check **Use Same Shape for All Inks**, so Ellipse will be chosen each time.

14. Click the down arrow next to Ink and choose another channel. Configure the same settings—**25** to **45** lpi, Angle **25**, and **Ellipse**.

15. Click the down arrow next to Ink and choose another channel. Configure the same settings—**25** to **45** lpi, Angle **25**, and **Ellipse**.

16. Click the down arrow next to Ink and choose another channel. Continue in this manner until all channels have been configured. Configure the same settings—**25** to **45** lpi, Angle **25**, and **Ellipse**.

 Tip:

Some printers always use an angle of 45 degrees when printing spot colors. You'll have to experiment to find what's best for you and the equipment you have available.

17. If you are printing to an imagesetter, check **Use Accurate Screens**. Click **OK**.

18. With the screens configured, place a check mark next to **Calibration Bars**, **Registration Marks**, and **Labels**. Check any additional marks as desired.

19. Click the **Print** button.

20. In the Print dialog box, use the drop-down list to choose the appropriate PostScript printer or imagesetter. I'll choose my generic PostScript printer, whose driver I installed from the Photoshop 7.0 installation CD. This driver will be used, and my PostScript printer will output the separations.

21. Click the **Properties** button.

22. Configure the settings for the printer. Make sure to pick the appropriate paper type too. I print at 600 to 1200 dpi, but you'll want to experiment with your own inks and papers before committing to a resolution. If applicable, set the contrast, toner darkness, and other attributes.

 Tip:

Read your printer's documentation to see how to get the best print possible. Compare this information with what your papers, films, acetates, and vellums suggest.

23. Click **OK** and **OK** again to print.

If the print doesn't come out as desired (for instance, if it's pixelated, too light, or the wrong size), you'll have to start over or at least reconfigure the image resolution and printer configurations. Read Chapter 22 on spot color separations, Chapter 27 on page setup and the print dialog boxes, and Chapter 28 on specialty papers.

Printing Indexed Color Separations

Indexed color separations are created in Photoshop when you want to choose the colors and the number of colors to print at the press. Index separations use random square dots called stochastic or diffusion dither (not halftones), so you won't need to pick a dot shape. In addition, the actual size of the dot is determined by the image itself, so you won't need to specify a frequency or angle either. This makes outputting color separations quite simple.

✖ Caution!

Because the size and quantity of the dots is created automatically, you'll want to have an image that is between 175 dpi and 200 dpi. This will allow for a 65 lpi dot.

To output an indexed color separation, perform the following steps:

1. Open the file **PoolBalls.psd** from the Chapter 29 folder on the companion CD. This image has already been indexed and separated.

2. In the Channels palette, place an eye icon next to all of the channels that you want to print. You won't want to print the Shirt Color channel, and you might only want to print a couple of channels as a test before printing out all of the others. Whatever the case, make the appropriate selections. See Figure 29-11.

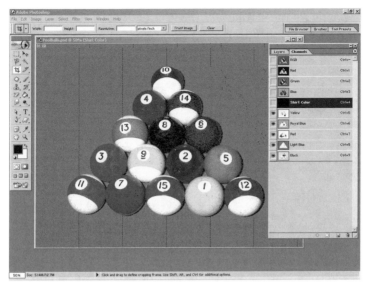

Figure 29-11: Selecting the channels to print

3. Verify that you have a PostScript printer or imagesetter available.

4. Choose **Print with Preview**.

5. If desired, check **Center Image**, **Scale to Fit Media**, and **Show Bounding Box**.

6. Verify that Show More Options is checked.

7. Place a check mark next to **Calibration Bars** (if available), **Registration Marks**, and **Labels**.

8. Click the **Print** button.

9. In the Print dialog box, use the drop-down list to choose the appropriate PostScript printer or imagesetter. I'll choose my generic PostScript printer, whose driver I installed from the Photoshop 7.0 installation CD. This driver will be used, and my PostScript printer will output the separations. (I've printed out indexed prints from my inkjet printer too, but the print was unusable because of the quality of output.)

10. Click the **Properties** button.

11. Configure the settings for the printer. Be sure to pick the appropriate paper type too. I print at 600 to 1200 dpi, but you'll want to experiment with your own inks and papers before committing to a resolution. If applicable, set the contrast, toner darkness, and other attributes.

 Tip:

Read your printer's documentation to see how to get the best print possible. Compare this information with what your papers, films, acetates, and vellums suggest.

12. Click **OK** and **OK** again to print.

If the print doesn't come out as desired (for instance, if it's pixelated, too light, or the wrong size), you'll have to start over or at least reconfigure the image resolution and printer configurations. Read Chapter 24 on indexed color separations, Chapter 27 on page setup and the print dialog boxes, and Chapter 28 on specialty papers.

Printing Simulated Process Color Separations

Simulated process color prints are printed like true process color prints, except the configuration of the lpi and angle are different. Although theories differ, we get pretty impressive results using 55 lpi for all frequency settings (although lots of printers use 65 lpi) and 25 degrees for all angles settings. We also use an elliptical dot, although some printers prefer circular.

To print a simulated process color separation:

1. Open the simulated process image to print and verify that you have a PostScript printer or imagesetter available. From the Channels palette, place an eye icon next to each channel that you'd like to print. Do not print the shirt color.

2. Choose **Print with Preview.**

3. If desired, check **Center Image**, **Scale to Fit Media**, and **Show Bounding Box.**

4. Verify that Show More Options is checked.

5. Because there are halftones in the image, you'll need to set Screen options. Click the **Screen** button.

6. Uncheck **Use Printer's Default Screens**, as shown earlier in Figure 29-8.

7. Click the down arrow next to Ink, and choose the first ink color you want to print from the list.

8. For Frequency, choose **55** lpi.

9. For Angle, type in **25**.

10. For Shape, choose **Ellipse**.

11. Check **Use Same Shape for All Inks** so that Ellipse will be chosen each time.

12. Click the down arrow next to Ink and choose the next color to print. Configure the same settings—**55** lpi, Angle **25**, and **Ellipse** for each of the remaining ink colors.

✎ **Note:**

If you have spot color channels to configure along with the process color channels, you'll need to configure those in the Screen dialog box before closing it. Use the same frequency listed above and 15 to 45 degrees for the angle for each spot channel. Again, you'll need to experiment with your presses, inks, screens, etc.

13. If you are printing to an imagesetter, check **Use Accurate Screens**. Click **OK**.

14. With the screens configured, place a check mark next to **Calibration Bars** (if available), **Registration Marks**, and **Labels**. Check any additional marks as desired.

15. Click the **Print** button.

16. In the Print dialog box, use the drop-down list to choose the appropriate PostScript printer or imagesetter. I'll choose my generic PostScript printer, whose driver I installed from the Photoshop 7.0 installation CD. This driver will be used, and my PostScript printer will output the separations.

17. Click the **Properties** button.

18. Configure the settings for the printer. Be sure to pick the appropriate paper type too. I print at 600 to 1200 dpi, but you'll want to experiment with your own inks and papers before committing to a resolution. If applicable, set the contrast, toner darkness, and other attributes.

 Tip:

Read your printer's documentation to see how to get the best print possible. Compare this information with what your papers, films, acetates, and vellums suggest.

19. Click **OK** and **OK** again to print.

If the print doesn't come out as desired (for instance, if it's pixelated, too light, or the wrong size), you'll have to start over or at least reconfigure the image resolution and printer configurations. Read Chapter 25 on process color separations, Chapter 27 on page setup and the print dialog boxes, and Chapter 28 on specialty papers.

Summary

In this chapter you learned how to print true spot color images, spot color images with halftones, process color images, simulated process color images, and indexed color images. Each requires specific settings for lpi, frequency, and angle, and each has additional printer requirements.

While theories vary about the settings suggested in this chapter, I've tried to offer industry standards, what works for our shop, and what I consider the best settings for the general public (beginning screeners in particular). Once you've tried these settings and output options, you can tweak them to suit your specific tastes, needs, and equipment.

Chapter 30

Specialty Printing

Sublimation and heat transfers were introduced briefly in Chapter 17, but now that you're ready to print them, there's more to talk about! In this chapter I introduce how to print heat transfers, sublimation, and numbers in Photoshop and what types of printers, papers, and inks you'll need to do so. I also introduce CAD cutters and how Photoshop can and cannot be used to produce prints and how using vinyl and thermal film differs from other print options.

Of the three options (heat transfers, sublimation, and CAD cutting on vinyl), heat transfers are the least expensive, with sublimation fairly close behind. CAD cutters can be expensive and beyond the reach of many smaller shops. In addition, using a CAD cutter generally requires that another program be used as a liaison between Photoshop and the cutter itself. For all three options you need a heat transfer press, but for sublimation you also need a new (sublimation) printer and inks, and for CAD cutting you need a CAD printer/cutter, color ribbons, film, and various other accessories. Heat transfers are the least expensive because they can be output on your in-house color laser copier, laser printer, thermal printer, or inkjet printer using inks you already have; all you have to buy is the paper.

Numbers are an issue for screen printers as well. Numbers can be printed using heat transfers, sublimation, and other methods. Numbers can be screen printed using a stenciling system, where a special press holds screens with all (or some) of the numbers ready to print when you need them, and numbers can also be output from a CAD cutter and used with a heat press. Numbers can also be purchased that are ready to use on your heat press, or you can create numbers using heat transfer paper. In this chapter, we learn about printing using these techniques.

Tip:

If you skipped Chapter 17, go back and read it now. It explains the differences between heat transfers, sublimation, and screen printing and when you should and should not use them.

Printing Heat Transfers

The least expensive way to produce one-of-a-kind artwork, limited run jobs, and artwork that is too difficult to screen print and/or too expensive to embroider is to use a heat transfer. Heat transfers can be created from your existing inkjet printer and inkjet inks, your color laser copier, laser printer, or your existing thermal printer, making it a perfect option for both small and large shops alike.

 Tip:

If a client wants ten shirts that have 25 colors, screening the shirt isn't an option for them since the screen fees alone would put the item out of reach. This is a great time to consider a heat transfer.

Heat Transfer Papers and Inks

When printing a heat transfer, you have to make sure you have the correct paper for your printer. There are several manufacturers to choose from; you'll just need to call and ask for a brochure. We get our papers from Xpres, which offers several types of papers. Some of the types of papers that you can purchase include:

■ **Ink Jet Transfer:** Use for creating heat transfers using an inkjet printer and regular inkjet inks. These transfers can be peeled after being applied (using a heat press) either hot or cold and produce a satin, glossy finish.

■ **Color Laser Copier:** Use when printing heat transfers using a color laser copier. This paper feeds easily into copiers and will transfer to T-shirts, sweatshirts, mousepads, caps, tote bags, and a variety of other substrates.

- **Color Laser, Alps, and Citizens dry resin**: Use when printing on any of these specialty printers.

- **Thermal**: Use when printing to a thermal printer or a color laser printer. These types of prints can usually be peeled hot or cold.

- **Color laser for glass, plastics, woods, ceramics, metals**: Use this specialty paper when printing from a laser copier for adherence to these materials.

Besides purchasing the right paper for the printer that you have, making sure you get the paper you need for the job, don't spend more than you need to. If you want to print using a laser copier and a color laser printer, purchase a paper that can do both. Verify when purchasing that the paper can be used to print on your specific substrate also. Some papers can only be used on polyester, for instance.

 Tip:

If you don't have a heat transfer press yet, I'd strongly suggest buying one. You can get a complete system with various papers and inks for under $2,000, and the money you can profit from with this will be well worth the investment.

Printing from Photoshop

Printing a heat transfer from Photoshop requires that the image be flipped, the printer properties be set to best or high quality, and the paper be inserted the correct way in the printer.

1. Open a file to print using a heat transfer. If you don't have a file, you can use the NewLight.psd file in the Chapter 30 folder on the companion CD.

2. Choose **File>Print with Preview**.

3. Check **Emulsion Down**, as shown in Figure 30-1. This will flip the image.

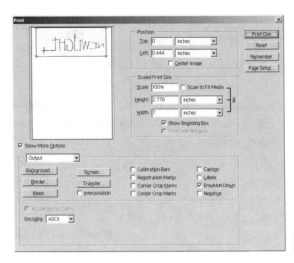

*Figure 30-1: Printing a
heat transfer*

4. Uncheck **Center Image** and change the Top number to **0**. Change
   the Left number to **0.44**. This will allow you to reuse the rest of the
   paper for another job. This is also shown in Figure 30-1.

5. Click the **Print** button.

6. In the Print dialog box, select the printer to use and click
   Properties.

7. Read the documents that came with the paper and printer you are
   using to determine the print quality. At our shop, on our Alps 5000,
   600 dpi is usually fine; on our inkjets, we choose Best Quality or
   Photo Quality. Given the option though, we do not up the ink value
   slider. Doing so causes the print to blur and/or smudge. You'll have
   to test yours to find what's best.

8. Click **OK**.

9. Place the paper in the printer. There will be writing on the side of the
   paper that you don't want to print on, so insert the paper accordingly.

10. Click **OK** again to print.

At the heat press, follow the instructions carefully. Make sure you are
using the correct pressure, time, and heat settings. If you aren't careful,
the image might not adhere the way you want and may peel around the
edges.

 Caution!

Don't put papers meant for inkjets in laser printers and vice versa. Doing so could
harm the inner workings of the printer and cause problems down the road.

Printing Sublimation

Printing with sublimation requires you have a sublimation printer and sublimation inks, along with special papers for printing. Although sublimation can be used for printing T-shirts, caps, and totes, we use sublimation mostly for printing coffee cups, mouse pads, luggage tags, clipboards, and similar materials.

 Tip:

Clean the sublimation nozzles once a month or so. Doing this will increase the life of the printer.

Sublimation Papers and Inks

To print sublimation, you'll need a sublimation printer. These can be purchased on the Internet and at specialty print stores. Some printers accept both regular inkjet cartridges and sublimation cartridges. You'll need to verify that your printer can accept sublimation cartridges before trying to print using sublimation paper.

Depending on the printer and the size of the sublimation ink set that you purchase, a set of sublimation cartridges runs around $300. The required paper for our sublimation printer is $15 for 100 sheets.

Printing from Photoshop

You can print sublimation items directly from Photoshop. Once the image has been created:

1. Open a file to print using sublimation. If you don't have a file, you can use the NewLight.psd file in the Chapter 30 folder on the companion CD.

2. Choose **File>Print with Preview**.

3. Check **Emulsion Down**, as shown in Figure 30-1. This will flip the image.

4. Uncheck **Center Image** and change the Top number to **0**. Change the Left number to **0.44**. This will allow you to reuse the rest of the paper for another job.

5. Click the **Print** button.

6. In the Print dialog box, select the printer to use and click **Properties**.

7. Read the documents that came with the paper and printer you are using to determine the print quality. At our shop, on our Epson C60, we choose 720 dpi and configure it from the Custom settings. You'll have to test yours to find what's best.

8. Choose the correct paper type from the Paper Type drop-down list.

9. Click **OK**.

10. Place the paper in the printer.

11. Click **OK** again to print.

If you are using a heat press, follow the instructions carefully. Make sure you are using the correct pressure, time, and heat settings. If you aren't careful, the image might not adhere the way you want and may peel around the edges. If you are using a cap press, mug press, or something similar, heed the same warnings.

CAD Cutters

More expensive and much more complicated than using sublimation or heat transfers are CAD cutters. These printer/cutter units can be purchased from various Internet sites and specialty print shops. They can be used to adhere full color prints onto dark garments with no color limitations (unlike heat transfers and sublimation).

CAD Cutting Films and Inks

CAD cutters use thermal film to produce full color prints at 600 dpi or higher. Resin ink cartridges are used, which can be similar to the ribbon cartridges that you might have seen with Alps and similar printers. The printer/cutter automatically prints and cuts out the design, and you peel it off and apply it to the substrate using a heat transfer machine. You'll have to read your cutter's documentation to purchase the correct inks and films.

 Tip:

Most larger print shops have a CAD cutter. With these, they create decals for cars and trucks, print posters and banners for various shops and merchandise, and more.

Printing from Photoshop

Although most CAD cutter/printers come with their own software, emerging technologies will arise that allow you to print directly from Photoshop to the CAD cutter. At this time though, using Photoshop for output to a CAD cutter isn't a viable option for most companies. If you must create the image in Photoshop, you'll have to export it to a program like Adobe Illustrator and then on to the CAD cutter's own software program. Your best option at this time is to create the design in the program that comes with the CAD cutter. You can also scan a design into these programs if you have a hard copy of it available.

Printing Numbers

I've found that putting numbers on team shirts is just about the worst job ever! You have to look at the shirt size and choose the correct number for the jersey first and then, depending on your system, go through the process of getting the numbers on the shirt.

If it's a heat transfer, you'll need to pull the numbers, lay them out for each shirt, and line them up on the press before printing. If it's a stenciling system, you'll have to spend time cleaning all of those screens, taping them, and cleaning them again. In the following sections, I outline some different ways to put numbers on shirts—you can choose your poison!

Use Heat Transfers and Sublimation

There are two ways to print numbers using a heat transfer. You can purchase the numbers from your local dealer, or you can print them out on heat transfer or sublimation paper. With either, you use the heat press to apply them.

Heat transfers using commercially produced numbers are the easiest for us and our method of choice. Applying numbers via heat transfer doesn't cause the mess that a screen would and is generally faster. We purchase numbers from our local dealer and try to keep at least four colors in stock.

Printing using numbers printed on heat transfer or sublimation paper directly from Photoshop is an option too but is generally more expensive. However, if you rarely print numbers, this might just be the way to go.

Purchase Paper Stencils

You can create one- to three-color outlined numbers using paper stencils that you purchase from your dealer. These paper stencils adhere to the screen mesh as you print. Once you've printed the number, you just discard the stencil. These stencils are sold in sets that usually come with 200 or so 1s and 100 or so of the other numbers. Medium-sized shops tend to go this way.

Employ a Stenciling System

Large shops that do quite a bit of numbering often choose a stenciling system. Screens are created for a set of numbers and attached to a press where they can then be screen printed. The press is used only for numbering, so the screens stay in there all of the time (unless they're being cleaned or replaced). A one-color numbering system can be purchased for less than $1,000.

Tip:

I've read that these systems are often more trouble that they're worth. Research this option fully before committing to it.

Use Vinyl Numbers (CAD Cutting)

You can create awesome-looking numbers using a CAD cutter. If I had one, I'd use it for numbering! Numbers can easily be created inside the CAD cutter's software and output and adhered easily.

Summary

In this chapter you learned about printing heat transfers, sublimation, and numbers and how a CAD cutter can also be helpful in your shop. Heat transfers and sublimation require special inks and papers, and you also need a heat transfer press. CAD cutters require special printers, films, and software.

Numbers can be printed in a variety of ways, including heat transfer, sublimation, CAD cutters, or by using a variety of manufactured items. These items include paper stencils and precut numbers that can be screen printed and transferred using a press, respectively.

Glossary

Action files: Recorded actions that can include adding text effects, image effects, and production actions, such as changing a custom RGB file to grayscale or saving a file as a JPEG, and will increase the efficiency in which you perform oft-repeated tasks.

Actions palette: Lets you record, play, edit, and delete specific actions or load action files.

Additional options: These are available when a pop-up palette is opened and denoted by a right arrow located in the top-right corner of the palette. Clicking on this arrow brings up the additional options.

Airbrush: Simulates traditional airbrush techniques by gradually adding paint similar to a spray paint gun or a spray paint can. The airbrush icon is located on the options bar when a brush is selected.

Align: Allows you to align layers or selections within an image. There are several ways to align objects: top, vertical center, left, horizontal center, and right.

Aligned: Use when repairing flaws in images (such as when using the Healing Brush or Clone Stamp tool). Place a check in the Align box if you need to release the mouse button while working and still keep the sampling point; sampled pixels are thus applied continuously. Uncheck the box to apply the pixels from the original sampling point each time. Aligning can also mean to left align text, center text, or right align text.

Alpha channel: A spot color channel in the Channels palette that you create using the Color Range tool.

Anchor point: As lines and curves are drawn using the Pen tool, anchor points are created that define the line, its endpoints, and its curves. Anchor points can be added or deleted from a shape, and they can be edited.

Angle: Controls the angle of the brush stroke. Angling creates a calligraphic look.

Anti-Aliased/Anti-aliasing: Anti-aliasing is the process of smoothing edges around a selection. It differs from feathering in that it does not blur the edges but instead softens them by blending the colors of the outer pixels with the background pixels. This results in no loss of detail. You must choose anti-aliasing before selecting; it cannot be added after a selection has been made.

Art History Brush: Allows you to change an image to make it look like some other type of artwork—artwork that is older, such as impressionist artwork, an oil painting, or a watercolor. These changes are unlike filters and similar tools because they allow you to brush over only part of the image to make the changes and do not apply the change to the entire image or layer.

Auto Color: Adjusts the colors in an image by searching the image for shadows, midtones, and highlights instead of basing those adjustments on the histogram settings. Auto Color is located at Image>Adjustments.

Auto Contrast: This command adjusts the contrast of an image but does not repair color-related problems such as colorcasts. By enhancing the contrast of the image, whites appear whiter and blacks appear blacker, and everything in between changes accordingly.

Auto Erase: Available with the Pencil tool, checking this box allows you to paint the background color over areas of foreground color. This, in essence, erases what has been previously drawn with the foreground color.

Auto Levels: A command in the Image>Adjustments menu that sets highlights and shadows in an image by defining a black point and a white point based on the majority of colors in the image and the lightest and darkest points. With the black and white points set, it configures the intermediate colors accordingly.

Auto Select Layer: Automatically selects the layer you intend to work with as determined by where you click with the mouse.

Background button: When printing, the Background button lets you select a color from the Color Picker that will be printed on the page outside the image area. For instance, if you are printing slides for a film projector, you might want the background to be a specific color.

Background color: The background color can be configured from the toolbox and is used when creating gradient fills, creating a new file using the background color, or filling in an erased area of the image.

Background Eraser tool: Lets you erase on a layer in such a way as to maintain the integrity of the foreground and other layers and works by dragging the mouse.

Baseline Shift: Baseline Shift is used to specify how much the text deviates from its normal baseline.

Batch Rename: Allows you to rename multiple files simultaneously.

Black Generation: This setting in the Color Settings dialog box determines the amount of black ink used in the CMYK separation. This value is used to determine how dense the darkest shadows in the image will appear. By keeping the values at light or medium, you are preventing loss of color intensity in the image at press time.

Bleed button: When printing, use this button to create crop marks inside (instead of outside) the image. This allows you to trim the image if needed inside the graphic instead of outside of it. You can specify the width of the bleed.

Blending modes: A layer's blending mode determines how the layer's colored pixels will mix (relate) with the underlying pixels in the image. By default, there is no blending of layers, but by choosing and applying a blending mode, you can change this. When the blending mode is changed, the order of the image's composition is changed too. Blending modes are generally used to create special effects like adding soft light or hard light or to change the color, saturation, hue, luminosity, or other attributes of how the layers can be combined.

Blur tool: Blurs an area of the image using any brush you select.

BMP files: Bitmap files, which are pixel-based files usually considered standard Microsoft Windows files. Bitmap files only support RGB color spaces and 1, 4, 8, or 24 bits per channel.

Border button: When printing, use this button to create a border around the image's printed area. The border is black and can be between 0.000 and 0.150 inches.

Bounding box: A square or rectangle around an image that allows it to be resized or distorted. When printing, check Show Bounding Box. Checking this option adds a bounding box around the image so it can be resized using the corner handles.

Brush tool: The Brush tool allows you to select a brush, choose its characteristics, including size, shape, spacing, roundness, hardness, angle, diameter, mode, opacity, and more, and then use the brush for various types of artwork

Brushes palette: Here you can create or access thousands of types of brushes and configure them to meet any drawing need.

Burn tool: The Burn tool is used to darken areas of an image or print.

Cache: An area of the hard drive where information is stored about the thumbnails, metadata, and ranking information in your images.

CAD cutter: CAD cutters use thermal film to produce full color prints at 600 dpi or higher. Resin ink cartridges are used, which can be similar to the ribbon cartridges you might have used with Alps and similar printers. The printer/cutter automatically prints and cuts out the design, you peel it off, and apply it to the substrate using a heat transfer machine. You'll have to read your cutter's documentation to purchase the correct inks and films.

Calibration: Brings a device like a monitor, scanner, or printer to an absolute standard that ensures consistency across devices. Calibrating is especially necessary when files are being passed from one person to another; what a client sees on their computer, compared to what you see on your computer, compared to what the service bureau sees on their computer can differ outrageously.

Calibration bars: When printing, check this option to print an 11-step grayscale step wedge moving from 0 percent black to 100 percent black in 10 percent increments.

Center crop marks: Prints marks where the image should be trimmed. These marks can also be useful if you are printing out an image for a demonstration using a slide projector, for package design work, or for any other type of work that requires CMYK printouts be aligned exactly.

Channels: Channels are located in the Channels palette and created automatically when a color mode is chosen and determined based on the colors in the image. In RGB mode, for instance, there are three channels: red, green, and blue.

Clear: This command enables you to delete a selection without placing that selection on the clipboard. It's similar to the Cut command. Make sure if there are multiple layers in an image that you've selected the layer you want to work with from the layers palette.

Clone Stamp tool: Lets you duplicate any area in an image and "paint" that area over any other part of the image.

Clip art: Non-photographic graphic images that can be either vector or bitmap in form. Images in clip art collections are generally categorized by type, such as animals, vehicles, monuments, people, borders, edges, etc. These images can be edited, colored, and resized as required by the user.

CMYK mode: A color mode that uses cyan, magenta, yellow, and black to create its colors. CMYK mode assigns colors to pixels in percentages that are determined by the inks used (and have configured in the Color Settings). Color values range from 0 to 100 percent. For instance, a teal color might have 51 percent cyan, 4 percent magenta, 19 percent yellow, and 0 percent black. You can see these numbers in the Info palette. All zeroes produces a pure white.

Color gamut: The range of colors that a specific color mode can print in. The RGB color gamut can produce over 16 million colors, while the CMYK color gamut produces substantially less. A gamut is also the range of colors that a system can print or display.

Color models: Established models for creating and reproducing color. There are many color models, including RGB, CMYK, HSB, indexed, and more. As a screen printer, you'll mainly be concerned with RGB and CMYK color modes, although indexed color can be useful as well, depending on your needs.

Color palette: Displays information on the current foreground and background colors and allows you to change the colors as desired and/or base the colors on different color models.

Color Sampler: Like the Eyedropper tool, this allows you to match a color exactly by clicking on an area of the image and then offers information about that color. The Color Sampler tool is located with the Eyedropper in the options bar. This tool lets you take a snapshot of up to four color samples in an image and lists them in the Info palette. This is useful when you need to compare one color to another or when you need to see the changes in colors after applying image transformations.

Color Table: When selecting indexed colors, the Color Table allows you to select custom indexed colors for separations.

Commit: The check mark on the options bar that is used to accept a recently made change to an image.

Contiguous: Used with tools such as the Magic Eraser, the Paint Bucket, and the Magic Wand to specify how colors will be selected, applied, or erased. When Contiguous is checked, the resulting selection only includes pixels that are adjacent to each other. Otherwise, all pixels of the preferred color are selected.

Convert Point tool: A hidden tool in the Pen tools section of the toolbox, it can be used to change a smooth point, like that on a curve, to a corner point, like that on a rectangle or square. Clicking and dragging with the tool achieves this.

Copy: Copies the selection and leaves the image on the original file or image, while at the same time placing it on the clipboard for later use with the Paste commands. Copying a selection, a layer, or text allows you to quickly place the information in another file or the same one without having to recreate it.

Copy Merged: This command makes a merged copy of the visible layers in an image or selected area and places it on the clipboard. This command allows you to copy multiple layers at once.

Contact sheet: A sheet that contains thumbnails of images. Contact sheets can be used to catalog images on your computer, in your digital library, for your library of logos and designs, or to offer choices for different photos or logos to clients. You can automatically create a contact sheet using the File>Automate>Contact Sheet II command.

Corner crop marks: Print marks where the image should be trimmed. These marks can also be useful if you are printing out an image for a demonstration using a slide projector, package design work, or any other type of work that requires CMYK printouts to be aligned exactly.

Crop tool: The Crop tool lets you remove extraneous portions of an image or file by selecting a specific portion of the image and deleting the area outside of it.

Curves tool: Allows you to control your color changes precisely and from the entire tonal spectrum. The Curves tool also allows you to preview changes as you make them, as well as view the changes to the ink values in the Info palette at the same time.

Custom shapes: Vector-based clip art that comes with Photoshop that is available from the toolbox under Shapes. Choose the custom shape from the pop-up palette in the options bar.

Cut: A command that is used in many software programs to remove a selection from the file. You can cut text, layers, and manual selections and thus remove them completely from the image. Cutting places the deleted selection onto the clipboard, where it can then be pasted into the same image or another one.

DCS: Desktop Color Separations format is a version of the standard EPS format that lets you save not only the file or image but also its CMYK or multichannel color separations you see in the Channels palette. DCS 2.0 allows you to save spot channels too. These files can then be exported to various other graphics programs, and their separations can be printed on PostScript printers.

Diameter: Controls the size of the brush and can be set using the slider or by typing in a number.

Direct Selection tool: Use this tool when you want to edit the paths that you've created. Paths allow you to create custom outlines of shapes for rious uses, including creating a custom shape, using the shape or path as a mask to hide areas of a layer, or for using it as a clipping path.

Discontiguous: This is a Limits option that specifies that erasures are performed underneath the brush.

Distort: A Transform tool that allows you to move an image in any direction at all. Distort is also a filter that allows you to manipulate an image drastically, offering special effects.

Distribute: Allows you to distribute layers or selections within an image. There are several ways to distribute objects: top, vertical center, left, horizontal center, and right.

Dither: Reduces visible banding related to gradients when using the Gradient tool.

Docking: The Palette Well offers a place to dock palettes that you don't want on the screen but you still want to have access to without having to use the Window menu. To dock a palette, simply drag it from its place in the workspace to the Palette Well.

Dodge tool: Used to darken areas of an image or print. The Dodge tool's name comes from the traditional photographer's method of reducing the amount of light made available when exposing the film to get the picture.

Dot gain: The inherent "growth" of a halftone dot when printed on paper, vellum, or film. A small dot can grow as much as 50 percent or more when printed. Dot gain can also occur when the ink is printed on the shirt.

dpi: Dots per inch. This describes how many dots per inch can be printed on a page and is a measure of how good a printer is. Generally, printers can print many more dots per inch than the pixels per inch that need to be printed.

Duplicate: Used to duplicate an entire image and is useful when you want to make changes to a file, such as a photograph, without applying any changes to the actual file that's saved on the hard drive. Duplicate is a choice in the Image menu.

Edge Contrast: Use this option with the Lasso tools to define the Lasso's sensitivity to the edges of the selection that you're trying to lasso. Values can range from 1 percent to 100 percent. A lower value detects low-contrast edges (those that don't have much contrast with their backgrounds), and a higher value detects edges that contrast sharply with their backgrounds. Configuring this prior to and during a selection can make selecting an object manually much more efficient (combine with the Zoom tool for best results).

Edit: From the Edit menu, you can undo the last step taken or "undo an undo" by choosing Step Forward. You can cut, copy, and paste a selection

from the clipboard, fill a layer with a color or pattern, check the spell
text, and transform images in any number of ways. The Edit menu is a
place to configure custom color settings or set preferences for file hand
cursors, the display, transparency and gamut, units and rulers, memory a
image cache, and more.

Emulsion Down: When printing, check this box to denote that the paper
used is emulsion side down and must be printed the opposite of what is
shown on the screen. If this is checked, Photoshop flips the image around so
it'll print correctly.

EPS DCS2: These files are variations of EPS files. DCS stands for Desktop
Color Separations file. This file type allows you to save color separations as
CMYK files. The DCS2 format also allows you to export images containing
spot channels, which regular EPS doesn't support. To print DCS files, you
must have a PostScript printer.

EPS File Format: EPS files are Encapsulated PostScript files and contain
both raster- and vector-based images. EPS files can be edited in Adobe Illustrator as well as Photoshop, and some EPS files from third-party clip art
companies can be edited in other programs such as CorelDRAW and Arts &
Letters.

Eraser tool: Erases to the background layer by dragging the mouse.

EXIF: Information obtained from a digital camera such as date and time,
resolution, ISO speed rating, f-stop, compression, and exposure time.

Extract: From the Filter menu, this lets you remove an object or objects
from an image and works when other options don't (like the Background
Eraser tool or the Magic Eraser tool). With the Extract option, you can trace
around an image to select it for removal, using a large highlighter-type pen,
fill that area with color, and extract it from the image

Eyedropper tool: Like the Color Sampler tool, this allows you to match a
color exactly by clicking on an area of the image and then offers information
about that color.

Fade: The Fade command appears in the Edit menu after a filter has been
applied and allows you to change the blending options for that filter. The
Fade command also appears after using a painting tool, using an eraser, or
making a color adjustment. The Fade dialog box has two options: changing
the opacity and changing the blending mode.

Feather: Feathering is the process of blurring edges around a selection.
Blurring the edges helps the selection blend into another object, file, or
selection when it is moved, cut, copied, and/or pasted.

le: From the File menu, you can choose to open a file, save a file, and ʹowse for a file, and you can print, print one copy, or print with a preview. ʹou can import or export files too or save a file for the web. Files contain the image and all data.

File browser: Allows you to search your physical drives (hard drive, CD-ROM drive, DVD drives, digital camera drives, floppy drives, and zip drives) for files that you've either previously created or need to open.

Film: Films enable printers to produce high-quality film positives using a printer. Inkjet films require inkjet printers, and other types of films can be used for laser printers. Films create extremely dense positives, where the black is really black, thus it creates a wonderfully perfect screen.

Filters: Filters allow you to change the look of an image or layer simply by choosing the desired look from the menu options and configuring any dialog boxes that appear.

Flattening: Like merging, flattening an image combines all of the layers into a single layer.

Flow: Used to specify how quickly paint is applied when using a Brush tool like the Airbrush. A heavier flow lays on more paint more quickly; a lower flow lays on less.

Font: Used to create text. Fonts are categorized by family, style, size, and other attributes.

Foreground color: The foreground color can be configured from the toolbox. The foreground color is used when paint tools are chosen and when Fill and Stroke tools are selected. When using a brush or the Paint Bucket tool, the foreground color will be applied. The foreground color is also used by some of the special effect filters.

Frequency: Use this option with the Lasso tools to determine at what frequency or how often anchor points are added as you trace around the object. Values from 0 to 100 can be used, and higher values add more anchor (fastening) points. Frequency is available when using the Pen tool too, with values ranging from 5 to 40.

GCR: Gray Component Replacement is an extension of UCR in that it replaces the neutral colors in the image as well as the colored areas with equal amounts of cyan, magenta, and yellow throughout the tonal range of the image. The gray component is replaced with black ink. GCR is a better option for most high-quality print work, thus the reasoning behind choosing it for our CMYK custom settings.

GIF: Stands for Graphics Interchange Format and is generally used f(that are considered line art or have only a few colors. GIF images are for images containing less than 256 colors, so they're not good for phot graphs. The GIF format supports grayscale and RGB color spaces.

Gradient tool: Fills a closed object with a range of colors that fade into e other.

Grayscale: This color mode uses up to 256 shades of gray (or black). Every pixel in the image is defined by its brightness values between 0 and 255 or its percentage of black ink coverage (0 percent to 100 percent).

Halftones: Halftones are dots of a specific shape, such as an ellipse or a circle. Halftones dictate how much of each color goes on the material at press time. Varying how large or small the dots are determines the actual color printed on the shirt. Because halftone dots are so small, they fool us into thinking that we are seeing the real image, when in reality we are just looking at a combination of dots.

Hand tool: Allows you to scroll through an image that doesn't fit completely in the viewing window. It's like using the scroll bars at the bottom and right side of the window, except you do the moving with the mouse by dragging. When the Hand tool is chosen, the cursor becomes a hand.

Handle: Small squares that appear around an object when transforming it that allow you to move, resize, reshape, or distort the image.

Hardness: Controls a brush's hard center and can be set using the slider or by typing in a number. Hardness can be compared to using a pencil by pressing hard to create a darker and more forceful print; lower this number for a softer effect.

Healing Brush tool: The Healing Brush let you correct imperfections in images such as dirt, smudges, and even dark circles under a subject's eyes. You can match the background texture, lighting, and shadows or shading to "cover up" these flaws.

Heat transfers: Used when names, numbers, one-of-a-kind artwork, artwork with many different colors, gradients, and process color, and short runs are desired. With a heat transfer, there are no screens to burn, and you (should) get what you see on your computer screen. Heat transfers can be used on mouse pads, can coolers, puzzles, tote bags, and similar products, and they are quite easy to produce in Photoshop. You use a heat transfer press to apply the transfer to the product.

Hidden tools: In the toolbox, many of the icons have arrows in the bottom-right corner. This signifies that there are additional tools located derneath the tool that is showing. Selecting a hidden tool from the toolbox an be achieved by clicking, holding, and choosing the tool you want from the resulting list of tools.

History Brush: You can use the History Brush to paint over something that you've recently added to an image to erase it.

History Palette: Shows the list of steps taken to create the image that you are currently working on. The History palette helps you correct errors (by storing what you've done to a file previously) and allows you to "go back" to a point before a particular edit was made simply by clicking on the appropriate step.

HSB: This mode uses a color's hue, saturation, and brightness to define it. Hue is defined by its location on the color wheel and is denoted by a number from 0 to 360 degrees. Saturation is the purity and strength of the color and is defined by the percentage of gray in the image (0 to 100 percent). Brightness is how light or dark a color is and is defined by a percentage (0 percent is black and 100 percent is white).

ICC profiles: Color space descriptions that can be configured or installed for a specific device like a scanner or printer. ICC stands for and was defined by the International Color Consortium as a cross-platform color standard.

Image: From the Image menu choices, you can make adjustments to the image concerning color, hue, saturation, and other attributes, as well as make changes to the color mode. Other options allow you to duplicate, trim, rotate, crop, and trap the image, and change the image size.

Image Ready: A second application that ships with Photoshop 7.0 and is used mainly for web design.

Import: Available from the File menu, this command lets you import files from a scanner or digital camera and import PDF images, annotations, and WIA support. PDF (Portable Document Format) is the primary file format for Adobe Illustrator and Adobe Acrobat.

Impressionist: Adds an impressionist effect (like Monet's art) when the box is checked while using the Pattern Stamp tool.

Indenting text: Left indent indents a paragraph from the left edge of the paragraph, right from the right edge, and first line to only indent the first line of the paragraph.

Indexed color: This mode uses from 1 to 256 colors. You can convert an RGB image to an indexed color image, and Photoshop will look at the colors and convert them to the colors available in the indexed color model. Indexed color can be used for web images but is used in screen printing as well.

Screen printers can use indexing to color separate an image using on
colors, and those colors can be hand picked.

Info palette: Displays color information about the color directly under
the mouse pointer and displays additional information depending on the
chosen.

Interpolation: Photoshop's way of figuring out what should be in a specifi
pixel when enough information isn't given, such as when you resample an
image. If you start with a small image and try to double the size, Photoshop
has to guess at what's supposed to be in those extra areas. If you take a large
image and reduce its size, it has to guess at what to throw away. There are
several types of interpolation: Bicubic, Bilinear, and Nearest Neighbor.

JPEG: Stands for Joint Photographic Experts Group and is sometimes also
written JPG. JPEG files are lossy, meaning that as they are compressed, they
lose detail. When the file is changed from a JPEG to another format, those
compressed or lost pixels must be reconstructed. This usually results in jagged edges in the design.

Justify Text: Justifies all lines of text in the paragraph and leaves the last
line justified either left, center, or right. (For vertical text, it is top, center,
and bottom.)

Kerning: Kerning determines how much of a gap to have between specific
letter pairs. Letter pairs like AV and Ky often seem out of sync with the
other letters in the text because of how the sides of the letter pairs line up
with each other. Kerning can be used to add to or diminish the space to
remove this natural occurrence.

Labels: When printing, check this to print the file name above the image.

Lasso tools: There are three Lasso tools: the Lasso tool, the Polygonal
Lasso tool, and the Magnetic Lasso tool. The first two choices let you draw
around an object using curves and line segments, respectively, and the third
lets you draw around an object and have the drawn lines snap to the object
(based on calculations determined by color differences in the object and the
background).

Layer: Layers are like transparencies, which are clear plastic sheets of
material that can be printed on. The transparencies can be printed and
stacked on top of one another to form a complex picture, and single transparencies can be removed from the stack for editing or removal. When you
create artwork in Photoshop 7.0, you can create it on layers similar to these
transparencies—text on one layer, background image on another, and

538

:haps a selection pasted from another file on another. These layers can
.en be edited independently of each other, making the editing process more
:fficient and precise.

Layer masks: Used to obscure entire layers and layer sets. By using masks,
you can apply special effects without actually affecting any of the original
data on that layer. After you've found the perfect effect, you can then apply
the changes. The changes can also be discarded. Layer masks are created
using the painting and selection tools.

Leading: Leading is the amount of space between lines of text in a
paragraph.

Limits: Allows you to choose from Contiguous, Discontiguous, and Find
Edges when using the Background Eraser tool. Contiguous erases colors
that are next to the original sample, Discontiguous erases underneath the
brush, and Find Edges looks for and finds the edges of an image and erases
to those edges.

Line screen: Also called screen ruling, line screen is how many lines of
halftone dots appear per linear inch on a printed page, positive or negative.
Line screen is measured in lines per inch (lpi). Lines per inch is limited by
the output device and the paper or film you print on. Common lpi for screen
printers range from 55 lpi to 65 lpi. Newspapers print around 85 lpi and magazines around 133 or 155 lpi.

Line tool: Allows you to draw straight lines using the mouse. The Line tool
is located with the other Shape tools and draws vector-based lines.

lpi: Lines per inch is a term used by offset printers, screen printers, and
other graphic artists to describe how many lines or dots per inch will be in a
halftone screen. Screen printers generally output their images at 55 to 65 lpi,
depending on the type of print process (spot or process) and other factors
such as the type of screen used and its mesh count and the type of ink used.

Magic Eraser tool: Lets you erase by clicking with the mouse and erases
all pixels similar in color to the area you click on.

Magic Wand tool: Allows you to make a selection automatically, based on a
color, without having to physically trace the outline by clicking in a specific
area with the mouse. Options for the Magic Wand are set in the options bar.

Magnetic Pen tool: A variation of the Freeform Pen, this Pen tool snaps to
the edges of an image, making tracing around an image easy.

Marquee tools: There are four Marquee tools—rectangular, elliptical, single
row, and single column. These tools allow you to select portions of an object,

file, photo, or subject for editing. These selections must be elliptical, gular, circular, or 1 pixel wide or thick.

Menu bar: The bar at the top of the Photoshop interface that contains eral headings: File, Edit, Image, Layer, Select, Filter, View, Window, and Help.

Mode: Mode options allow you to control how you want pixels to be affect by the application of the painting or editing tool you choose. Modes, also called blending modes, are generally used for creating special effects.

Moiré: The unwanted addition of patterns on a print or scan. These patterns are usually caused when two similar repetitive grids are placed on top of one another. Screens and their inherent mesh pattern when combined with the halftone dots and their inherent dot patterns can cause the print to have unwanted lines and patterns. You can also get moiré when you scan an image that has already been halftoned, like a photograph from a magazine. If you get moiré patterns when scanning, use a "Descreen" option if one exists, scan the image at twice the final size, and then resize the image as needed and experiment with other settings.

Move tool: Allows you to move a selected part of an image, align layers, and distribute layers in an image. When the Move tool is selected, a box is placed around the selected part of the image. This box can be used to move the selection and edit its shape and size.

Navigator palette: Allows you to quickly change the viewing area of the file that you are working on.

Negative: When printing or working with a file, use the Negative option to invert the entire image, including background color and masks. When printing, Photoshop converts the entire image to a negative but not the preview or on screen version. When printing a negative, white becomes black and black becomes white.

Notes tool: Use this tool to add both written and audio notes to Photoshop files. These notes can work in tandem with other Adobe products such as Adobe Acrobat Reader.

Opacity: Used to specify how transparent a layer should be, either on its own or in regard to other layers.

Options bar: This bar is located at the top of the interface underneath the menu bar and changes each time a new tool is selected. The options bar contains choices for configuring and working with the various tools in the toolbox.

...ge Setup dialog box: An area where paper, orientation, and margins can ...e set and access to the printer properties is available.

Paint Bucket tool: The Paint Bucket tool fills a closed object with a solid color.

Palette: These are located on the right side of the interface. They are contained in rectangular boxes and offer tools to help you modify, monitor, and edit images. Palettes are stacked together, and each rectangular box holds two or three separate palettes.

Palette Well: Located on the options bar in the top-right corner of the interface. Palettes can be dragged from the work area to the Palette Well. This effectively removes the palette from the work area, while keeping the palette handy and easily accessible. You won't be able to see the Palette Well unless you have your screen resolution set at 1024 x 768 or higher.

Pantone colors: Industry standard colors that are represented by names and numbers.

Pantone Matching System (PMS): An ideal way to ensure true colors when you print. Pantone colors include Pantone Yellow, Pantone Red, Pantone Purple, etc., with various shades in between with names like PMS251 and PMS262.

Paragraph Type: A way to type in paragraphs where all of the letters typed in wrap to new lines based on the size of the bounding box. Using this option, paragraphs of text can be entered, and if more space is required, the bounding box can simply be resized. Compare to point type.

Paste: This command pastes the selection (from Cut or Copy) into another part of the image or into a new image as a new layer.

Paste Into: This command pastes a selection into another part of the image or into a new image as a new layer, and the destination's selection border is converted into a layer mask. You can then decide if you want to apply the mask or discard it.

Patch tool: Similar to the Healing Brush tool, this allows you to choose a part of the image and use it as a sample for repairing another part of the image. The Patch tool combines the selection power of the Lasso tools with the correction properties of the Healing Brush and other cloning tools.

Path Selection tool: Use this tool when you want to edit the paths that you've created using the Pen or Shape tools.

Pattern Stamp tool: Allow you to paint with a specific pattern from the pattern library or from your own pattern creations.

PDF: Stands for Portable Document Format and is used mainly for d[ ] ments. PDF file format preserves fonts, page layout, and other docum[ ] information and can be imported into Photoshop for editing. PDF files [ ] platform independent, meaning almost any computer OS can be used w[ ] opening them. PDF files are not used in Photoshop for creating artwork.

Pen pressure: If you use a stylus tablet, you can set pen pressure. This allows you to draw on the tablet and have the resulting amount of pressure you use while drawing applied to the tool you're using on the screen. Pen pressure is available with several tools, including the Pen tool and some Brush tools.

Pen tool: The Pen tool is used for drawing paths and custom shapes. As lines and curves are drawn, anchor points are created that define the line, its endpoints, and its curves.

Pencil tool: The Pencil tool allows you to select a brush, choose its characteristics including size, shape, spacing, roundness, hardness, angle, diameter, mode, opacity, and more, and then use the brush for various types of artwork.

Perspective: A Transform tool that allows you to apply perspective to an image.

Photorealistic images: These images are generally created using actual pictures of things, such as animals, motorcycles, carnival rides (Ferris wheels, roller coasters), rock and roll bands, landscapes, seascapes, moonscapes, sunsets, or mountain scenes. Photorealistic images are generally printed using process techniques but can be created using indexed color as well.

Pixel: Images such as photos are made up of pixels, which are small squares that contain color. An image's resolution is determined by how many pixels there are in the image per inch. Monitors display output using pixels as well. Monitors display output at 72 ppi.

Point Type: A way to type a paragraph where each line of text that you add is independent of the other lines; it does not wrap to the next line. If you run out of space in the work area, the letters that don't fit on the page won't show. Compare to paragraph type.

Polygons: Closed shapes like triangles, squares, rectangles, and octagons, these are shapes that have three or more sides.

Pop-up palette: Some palettes are not available from the window menu choices and instead appear when a specific tool is chosen and is being configured. These are available from the options bar and denoted by a small arrow. Click on the arrow to access the palettes.

PostScript: A page description language for medium to high resolution print devices. The language consists of software commands and protocols that allow you to send data (including picture and font information) from your computer to the printer for output. PostScript is device independent, allowing different computers and printers to communicate independently of platforms.

ppi: Image resolution is a ratio of pixels per inch; the more pixels you squeeze into each inch of the image, the higher the resolution. Higher resolution means a better quality image.

Preserve Exact Colors: Check this when creating indexed colors to make any pure color a spot color.

Preset Manager: A dialog box that allows you to manage all preset items in one place. Changes made here affect all of the presets you see when accessing them from any area of Photoshop. The Preset Manager is available from Edit>Preset Manager.

Print Selected Area: This check box is available if you've used a Selection tool to select a specific area of the image prior to opening the Print dialog box. When this box is checked, only the selected area is printed.

Process color: Used when you want to print photorealistic prints. Process color printing requires that you create four unique halftone screens, one for each of the four colors (CMYK). These screens are really just dots on a page that control how much ink should be put in a particular part of the image.

Proprietary file format: A proprietary format means the file can only be opened in the program in which it was created, such as Arts & Letters' GED files, Adobe Photoshop's PSD files, Paint Shop Pro's PSP files, CorelDRAW's CDR files, and other file formats.

PSD file format: Photoshop's own format for saving files. Files saved in this format retain layer and channel information. The image's resolution and spot color channels are also saved, as is image bit depth. PSD files save information about the file, including its layers and channels, so that those items can be continually edited.

Range: Used with the Dodge and Burn tools, this allows you to select a tonal range to lighten or darken (midtones, highlights, or shadows).

Raster data: This data is defined by its colors and pixels and is not defined mathematically. Digital pictures are raster data. Some tools in Photoshop can only be applied to raster data or raster images.

Rasterize: Converting vector data to raster data. Performing this conversion is called rasterizing.

Registration marks: When printing, these marks are used to print r on the image for alignment on the press (bull's-eyes and star targets).

Resolution: Resolution determines how many pixels are shown per un. (such as inch or centimeter) in an image. Higher resolutions contain mor pixels (thus more detail) than lower resolution images.

Reverse: Reverses the chosen gradient's colors. Used with the Gradient tool.

Revert: Located in the File menu, the Revert command returns the file to the condition it was in the last time it was saved.

RGB mode: A color mode that uses red, green, and blue to create the colors you see. Monitors use RGB mode to output color, and RGB mode is Photoshop's default.

Rotate: A Transform tool that allows you to rotate an object around its center point. The center point can be changed.

Roundness: Controls how round the brush stroke will be. A setting of 100 percent creates a circular brush stroke; 0 percent creates a linear brush stroke.

Sample size: The Eyedropper can be used to take a sample of a color for multiple uses, including choosing a foreground color, using the Healing Brush, and using the Background Eraser. The sample size of the Eyedropper can be changed from the sample size window. It is usually best to keep the sample size small. You can choose from point sample, 3 by 3 average, or 5 by 5 average.

Scale: A Transform tool that allows you to enlarge or reduce an image's size horizontally, vertically, or both.

Scaled Print Size: Scale determines how large or small the image should be printed in relation to the actual size of the image itself. A choice of 100 percent, the default, prints the page as you see it using its actual size.

Screen button: Use the Screen button when printing to set screen frequency, angle, and dot shape for each of the ink colors (CMYK) in the process print.

Screens: When screen printing images onto fabric, you use screens to physically transfer the ink onto the shirts and other materials. These screens are created from printouts that you print from your PostScript printer. These printouts can be created on vellum, film, or similar paper.

Selective Color: A powerful command that allows you to work with and adjust colors independently of one another.

hape tools: Shape tools include rectangle, rounded rectangle, ellipse, poly-
;on, line, and custom shapes. Shape tools are used by graphic artists for
creating logos, setting type boundaries, creating custom artwork, creating
trademarks, and more. Shapes are vector images too, meaning they can be
resized without distortion. Photoshop comes with many custom shapes,
including animals, check marks, hands, feet, puzzle pieces, pens and pencils,
phones, international symbols, and more.

Sharpen tool: Sharpens an area of the image using any brush that you
choose.

Show Bounding Box: Available from the options bar when you choose the
Move tool or the Path Selection tool. Checking this box allows you to see the
bounding box that surrounds a selected object, which in turn makes it easier
to move, resize, and rotate a selection.

Simulated process color separations: Sometimes called fake process
color separations, these are created when you want to print an image on a
dark-colored shirt. Common images and clients for simulated process color
prints include rock bands, fantasy groups, animals, motorcycles, and photographs. Simulated process color differs from true process color because
these images are not printed using CMYK inks like regular process prints
are. These images are printed using "regular" colors like red, black, orange,
yellow, blue, white, etc., and are printed with all-purpose inks.

Skew: A Transform tool that allows you to slant an image vertically or
horizontally.

Slice tool: Slices are generally used to define areas of an image that will
later be used for animating for a web page, as links to URL addresses or for
rollover buttons.

Smudge tool: Smudges an area of the image using any brush you choose.

Source (Sampled or Pattern): Used when repairing flaws in images (perhaps with the Healing Brush) to determine how exactly an image will be
repaired. Sampled uses pixels from the current image, and Pattern fills the
area with a pattern you select from the Pattern pop-up palette.

Spacing: Controls the distance between the brush strokes when using a
brush. Increasing the spacing creates a skipping effect; decreasing the spacing creates less of a skipping effect (or none if set to 0).

Splitting channels: To send process color separations to programs that
don't accept DCS 2.0 files, you can split channels to create a separate file for
each channel that you've created. When splitting channels, Photoshop
renames them and places them on the screen one by one as they're created.
With these separate files, you can do a File>Save As command on each file,

and then you can send them to a service bureau or import them into a program. To split the channels, simply click the right arrow in the Chai palette and choose Split Channels. Don't do this until you're sure thoug. this can't be undone!

Spot color: Images that have a limited number of colors in the design. Ge erally, spot color prints are the easiest kind of images to both screen print and color separate.

Step Backward: Like the Undo command, you can revert to a previous state. With Step Backward you can undo even after you've saved the image with the state change.

Step Forward: Allows you to move forward one state. Moving forward is the opposite of moving backward and is only available after using the Step Backward command from the Edit menu.

Stochastic: Indexed separations use random square dots called stochastic or diffusion dither. These dots are not halftone dots and are used only in indexed color separations.

Strength: Used with Blur, Sharpen, and Smudge and specifies how strong the stroke should be. Lower numbers reduce the strength; higher numbers increase the strength.

Styles palette: Lets you apply a preset style to a selected layer, which can be the foreground or background or load different libraries of styles.

Sublimation: Printing with sublimation requires that you have a sublimation printer and sublimation inks, along with special papers for printing. Although sublimation can be used for printing T-shirts, caps, and totes, it is mostly used for printing coffee cups, mouse pads, luggage tags, clipboards, and similar materials.

Swatches palette: Allows you to choose a foreground or background color and allows you to add or delete colors from the swatches library of colors.

Third-party color separation software: Software you purchase from a third-party company not affiliated with Adobe. This software will create color separations automatically, using macros to do the work that you'd normally have to do.

TIFF files: Tagged Image File Format files (also called TIF files) that are widely used files in graphic design. TIFF files are raster-based and support almost all color spaces. TIFF files can be compressed using a lossless compress scheme, making them better for saving than JPEG files.

Tolerance: This option is available with several tools and used to set how "tolerant" a tool is with regard to the colors with which it is working. For stance, when using the Paint Bucket tool to fill an area with color, the tolerance level determines how close the color must be to the original color (where you click) before it gets filled. Values can be from 0 to 255. A lower number only fills colors very similar to where you click; a higher number fills a broader range of colors. Tolerance can also be set for the Magic Eraser tool, the Art History Brush, and the Magic Wand tool.

Tool Presets palette: Lets you load, save, and replace tool preset libraries for quick reference. Saving custom preset tools allows you to reuse these tools without recreating them each time. Each tool in the toolbox has its own icon in the left corner of the options bar, and there is a down arrow beside it. Clicking on this arrow brings up the tool presets. Here, you can save and reuse tools and tool settings, as well as load, edit, and create libraries of tools you use most often.

Toolbox: Located on the left side of the screen, it's where you'll find the tools you need to create your artwork and perform editing tasks. From the toolbox you can access the selection tools, Shape tools, Type tools, the Crop tool, Eraser tools, Zoom tools, and more.

Tracking: Tracking keeps equal amounts of space across an entire range of letters, such as in a paragraph.

Transfer button: When printing process color separations, this button allows you to compensate for dot gain and loss from inside the Print dialog box. However, since dot gain is taken into account and dealt with appropriately when configuring the color settings from the Edit menu, this is best left at its defaults.

Transparency: When an area of an image is "erased to transparency," there is a checkered background showing. There is nothing on that part of the image.

Trim: The Image>Trim command automatically trims an image (which is like cropping) based on attributes you specify in the Trim dialog box. This trimming can be based on transparent pixels in the image, the top-left pixel color, or the bottom-right pixel color. With that choice made, the trimming can be done from the top, bottom, left, or right sides of the image or a combination of these.

Tsume: Reduces the space around a character. The character is not squeezed or stretched as a result of this action, only resized.

TWAIN: A proper name that is often followed by the words compliant driver or compliant application. TWAIN-compliant hardware, such as scanners, allows you to use your scanner and scan an image from various applications that are also TWAIN compliant. (This is what makes the File>Import command work.) Other hardware can be TWAIN compliant too, such a tal cameras and virtual devices, explaining why some digital cameras, scanners, and similar hardware work from inside Photoshop and others don't.

Type Mask tools: Allows you to create a selection in the form of typed le ters. These selections can be moved, copied, or filled with color just like an other selection can. Type selections are best created on a normal image laye and not a type layer, since the type is created from the underlying image.

Type tools: There are four Type tools: the Vertical Type tool, Horizontal Type tool, Vertical Mask Type tool, and Horizontal Mask Type tool. These tools are used to add words to an image. With a Type tool selected, you can set options for font, size, color, alignment, and more.

UCA: UCA adds cyan, magenta, and yellow where black is present in a photograph or neutral colors in an image. UCA gives density to an image and increases ink coverage. UCA is not generally desirable in offset printing or screen printing and should be set to 0 percent.

UCR: A choice in the Color Settings dialog box. Choosing UCR before printing reduces the amount of C, M, and Y ink in the darkest neutral areas of the image when the colors exceed the specified ink weight configured in the Color Settings dialog box. Thus, UCR is better suited for newsprint where ink is heavily restricted.

Undo: The Undo command is usually accompanied by the name of the last tool used, such as Undo Paint Bucket or Undo Trim. Undo simply moves back one step and reverses the last action taken. The Undo command is not available after a file has been saved.

Unsharp Mask: Available from Filter>Sharpen>Unsharp Mask. Increasing the values in this dialog box makes the edges, pixels, and colors in the image sharper (they'll stand out more) so that when you lose sharpness during the print process, the final product will look similar to the original.

Use All Layers: To apply a selected tool to all of the layers in the image, place a check in this box. For instance, when using the Magic Wand to select a specific color, you can choose to apply the selection to all of the layers in the image instead of the default of only the active layer.

Vector data: Type and shapes are vector data. Vector data is computed mathematically, and the object or type is defined by it geometric shape. Type, shapes, and vector masks are all considered vector data.

vector masks: Created from paths, these masks can be used to mask (or hide) part of a layer, they can be edited by configuring styles or adding special effects, and they can be used to reveal specific areas of a layer. Vector masks are created with the Pen and Shape tools.

Vector type layers: These type layers are the optimal choice when possible because they are printed as vector data and are thus much cleaner, less pixelated, and a whole lot easier to screen print than rasterized type.

Vellum: A paper used in both laser and inkjet printers for outputting color separations. The vellum is then used to burn the screen used at the printing press.

Warping: Allows you to configure the type so it isn't simply added to the document in a straight horizontal or vertical line. When the type is added, the warp icon appears in the options bar. Warping can also be achieved using Layer>Type>Warp Text, and in some cases you won't have the option to choose in what orientation you want the warp to occur (vertically or horizontally).

White plate: Also called a white printer or negative white printer, a white plate is like a spot color for the white in the image.

WIA Support: WIA stands for Windows Image Acquisition. This allows your digital camera, scanner, Photoshop, and Windows XP or ME to work together to acquire images.

Workspace: Once you have the workspace just the way you want it, you can save that configuration using the Window>Workspace>Save Workspace command. Type in a name for the workspace in the Save Workspace dialog box, and it becomes available from the Window>Workspace choices.

Zoom tool: Works much like any Zoom tool in any other graphics program. Simply choose the Zoom tool and click on an area of the image to zoom in or out. When the Zoom tool is chosen, the options in the option bar change, offering Zoom In and Zoom Out along with choices to resize the window to fit on the screen and other options.